to Helen

Preface

As the most recent fire, flood, earthquake or automobile crash demonstrates, we live in a risky world. Your welfare depends to a considerable extent on your ability to handle risk. This book can help you acquire the knowledge and skill you need.

The book is operational. It is concerned with what you need to *know* and what you need to *do*. As you proceed chapter by chapter, you learn how to manage risk and make the best use of insurance. Because insurance and your risk situation are complex, we discuss fundamental principles first and then apply them to real world situations. To keep the book a reasonable length for an introductory course, only topics that meet one or both of the following tests are included:

1. Is this essential for the reader's understanding?

2. Will this help him or her as a consumer?

Because the field of risk and insurance is so broad and dynamic, you won't know all there is to know about it when you finish this book. You will, however, have a great deal of knowledge and skill that will help you as a consumer and provide a foundation for further study.

Consumer Applications at the end of each chapter demonstrate how to use what you learned from it. For example, after the chapter on risk, we discuss how to handle the risks of academia, how to prevent car theft, and how to protect your home. After the chapter on managing home risks, we discuss how to shop for home insurance and how to reduce your home insurance costs.

Discussion Questions for each chapter provide the basis for class discussion that ranges beyond material included in the text. Short

Cases offer an opportunity to practice using what you have learned from the chapter.

Specimen insurance policies are included in appendixes A through D for reference as you read about them in the text. Addresses and telephone numbers of state insurance departments are listed in *Appendix F* so you can call or write for help when you have an insurance problem. The *Glossary* provides a handy reference for insurance terms you need to know.

Students can test their knowledge and reinforce what they have learned by using the *STUDY GUIDE* prepared by Professor John H. Thornton of North Texas State University. It includes fill-in questions, multiple choice and true or false questions as well as definitions for each chapter. A valuable tool for instructors is the *INSTRUCTOR'S MANUAL*, which provides suggested answers for *Discussion Questions* and case problems as well as a test bank.

This book lists one author, but it is the product of countless suggestions and a great deal of help from many people. Professors Robert S. Cline of the University of North Carolina-Greensboro, Gary W. Eldred of the University of Central Florida, Barry B. Schweig of Old Dominion University, and James A. Wickman of the University of Washington, made detailed comments on the manuscript. Professors William R. Feldhaus of Georgia State University, Robert A. Hershbarger of the University of Missouri-Columbia, Blair M. Lord of the University of Rhode Island, George E. Rejda of the university of Nebraska-Lincoln, and Salama A. Salama of East Texas State University made valuable suggestions on organization and content.

I am also indebted to Professors Terrence E. Williamson of the University of South Dakota and John H. Thornton for their contributions to chapter cases. Dr. Joseph Bonnice of the Insurance Information Institute, Joseph Eudy of the General Adjustment Bureau, Richard E. Harris and Charles Koon of Insurance Services Office, Douglas Broom and Charles Potok of the South Carolina Insurance Department, Dr. K. Edwin Graham of the American Council of Life Insurance, Conner Harrison of Seibels-Bruce Group, and Gloria Robinson of the Columbia Social Security Office were generous with their help.

Charles S. (Steve) Boland, a graduate student at the University of South Carolina while the manuscript was underway, drafted charts and tables and helped with research. Mrs. Betty C. McLees and Ms. Melinda Ford, of the U.S.C. Insurance Studies Center, provided invaluable aid in typing and retyping the manuscript, proofreading, and research. I am deeply grateful for their cheerful and efficient help.

This edition reflects the fact that what I think is most valuable for the beginning student, how much material can be dealt with effectively in one term, and how to present it, is constantly changing. I look forward to, and will appreciate, your comments.

JLA

Contents

Chapter One:
RISK

INTRODUCTION

Risk is a major component of our environment. We are surrounded by innumerable risks from birth to death. It is as pervasive as the air we breathe. Mere survival requires awareness of risk and how to cope with it. While we are familiar with many of the risks we face, all too often the more crucial ones escape our attention or we fail to appreciate their significance. As background for later discussion, and to help us become risk conscious as well as develop a risk point of view, we will discuss the following in this chapter:

1. The nature of risk

2. Kinds of risk

3. Factors affecting risk

4. Methods of handling risk.

NATURE OF RISK

Risk is the possibility of loss. Loss, in turn, is usually thought of as a reduction or disappearance of value. But, defining loss in economic terms is too narrow. There is an implication that loss must be measurable or, at least, describable in terms of some economic unit

such as dollars.[1] Many losses, however, cannot be measured or described in economic terms designed to indicate value. For example, the death of a family pet may be felt as a great loss to some members of the family but be neither measurable nor describable as a disappearance in value, at least in economic terms.

For these reasons, the term "loss" as used in this text means an unfavorable deviation from expectations. It is the possibility that something we do not want to happen will happen or that something we want to happen will fail to do so. It may or may not have economic implications, but whatever it is the development is one to be avoided and its occurrence is unfavorable. For our purposes then, risk may be defined as either (1) the possibility of loss, or (2) the possibility of an unfavorable deviation from expectations.

We *expect* but we are not sure; i.e., we are not certain. Most of our expectations are positive. That is, we *expect* our car to be where we parked it when we return. We do not expect it to be stolen. We *expect* to survive this year. We do not expect to die prematurely. We *expect* our home to remain standing and in good condition when we return from work. We do not expect to find that it has been damaged or destroyed.

Expectations are not necessarily verbalized or thought about consciously. When you park your car you do not say, "I know (expect) my car will be here in the same condition as it is now when I return." Nor does this thought actually cross your mind—at least not every time you go through the habitual, almost automatic, motions that are involved. That such an expectation is held, either consciously or subconsciously, is nonetheless indicated by your behavior. You do park your car and you do return to it. If it is missing or damaged when you return, you are surprised because such a development is contrary to your expectations.

When we realize that our expectations are held with less than absolute certainty—we *expect* rather than *know*[2]—we are aware of the possibility that actual events may differ from those we expect. Such a possibility is significant because it may result in a loss. Because there is merely the possibility of such losses and we cannot be sure whether they will or will not occur, the presence of risk is a source of

---

1. This usage probably evolved from the insurance practice which involves payment of funds upon the occurrence of a specified event. In most cases, the obligation of the insurer is stated in dollars and the insured is presumed to have suffered a loss equal to or greater than the dollars received from the insurer under the terms of the insurance contract. From the insurance point of view, defining loss as a reduction or disappearance of value is understandable.

2. Some people think they know; that is, they have no doubt about their expectation. They are subject to risk but do not realize it. As we shall discuss later in this text, recognition of risk is a major step in risk management.

uncertainty. Uncertainty is a state of mind which most people find unpleasant.[3]

KINDS OF RISK

Risks may be classified as either pure or speculative. A speculative risk involves the possibilities of loss, gain or no change. Wagering, for example, is a speculative risk. People who wager may gain or lose, depending upon the outcome of the subject of the wager. Similarly, when you buy shares of common stock you assume a speculative risk. In entering the transaction you expose yourself to the possibility of gaining, losing, or breaking even.

In contrast to speculative risk, pure risk involves only the possibilities of loss or no change. Your home is exposed to the risk of loss by fire, for example, but there is no possibility of gain from the same risk. On the other hand, as a homeowner, you are also exposed to the speculative risk that various forces may either increase or decrease the value of your property. When you own property you are exposed to this speculative risk as well as the pure risks associated with property ownership. The possible outcomes which may result from pure and speculative risks are illustrated in Figure 1-1.

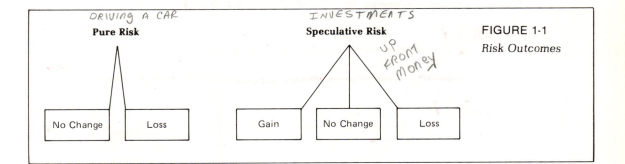

FIGURE 1-1

Risk Outcomes

Pure risks classified.

The pure risks which confront individuals, families, firms, and other organizations may be classified as personal, property, or liability:

Personal risks.   Because all loss is ultimately borne by people, it could be said that all risks are personal. Some, however, such as loss of in-

---

3.   There are exceptions to this statement. For example, many people enjoy the uncertainty connected with betting on a horse race or a ball game. In such cases, however, there is a chance of a gain as well as a chance of loss. Perhaps the contemplation of such gain has a stronger psychological effect than the uncertain possibility of a loss. Many who bet do not enjoy the uncertainty involved but endure it because of the possibility of gain. The type of risk to be discussed in this text is that which involves only a chance of loss. Such risks cause unpleasant uncertainty.

come or assets as well as mental or physical suffering, are most direct in their impact on people. Therefore, the risks of premature death, sickness, disability, unemployment, and dependent old age are classified as personal.

FIRE, THEFT, — **Property risks.** Property owners are exposed to the possibility of both direct and indirect (loss of use) losses. If your car is damaged in a collision, the direct loss is the cost of repairs. The indirect loss is the time *WATER DAMAGE* and effort required to arrange for repairs, loss of use while repairs are being made, and the additional cost of renting another car as opposed to driving your own.

Liability risks. You are exposed to the possibility of loss by having to defend yourself against a suit, or becoming legally obligated to pay for damage to the person or property of others. Under our legal system, we are often held responsible for causing damage to others.

FACTORS AFFECTING RISK

Loss is what pure risk is all about. If there were no possibility of loss, there would be no risk. So, factors which cause or contribute to loss are significant in the analysis of risk. Two of these factors which work together to cause losses are *perils* and *hazards*.

Perils

Perils are the immediate cause of loss. The reason we are surrounded by risk is because our environment is filled with perils such as flood, theft, death, sickness, excessive radiation, and many others.

Hazard   *Contributing factors to Perils*

Hazard is the condition that lies behind the occurrence of losses from particular perils. Hazard increases the probability of a loss as well as its severity. Certain conditions are referred to as being "hazardous." For example, during the summer when humidity declines and temperature and wind velocity rise in heavily forested areas, the fire danger goes up. Conditions are so hazardous that an uncontrollable forest fire could start very easily. The more hazardous conditions are, the greater the probability of loss.

KINDS OF HAZARDS

> Physical
> Moral
> Morale

Physical Hazard. Physical hazards are the physical aspects of property that influence the chance of it being damaged or destroyed. Location, construction, and use are physical hazards which affect risk. The location of a building affects its susceptibility to loss by fire, flood, earthquake, and other perils. If it is located near the fire department and a good water supply, there is less chance that it will suffer a serious loss by fire than would be the case if it were in an isolated area where there was neither water nor fire fighting service.

Construction affects the probability of loss. While no building is fireproof, some types of construction are less susceptible to loss from fire than others. What is susceptible to one peril, however, is not necessarily susceptible to all. For example, a frame building is more apt to burn than a brick building, but it will suffer less damage from an earthquake.

Use or occupancy also affects the chance of loss of property. A building will have a greater probability of loss by fire if it is used for a fireworks factory or a dry-cleaning establishment than it will if it is used as a grocery store. Automobiles used for business purposes are exposed to greater chance of loss than those that are not.

Moral Hazard. Moral hazard also affects the probability of loss. Dishonesty or lack of integrity in an individual can increase the chance of loss to 100 percent. Dishonest people can burn their own homes or rob their own stores in order to collect the insurance. When such people buy insurance, loss becomes a certainty. Because (as will be shown later) the operation of an insurance mechanism involves the law of chance, moral hazard may make a risk uninsurable.

Morale Hazard. Morale hazard as distinguished from moral hazard does not involve dishonesty. Rather, it is an attitude of carelessness and lack of concern that increases the chance a loss will occur. Poor housekeeping (such as the accumulation of trash in the attic or basement) and careless cigarette smoking are examples of morale hazard that increase the probability of loss by fire.

METHODS OF HANDLING RISK

The method used to handle a risk depends upon its nature and the circumstances of the person or firm exposed to it. One or more of the methods shown below may be used with regard to a particular risk.

HANDLING RISK

1. avoidance
2. loss prevention and control
3. retention
4. transfer

Avoidance

Personal, property, and liability risks in general cannot be avoided, but specific exposures to such risks can be. In many cases, however, avoidance may be possible but not feasible. For instance, it is possible to avoid the risk of drowning by staying away from the water. Of course this precludes all forms of water transportation as well as transportation over or near water; boating, water-skiing, swimming, and other water sports are also prohibited. To make the list complete, it also precludes taking a bath—except in a shower bath. Without going this far, however, you can avoid the risk of drowning that is associated with water sports by refraining from them.

The risk of loss to specific pieces of property can be avoided by neither owning nor being responsible for them. This is one reason some people prefer to rent property rather than to own it. The rental agreement may, however, shift some risks from the owner to the renter so efforts to avoid ownership risks must include refusal to sign agreements including such clauses. The risk of liability related to automobile ownership and operation can be avoided by neither owning nor operating an automobile, nor being in a position of responsibility for a person (or firm) who does.

The risk to a corporation that all of its top management team may be killed in a crash of the company's aircraft may be avoided by following a practice of limiting the number of such executives who may be in the plane at the same time. So far as one specific executive is concerned, however, the only way to avoid the aircraft risk is to keep him or her on the ground. This illustrates the point made earlier that the way in which a risk may be handled depends upon its nature and who is exposed to it. Some families avoid exposure to loss of both parents in a single aircraft crash by following the practice of the father and mother taking different flights to their destination. Such avoidance is possible only when there is more than one unit exposed to the risk.

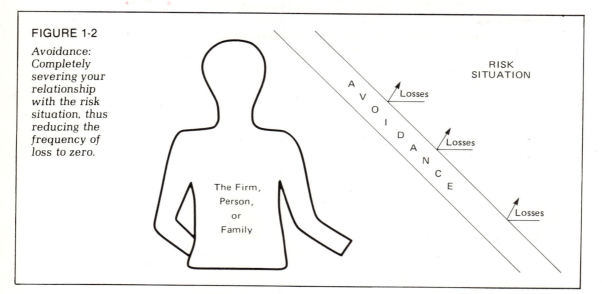

FIGURE 1-2

Avoidance: Completely severing your relationship with the risk situation, thus reducing the frequency of loss to zero.

Loss Prevention and Control

Loss prevention efforts are aimed at reducing the probability of a loss occurring. The objective of control efforts, on the other hand, is to reduce the severity of losses. If you want to ski in spite of the risks involved, you may take instruction and training to improve your skill and reduce the likelihood of falling or crashing into a tree. At the same time, you will engage in a physical fitness program to toughen your body to withstand spills without serious injury.

The magnitude of losses suffered by a firm during a year is a function of the frequency and severity of accidents, fires, and other loss-causing incidents. Frequency is a measure of how often such incidents occur; e.g., the number of injuries that occur in a plant during a specified period of time. Severity is a measure of the damage caused by each incident. Loss prevention and control efforts are directed toward reducing both frequency and severity. For example, attempts are made to prevent the occurrence of fire. Because some fires will occur in spite of such efforts, however, it is necessary to reduce their severity by quick suppression of those that start.

Similar efforts are made in your household. For example, you prevent the accumulation of oily rags, sawdust, and trash in your workshop because such refuse is susceptible to fires. You may also have a fire extinguisher in your shop to suppress any fire that starts in spite of your prevention program. If you have not already done so, it would be a good idea to have smoke and heat alarms installed in the workshop as well as other areas of your home. They don't prevent fires, but they can help reduce the severity of losses.

The goal of loss prevention and control is to reduce losses to the minimum that is compatible with human activity. At any given time, economic constraints place limits on what may be done although what is considered too costly at one time may be readily accepted at a later date. This is influenced as much by our sense of values as it is by our wealth although these two factors may be interrelated. Thus, little effort may be made to prevent injury to employees during one era because employees are regarded as inexpensive and expendable. A generation or two later, however, such injuries are prevented because they have become too expensive as a result of changing concepts of the value of human life.

Retention

When you engage in an activity, you assume the risks involved. If you decide to bear the burden of possible losses, you have retained the risk. Retention may also occur when the person exposed to a risk is unaware of it. Millions of people have retained the risk of cancer from cigarette smoking without knowing there was a risk. Many people rationalize the retention of this risk currently by pretending that it does not exist.

Some risks are retained because their significance is underestimated. Many people retain the liability risk not because they are unaware of it but because they think they are unlikely to suffer such a loss. Their decision is based on ignorance. They in effect say, "It won't happen to me." What they fail to consider is that it *can* happen to them and if it does it may very well prove to be a financial disaster. A similar attitude causes some families to retain the risk of disability or death of the person who is the sole or main source of income. Many young people are guided by the frequency of such losses among persons of their age group rather than their severity when the decision to retain the risk is made.

Other risks are retained because the possible losses are so unimportant that they are given little thought. If such losses do occur, they may be somewhat inconvenient but they are not burdensome. For example, there is a possibility that your shoelace may break today or that your inexpensive ballpoint pen may be lost, but you retain such risks because the loss is insignificant.

Finally, there are cases in which part or all of an important risk is retained after more or less careful consideration has been given to its analysis and the alternative methods of handling it. The arrangement made for sustaining the burden of losses which occur may be merely to charge them off as an operating expense. Or, some estimate of long-term average losses may provide the basis for the creation of a fund from which to pay for losses sustained. Such a fund may be in the form of cash or near-cash, or it may merely be a bookkeeping entry which represents an unidentified portion of the firm's assets.

The extent to which risk retention proves to be feasible depends upon the accuracy of loss predictions and the arrangements made for loss payment. When the risk is of such a nature as to be insurable and when the method of retention is highly formalized, it is sometimes said that the firm has "self-insured" the risk. Full discussion of this concept will be postponed until after the nature of insurance has been analyzed.

Transfer

As noted earlier, avoidance of risk involves staying out of the game, so to speak. We avoid a risk by avoiding the activity or situation which creates it. Transfer of risk, on the other hand, is a method of having our cake and eating it, too. We stay in the game but shift the risk to someone else. Transfer can be accomplished only when the risk and the activity or situation involving it are separable. For example, motorcycle racing involves the risk of injury which may cause pain, loss of income, and medical expense. The dollar cost of lost income and medical expense can be separated from the activity and shifted by having someone else, such as the employer, bear the loss. But the pain cannot be borne by someone else. That risk cannot be separated from the activity. Moreover, transfer of risk is not always complete, nor is it always dependable. Some risks may be transferred through the form of business organization. Others are transferred by contractual arrangements.

Form of business organization. A serious risk confronting the owner or owners of a firm involves the matter of responsibility for the payment of debts and other financial obligations when such liabilities exceed the assets of the firm. If the firm is organized as a *sole proprietorship*, the proprietor faces this risk. His or her personal assets are not separable from those of the firm because the firm is not a separate legal entity. The proprietor has unlimited liability for the firm's obligations. The owners of a *partnership* occupy a similar situation, each partner being liable without limit for the debts of the firm.

Because a *corporation* is a separate legal entity, investors who wish to limit possible losses connected with a particular venture may create a corporation and transfer such risks to it. This does not prevent losses from occurring but it transfers the burden to the corporation. The owners suffer indirectly, of course, but their loss is limited to their investment in the corporation. A huge liability claim for damages may take all the assets of the corporation but other assets held by the firm's owners are not exposed to this risk. This method of risk transfer is used to compartmentalize the risks of a large venture by incorporating separate firms to handle various segments of the total operation. In this way, a large firm may transfer parts of its risks to separate smaller firms, thus placing limits on possible losses to the owners.

Contractual arrangements. Some risks are transferred by guarantee included in the contract of sale. A noteworthy example is the warranty provided the purchaser for some makes of automobiles. When automobiles were first manufactured, the purchaser bore the burden of all defects which developed in the course of use. Somewhat later, automobile manufacturers agreed to replace defective parts at no cost, but the purchaser was required to pay for any labor involved. Currently, the manufacturer not only replaces defective parts but also pays for labor in making the repairs. The owner has, in effect, transferred a large part of the risk of purchasing a new automobile back to the manufacturer. The purchaser, of course, is still subjected to the inconvenience of having repairs made, but he or she does not have to pay for them.

Similar warranty contracts are now available to transfer the risk of repair losses from the purchaser of many household appliances to the manufacturer. As the nature of the durable goods we buy becomes more complicated and the cost of repairs rises, such a transfer of risk becomes an important consideration in making a choice among competing brands.

Bailments provide another method of transferring risk. A bailment exists when personal property is placed in the hands of another for safekeeping, servicing, processing, and so on. The arrangement usually provides that the bailee—the person or firm holding the property—is responsible to the owner only for damage to the property which results from the bailee's negligence. The bailment, however, may provide an opportunity for the owner to transfer specified risks to the bailee by contract. This is quite common in fur storage, for example. The owner of a fur is encouraged to store it by promises that the storage company will be responsible for any loss to furs while stored. The bailee, in turn, transfers the risk to an insurance company.

Leases and rental agreements often transfer risk from one party to another. A typical rental agreement, for example, provides that the property rented shall be returned to the owner in good condition, except for ordinary wear and tear. When you sign a lease for an apartment, such a provision places the burden of possible loss or damage to the property on you. Many people underestimate the risk they assume by signing such an agreement. Some leases contain a *hold-harmless clause* designed to shift certain risks from owner to tenant. This clause specifies that the tenant agrees to hold the owner harmless from liability arising out of the ownership or use of the premises during the term of the lease. Many tenants who sign leases do not realize that they have agreed to pay for losses which would normally be paid by the owner. On the other hand, if the tenant cannot pay, the burden will be borne by the owner.

√ *Contracts of suretyship* are another risk transfer device. In such a contract, a third party (known as the surety) guarantees that it will perform as specified in the contract if the person who is obligated fails to do so. A co-signer of a note is a surety who says to the creditor, "If the person who signed this note and to whom you loaned this money does not repay it in accordance with the terms of the note, I will." This transfers the risk of default from the creditor to the surety. When you endorse a check for deposit in your bank account, you are acting as a surety. If the check bounces, you are responsible for reimbursing the bank.

Clearly, it is neither possible nor feasible to list, much less discuss, all the methods of transferring risk. They are limited only by one's imagination. Those discussed above merely illustrate some of the possibilities. Perhaps the most important arrangement for the transfer of risk is insurance. Its nature is discussed at length in Chapter 3.

Consumer Applications
Handling Personal and Property Risks

Are the risk handling methods we have discussed applicable to your risks? Let's apply them to the academic risk and the car theft and home burglary risks.

Handling Academic Risk

Academic Risk Avoidance

Let's take a look at some of the ways you can deal with risk by examining what you do in a risk situation common to the college environment. The situation arises at registration. The risk is that you will register for a course in which (1) you will get a poor grade, and/or (2) you will die of boredom. What do you do?

First, you check with your friends for recommendations. You ask them two questions: (1) is the course worth taking? (2) which professor is best (or, least objectionable, as the case may be)? Second, you look at your alternatives. If the course is required, you look for the best professor. In this, you are guided by your own standards. If you can't get into his or her section this term, you postpone the course to another term. If the course is an elective, you may cross it off your list because several students whose opinion you value have told you "it's lousy, no matter who teaches it." Or, if the word is, "the course is OK if you get Professor Snodgrass," you try to get into that professor's section. If you can't get into Pro-

fessor Snodgrass' section, you postpone taking the course.

Academic Risk Transfer

In all these moves, you've investigated the risk situation and, if possible, avoided a situation in which the probability of loss was unacceptable when compared with what you might gain from it. What you have done is illustrated in Figure 1-2 on page 8.

But suppose the course is required, there is only one section, and this is the last term you can take it? If you are a valuable member of the football or basketball team in the right university, your faculty advisor can arrange for someone else to take the course for you. You transfer the risk of boredom and bad grades. This does not completely eliminate the risk, however, because your substitute may get a bad grade. Unless the athletic department moves quickly to have your first substitute's grade changed to something more satisfactory, you may be in academic trouble.

Academic Loss Prevention

Most students do not have the risk transfer option. They sometimes wind up in a required course offered by a professor they don't like and are stuck with it. What can they do? Loss prevention and control is a must. An experienced friend may make the suggestions shown below.

ACADEMIC LOSS PREVENTION

1. Buy the required textbooks.
2. Read them.
3. Study them.
4. Attend class regularly.
5. Stay awake in class.
6. Ask questions in class (this involves thinking).
7. Ask your professor for guidance; he or she may be flattered.

Following your friend's advice may not prevent boredom but it may prevent your receiving a bad grade.

Preventing Car Theft

The risk handling skill you have acquired in the academic environment is readily transferrable to other risk situations. If you want to prevent theft of your car or something in it, the following suggestions may help:

1. Always lock the doors when you leave the car even for a few minutes. Nearly 80 percent of all cars stolen were left unlocked.
2. Don't leave keys in the car. About 40 percent of stolen cars had keys left in the ignition.
3. Drive with the doors locked; when you stop at an intersection, be ready to move in case someone tries to get in.
4. Check before entering your car to see if it has been disturbed or if someone may be hiding on the floor in the back.
5. Never pick up hitchhikers. Most of them are nice people but it's hard to tell which are and which are not. Appearance can be deceiving.
6. Don't park your car in an unlighted area and don't leave packages or other items in sight on the seats of your car. They attract thieves.

Protecting Your Home

Burglary, especially residential, is a crime of convenience. With so many houses easy to get into, why bother with one that may be difficult or one in which you may get caught? The following loss prevention suggestions may help make your home undesirable from a burglar's point of view:

1. Have a ferocious dog. A professional burglar who had a long and successful career in Philadelphia never entered a house that had a dog. Why take a chance on being discovered? Only an amateur would be so foolish.
2. Have someone stay in the house if you are gone, or use timed lights to make the burglar think someone is at home.
3. Install dead-bolt locks; the spring type are a cinch for a skilled burglar.
4. If you are going to be gone for some time:
   a. Don't stop newspaper or mail deliveries if you can get a neighbor to pick them up for you. By stopping delivery, you inform strangers you will be gone.
   b. Notify the police before leaving; they may check your home.
   c. Don't leave notes pinned to the door announcing that you are away and when you will return.
   d. Keep garage doors locked, especially if the garage is attached to the house.
   e. In winter, have snow shoveled from the walks and have a friend drive a car up and down the driveway to give the impression that someone is at home. In summer, arrange to have the lawn mowed.

f. Leave a car in the driveway to prevent thieves from backing a van close to your doorway and to give the impression that the house is occupied.

5. Whenever you have been gone from home for any length of time, be wary if the entry door is open or unlocked. There may be an intruder inside and it may be very dangerous for you to surprise him or her, especially if there is no other exit. A professional thief will always have an escape route, but a trapped amateur may kill you.

Discussion Questions

1. Risk is sometimes defined as "uncertainty with regard to the occurrence of an event." Is it possible for an individual to be certain and yet be exposed to risk? Please explain. *Pg 4*

2. In a particular situation it may be difficult to distinguish between moral hazard and morale hazard. Why? *Pg 7*

3. Although an industrialized society provides a higher level of living than a primitive society, it may also expose its members to a greater number of risks. How do you account for this? Does it mean that a primitive society is safer than an industrialized society? *MORE HAZARDS*

4. Does the transfer of risk eliminate uncertainty? Why or why not? *Pg 10*

5. How do you account for the fact that, for many people, the safest place to be is at work? *10,11*

6. What do we mean by the term "premature death"? When you define this term, are you looking at the loss from an economic point of view? If so, is the death of a young, totally disabled person premature?

7. Inflation causes both pure and speculative risks in our society. Can you give some examples of each? How do you handle such risks? *pg 5*

8. Some people who have complete health insurance coverage have a tendency to "stay a little longer" in the hospital or "have a few more tests, just to be sure I've recovered." Is this tendency a moral hazard, a morale hazard, or simply common sense? Please explain. *Pg 7*

9. Proprietors have unlimited liability for the obligations of their proprietorship and partners are in the same position with regard to partnerships. Liability of those who own a corporation, on the other hand, is limited to their investment. Why should proprietors and partners have greater liability than stockholders? Isn't this a form of discrimination against small business? *pg 10,11*

10. Transferring risk to someone whose ability to bear loss is less than yours is hardly an effective way to handle risk. Nevertheless, many landlords who are better off financially than most tenants include a hold-harmless clause in leases or rental agreements. Why? Pg- 12

Cases

JJM

1-1 One medical practice that has been widely discussed in recent years involves "defensive medicine," in which a doctor will require more medical tests and x-rays than might have been the case in the past—not because of the complexity of the case, but because of the danger that the doctor may be sued by the patient for medical malpractice. The extra tests will establish that the doctor did everything a reasonable and prudent doctor would have done to try to diagnose and treat the patient.

1. What does this tell you about the burden of risk?

2. What impact does this burden place on you and your family in your everyday life?

3. Is the doctor wrong to do this, or is it a necessary precaution?

4. Is there some way that this situation could be changed?

1-2 Thompson's Department Store has a fleet of delivery trucks. The store also has a restaurant, a soda fountain, a baby-sitting service for parents shopping there, and an in-home appliance service program.

1. Name three perils associated with each of these operations.

2. For the pure risk situations which you noted in part 1, name three hazards which could be controlled by the employees of the department store.

3. If you were manager of the store, would you want to have all of these operations? Which—if any—would you eliminate? Explain why you would keep or eliminate each.

1-3 Omer Laskwood was overheard saying to his friend, Vince, "I don't carry any life insurance on my life for my family because I'm young and I know from statistics few people die at my age. I may race a stock car on weekends for a hobby but statistics are still on my side. I'm a young man."

1. What are your feelings about this statement?

2. How does Omer perceive risk relative to his particular situation?

3. Are there other risks Omer should consider?

1-4 The "city fathers" of Flatburg are very proud of the newly proposed airport they are discussing at a council meeting. When it is completed, Flatburg will finally have regular commercial air carrier service. Some type of fire protection is needed at the new airport but Flatburg can not afford to purchase another new fire engine. They could use the downtown facilities, or they could move the downtown facilities five miles out to the airport. Someone suggested a compromise—move them halfway. As the city fathers left their council meeting that evening they had a number of questions on their minds regarding this problem.

1. What questions would you raise?

2. How would you handle this problem?

Chapter Two:
RISK MANAGEMENT

INTRODUCTION

Risk management is an organized method for dealing with the pure risks to which an individual, family, firm, or other organization is exposed. The person who is primarily responsible for it in a firm is known as the *risk manager*.

Risk managers are responsible for identifying all pure risks to which the firm is exposed and creating programs to handle them. They are expected to protect the firm's income and assets from pure-risk losses as much as possible with maximum certainty at minimum cost.

In this chapter we will discuss the following:

1. What the risk manager does.

2. How the risk management process can be used by the family.

3. How it can be used by the firm.

WHAT THE RISK MANAGER DOES

Anyone who has an income or assets makes some effort to deal with the pure risks to which they are exposed. Thus, most of us are risk managers. We are responsible for protecting ourselves and our families against personal, property, and liability risks. Professionals who have this responsibility in the firm use the process of risk management, which involves the following steps:

1. Identify risks.

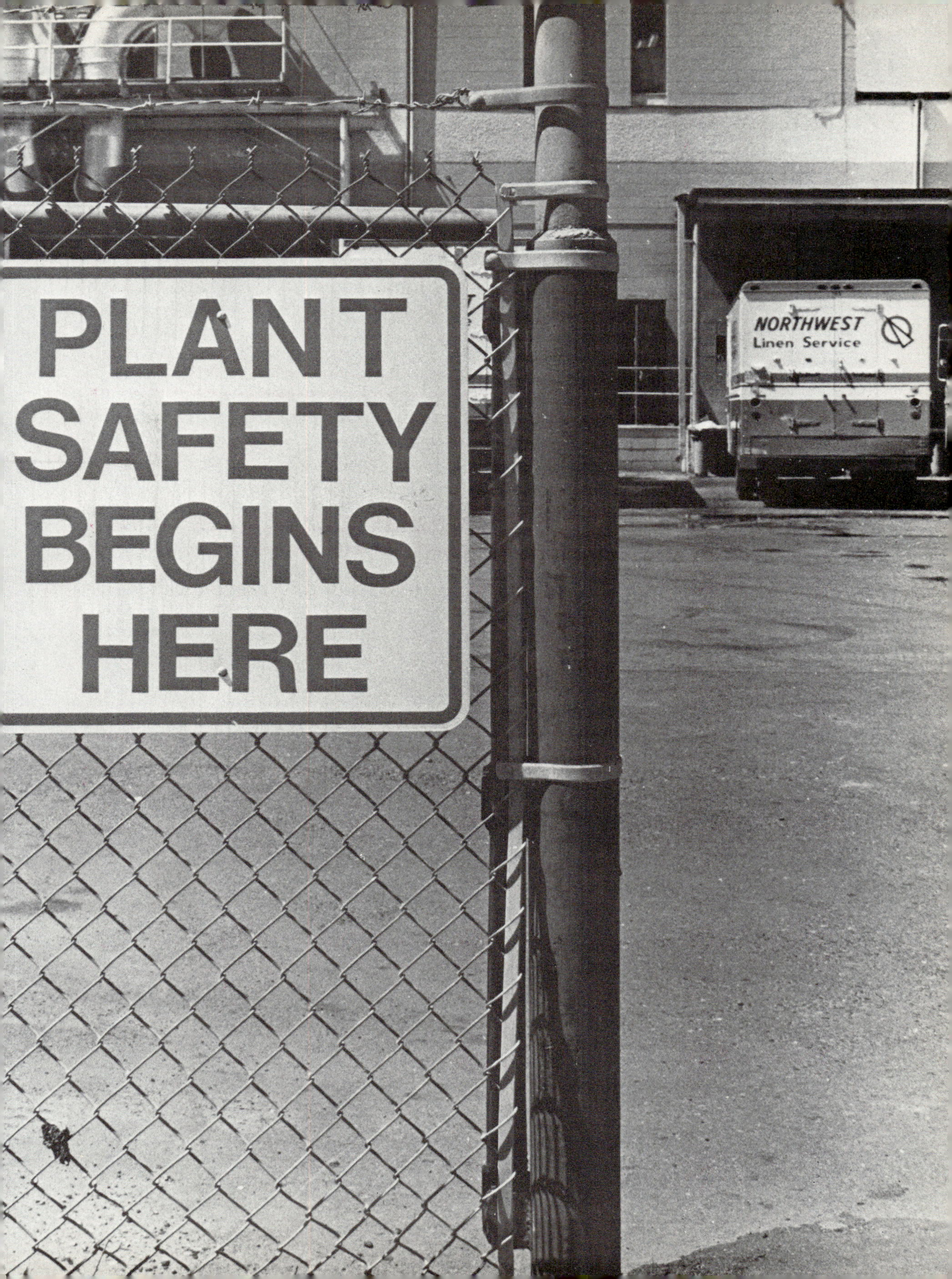
PLANT
SAFETY
BEGINS
HERE
NORTHWEST
Linen Service

2. Evaluate risks. *(MEASUREMENT)*

✱ 3. Select best method or methods for handling such risks. *CHOICE, AND USE OF METHODS OF TREATMENT.*

    a. Avoidance

    b. Loss prevention and control

    c. Retention

    d. Transfer

✱ 4. Implement the program. *(ADMINISTRATION)*

✱ *DIFFICULT*

5. Review program continuously.

Identifying risk is the most important and most difficult step. It is the most important simply because a risk which is not identified cannot be dealt with intelligently. We cannot do anything about a risk unless we are aware of its existence. Risk identification is especially difficult in a firm because no one can know all about every activity in which the firm is involved and every piece of property in which it may have an interest. Methods used to identify risks are discussed later in this chapter.

Risk evaluation means deciding how important a risk is. The best measure of importance is the potential size of a possible loss. If it is large enough to cause ruin or serious financial difficulty, a risk is clearly significant. At the other extreme, if the potential size of a possible loss is small, the risk may be relatively unimportant, especially if the probability of such a loss is low. If the probability of small losses is high, however, the risk is important enough to warrant attention. In all cases, of course, the significance of a risk is influenced by the ability to bear losses. A risk which is unimportant for a wealthy family or a large firm may be very significant for those with less financial strength.

Selecting the method of handling the risks which have been identified and evaluated as being important enough to justify attention requires consideration of the probability and potential size of possible losses as well as the ability to bear losses. Some risks must be avoided because they are unbearable for either financial or humanitarian reasons, but cannot be transferred. Others may be small enough in terms of potential loss and sufficiently amenable to loss prevention and control measures to justify retention. Still others can and should be transferred.

After identifying risks, evaluating them, and deciding upon the best method or methods of handling them, the risk manager must take whatever steps are required to *implement the program*. This means, for example, that loss prevention and control action must be taken, reserves established for risks that are to be retained, and the actual transfer arranged for those risks which are to be transferred. When insurance is the transfer mechanism, it must be purchased.[1]

---

1. Buying insurance is discussed in Chapter 7.

Continuous review of the risk management program is essential to keep it current because risk exposures to the family or firm change constantly.

FAMILY RISK MANAGEMENT

The family risk manager must identify all the risks to which the family's income, assets, and general welfare are exposed, evaluate them, select the appropriate method for handling them, implement the program, and review the program at regular intervals or whenever there is a significant change in the family's situation. It is not necessary for him or her to perform this function alone. Top quality insurance agents are willing and able to provide advice and counsel without charge. A professional life and health insurance agent can help with the personal risks and a professional property insurance agent can do the same with regard to property and liability risks.[2]

Identifying Risks

The first step in family risk management is risk identification. One need not be completely pessimistic in order to avoid overlooking a significant risk, but too cheery a view of the world can cause serious omissions. It is better to identify an unimportant risk than overlook one that could lead to serious loss.

Individuals and families are exposed to innumerable risks. For example, an individual may lose his or her income or property or be subjected to unusual expenses. When income is in the form of wages or salary, it may be lost as a result of unemployment, disability, death, or forced retirement. Disability of the family income producer not only reduces income but also increases expenses because of the need for hospital and medical care. Sickness or injury sustained by other members of the family may result in large, unplanned expenses for medical care. A major risk is the possibility of claims resulting from liability for bodily injury or property damage to others. Finally, the family may lose property as a result of fire, theft, windstorm, collision, or other perils.

After considering all these possibilities the family risk manager may organize the risks by creating a list such as Table 2-1.

Evaluating Risks

Evaluating family risks involves determining which are unbearable, which are difficult to bear, and which are relatively unimportant. Unbearable means risk of a loss so large that family finances would be so disrupted that bankruptcy would result. Difficult to bear means the possibility of a loss that would seriously reduce the family's level of liv-

---

2. Selection of an insurance agent is discussed in Chapter 7.

TABLE 2-1

Family Risks

	RISK	POSSIBLE LOSS
Personal		
Husband	Disability	Income, services and extra expense
Wife (employed)	Disability	Income, services and extra expense
Wife (not employed)	Disability	Services and extra expense
Husband	Death	Income, services and extra expense
Wife (employed)	Death	Income, services and extra expense
Wife (not employed)	Death	Services and extra expense
Child	Disability	Extra expense
Child	Death	Extra expense
Property		
Home	Damage or destruction	Asset and extra expense
Automobile	Damage or destruction	Asset and extra expense
Other property	Damage or destruction	Asset and extra expense
Liability		
Related to activities	Liability	Assets and extra expense
Related to property	Liability	Assets and extra expense

Note: The psychological loss that may be caused by the death or serious disability of a family member is not listed but does have a bearing on the relative significance of the various risks.

ing but not lead to bankruptcy. Relatively unimportant means the possibility of a loss that would not materially affect the family's living standards.

In determining the significance of a risk, two aspects of the possible loss are considered: (1) the severity of possible losses as measured by their potential size, and (2) the loss frequency or number of losses that may be expected during a specified period of time. For any particular

Perhaps the greatest financial loss that can befall any family is the

---

TABLE 2-2

Risk Evaluation

SEVERITY	FREQUENCY	EVALUATION
High	High	Unbearable
Low	High	Bearable
Low	Low	Relatively unimportant
High	Low	Unbearable

---

total disability of the main income-earner. In such a case, the income stops but family expenses rise because of medical costs. Such a risk is clearly unbearable for most families. Death of the main income-earner also stops income and is, therefore, unbearable although the risk may have less economic significance than disability because family expenses do not rise. In fact, they may decline. The liability risk is probably next in order of significance because the maximum possible loss is extremely high. But the serious illness of any member of the family, which could lead to unbearable medical expenses, may also be a financial catastrophe for the family. Death of a mother whose contribution to the family income is in the form of services rather than money earned through outside employment might not be unbearable financially but should surely be classified as difficult to bear.[4] Death of a child, on the other hand, has little economic significance to the family. This does not mean, however, that the risk is unimportant. Psychological losses can be far greater than any financial loss.

Some of the property risks to which the family is exposed can be classified as unbearable although they are not as important as those just discussed. Total destruction of the family home could completely disrupt the family's financial situation if the outstanding balance on the mortgage had to be paid out of the family's income and assets rather than by an insurance company. Total destruction of an automobile being

---

3. The number of categories could, of course, be expanded to include very high, high, medium high, etc. For a discussion of measuring potential frequency and severity of losses, see Williams, C. Arthur, Jr., and Richard M. Heins, *Risk Management and Insurance*, (3rd ed., New York: McGraw-Hill, Inc., 1976) Ch. 4.

4. Some estimates of the cost of replacing a homemaker's services are $12-14,000 plus per year. For some families, such an expenditure would lead to bankruptcy.

purchased on the installment plan could also cause an unbearable loss if the unpaid remaining balance had to be paid by the family instead of an insurance company. The relative significance of such risks does not matter, however, because lenders usually insist upon having the unpaid balance on such loans protected by insurance.[5]

With regard to much of the other property owned by a typical family, the risk is either bearable or relatively unimportant. Many people do have valuable property, such as art, antiques, and so on, and the loss of these could be large in terms of dollars but not unbearable so far as family finances are concerned. The risk with regard to most other family property can be classified as relatively unimportant.

Selecting the Method

After all the risks confronting the family—and there are far more than those just discussed—have been identified and evaluated, the next step in the risk management program is to decide upon the method for handling them. Some risks should be avoided, for others loss prevention and control may be effective, some may or must be retained, and others should be transferred.

Avoidance. When the significance of the loss which may be suffered is understood, it may be obvious that certain risks should be avoided. For example, some people abandon dangerous hobbies because of responsibility to children who are dependent upon them. Hang gliding may be an appealing sport when you are single and no one is dependent on you, but the risk may become too significant when you have a family. Although you can insure your life, this step takes care of only the financial aspect of your death. Some couples avoid the possibility of simultaneous death by taking separate flights when they travel by air. It is possible, of course, that both flights may crash, but the probability is extremely low.

The avoidance of a great many risks is simply impractical. For example, you may be killed on the way to work, regardless of your mode of transportation, but the risk is unavoidable unless you quit your job and stay home. Clearly, the price of avoidance can be too high.

Loss prevention and control. The probability of loss may be reduced through action taken by members of the family. Many people make concerted efforts to prevent accidental injury or illness and to prolong their lives by leading a safe and sane existence, getting adequate medical care, driving carefully, and so on. In some cases, the result of their efforts is reflected in insurance rates. For example, in many jurisdictions careful drivers receive a discount on their automobile insurance premium. People whose conduct makes them poor risks for life and health insurance either pay a higher than average premium or find it

---

5. If the home has increased in value since the loan was made, however, having just enough insurance to pay the original amount of the loan does not provide adequate protection for the owner.

impossible to obtain insurance at all. Many people lead a cautious existence and manage to avoid becoming liable to others for damages; they may also prevent loss to their property.

It is quite possible that if everyone pursued such an exemplary policy, total losses would decline and the cost of insurance would go down. Unfortunately, such action on the part of the individual or family may reduce the probability of loss somewhat and even prevent certain losses, but it does not eliminate the risk—there is still the possibility of a loss and it may prove to be unbearable.

When prevention is not certain and avoidance is either impossible or not feasible, the only alternatives for handling a risk may be retention or transfer.

Retention. After every effort has been made to avoid the risks confronting the family or to prevent losses which may occur, there will still be some risks which cannot be avoided or transferred, and some losses which cannot be prevented with certainty. Such risks must be retained and borne by the individual or the family. The financial aspect of illness, for example, can be transferred, but the mental and physical suffering must be retained. There is no way to transfer such a risk, nor can it be avoided.

On the other hand, some risks are retained because they are relatively unimportant. The possible loss of an inexpensive pocket calculator or this textbook are examples of this kind of risk. These risks are retained because they do not involve a serious burden. It is a waste of premium dollars to transfer them by purchasing insurance.

In some cases, however, risks are retained because of ignorance. The person or family exposed to them is simply unaware of their existence, or of the potential size of possible losses. In other words, they have either not been identified or they have been improperly evaluated. Some pilots, for example, fly without liability insurance. Such unconscious retention of risk can be avoided by reviewing the family's risk management program.

Transfer. Clearly, when major risks cannot be avoided and loss cannot be prevented with certainty, the risk manager must transfer those which are insurable to an insurance company if the family is to avoid exposing itself to possible serious losses. Insurance and how to buy it are discussed in Chapters 3 through 7.

Implementing the Program

Implementing the program means *doing* all the things we have discussed thus far. Identifying risks, evaluating them, deciding which method to use in handling them—these essentially represent the planning stage. Utilizing the plan requires action. If it has been decided that certain risks should be avoided, for example, then they must be avoided. This may be more difficult than it sounds. Giving up a favorite—but dangerous—hobby is like going on a diet; it is easier to plan than to do. If the program indicates that loss prevention efforts—such as proper exercise prior to the skiing season—may prevent, or reduce the severity of, accidental injury, the loss prevention program must be followed. If the risk of a large deductible on medical insurance or automobile collision insurance is to be retained, the risk manager may decide to accumulate a cash reserve to take care of such contingencies. Until the reserve is accumulated, that portion of the program has not been implemented. For those risks which are to be transferred to an insurance company, implementation means the purchase of insurance to cover them.

Risk identification and evaluation, loss prevention and control, retention and transfer, are the steps a risk manager follows in making decisions and taking action. Until the action is taken, the program has not been implemented.

Continuous Review

The family risk manager's job is never done; he or she must engage in virtually continuous review to keep the risk management program up to date. Property owned by the family changes in nature, amount, and value almost continuously. Activities of family members change; some risks may disappear while new ones come along.

A few examples may illustrate these changes. Suppose that at the time the program is implemented, the family has a new automobile and the risks entailed are covered by a policy which includes collision coverage with a $250 deductible. As the car becomes older and declines in value, it may be well to drop the collision coverage if family finances permit bearing the risk of a total loss.[6] At the same time, the replacement value of the family home may be increasing as a result of rising construction costs. Is the present amount of coverage adequate? A member of the family buys an expensive camera. Is it covered by the Homeowner's Policy? If so, is there any special limit applicable to such coverage? The family decides to take a trip to Europe. Of the special risks involved, which are already covered by insurance, which will require additional insurance, which may be retained, which should be avoided, and what loss prevention steps should be taken? A review of the risk management program requires that such questions be raised.

BUSINESS RISK MANAGEMENT

Business risk management and family risk management are very similar; both have the same objectives and follow the same process. There are some differences, however, and these will be discussed in this section. The differences lie in the authority of the risk manager, the alternatives available, the complexity of the task, and some of the approaches used in the risk management process.

---

6. Remember that after a deductible of $100, unreimbursed casualty losses are a deductible item for income tax purposes.

Authority

In a small firm, the owner performs the risk management function; he or she establishes policy and makes decisions. In larger firms, the authority of the risk manager depends upon the policy adopted by top management. He or she may be authorized to make decisions with regard to routine matters but restricted to making recommendations in others. For example, he or she may have the authority to continue insuring the workers' compensation risk but a decision to retain it would be made by top management. Avoidance may also involve decision making at higher levels because it frequently requires sacrificing an opportunity to make profits. For example, a new product may have potential for both great profits and huge liability losses. The liability risk can be avoided only by keeping the product off the market, but if that is done the profits it could generate are foregone. In such a situation, the risk manager is an adviser to top management rather than a decision-maker.

Alternatives

In some respects the business risk manager has greater flexibility than a family risk manager, at least in the case of a large firm. Because a large firm has the financial strength to bear the burden of rather large losses, it can retain all or a portion of risks which would be unbearable for a small firm or the typical family. Moreover, the risk manager of a large firm may be able to predict losses more accurately than a family risk manager. For example, if the firm has 50,000 employees, it may be possible to predict losses related to employee injuries on the job so accurately that the risk involved can be retained and self-insured. A family risk manager cannot make such accurate loss forecasts because the family has relatively few members; both the size and frequency of losses are hard to predict accurately.

On the other hand, responsibilities imposed upon the firm by law may reduce the flexibility of the business risk manager compared with the family risk manager. The Occupational Safety and Health Act (OSHA) of 1970 established the Occupational Safety and Health Administration and gave it the authority to set safety and health standards for virtually all employers. Through its authority, minimum safety standards for working conditions have been established and compliance with these standards is required by law. In effect, the minimum loss prevention and control program for workers is set by law rather than the risk manager.

Complexity

Risk management is more complicated for a firm than it is for a family for a number of reasons. First, the average firm has far more and greater variety of property exposed to risk than does the average family. Second, firms engage in a broader range of activities that expose them to the possibility of loss. Third, the responsibility of the firm for the actions of others is far broader than in the case of the family. No family has 5,000 members, but many firms have that many employees, any one of whom may get into trouble. Fourth, firms have certain responsibilities imposed by law—such as workers' compensation—which expose them to loss. Fifth, many firms either voluntarily or involuntarily (through union pressure) assume part of the life and health risks to which their employees are exposed. Finally, as mentioned earlier, large firms have more alternatives in handling risk than does the family.

Risk Identification

Business risk managers use the following approaches to identify every risk to which the firm is exposed:

1. Advice from insurance agents and brokers and risk management consultants

2. Insurance policy checklists

3. Risk analysis questionnaires

4. Financial statement analysis

5. Flow chart analysis

6. Communication with other departments in the firm

7. Inspections of the firm's facilities and operations.

Advice from insurance agents and brokers. This may be too insurance oriented in the sense that uninsurable risks are ignored, but professionals in the field have become risk management oriented. They can render valuable service in both identifying and evaluating risks.

Insurance policy checklist. These list the policies or types of insurance needed by various kinds of organizations. They are entirely concerned with insurable risks, but risk managers who bear this shortcoming in mind find them useful. Insurable risks confronting the firm are not the only risks, but they are a large part of the total.

Risk analysis questionnaires. These are designed to identify risks and compile information needed for their evaluation. Because every firm is unique in some respects, some risk managers develop their own checklists by modifying insurance policy checklists and published risk analysis questionnaires.

Financial statement analysis. This involves an examination of both the balance sheet and income statement, as well as financial forecasts and budgets. Current statements provide clues to the present property exposures of the firm, while forecasts and budgets reveal risks which will arise in the future. Budgets, for example, show planned expenditures for future operations and purchases of property. The risk manager must know about such plans so that the risks involved can be identified and timely recommendations made. Advice concerning fire prevention and control is more helpful while a new structure is in the planning stage than after it is constructed.[7]

Flow chart analysis. These charts depict graphically the operations of the firm, starting with inputs at one end and progressing through various processes and locations to output at the other end. Used in conjunction with a checklist, they are helpful in identifying possible losses to property and operations. Bottlenecks in the various processes, which create a situation in which a small direct loss can lead to a large indirect loss by shutting operations down, may be readily identified.

Communication with other departments. This has the dual purpose of making everyone risk conscious and finding out what is going on. No one can possibly know about everything that goes on in the firm, so such help is essential. In addition, employees who are risk conscious can help directly by identifying risks and keeping the risk manager informed of changes in activities, processes, property, and products. This will alert him or her to new possibilities for loss. A new activity, for example, may require inspection to assure that all OSHA regulations are complied with. New processes and products may create a liability risk. Newly acquired property may or may not be covered by present insurance. Some common business risks are shown in Table 2-3.

TABLE 2-3

Common Business Risks

	RISK	POSSIBLE LOSS
Personal		
Employee	Disability	Income, services, extra expense
Employee	Death	Income, services, extra expense
Property		
Buildings, equipment	Damage or destruction	Asset, income, extra expense
Trade secrets	Theft	Income
Inventory	Damage or destruction	Asset, income
Liability		
Activities	Product liability	Asset, income, extra expense
Activities	Pollution	Asset, extra expense
Property	Liability	Asset, extra expense

7. Example: Should the new structure have a fire suppression sprinkler system? If the answer is yes, the cost can be reduced considerably by having it installed while the building is under construction rather than after it has been completed.

Risk Evaluation

As with risks to which the family is exposed, some are unbearable, some are difficult to bear, and others are relatively unimportant. If the significance of a risk is overestimated, resources may be wasted in dealing with it. On the other hand, if it is underestimated, the firm may be inadvertently left exposed to the possibility of serious loss. Accurate evaluation provides the basis for a priority list which shows the relative importance of each risk to the firm. The nature of each is then analyzed to determine the best alternative for dealing with it. The choice among alternatives is influenced by the relative significance of the risk and the feasibility of each alternative from the mechanical, engineering, and economic points of view.

Retention

Small firms are in the same position as the family with regard to retention. Large firms, however, are different in two respects. First, because of their large financial resources, they are able to bear the risk of losses which would be unbearable for most families. They are also able to bear the burden of larger deductibles. Second, they may have some significant risks for which loss experience is sufficiently stable to permit retention. A large firm, for example, may own enough automobiles so that annual physical damage losses can be predicted accurately. In such a case, a program of self-funding for losses may be feasible.

Consumer Applications
Identifying Property and Personal Risks

Because identifying risks is the crucial first step in the risk management process, you may want to get some experience doing it. One approach is the use of checklists which help remind us of what we have to lose. Most people who use them are pleasantly surprised to learn how well off they are in terms of possessions and income. Let's look at those associated with the home and the personal risks confronting an individual or family.

The Home Risk

The first checklist, Figure 2-1, deals with home property risks. If your house and other structures were already built when you bought them, it may not be possible to determine the original cost of all the different structures because the purchase price was a package deal. On the other hand, the original cost of any structures built after the house and land were purchased should be obtainable. Some people, for example, buy a house and build a garage, tool shed, or greenhouse later. Planting trees and shrubs is almost a continuous process, so their original cost can be identified. Replacement cost today is what it would cost to replace any structures new, without reference to depreciation of present structures. Actual cash value, on the other hand, means replacement cost less depreciation. Your local building contractor, realtor, swimming pool firm, and nursery can help estimate the replacement cost of the various items on the checklist.

SECTION A—THE HOUSE AND LAND			
Item	**Original Cost**	**Replacement Cost**	**Actual Cash Value**
House	_____	_____	_____
Garage	_____	_____	_____
Swimming Pool	_____	_____	_____
Tool Shed	_____	_____	_____
Workshop	_____	_____	_____
Greenhouse	_____	_____	_____
Stable	_____	_____	_____
Other	_____	_____	_____
Other	_____	_____	_____
TOTALS	_____	_____	_____

FIGURE 2-1

Checklist for Your Home Risks—Property

FIGURE 2-2   *Checklist for Your Home Risks—Contents*

SECTION B—CONTENTS*

LIVING ROOM	quantity	date of purchase	price paid
couch			
chairs			
rugs			
tables			
lamps			
drapes			
TV			
radio			
artwork			
other			

KITCHEN	quantity	date of purchase	price paid
table/chair			
stove			
refrigerator			
major appliances			
small appliances			
utensils			
curtains			
rugs			
artwork			
cookware			
other			

DINING ROOM	quantity	date of purchase	price paid
table			
chairs			
rug(s)			
silverware			
china			
linen			
glassware			
drapes			
artwork			
other			

DEN/FAMILY ROOM	quantity	date of purchase	price paid
couch			
chairs			
tables			
rugs			
TV & radio			
stereo			
curtains			
artwork			
other			

*This is an excerpt from an eleven page checklist.

Reprinted with permission by the National Association of Professional Insurance Agents.

The second checklist, Figure 2-2, is an excerpt from an 11-page inventory guide for homeowners.[8] By making a complete list of all personal property in every room in your house or apartment along with the date of purchase and the price paid for each item, you will have a basis for determining the current value of your possessions. What you will find is that you have far more possessions to lose than you realized. The more you have, the more you are exposed to the possibility of loss.

In addition to helping you identify your property risks, such an inventory can prove to be a valuable aid when a loss occurs. Suppose, for example, that your home is burglarized. How can you prove the extent of your loss to the insurance company? An up-to-date inventory of your possessions will take care of that problem. If you don't have an inventory, you may have difficulty proving what the burglar took because you can't remember all the things you had.

The Personal Risk

If your home and its contents are worth $150,000 and a fire totally destroys it, you have lost $150,000 unless you have adequate insurance. What is the loss to your family if the person whose income provides support dies? We are all aware of this risk, but we choose not to think about it. We will discuss it in detail in Chapter 13 but you can get some idea of the financial significance of the risk by filling out a form like the one illustrated in Figure 2-3.

What this process does is simple but startling. It shows you the net contribution to the family budget made by the family income earner. It looks at the income earner from the investment point of view: how much is the net income stream from an investment worth? If your gross annual salary is $50,000, your net contribution to the family budget is that amount less taxes and other payroll deductions and the cost of maintaining you. If the net

```
Gross Income                                    _____   FIGURE 2-3
Less
    Income Taxes              _____                      Net Annual
    Social Security Taxes     _____                      Family Income
    Other payroll deductions  _____                      Lost by Death
    Personal Maintenance                                       of an Income
        Food          _____                                Producer
        Clothing      _____
        Transportation _____
        Recreation    _____
        Other         _____
    Total Personal Maintenance    _____
    Personal Insurance Premiums   _____
    TOTAL                                       _____

NET ANNUAL INCOME LOST                          _____
```

8. Homeowners & Renters Insurance & Inventory Guide, available free from Professional Insurance Agents, P.O. Box 6803, Washington, D.C. 20020.

contribution figure is $20,000 annually, what is the total loss to the family in the event of your death? You can estimate this the same way you would the value of any other income-producing asset.

Discussion Questions

1. The newspaper article says, "Little Becky Burrows, age 2, wandered away from the family picnic at Riverview Park yesterday afternoon. Her body was recovered from the river three miles downstream by a fisherman late last night." What does this story suggest to you about family risk management?

2. What type of skills should a risk manager have? Must he or she be an insurance expert?

3. Some risk managers say they are responsible for all their firm's pure risks but have inadequate authority to fulfill their responsibilities. What authority do you think the risk manager should have?

4. Architects design buildings to be functional and attractive. What contribution can a risk manager make during the planning stage?

5. What governmental agencies other than OSHA are involved in risk management for families, individuals, and firms?

6. Some people have an aversion to risk identification and evaluation. They say it's a dreary way of looking at the world. "If all you think about is risk, it spoils all the fun." How do you react to this attitude?

7. What is meant by the statement that "what you do for recreation is influenced by your family responsibilities"?

8. Some firms provide annual medical examinations, weight control programs, exercise facilities, and other health related programs for employees. Do you think this is just another form of compensation or may there be other reasons for such programs?

9. Economics is sometimes called the "dismal science" because it deals with problems of scarcity. Considering the fact that risk management is concerned with risk (the possibility of loss), do you think it merits a similar label? Why or why not?

10. It has been said that, "the most important thing in the world is to know what is most important *now*." What do you think is the most important risk for you now? What do you think will be the most important risk you will face 25 years from now?

Cases

2-1 Brooks Trucking has never had a risk management program. It provides trucking services over a 12-state area from its home base in Cincinnati, Ohio. Elmer Dean, Brooks Trucking's Financial Vice President, has a philosophy that "lightning can't strike twice in the same place." Because of this, he does not believe in trying to practice loss prevention or loss control.

1. If you were appointed its risk manager, what are the first three things that you would do to identify the pure risk situations facing Brooks? *Ident – Past & Present / Eval – more Imp. / loss Prev.*

2. Do you agree or disagree with Elmer? Why?

2-2 Fred Gregg is an independent oil driller in Oklahoma. He feels that the most important risk he has is property damage to his drilling rig, because he constantly has small, minor damage to the rig while it is being operated or taken to new locations.

1. Do you agree or disagree with Fred?

2. Which is more important, frequency of loss or severity of loss? Please explain.

2-3 Howard Smith does not believe that risk management can properly be used by a family. "After all," he argues, "my family is such a small group of people that I cannot predict when losses will happen. I can't manage risk—it's too uncertain."

1. Explain why you agree or disagree with Howard.

2-4 As an agent for an independent insurance agency you have been pondering a presentation you have to make to the Lady's Sports Car Club. Your task is to explain to them how a family moves through various growth stages. Examples would be newly married, young children at home, children in high school and college, and finally the "empty nest" retirement years. The methods by which a family handles risk associated with these changes varies through the years. Your task is to give examples of how the risk varies and how it can be successfully dealt with by the family during its lifetime.

1. Set up examples to explain these family changes and the changing risks associated with them.

2. Note the obstacles that could surface through the years within a family that would make it difficult for them to transfer various forms of risk.

Chapter Three:
INSURANCE

INTRODUCTION

As noted in the last chapter, risk may be avoided, reduced, or eliminated by loss prevention, retention, or transfer. The most common way to transfer risk is to buy insurance. This chapter deals with the following questions about insurance:

1. What is insurance?

2. How does it work?

3. What risks are insurable?

4. What is self-insurance?

5. What is reinsurance?

WHAT IS INSURANCE?

Everybody knows what insurance is—or do they? Sometimes a person will say, "I'm not going to buy insurance on my camera. I will insure it myself." As we shall see, such a person is not insuring his or her camera but is, instead, simply bearing the burden of any loss that may occur.

A brief survey of insurance literature reveals differences of opinion among authors concerning how the term should be defined. In whatever way they define the term, however, their use of it indicates that they are all referring to the same thing when they say "insurance." Because the following definition best describes what we think insurance is by incorporating its essential features, we will try to adhere to it consistently:

> Insurance is a social device which combines the risks of individuals into a group, using funds contributed by members of the group to pay for losses.

The essence of the insurance scheme is that it is a *social device*, that it involves the *accumulation* of funds,[1] that it involves a *group* of risks, and that each person or firm who becomes a member of the group *transfers* his risk to the whole group.

Purpose of Insurance

The fundamental purpose of insurance is to reduce the uncertainty and worry caused when we become aware of the possibility of loss. It does this by spreading the economic burden of losses among members of the group. Insurance does not prevent loss, such as your car being stolen, but it relieves you of the financial burden.

An insurance scheme reduces uncertainty for the individual members of the group by averaging loss costs. The premium you pay is assumed, on the basis of predictions, to be your share of losses suffered by the group. In exchange for this contribution, you are assured that the group will pay for your losses. You transfer your risk to the group and average your loss costs, thus substituting certainty[2] for uncertainty. You pay a *certain* premium instead of facing the uncertainty of a potentially large loss.

Insurance and Gambling

Not infrequently one hears a remark to the effect that "the insurance company is betting that my house won't burn and I'm betting that it will." Such a reference to insurance makes it difficult to distinguish from gambling. It is true that in both gambling and insurance money changes hands on the basis of chance events. You pay a premium to insure against loss to your house caused by fire. If no fire occurs, the insurance company keeps the premium and you receive no money.[3] On the other hand, if a fire occurs, the insurance company pays for the loss. Similarly, if you bet Jon Smith $100 that East will win its ball game with West, money will change hands on the basis of what is to you and Smith a matter of chance.

In spite of the similarity of these insurance and gambling transactions, there is a fundamental difference between them. In gambling the risk of loss is created by the transaction itself, while in insurance the risk exists without the transaction. You are not exposed to a possibility of loss in connection with the East-West ball game until you make a

---

1. As a rule, funds with which to pay losses are accumulated in advance but some insurance schemes are operated on an assessment basis which provides for contributions to the group by its members after a loss has occurred.

2. With regard to the financial aspect of the risk.

3. It would be incorrect to say that you receive nothing for the premium payment. You get peace of mind from being relieved of the uncertainty of financial loss.

wager with Smith. You are, however, exposed to the possibility that fire will damage your home whether or not you insure it. Thus, gambling is an activity which creates risk for the participants whereas insurance is a device which transfers existing risk from one party to another.[4]

HOW INSURANCE WORKS

A definition and indication of the purpose of insurance, as well as the way in which it differs from some other activities involving chance events, provides some indication of what it is. Real understanding, however, requires an analysis of how it works. This section, therefore, is devoted to a discussion of the basic principles of risk assumption, probability, the law of large numbers, and the problem of adverse selection. Some familiarity with these principles is essential to an understanding of insurance.

Risk Assumption

Financial aspect.   Insurance is created by an insurer which, as a professional risk-bearer, assumes the financial aspect of risks transferred to it by insureds. Most insurance contracts are expressed in terms of money although some indemnify insureds by providing service. A life insurance contract, for example, obligates the insurer to pay a specified sum of money upon the death of the person whose life is insured. A liability insurance policy, on the other hand, not only requires the insurer to pay money on behalf of the insured but also to provide legal and investigative services needed when the event insured against occurs. The terms of a health insurance policy may be fulfilled by providing medical and hospital services for the insured when he or she is ill or injured.

Whether the insurer fulfills its obligations with money or services, the burden it assumes is financial. The insurer does not guarantee that the event insured against will not happen. Moreover, it cannot replace sentimental values or bear the psychological cost of a loss. A home may be worth only $80,000 for insurance purposes but have many times that value to the owner in terms of sentiment. The death of a loved one can cause almost unbearable mental suffering which is in no way relieved by receiving a sum of money from the insurer. Neither of these aspects of loss can be measured in terms of money, therefore, such risks cannot be transferred to an insurer. Because these noneconomic risks create uncertainty, it is apparent that insurance cannot completely eliminate it.

Prediction.   As a device for handling the financial aspect of risk, insurance is feasible because insurers are able to combine the risks of individuals into a group and pay losses with funds collected from its members. The function of insurers is to assume risk and the purpose of

---

4.   You cannot buy insurance unless you are actually exposed to the possibility of loss. If you could, the transaction would be gambling.

insurance is to reduce uncertainty. A common question, then, is why is the insurer better able to assume a risk than the insured? That is, in what respect is the situation of the insurer and the insured different? Clearly, if they are not different, the insured is no better off transferring his or her risk than retaining it.[5]

It is sometimes said that the difference lies in the fact that the insurer has greater financial resources than the insured. This is usually the case, but not always. Occasionally, the insured is larger than the insurer. In any event, the insurer is obligated to a large number of insureds, so the size of its financial resources compared with those of anyone of its insureds is not a measure of its ability to bear a risk. Moreover, if the only difference between the insurer and the insured is financial ability to bear losses, the transfer agreement is a mere speculation.[6]

Another suggestion is that the insurer may differ from the insured in its ability to prevent losses. This is perhaps true in general, but complete elimination of the possibility of a particular individual suffering a loss is in most cases impossible. Thus, uncertainty remains. With reference to one risk confronting one individual, the position of the insurer and the insured is virtually identical.

The fundamental difference between the insurer and the insured is in predicting future events. So far as you are concerned, the insurer has no greater ability to predict than you. The insurer, however, does not have to make the same prediction as you do. You must predict what will happen to you as an individual. The insurer, on the other hand, makes predictions with regard to all insureds as a group. When a large number of risks or exposures is combined into a group, the risk faced by the insurer is not the same as that to which you are exposed nor is it merely the sum of the risks of all members of the group. The difference between the insurer which assumes a risk and the insured who transfers it is that the insurer can make more accurate and reliable predictions with regard to its risk. The reason for this difference lies in the concept of pooling.

Pooling. In Chapter 1 we defined loss as an unfavorable deviation from expectations and risk as the possibility of a loss. Your risk is a function of *your* expectations and the state of the world which can cause actual events to deviate from those you expected. The insurer's risk is defined in the same way but it is not identical with yours because the insurer's expectations are different. You do not expect losses but know that they are possible, whereas the insurer expects events which are—to you—losses.

The difference between you and the insurer is not that the latter's predictions for the individual insured are more reliable but rather that the insurer can make predictions for the group which are more reliable

---

5. Transferring a risk to someone whose ability to bear it is no greater than yours does not reduce uncertainty.

6. This is virtually the case with the insuring of unique risks.

than your predictions for yourself. Thus, *pooling changes the nature of the risk and improves predictions.* This, in turn, results in smaller deviation from expectations. A brief discussion of probability and the law of large numbers may help clarify this point.

Probability

An insurer which assumes risks does so with the expectation of substituting average losses for actual losses, thus reducing uncertainty for insureds. Because the funds which are used to pay for losses suffered by insureds are typically collected from members of the group in advance, the insurer must be able to predict losses accurately. The fee (premium) charged for assuming a risk is based on such predictions and the predictions, in turn, are based on probability estimates.

A person who says "there is a great chance" that something will happen or "there is little chance" that it will happen, is thinking in terms of probability. *Probability is a measure of the chance of an occurrence.*[7] When there is no possibility of an occurrence, the probability is 0. When an occurrence is a certainty, the probability is 1. Probability may be expressed as a fraction or as a percentage. If there are two possible outcomes, each of which is equally probable, the probability of either is 1/2 or 50 percent. The numerator is the number of favorable—or unfavorable—possibilities, while the denominator is the number of all possible outcomes.

Deductive estimates. Estimates of probability may be made through either deductive or inductive reasoning or the use of both methods. The deductive approach involves ascertaining all the factors which can influence the outcome and using logical reasoning to arrive at an estimate. For example, if you examine a coin and determine that it has two sides, is perfectly balanced, and has such a narrow edge that it is impossible for the coin to stand on edge, you can conclude that if you flip the coin it will come up either heads or tails. Because the coin is perfectly balanced, it may be concluded that, unless there is interference with the process, the chance of the coin landing heads up is as great as the chance that it will land tails up. When the coin is flipped, there are only two possible outcomes. If one is chosen as the favorable outcome, it can be seen that there is one chance out of two that such an outcome will occur in any one trial. Thus, it may be concluded that there is a probability of 1/2 or 50 percent that, in any given trial, heads will come up. Since it is known that either heads or tails *must* come up when the coin is flipped, it may be concluded that there is the same probability that tails will come up. When the number of possible outcomes of an event is known, the probability of any one in particular is 1 minus the sum of the probabilities of all the others. In the coin-flipping illustration, there are only two outcomes possible, so the probability of each is 1 minus the probability of the other; in this case, 1/2.

7. Probability is a concept with several meanings. It is used here in the statistical or frequency distribution sense. Relative frequency refers to the proportion of the time an event occurs and probability is measured in terms of relative frequency.

The probability of getting a desired number with the roll of a die may be estimated in a similar fashion. Because the die has six sides, there are six possible outcomes if it is perfectly balanced and no attempt is made to influence which side comes up. The probability of rolling a specific number is 1/6, because it is one of six possibilities. Because there are five other possibilities each of which has a probability of 1/6, the probability of rolling a specific number is 1 minus 5/6 or 1/6.

Inductive estimates.   As noted above, use of the deductive method requires that all factors which may affect an event must be ascertainable. Unfortunately for those who are responsible for insurance company price-making, such a situation seldom prevails. In calculating the probability of death for the purpose of creating life insurance premium rates, for example, it is impossible to determine every factor which may influence the death rate. Under such circumstances, probability estimates must be made through the inductive process. This method, which is also referred to as the *empirical method,* involves observing what has happened in the past and assuming that the same will happen in the future if the same conditions prevail. Using this approach, an estimate of the probability of getting heads (or tails) when a coin is flipped can be made by simply flipping the coin to see what happens. After making note of what is observed, it may be concluded that the same would happen in the future and that such observations provide the basis for a calculation of the probability of a particular outcome.

Here, however, a problem may arise. Suppose the coin is flipped twice and tails appear both times. Does this justify the conclusion that there is no probability of heads coming up? Or, suppose the coin is flipped ten times and shows two heads and eight tails. Does this mean that the probability of heads is 1/5 and the probability of tails is 4/5? Since it has already been established deductively that there is equal probability of getting heads or tails, it may seem at this point that the coin being used in the experiment is not perfectly balanced or that the deductive conclusion was in error. This, of course, is a possibility. However, suppose the coin *is* perfectly balanced. Then can it be concluded that the estimates of probability arrived at inductively are accurate? The answer is no. This is because the law of large numbers has not been considered.

Law of Large Numbers

If we had continued to flip the coin for an indefinite period instead of stopping after ten trials, the distribution of heads and tails would have approached 50 percent each more closely as the number of trials increased. This experiment would illustrate the law of large numbers which states that the larger the number of trials, the more nearly experience will approximate the underlying (true) probability. Thus, if the probability of heads is 50 percent, results should more and more closely approach 50 percent heads as the number of trials increases. Those who make the experiment find that this is correct, but are surprised at how large a number of trials is involved. One experiment involving more than 70,000 tosses of the coin resulted in a distribution of heads and tails which was not quite 50–50.

The unique contribution of pooling to the insurer as a risk-bearer should now be apparent—it is a function of the law of large numbers. Insurer operations are affected by this law in two ways. First, if accurate estimates of the probability of an occurrence are to be made, a large number of cases must be considered. If the inductive method is used to determine, for example, the probability of death during age 25, a large number of cases must be observed in order to derive an estimate that is useful.

The second way the law of large numbers affects insurer operations stems from the fact that, after an estimate of probability has been made, it can be used as the basis for predicting future experience *only* when dealing with sufficiently large numbers. If, for example, an insurance company provides one person with $10,000 of life insurance for one year in exchange for a $100 premium, it will either make $100 or lose $9,900 on the transaction. That is, either the person whose life is insured will die during the year or he will not. There is some probability that a person his age will die during the year but even if the insurance company knows exactly what that probability is such information is not helpful in predicting the outcome so far as one individual is concerned.

So far as an individual is concerned, knowing the probability of death during the coming year is no help in predicting the future. With respect to one individual's life, the insurance company is in no better position to make predictions than is the individual. Given a large number of similar lives, however, the insurer can make accurate predictions concerning what will happen to the group. While there is no way of predicting which of the people whose lives are insured will die, it is possible to make fairly accurate predictions for the group based on the underlying probability. The insurer does not need to know what will happen to any one person—that is the individual's problem. All it needs is an accurate prediction for the group. The basis for this is probability and the law of large numbers. Their use is made possible through the concept of pooling.

Adverse Selection

Adverse selection is the tendency of people who have a greater probability of loss than the average to seek insurance. It can result in greater losses than are expected on the basis of past experience. Insurers try to prevent this by learning enough about applicants for insurance to identify such people so they can either be rejected or put in a group whose members have a loss probability similar to theirs. This is the purpose of medical examinations for older applicants for life insurance or anyone who applies for a large amount of insurance.

Some insurance policy provisions are designed to reduce adverse selection. The suicide clause in life insurance contracts, for example, avoids liability to the applicant who purchases life insurance in contemplation of taking his or her own life. The pre-existing conditions provision in health insurance policies is designed to avoid paying benefits to people who buy insurance because they are aware of a physical ailment which will require medical attention and/or disable them.

IDEAL REQUISITES FOR INSURABILITY

Are all pure risks insurable? No. The insurance device is not suitable for all risks. Many are uninsurable. So that you may understand why some risks cannot be insured, this section is devoted to a discussion of the requirements which must generally be met if a risk is to be insurable. As a practical matter, many risks which are insured meet these requirements only partially or, with reference to a particular requirement, not at all. Thus, in a sense, the requirements listed describe those which would be met by the ideal risk. Nevertheless, the bulk of the risks insured fulfill—at least approximately—most of the requirements. No insurer can safely disregard them completely.

A risk which was perfectly suited for insurance would meet the following requirements:

1. The potential loss would be significant but the probability would not be high, thus making insurance economically feasible;

2. The probability of loss would be calculable;

3. There would be a large number of similar exposure units;

4. Losses which occurred would be fortuitous;

5. Losses would be definite;

6. A catastrophe could not occur.

Economic Feasibility (*IMPORTANT*)

For insurance to be economically feasible, the possible loss must be significant to the insured and the cost of insurance must be small compared with the potential loss. If the possible loss is not significant to those exposed to the risk, they will not be interested in transferring it to an insurer. Retention of many risks is almost automatic because the loss would not be a burden. You may expect to lose your ballpoint pen but do not consider insuring yourself against the risk because such a loss is not important—it would be inconvenient, perhaps, but not burdensome. If all the people who own automobiles were wealthy, it is doubtful that much automobile physical damage insurance would be written because such losses would not be significant to the wealthy owners. Insurance is feasible only when the possible loss is large enough to be of concern to the person who may bear the burden.

The possible loss must also be relatively large compared with the size of the premium. If the losses the insurer pays plus the cost of operations are such that the premium is equal to or nearly as large as the potential loss, insurance is not economically feasible. When the probability of loss is high, budgeting is preferable to insurance. This explains why automobile physical damage insurance, for example, is available only subject to a deductible. The deductible eliminates claims for small losses. Small losses have such high probability that the premium for covering them would be very large compared with the size of losses. Insurance is best suited for risks involving large potential loss but low probability. Large losses are important to insureds because they cannot bear them, and low probability makes possible a premium relatively small compared with the possible loss.

Probability Calculable *(CALCUABILITY)*

For a risk to be insurable, it must be possible to calculate the probability of loss fairly accurately. Insurance premium rates are based on predictions of the future which are, in turn, based on estimates of probability. While some probabilities, such as that of getting a particular number when a die is rolled, may be determined deductively, others must be calculated inductively on the basis of past experience. Probability estimates based on experience are useful for prediction, however, only when it is safe to assume that factors shaping events in the future will be similar to those of the past. When such an assumption cannot be made, past experience is not a valid guide to the future. That is, the relative frequency of an occurrence in the past does not indicate the probability of its occurrence in the future unless all conditions affecting the occurrence are the same in the future as they were in the past. This is why marine insurance becomes unavailable from commercial insurers upon the outbreak of a major war. Past war experience does not necessarily indicate what will occur because each war brings new weapons of destruction, and deductive reasoning cannot be used as the basis for predictions because of the impossibility of weighing all the factors that may influence losses. When the probability of the loss to be insured against cannot be calculated fairly accurately, the risk is uninsurable.

Mass and Similarity

Mass.   A major requirement for insurability is *mass;* that is, there must be large numbers of exposure units involved. In the case of automobile insurance, there must be a large number of automobiles. In life insurance, there must be a large number of persons. An automobile insurance company cannot insure a dozen automobiles and a life insurance company cannot insure the lives of a dozen persons. You will recall that arriving at accurate probability estimates requires observation of a large number of events. After the probability of loss has been estimated, it can be relied upon for prediction only with reference to a large group. The insurance company is in no better position to predict losses for you than you are for yourself.

How large is a "large group"? For insurance purposes, the number of exposure units needed in a group depends upon the extent to which the insurer is willing to bear the risk of deviation from its expectations. Suppose the probability of damage to houses is 1/1,000. An insurer might assume this risk for 1,000 houses with the expectation that it would have one claim during the year. If no houses were damaged there would be a 100 percent deviation from expectations but such a deviation would create no burden for the insurer. On the other hand, if two houses were damaged, the claims to be paid would be twice the number expected. This could be a severe burden for the insurer. By increasing the number of houses insured to 10,000, the expected losses increase to ten but the stability of experience is increased. That is, there is a *proportionately* smaller deviation from expected losses than with a group of 1,000 houses. Similarly, if the group is increased to 100,000 houses, the variation of actual from expected losses will increase in absolute terms but decline proportionately. The number required to assure that actual experience will be the same as that expected on the basis of probability is infinitely large. The number required for practical purposes is a function of the amount of risk the insurer is able and willing to bear.

Similarity. The risks to be insured and those whose observed experience is the basis for loss probability estimates must be similar. The risks assumed by insurers are not identical regardless of how carefully they may be selected. No two houses are identical even though physically they may appear to be. They cannot have an identical location and they are occupied by different families. Nevertheless, the units in a group must be reasonably similar if predictions concerning them are to be accurate.

Moreover, probability calculated on the basis of observed experience must also involve units which are similar to each other. Observing the mortality experience of a group of people whose age, health, and occupations were all different, for example, would not provide a basis for calculating the probability of death for a group of male clerical workers whose age, health, and other characteristics were similar to each other. Probability estimates based on experience require that the exposure units observed be similar to each other. Moreover, such estimates are useful only in predicting risks similar to those whose experience was observed.

5. **Losses Fortuitous**   ACCIDENTAL

The risks assumed by an insurer must involve only the *possibility* of loss to the insured. Loss must be fortuitous: i.e., a matter of chance. Ideally, the insured should have no control or influence over the event to be insured against. In fact, this situation prevails only with respect to perils such as earthquakes and weather. As mentioned in Chapter 1, both moral and morale hazards influence the probability of loss. Prediction of loss experience is based on probability which has been estimated by observing past experience. Presumably, the events observed were, for the most part, fortuitous occurrences. The use of such probability estimates for predicting future losses is based on the assumption that they will also be a matter of chance. If this is not the case, predictions cannot be accurate.

6. In TOTAL
Regu Are
not Absolute
-/ou Pppen all Reg

3 Losses Definite *(Definitely Losses)* ENDING PT.

Losses must be definite in time and place because in many cases, insurers promise to pay for losses if they occur during a particular time and at a particular place. For example, the contract may cover loss by fire at a specified location. In order for this contract to be effective, it must be possible to determine *when* and *where* such loss occurred. If this cannot be established, it is impossible to determine whether the loss is covered.

The fact that, in many cases, it is difficult to determine objectively whether a person is sick makes the risk of sickness difficult to insure. On the other hand, risk of death meets the requirement of definiteness almost perfectly as death is ordinarily easy to establish. Only when the insured disappears mysteriously does a problem arise. One other reason the requirement of definiteness in time and place is essential is that it is necessary to accumulate data for future predictions. Unless such data can be accurate, it cannot provide the basis for useful predictions.

4 No Excessive Catastrophe Risk

The possibility of a catastrophe loss may make a risk uninsurable. When an insurer assumes a group of risks, it expects the group as a whole to experience some losses but that only a small percentage of the group will suffer loss at any one time. A relatively small contribution by each member of the group will be sufficient to pay for all losses. If it is possible for many or all insureds to suffer a loss simultaneously, however, the "relatively small contributions" would not provide sufficient funds. Thus, a requisite for insurability is that there must be no catastrophe risk. There must be limits beyond which insurers can be reasonably sure losses will not go. Insurers build up surpluses to take care of deviations of experience from the average, but such deviations must have practical limits. If they cannot be predicted accurately and with confidence, it is impossible to determine either insurance premium rates or the size of surpluses required.

Catastrophe losses may occur in two circumstances. In the first, all or many units of the group are exposed to the same loss-causing event. For example, if one insurer had assumed the risk of damage by earthquake for all houses in Southern California, it would have suffered a catastrophe loss in 1971 when many houses were damaged simultaneously. A second type of catastrophe exposure exists when the units in a group are interrelated in such a way that loss to one leads to loss to another with a chain reaction resulting in a loss to all. If one insurer assumes the risk of damage by fire for all buildings in a congested area, it may suffer a catastrophe when a fire which starts in one building leads to the destruction of the whole area.

The existence of the catastrophe exposure explains why insurance companies limit the amount they will commit themselves for on any one risk and why fire insurers limit their total commitments in any one city or area of a city. Moreover, certain perils such as nuclear energy are difficult to insure, partly because of the catastrophe exposure and partly because there is limited experience upon which to base predictions.

SELF-INSURANCE

Nature

As the most sophisticated form of risk retention, self-insurance differs significantly from mere failure to buy insurance. It involves establishing a scheme for handling risk which is fundamentally the same as insurance except that the risk is not transferred to an insurance company.

Example of Self-Insurance

Suppose a firm has one salesperson and owns one automobile worth $10,000. The firm is exposed to a large number of risks in connection with the automobile but let us give our attention to that of damage to the vehicle by windstorm. The firm may insure against this loss by transferring the risk to an insurance company or it may retain the risk and pay for losses as they occur. If it shifts the risk to an insurer, annual cost of wind damage becomes certain. The cost equals the insurance premium. If the risk is retained, annual losses caused by wind are entirely uncertain. They may be any amount from zero to $10,000. The probability of such losses cannot be determined on the basis of past experience because the number of units exposed to loss in the past is too small. Even if the probability of loss could be determined, however, it would not be useful in predicting future experience. The firm is in the same position as an individual automobile owner in this respect.

In contrast, suppose a second firm has a fleet of 5,000 automobiles, each worth $10,000, and each used by a different employee in a different part of the country. Because this group is fairly large, its past experience may provide a reliable indication of the cost of wind damage to be expected in the future. The owners of the fleet cannot predict what will happen to any particular vehicle, but their predictions for the group as a whole may be reasonably accurate. With this data available, the firm may establish a fund from which to pay for windstorm damage to its automobiles instead of paying premiums to an insurance company to perform the same operation. Through pooling, the magnitude of deviations from expectations is reduced to manageable proportions. This places the self-insuring firm in a position similar to that of an insurer which assumes the windstorm risk of a large number of automobile owners. The risk each bears is the possibility that damage to the automobiles in the pool will be greater than that predicted. With 5,000 automobiles in its fleet and a fund from which to pay the cost of damage caused by windstorm, the firm is, in effect, operating its own insurance scheme. It is a self-insurer.

Requisites for Self-Insurance

A risk perfectly suited for self-insurance would have the same characteristics as one ideally qualified for insurance. That is, the potential loss would be significant but the probability would not be high, the probability of loss would be calculable, there would be a large number of similar exposure units, losses would be accidental and definite, and a catastrophe could not occur. To what extent does the example of self-insurance just described meet these criteria? Is the potential loss from windstorm significant and is the probability low? A firm which operated a fleet of 5,000 vehicles over a period of years could have records which would provide the answer to this question. If such damage has been frequent but slight, it may be handled on a maintenance basis and there is no need for a self-insurance plan. On the other hand, if such losses have been infrequent but severe when they did occur, either insurance or self-insurance is economically feasible. As indicated earlier, the probability of windstorm damage may be calculated and used for predicting future experience because the fleet has a fairly large number of (relatively) homogeneous units. Because windstorm damage cannot be caused intentionally, such damage is accidental. It is also possible to determine when and where it occurred as well as the cost of repair or replacement of the damaged vehicle. Thus, the risk meets the requirement of definiteness.

Could a catastrophe occur? That is, could all or a large number of the vehicles in the fleet suffer windstorm damage simultaneously? Because each automobile is operated by a different employee in a different part of the country, such a catastrophe is unlikely. Suppose, however, that once a year all the employees who drive these automobiles use them to attend a convention sponsored by the firm. Suppose, also, that during the convention a hurricane strikes the city and all of the cars are badly damaged. Will the firm have enough money in its self-insurance fund to pay for the damage? Probably not, because the size of the fund is based on the assumption that only a few vehicles will be damaged by windstorm each year. When all automobiles in the fleet are concentrated in one location, the self-insurance scheme is exposed to the possibility of a catastrophe. If such an exposure cannot be avoided or shifted, self-insurance is not feasible. It might be avoided by having all participants in the annual convention leave their cars at home and use public transportation. It might be shifted by transferring the risk of large losses caused by one storm to an insurance company.

REINSURANCE

Nature

Reinsurance is an arrangement by which an insurance company transfers all or a portion of its risk under a contract (or contracts) of insurance to another company. In effect, the insurance company that has issued policies of insurance purchases insurance from another company. This protects it against all or a part of the losses against which it is insuring its policyholders. For example, a company which insures a building for $100,000 against loss by fire may make an agreement with a reinsurer which requires the latter to pay half of all losses under the policy. In the event of a $10,000 loss, the insurer would pay the insured $10,000 and then collect $5,000 from the reinsurer.

In this process, the company transferring the risk is called the *ceding company* while the company assuming the risk is called the *reinsurer*. When there is a claim on a policy, the reinsurer is liable to the ceding company, not the insured. The insured has a contract with the insurer, not the reinsurer.

The amount which the ceding company is willing to bear is called its *retention*. The size of the retention is influenced by such factors as the size of the surplus of the company and its experience with the type of risk being considered, as well as the temperament of its management. As a general rule, new and small companies establish retention limits which are smaller than those of older and larger companies.[8]

Some companies specialize in reinsurance, but the bulk of such business is done by insurance companies that sell both insurance and reinsurance. Thus, a company may act as both an insurer and a reinsurer, ceding part of its risks to another reinsurer and accepting a portion of other insurers' risks.

Purpose

The main reason for reinsurance is that the ceding company wants to protect itself against losses in individual cases beyond a specified sum, but competition and the demands of its agency force may require issuance of policies of greater amounts. A company that issued policies no larger than its retention would severely limit its opportunities in the market. Many insureds do not want to place their insurance with several companies but prefer to have one policy with one company for each risk. Furthermore, agents who represent companies offering insurance find it inconvenient to place insurance in small amounts when they are insuring a large risk. In addition to its concern with individual cases, a company must protect itself from catastrophic losses in a particular line (e.g., windstorm) or a particular area—such as a city or a block in a city—or during a specified period of operations, such as a calendar year.

A company offering a particular line of insurance for the first time may want to protect itself from excessive losses and also take advantage of the reinsurer's knowledge concerning the proper rates to be charged and underwriting practices to be followed. In other cases, a company which is expanding rapidly may have to shift some of its liabilities to a reinsurer in order to avoid impairing its capital.[9]

Significance to Insured

Reinsurance is significant to the buyer of insurance for a number of reasons. First, reinsurance spreads the risk and increases the financial

---

8. Some new life insurance companies reinsure *all* of their business for the first few years of operation until they become well established.

9. The immediate effect of issuing a policy of insurance is to add more to liabilities than is added to assets. This is because most expenses in connection with issuing the policy are incurred immediately but no allowance is made for this fact in the requirements for establishing reserves. This causes a short-run drainage of surplus which can be relieved through reinsurance.

stability of insurers. This makes a policy of insurance "surer" than it would be otherwise. Second, reinsurance facilitates placing large or unusual risks with one company, thus reducing the time spent seeking insurance and eliminating the need for numerous policies to cover one risk. This reduces costs for both buyer and seller. Third, it helps small insurance companies stay in business, thus increasing competition in the industry. Without reinsurance, small companies would find it much more difficult to compete with larger companies.

RETROCESSION !

Consumer Applications

Looking at Insurance
From an Insurer's Point of View

What use can you make of our discussion of what insurance is and how it works? First, you can adopt a financial point of view. You can analyze your situation and the risks you face as if you were an insurer considering insuring them for someone else. Second, you can bear in mind that an insurer differs from you in two respects:

1. It has more money and can bear larger losses.
2. It can predict more accurately.

Thus, you have to be more conservative than an insurer with regard to your risks. You can, however, get some practical knowledge about how to handle them by observing what insurers do.

WHAT DO INSURERS DO?

1. Estimate the possible size of loss.
2. Estimate the probability of loss.
3. Spread the risk by pooling.
4. Accumulate funds to pay losses.
5. Retain only what they can bear.
6. Reinsure what they cannot bear.
7. Refuse to assume risk for inadequate premium.

What Should You Do?

If you look at each risk to which you are exposed as if you were an insurer, you can use your knowledge of what insurers do as a checklist. For example, let's look at the risk of flunking this course from an insurer's point of view. What is the possible size of the loss in terms of dollars? You would lose the cost of fees and tuition, the time you spent on the course, and the net cost of the textbook (purchase price minus resale to the bookstore). You would also suffer boredom and frustration, and although attaching a dollar value to that is difficult, you could make an estimate. To summarize the possible size of the loss:

Tuition and fees	$ 75.00
Textbook	10.00
Time (45 hours @ $5 per hour)	225.00
Total	$310.00

The time cost is an hour for each of 45 class meetings. Instead of taking the course, you could have worked during those hours. Your time may be worth more or less than $5 per hour, depending on your opportunities. If you spent any time outside of class studying, of course, the total value of time lost would be greater than we have shown. On the other hand, further expenditure of time might decrease the probability that you would fail the course.

Would an insurance company sell insurance for this risk? Probably not. The loss would not be fortuitous, a matter of chance. You, as the insured, have some control over the event insured against. If you bought insurance and then decided you would rather have the money than credit for the course, there would be a moral hazard. If you are lazy and disinterested, there would be a morale hazard. If you cannot insure this risk, what should you do?

Self-Insurance and Retention

What about the risk that your car may be stolen or damaged in a collision? Can you self-insure the risk? No, because you cannot predict losses accurately. On the other hand, if the car is worth only a few hundred dollars, you may be able to retain the risk if the possible loss is bearable. Similarly, you can retain the risk of small losses which are regular enough to be predictable. They, in effect, become an expense item in your budget. They are like the losses an insurance company expects in the normal course of operations.

How large can your retention be? In deciding that, you can be guided by what insurers do. Their retention is influenced by the size of their surplus; the larger the surplus, the larger their retention. If you have several thousand dollars in a savings account, your retention can be rather large because you have the cash to pay for small losses. If you have little or no savings and barely get from one payday to the next, your retention must be small. What is a disaster for one person may be a minor inconvenience for another.

Retention May Be a Mistake

Do you retain a risk because the premium for insuring it is "too high"? Why is the premium high? If the answer is because the possible loss is large and unpredictable, you should either avoid it or insure it. An insurer will not insure such a risk unless it can shift at least part of it to a reinsurer. If an insurer reinsures what it cannot bear, insuring the unbearable may be a good policy for you.

Don't Risk Too Much for Too Little

Do you expose yourself to risks for little or no gain? For example, do you leave your car unlocked or leave the keys in it simply because it is convenient for you? Would an insurer assume the risk that your car might be stolen in return for such a small premium? If an insurer would refuse such a deal, is it smart for you to accept it?

Discussion Questions

PERFORMANCE BOND

1. What is the difference between insurance and suretyship? Are there similarities? Why do some people insist there is no difference?

2. At one time, some banks issued cards to depositors which guaranteed that checks they wrote to specified merchants would not bounce. Was this a form of insurance or suretyship? Other?

3. When you buy a service contract on your new refrigerator, are you buying insurance? Please explain.

4. The Mt. St. Helens eruption caused tremendous loss. Would it be feasible to provide insurance against all losses caused by volcanic eruption? Why or why not?

5. Mr. Bramovitz and Mrs. Bramovitz each own small retail businesses. Mr. B. has 10 locations, each valued at $50,000, while Mrs. B. has one location valued at $500,000. Can either of these businesses self-insure against loss by fire? What information would be helpful to you in answering this question?

6. Occasionally, Company X will reinsure part of Company Y's risks and Company Y will reinsure part of Company X's risks. Doesn't this seem like merely trading dollars? Please explain.

7. Some large insurance companies cede part of their risks to a smaller company. In view of the fact that the large company is stronger financially than the small company, does this seem reasonable? Please explain.

8. Some people use the term "self-funding" instead of "self-insurance." How do you account for this preference?

9. Prof. Kulp said, "Insurance works well for some risks, to some extent for many, and not at all for others." Do you agree? Why or why not?

10. For the past week, the weather forecast every evening has been as follows: 50 percent chance of rain tonight, 40 percent tomorrow, and 50 percent tomorrow night. Much to your dismay, there has not been a drop of rain all week and you still have to water the lawn. Does this mean the meteorologists don't know what they are talking about? Please explain.

Cases

3-1 Hatch's Furniture Store has many perils which threaten its operation each day. Explain why each of the following perils may or may not be insurable. In each case, discuss possible exceptions to the general answer you have given.

1. The loss of merchandise because of theft when the thief is not caught, and Hatch's cannot establish exactly when the loss occurred.

2. Injury to a customer when the store's delivery person backs the delivery truck into that customer while delivering a chair.

3. Injury to a customer when a sofa catches fire and burns the customer's living room. Also, discuss the fire damage to the customer's home.

4. Injury to a customer's child who is running down an aisle in the store and falls.

5. Mental suffering to a customer whose merchandise is not delivered as Hatch's had agreed.

6. Embarrassment to a customer who is detained as a possible shoplifter.

3-2 Charles Wood does not really like to buy insurance. Instead, he will do whatever he can to treat risk in other ways. For instance, Charles says, "I self-insure my car against collision. It is old, and I can afford to pay for it even if it is totally lost in an accident."

1. Is this self-insurance?

2. What must Charles be able to do to self-insure?

3-3 Company A, the ceding company, and Company B, the reinsurer, are having a contractual dispute about the reinsurance treaty which they established for Mammoth Manufacturing's main plant. A sold Mammoth a $20,000,000 fire insurance contract, and then reinsured with B for $15,000,000 of the $20,000,000.

1. What is one possible major argument about this treaty, if the fire loss in question is $3,000,000?

2. How will this change, if the loss is $20,000,000?

3. Will this argument affect Mammoth's ability to collect from A? If so, how?

4. Should Mammoth have tried to find out about any reinsurance in effect before buying its coverage from A?

Chapter Four:
TYPES OF INSURANCE AND INSURING ORGANIZATIONS

INTRODUCTION

In Chapter Three we talked about what insurance is and how it works, what risks are insurable, and what self-insurance and reinsurance are. This chapter deals with some further questions about insurance, including the following:

1. Where did the social device called insurance come from? How did it develop?

2. What kinds of insurance are there?

3. Who provides insurance?

DEVELOPMENT OF INSURANCE

Because of a lack of reliable records, there are differences of opinion concerning the origin of insurance. Something similar to modern insurance may be discerned, however, in certain ancient practices.

Ancient Practices

Perhaps the earliest forerunner of property insurance was a scheme used by merchants in Babylonia several thousand years ago. They engaged salesmen to sell goods in faraway places. In order to assure the salesmen's return with the merchants' shares of the profits, the salesmen were required to pledge their own property as a guarantee. But a salesman who was robbed while away from home sacrificed the pledged property just as he would in the case of dishonesty. The unfair-

SURANCE
FIRE LIFE HEALTH

MSI
Insurance

SURANCE

FRED WING
AGENT

ness of this arrangement led to a new system in which the pledge was not forfeited if a loss was caused by robbery in a foreign land and was not the fault of the salesmen. Thus the risk was shifted from the salesmen to the merchant.

A similar shifting of risk had its origin in ancient Greece. When a Greek moneylender financed a voyage for a shipowner, the ship was pledged as collateral for the loan. The lender agreed, however, that the loan would be cancelled if the ship failed to return. In effect, the lender insured the ship for the amount of the loan.

The forerunners of modern life and health insurance are found in ancient Greece and Rome. In Greece, religious groups collected funds from their members to assure funeral services, providing what was probably the first form of burial insurance. The Romans adopted similar arrangements for life insurance. Their schemes, however, were open to the general public. In some cases, rather broad forms of coverage were developed for particular groups, such as soldiers.

Middle Ages

During the Middle Ages, the guilds contributed to the development of the insurance by establishing insurance schemes financed by regular payments from their members. Benefits were paid for a wide variety of losses, such as those caused by fire, shipwreck, theft, and flood. Benefits similar to those currently offered by health insurance companies were also made available through the guild system. Loss of sight, serious illness, and old-age dependency were compensable by insurance.

There is no general agreement concerning just when marine insurance contracts as they are known today came into existence. It appears, however, that contractual marine insurance may have been written as early as the middle of the fourteenth century. By the middle of the fifteenth century, rules governing the conduct of the business had been adopted by several Mediterranean port cities.

Modern Development

The development of ocean marine insurance was stimulated by a law in England in 1574 creating a Chamber of Insurance to sell such insurance. Later, instead of roaming the streets looking for business, underwriters adopted the practice of meeting in coffeehouses to transact business. One coffeehouse proprietor, Edward Lloyd, attracted insurance men to his establishment by gathering shipping news which he published as *Lloyd's News*. The popularity of his coffeehouse among underwriters ultimately led to the establishment of Lloyd's of London in 1769. During this same period, a marine insurance company was formed in Paris to compete with individual underwriters. Later, British law enabled King George to grant charters to two marine insurance companies. Subsequently, they were empowered to write fire and life insurance as well as marine.

Fire insurance developed slowly in spite of the fact that London had disastrous fires in every century from the eighth to the thirteenth. After four centuries without a conflagration, the Great Fire of London in 1666 caused such huge losses of property and life that attention was called to the problem of adequate fire insurance facilities. Dr. Nicholas Barbon responded to this situation by building houses to replace those which had been destroyed and offering fire insurance to the purchasers. In 1667, he established the world's first fire insurance company, known as the Fire Office.

One of the first life insurance policies to be offered by professional insurers was a term policy written by a group of marine underwriters in London on the life of William Gibbons, early in the sixteenth century. The first life insurance organization, as measured by modern standards, was the Society of Assurance for Widows and Orphans. It was established in London in 1699 for the purpose of paying a stipulated amount at the death of a member. Premiums were collected on a weekly basis and insureds were selected on the basis of health and age. The oldest life insurance company in existence today is the Society for the Equitable Assurance of Lives and Survivorship, usually called "Old Equitable." Established in England in 1756, it originated such practices as a grace period for premium payment and the payment of dividends to the policyholder.

Insurance Development in America

The major development of insurance in America began after the colonies became independent. Prior to that time most insurance was written by foreign insurers, although some small American marine insurers did a thriving business. Lack of capital hampered American insurers until 1792 when the Insurance Company of North America was established. Its success encouraged the formation of other companies and, by 1800, more than thirty had been created. Marine insurance grew as the American merchant fleet grew.

Fire insurance in America developed as a result of the formation of fire-fighting companies. Benjamin Franklin helped establish the Union Fire Company in Philadelphia in 1730, and the movement spread to other cities. Among the first American fire insurance companies was The Friendly Society in Charleston, South Carolina. Founded in 1735, it went out of business after a major fire swept the city in 1740. The Philadelphia Contributionship for the Insurance of Houses from Loss by Fire was formed in 1752. It issued perpetual policies financed by earnings from the large deposit made by insureds. Establishment of other fire insurance companies soon followed. The Insurance Company of North America began writing fire insurance in 1794 and by the end of the century fourteen insurance companies had been formed.

The nineteenth century saw the evolution of fire insurance companies to their present status. Early in the century, fire insurers were small and operated in relatively small areas. The disastrous fire of 1835 in New York City showed the necessity for spreading such risks. From that time on, fire insurance companies built their businesses on a much broader basis. As a result, they were able to survive disasters such as the Chicago fire of 1871 and the San Francisco earthquake and fire of 1906.

Early life insurance policies in America were issued by individual underwriters for short terms at high premium rates. The first permanent life insurance organization established in the United States was the Presbyterian Ministers' Fund in 1759. In 1794, the Insurance Company of North America became the first American commercial company to write life insurance. Later, it discontinued this activity. The oldest commercial insurance companies still writing life insurance are the New England Mutual Life Insurance Company (1835) and the Mutual Life Insurance Company of New York (1842). The number of life insurance companies grew continuously from that time on. Today, there are over 1,800 operating in the United States.

Other forms of insurance, such as inland marine and casualty insurance, developed during the nineteenth century. During that time, insurers were licensed only for specified lines of insurance. A company could write fire insurance but not life insurance. Or, it could write life insurance but not marine insurance. In order to fill the need for more than one kind of insurance, multiple insurers were created. This led to the formation of fleets, or groups, of companies to offer several different lines of insurance under one management. Eventually, a movement to abandon this system of compartmentalization was successful in getting changes in legislation. Today, all states permit multiple-line underwriting, which enables a single insurer to write all lines of insurance other than life insurance. This makes it possible to buy several lines of insurance in one policy, as we shall see when we discuss automobile and homeowner's insurance.

TYPES OF INSURANCE

With regard to a particular insurance policy, the following questions may be raised:

1. Is it personal or property? Commercial - Profit
2. Is it issued by a private insurer or a government agency? Co-ope
3. Is purchase voluntary or involuntary?

Figure 4-1 follows the pattern of these questions.

Personal or Property

Personal Insurance covers the personal risks of premature death, accidental injury and sickness, unemployment, and dependent old-age. Property insurance covers property risks such as direct and indirect losses to property which may be caused by the perils of fire, windstorm, theft, and so on. Property insurance is sometimes called "property-liability insurance" because it also includes insurance to cover the liability risk.

Private or Government

Insurance is provided by both privately owned organizations and state and federal government agencies. Measured by premium income, the

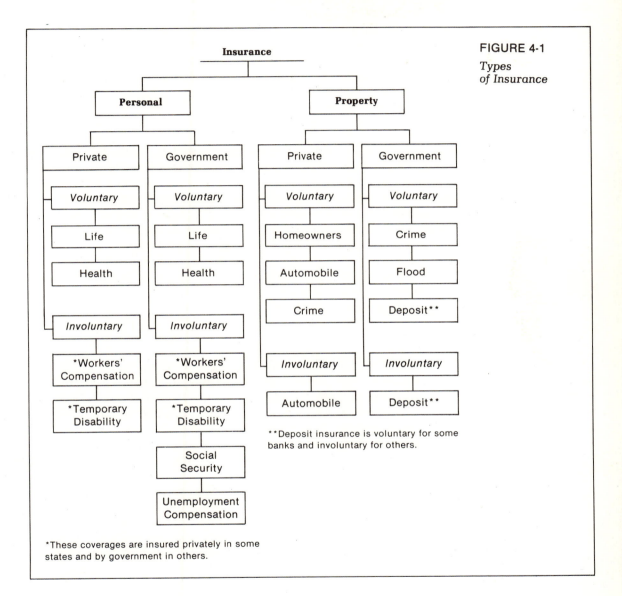

FIGURE 4-1

Types
of Insurance

Insurance

Personal — Property

Personal
- Private
  - *Voluntary*
    - Life
    - Health
  - *Involuntary*
    - *Workers' Compensation
    - *Temporary Disability
- Government
  - *Voluntary*
    - Life
    - Health
  - *Involuntary*
    - *Workers' Compensation
    - *Temporary Disability
    - Social Security
    - Unemployment Compensation

Property
- Private
  - *Voluntary*
    - Homeowners
    - Automobile
    - Crime
  - *Involuntary*
    - Automobile
- Government
  - *Voluntary*
    - Crime
    - Flood
    - Deposit**
  - *Involuntary*
    - Deposit**

**Deposit insurance is voluntary for some banks and involuntary for others.

*These coverages are insured privately in some states and by government in others.

bulk of property insurance is provided by private insurers. Largely because of the magnitude of the Social Security program, however, government provides about a third more personal insurance than the private sector.

Voluntary or Involuntary

Most private insurance is purchased voluntarily although some is required by law. In many states, for example, the purchase of automobile liability insurance is mandatory. Most government insurance is involuntary under certain conditions for certain people. For most people, participation in the Social Security program is required by law. Some government insurance, however, is made available to those who want it, but no one is required to buy it. Crop insurance, for example, is made available to farmers by a federal government agency, but purchase is voluntary.

PRIVATE INSURING ORGANIZATIONS

Insurance is provided by both private and government insuring organizations. Private insuring organizations are owned and controlled by private citizens rather than by the government. They engage in risk-bearing for a fee. In some cases, the objective is to make a profit. In other cases, it is to provide insurance at cost. Firms created to bear risk are known as insurers, insurance companies, or carriers.

Insurance is offered by several types of insurers:

1. Proprietary

2. Mutual

3. Reciprocal

4. Savings banks

5. Hospital-medical plans.

The first three types are sometimes referred to as *commercial insurers* in order to distinguish them as a group from organizations for which insurance is a sideline (savings banks), and hospital-medical plans, which originated as prepayment plans rather than risk-bearers. The various types of private insurers have more common characteristics than differences but we should be aware of their distinguishing features.

Proprietary Insurers

Proprietary insurers are owned by an individual or a group to render insurance service to other individuals or groups, usually for the purpose of making a profit.[1] Included in this classification are stock companies, Lloyd's of London, and Lloyd's Associations.

Stock companies. Stock insurance companies are organized in the same way as other privately owned corporations created for the purpose of making a profit. Individuals provide the operating capital for the

---

1. An exception may be the so-called "captive insurer." Such an insurance company is owned by the firm for which it provides insurance. It may or may not provide insurance to others, but its owners usually do not operate it to make a profit.

company by purchasing its stock. As stockholders, they own and control the firm. They are induced to invest their funds in the firm by the prospect that it will earn a profit. If the firm is operated successfully, the value of their initial investment will increase as the firm grows. Thus, they may benefit by both income and appreciation.

The insurance premium charged by a stock company is a fixed sum so that the insured knows exactly what such protection will cost. In their appeal to prospective insureds, stock companies emphasize the service they render and the fact that both the capital and surplus of the company, as well as the reserves, help to guarantee payment of claims made by insureds. The insurer bears the risk as an entity separate and apart from the insured.

Lloyd's of London.   The term "Lloyd's of London" refers to the oldest insurance organization in existence—the underwriters at Lloyd's in London. It has over 18,000 members, is licensed in two states in this country, and maintains a trust fund in the United States for the protection of American insureds. Lloyd's does not assume risks, but underwriters who are members of Lloyd's engage in the insurance business at that location under the supervision of a governing committee. The arrangement is similar to that of an organized stock exchange where physical facilities are owned by the exchange but business is transacted by the members. The financial condition of prospective members is investigated and those accepted are required to make a deposit with the governing committee. The liability of individual underwriters is unlimited; they are legally liable for their underwriting obligations under Lloyd's policies to the full extent of their assets.

Each underwriter is required to put premiums into a trust fund which makes them exclusively applicable to his or her underwriting liabilities until the obligations under the policies for which they were paid have been fulfilled. Underwriting accounts are audited annually by an auditor approved by the Committee of Lloyd's to assure that assets and liabilities are correctly valued and assets are sufficient to meet underwriting liabilities.

Individual members at Lloyd's operate through an underwriting agent who represents a number of underwriters. Insurance is placed through a broker who is authorized to do business at Lloyd's. Lloyd's underwriters do not assume all of one risk individually. Instead, they become members of a syndicate and the syndicate, in turn, assumes part of a risk. Thus, an individual underwriter may become liable for a fraction of 1 percent of the total liability assumed in one policy.

Lloyd's Associations.   There is no connection between Lloyd's Associations and Lloyd's of London. Lloyd's Associations—sometimes called "American Lloyd's"—are corporations, partnerships, or associations made up of individual underwriters who join together in offering insurance. Each underwriter assumes a specified portion of the liability under each policy issued. As a rule, underwriters specify a maximum amount of liability they are willing to accept.

Operations are carried on by an attorney-in-fact appointed by members of the association. He or she is compensated by a salary or a percentage of premiums.

There is a superficial resemblance to Lloyd's of London because of their name and the fact that risks are underwritten by individuals. They are not, however, subject to the strict supervision which characterizes Lloyd's of London, nor do they have the same financial strength.

Mutual Insurers

In a sense, all insurance is mutual. That is, the losses of the few are spread among the many by paying for them from premiums paid by all members of the group. There are, however, certain characteristics of mutual insurers which make them more "mutual" than other types of carriers. For example, a mutual insurance company is owned and controlled by its policyholders. There are no stockholders and no capital stock is issued. People become members of the company by purchasing an insurance policy from it. Officers who run the company are appointed by a board of directors which is elected by policyholders. The purpose of the organization is to provide insurance at cost rather than to make a profit. There are several types of mutual insurers, including county or farm, class or specialty, general, factory, perpetual, and fraternal.

County or farm mutuals. These mutuals are local insurance operations which offer fire insurance primarily on farm property. Some of them confine their writings to property located in small towns. Most of them, including some which are fairly large, operate on an assessment basis rather than collecting a premium in advance. Many, however, charge an annual assessment in advance and also retain the right to levy additional assessments if losses exceed expectations. The advance assessment provides funds to make more prompt loss payments than is the case when assessments follow losses. Some farm mutuals limit additional payments by insureds to one assessment, while in other cases there is unlimited liability. Considerable publicity has been given to a few instances in which mutual members have suffered severe losses because of this assessment feature.

Class or specialty mutuals. A number of mutuals specialize in the insuring of particular kinds of business firms or specific lines of insurance. Some specialize in insuring hardware stores or lumber firms, for example, while others concentrate on automobile insurance, boiler and machinery insurance, glass insurance, and so on, for all types of insureds. Many general mutuals started as specialty insurers. One mutual, for example, specialized initially in insuring glass but has now grown into a general mutual writing all lines. Nearly all of the class mutuals are now in the general insurance business, although many of them write substantial amounts of business in their original specialty class.

General mutuals. Many mutuals in both the life and property fields have grown to considerable size and operate over large areas of the country. This is particularly true in life insurance, where the largest insurers are mutuals. When the surplus of a mutual company reaches a size specified by the law of the state or states in which it operates, it is permitted to issue policies which are not assessable.[2] In such cases, premiums are paid in advance and are large enough to make possible the payment of dividends at the end of the year.[3] These large mutuals do a general line of business in the life and health or property insurance field as opposed to confining their efforts to a small geographic area or a particular type of insured.

Factory mutuals. These mutuals came into existence because a New England manufacturer felt that the rates he paid for insurance were too high. He persuaded other manufacturers to join him in organizing a mutual which specialized in insuring factories that met high standards of construction and emphasized the prevention of losses. There are now four factory mutuals organized as the Factory Mutual System.[4] These companies share risks through a reinsurance agreement and maintain an engineering division for inspection and service to policyholders.

Insurance provided by factory mutuals is limited to the larger and better risks because of high underwriting standards and the cost of inspections. The factory mutuals own a stock insurance company, however, which insures risks not eligible for factory mutual insurance.

Perpetual mutuals. Several mutuals provide fire insurance on brick and stone dwellings through the use of perpetual policies. The initial premium, or deposit, is large enough so that interest earnings are the equivalent of an annual premium. When losses and expenses are less than interest earnings, a dividend may be paid to policyholders. When a policy is cancelled, the deposit is refunded. One of the first companies to offer perpetual insurance was the Philadelphia Contributionship, which was established in 1752 under the leadership of Benjamin Franklin.

Fraternals. Fraternal societies are primarily social organizations. Many of them, however, offer life and health insurance to members on a mutual basis. When fraternals first began to experiment with insurance, their efforts were more social than scientific, and many insurance schemes ended in failure because premiums were not ade-

---

2. This usually means when the mutual meets the same financial requirements as those met by stock companies; i.e., when its surplus is as large as the capital and surplus required of a stock company.

3. Because mutuals are nonprofit organizations, dividends are simply a refund of the portion of premiums not needed rather than a share of profit.

4. The stock company counterpart of this association is the Factory Insurance Association.

quate to pay claims. In more recent years, their insurance operations have been subjected to greater regulation, which has tended to strengthen them financially. In the past, fraternals relied heavily on their ability to increase premium rates when more funds were needed, but currently there is a greater emphasis on adequate rates calculated in the same manner as other insurers. There is nothing inherently wrong with fraternal insurance and whether it is satisfactory depends upon management. Many fraternals offer reliable low-cost insurance.

Reciprocals

These insurers are similar to, but not identical with, mutuals. Both are formed to provide insurance at cost rather than to make a profit. Each policyholder in a reciprocal, however, insures part of the risk of each of the other policyholders. If there were 100 insureds in the group, for example, and each had the same value at risk, each would, in effect, say to the other, ''I will pay one percent of your losses if you will pay one percent of mine.'' The reciprocal itself is not liable to policyholders but they are liable to each other. In a mutual, on the other hand, assets belong to the mutual and the mutual corporation is liable to policyholders. The reciprocal holds assets contributed by the policyholders as premiums, but the assets are owned by the individual policyholders rather than by the reciprocal.

Reciprocals are also known as *interinsurance associations* or *interinsurance exchanges.* They are managed by an attorney-in-fact whose powers are enumerated in a power of attorney granted by the policyholders. Part of the premium is paid to the attorney-in-fact for his or her services in soliciting business and managing the operations of the reciprocal, and the balance is credited to the account of the insured. When losses are paid, each insured's account is charged with his or her proportionate share of the loss. At the end of the year, funds remaining in each account may be left in the reciprocal or paid back to each insured as a dividend.

There are only about 50 reciprocals left in this country. The bulk of reciprocal business is now written by interinsurance associations, which are more like mutuals than the pure reciprocals described in this section. They keep no separate members' accounts, and losses and expenses are not prorated among insureds. Furthermore, insureds do not have a claim to any portion of surplus funds. Reciprocals in their pure form are a declining type of insurance.

Savings Bank Life Insurance

Savings banks in Massachusetts, New York, and Connecticut may establish life insurance departments and/or act as agencies for other savings banks in the state which have done so. These banks sell the usual types of individual policies and annuities as well as group insurance. Business is transacted on an over-the-counter basis or by mail. No agents are employed to sell the insurance and no commissions are paid. Insurance is provided at a low cost because expenses are low and fewer policies are lapsed than in the life insurance industry as a whole.[5]

Hospital-Medical Plans

A number of insurance plans have been organized on a nonprofit basis to provide hospital and medical benefits for private groups. These plans are created by employers, unions, hospitals, medical societies, and others. They are different from the insuring organizations discussed previously in this chapter in at least two respects. First, some of them were created originally by purveyors of hospital or medical services as prepayment plans to assure that such services could be paid for by those who needed them. That is, they were not organized to assume risks but to pay for services. Second, some of them were organized by employers to provide benefits to employees or by consumers on a cooperative purchasing basis. The plans described in this section may be divided into two categories: (1) the Blues—Blue Cross and Blue Shield, and (2) independent plans.

Blue Cross. A Blue Cross plan is a nonprofit hospital service prepayment plan which meets the standards set up by the Blue Cross Association. There are 69 Blue Cross plans in the United States which have a membership of approximately 84 million persons. Each plan is locally autonomous; that is, it is formed and controlled in the area it serves by hospitals which wish to participate. The Blue Cross Association acts as the coordinating agency for the various plans, establishes minimum standards for membership, and provides national advertising as well as some advisory services.

Blue Shield. Blue Shield is the surgical-medical counterpart of Blue Cross. It is a nonprofit prepayment plan covering medical and surgical services which has been approved by the National Association of Blue Shield Plans. There are 69 such plans in the United States. About 90 percent of the doctors in private practice participate in the areas served by Blue Shield plans. Most plans are organized and controlled by a local medical society but they are coordinated with the local Blue Cross plan whose staff handles their daily operations. Most Blue Shield and Blue Cross plans are sold to members of eligible groups, but some have individual contracts available.

Independent plans. This is the name given to all accidental injury and sickness plans other than those provided by commercial insurers and Blue Cross and Blue Shield. These plans include paid sick-leave plans provided by employers, supplementary workers' compensation plans

---

5. A policy lapses when the insured fails to pay the premium. If a policy remains in force for a relatively short period of time, the insurer loses money on it because the bulk of expenses in connection with it are incurred during the first year. If the policy stays in force, such expenses will be recovered over a period of years as premiums are paid. A high lapse ratio increases the premium which must be charged for insurance.

under which a firm seeks to supplement workers' compensation payments, and a variety of medical expense plans. There are about 400 of the latter plans. Some are industrial plans which provide medical care through the employer or a union. Others are nonindustrial plans sponsored by medical societies (other than Blue Shield), a community, or a private group clinic. An example of the community plan is the Health Insurance Plan of Greater New York. More than 10,000,000 people are covered by independent plans providing some kind of hospital or medical benefits.

GOVERNMENT INSURING ORGANIZATIONS

Agencies of the federal and state governments account for nearly half of the insurance activity in the United States. To some extent, they fill a gap where private insurers have not provided coverage. In other cases, government insurers compete with private firms. This section summarizes those activities.

State Insuring Organizations

1. Most states have insolvency funds to assure that the burden of insurance company failure will not be borne by policyholders. Financing is provided by involuntary contributions from all insurance companies licensed in the state. The funds are responsible for obligations of insolvent companies to their policyholders. No benefits are paid to stockholders of defunct insurers.

2. Eighteen states have funds to insure the workers' compensation risk; some are monopolistic while others compete with private insurers.

3. The Wisconsin State Life Fund sells life insurance to residents of Wisconsin on an individual basis similar to that of private life insurance companies.

4. A state agency in Montana competes with private insurance in providing insurance against loss to growing crops caused by hail storms.

5. All states administer unemployment compensation insurance programs.

6. The state of Maryland operates a fund to provide automobile liability insurance to Maryland motorists unable to buy it in the private market.

7. Several states provide temporary nonoccupational disability insurance, title insurance, or medical malpractice insurance.

Federal Insuring Organizations

1. The Social Security Administration, which operates the Social Security program, is the country's largest single insurance organization.

2. The Federal Deposit Insurance Corporation insures depositors against loss caused by the failure of a bank. Similar insurance is provided for depositors in savings and loan associations by the Federal Savings and Loan Insurance Corporation.

3. The Federal Crop Insurance Corporation provides all-risk insurance for farm crops in certain counties.

4. Fair Access to Insurance Requirements (FAIR) plans have been established in a number of states under federal legislation. They are operated by private insurers as a pool to make property insurance available to applicants who cannot buy it in the regular market. Federal government reinsurance pays for excessive losses caused by riots and civil disorder.

5. The Federal Insurance Administration provides crime insurance through private insurers in areas where it is unavailable in the private market.

6. Federal government flood insurance is sold through private insurance agents in communities that have met federal requirements designed to reduce flood losses.

7. Several programs for veterans of the armed forces are provided by the Veterans Administration.

8. Several agencies insure mortgage loans made by private lenders.

Consumer Applications

Choosing the Right Insurer

Unless the insurance policy you just bought came from Lloyd's of London and you are thrilled to be insured at Lloyd's, the chances are you don't know what type of insurer issued it. And it may not make much difference. But it could make a difference because of the differences in insurance contracts and the way in which they define your relationship with the insurance company. How do you decide which type of insurer to choose?

Participating Versus Nonparticipating

Stock insurers usually sell fixed-premium policies which do not provide for policyholder participation in the company's experience. They are called nonparticipating or guaranteed cost. Mutuals, on the other hand, sell policies which provide that you may receive a return of excess premium, called a policy dividend.[6] Because the size of the dividend depends on the company's experience, such policies are called participating (par). As a policyholder, you share when the company has good experience.

Stock insurer agents say guaranteed cost policies are best because "you know what your insurance will cost." Mutual company agents counter that par policies are best because dividends reduce cost below that charged by stock insurers. From which type insurer should you buy?

Table 4-1 shows how par and non-par policies may be compared on the basis of cost. At first glance, it appears that the par policy is cheaper than the non-par. Its net cost at the end of the year is $190 compared with $200 for the non-par policy. In making your choice between the two, however, you should consider two facts:

1. The dividend cannot be guaranteed; it is illegal to guarantee policy dividends. If the dividend is $30, the par policy is $10 less than the non-par. But if the dividend is $15, the par policy costs $5 more than the non-par. When you buy a par policy, you are bearing part of the risk.
2. You give up the use of the difference between the par policy premium ($220) and the non-par premium ($200) for a full year. How much sacrifice does that involve?

Your choice between the two policies depends upon your answer to the following question: "Are you willing to pay an extra $20 now for the chance of getting $30 at the end of the year?" If you get the $30, you will make a 50 percent return on the $20 in one year. If the divi-

---

6. These companies are called advance-premium mutuals to distinguish them from the assessment mutuals discussed later in the chapter. Some advance-premium mutuals charge an initial premium lower than that charged by dividend-paying mutuals and then pay no dividends to policyholders. They are said to be paying dividends in advance.

dend is $20 instead of $30, however, you will have made no return. It is possible, of course, that you might double your money by getting a $40 dividend.

Suppose that the annual premium for the par policy is $210 instead of $220 and the projected dividend is $20. If you buy the par policy, you are giving up the use of $10 for a year for the chance to save $10 premium. Or, maybe do even better. Or, worse.

Your choice between par and non-par policies will depend on the difference in the premiums, the size of the projected premium, and how you feel about taking chances. If the mutual company has paid at least the projected dividend on similar policies for the last ten years, of course, your confidence in its projections may induce you to buy the par policy. But what if actual dividends have occasionally been less than those projected? Clearly, you should ask your agent for information about the insurer's past dividend record.

Assessment Versus Nonassessment Mutuals

Another choice you have is between a non-assessment mutual and an assessment mutual. The former sells nonassessable policies for which you pay only the stated premium. On the other hand, if you buy a policy from an assessment mutual, you may be required to pay additional premium. The contract may or may not place a limit on the assessment and you are legally obligated to pay them. Thus, you should be wary of buying a par policy from an assessment mutual. Suppose, for example, that you were presented the premium comparison shown in Table 4-2.

As you can see, the assessment policy offers a significantly lower projected net cost. Is the lower projected cost worth the risk of possible assessment? If the maximum assessment is some multiple of the initial premium, such as 3 times (another $300), would this

---

TABLE 4-1

*Premium Cost Comparison**

NON-PAR POLICY

Annual Premium (paid in advance)	$200.00
Total Cost Per Year	$200.00

PAR POLICY

Annual Premium (paid in advance)	$220.00
less: Projected Dividend (paid at year-end)	(30.00)
Total Cost Per Year	$190.00

*Many state insurance offices have figures available on premium cost comparisons. See Appendix F for the address and telephone number of your state insurance office.

TABLE 4-2

*Premium Cost
Comparison for
Assessment and
Nonassessment
Policies*

NONASSESSMENT POLICY

Initial Premium	$220.00
Projected Dividend	(30.00)
Projected Net Cost	$190.00
highest possible annual cost equals initial premium of	$220.00

ASSESSMENT POLICY

Initial Premium	$100.00
Projected Dividend	(0.00)
Projected Cost	$100.00
highest possible annual cost equals your share of insured loss experience, limited only by contract provisions, if any	

POSSIBLE UNLIMITED COST

make the lower cost attractive to you? If the contract is a pure assessment policy (no limit on assessment), which one would you choose? When you buy an assessment policy, you are assuming a risk.

Be sure you read the policy and understand your obligations before you buy it. Otherwise, you may assume a risk you have neither identified nor evaluated.

Discussion Questions

1. Why do you suppose The Friendly Society in Charleston, South Carolina went out of business after a major fire swept the city in 1740?

2. What arguments are there for and against buying fire insurance from a perpetual mutual?

3. Some people who deal with Lloyd's of London say, "United States insurers are

risk averters, while Lloyd's of London attracts risk seekers." Do you agree? Why or why not?

4. Why do you suppose crime insurance is unavailable in the private market in some areas? What is the effect of government providing crime insurance when private insurers do not?

5. Why are Lloyd's Associations called by that name? Do you think some people confuse them with Lloyd's of London? If so, what should be done about that situation?

6. Do you think all states should permit savings banks to engage in the life insurance business? Why or why not?

7. Blue Cross and Blue Shield are referred to as "nonprofit prepayment plans." Are they insurance companies? Please explain.

8. The Wisconsin State Life Fund sells life insurance to Wisconsin residents. Do you think other states should have a similar fund? Why or why not?

9. A person who buys insurance from a pure assessment mutual or a pure reciprocal transfers risk to the group but also assumes a risk. Does this seem rational to you? Please explain.

10. State insolvency funds protect policyholders against loss in the event of insurance company failure but they do not protect stockholders of defunct insurers. Do you think this discrimination is justified? Why or why not?

Cases

4-1 Terry Harvey lives in the hills above Los Angeles. He knows that the fire peril is significant because of the winds and the seasonal droughts which affect the area, but he loves the view and the prestige of the location, and he wants to stay there if he can. However, private insurers are balking about selling him fire insurance.

1. Do you think that private insurers should be compelled to sell Terry fire insurance?

2. If they are forced to do so, how much freedom should they have to set rates?

3. Should the government provide fire insurance to people like Terry, who live in areas which are especially subject to major perils?

4-2 Fair Access to Insurance Requirements (FAIR) Plans are operated by private insurers to make property insurance available in high-risk inner city areas not served by the regular market. Federal government reinsurance pays for excessive losses caused by riots and civil disorders.

1. Since the primary coverages sold are property coverages, and since these are sold directly to the public by pools of private insurers, do you feel that this program really is social insurance? Why or why not?

4-3 In recent years, some life and health insurers have moved into the property and liability insurance marketplace. This move occurred at a time when property and liability insurance was far less profitable than the life-health part of the industry.

1. Why would a life-health company make such a change, when it would have to spend a great deal of money to enter the property-liability marketplace, and when the profit outlook for this new business is not as good as for its existing lines of business?

4-4 An agent from a fraternal society recently contacted you and asked for an appointment. Your friend Bill told you all life insurance companies were alike and fraternals were just another form of life insurance company. Some investigation on your part is in order before the agent from the fraternal visits you.

1. What are the differences between life insurers—if any?

2. Was Bill correct in his assumption?

3. Which type(s) of insurers do you prefer? Why?

Chapter Five:
FUNDAMENTAL DOCTRINES

INTRODUCTION

The process of transferring a risk to an insurance company is commonly referred to as "buying insurance." The risk manager, in effect, buys a promise from the insurer. The written agreement between the insured and the insurer is called the policy or policy contract. The policy states in detail the rights and duties of both the insured and the insurer. The formation, interpretation, and enforcement of insurance contracts are influenced by the fundamental doctrines which have evolved in the process of putting insurance theory into practice during several centuries of development. In this chapter, we discuss the following:

1. Basic legal principles applying to insurance contracts

2. Requirements of a contract

3. Distinguishing characteristics of insurance contracts

BASIC LEGAL PRINCIPLES

Indemnity Concept

Many insurance policies are contracts of indemnity. This means the insurer agrees to pay for no more than the actual loss suffered by the insured. For example, suppose your house is insured for $100,000 at the time it is totally destroyed by an earthquake. If its value at that time was only $80,000, that is the amount the insurance company would pay. You cannot collect $100,000 because to do so would exceed the actual loss suffered. You would be better off after the loss than you were before.

The purpose of the insurance contract is to restore you to the same economic position you had prior to the loss, not to improve your situation.

Indemnity agreements have practical significance for the insurer and for society as a whole. If insureds could gain by having a loss, many would be tempted to cause losses. This would result in a decrease of resources for society, an economic burden for the insurance company, and ultimately higher insurance premium rates for insureds. Moreover, if losses are caused intentionally rather than as a result of chance occurrence, the insurer is unable to predict costs satisfactorily. A contract of insurance that makes it possible for the insured to profit through the occurrence of the event insured against violates the principle of indemnity and may prove to be poor business for the insurer.[1]

The doctrine of indemnity is implemented by several legal principles and policy provisions, including the following: (1) insurable interest, (2) subrogation, (3) the actual cash value provision, and (4) other insurance provisions.

Insurable Interest. If the occurrence of a contingency, such as a fire or auto collision, will cause loss to a person or firm, then an insurable interest exists. A person who is not subject to risk does not have an insurable interest. The law concerning insurable interest is important to the purchaser of insurance because it determines whether the benefits from an insurance policy will be collectible. Thus, all insureds should be familiar with the sources of insurable interest, the time it must exist, and the extent to which it may limit payment under an insurance policy.

Sources of insurable interest. There are many sources of insurable interest. The most common is ownership of property. As the owner of a building, you will suffer financial loss if it is destroyed by fire or other peril. Thus, you have an insurable interest in the building. If you financed your purchase with a loan from the bank and provided a mortgage on the building for security, the bank has an insurable interest in the building. A secured creditor has an insurable interest in the security but an unsecured creditor does not have an insurable interest in the general assets of the debtor. If part of the building referred to above is leased to a tenant who makes improvements in the space leased, such improvements become the property of the building owner. Because he or she will lose use of these improvements if they are destroyed, the tenant, too, has an insurable interest in them.

If a tenant has a long-term lease on terms more favorable than those presently available but the lease may be cancelled in the event that the building is damaged by fire to the extent of some specified portion of its value, the tenant has an insurable interest in the lease. This is called a

---

1. Some fire insurance policies provide for the payment of claims on the basis of replacement cost rather than the actual cash value of the property damaged or destroyed. If such a provision causes the insured to be in a better position financially than he or she was prior to a loss, it violates the principle of indemnity.

leasehold interest. A bailee who is responsible for the safekeeping of property belonging to others and must either return it in good condition or pay for it, has an insurable interest. You have an unlimited insurable interest in your own life and may have an insurable interest in the life of another.[2] An insurable interest in the life of another may be based on love and affection, such as that of the parent for the child, or it may be based on financial considerations. A creditor may have an insurable interest in the life of a debtor and an employer may have an insurable interest in the life of an employee.

Time insurable interest must exist. The time at which insurable interest must exist, in order for the right to payment under an insurance policy to be enforceable, depends upon the type of insurance. In property insurance, the interest must exist at the time of the loss. As the owner of a house, you have an insurable interest in it. If you insure yourself against damage to the house by fire or other peril, you can collect on such insurance only if you still have an insurable interest in the house at the time the damage occurs. Thus, if you transfer unencumbered title to another party prior to the time the house is damaged, you cannot collect under the policy because you did not have an insurable interest at the time of the loss.

As a result of the historical development of insurance practices, life insurance requires an insurable interest only at the inception of the contract. At the time the question of insurable interest in life insurance was being adjudicated in England, such policies provided no cash surrender values; payment was made by the insurer only if the person who was the subject[3] of insurance died while the policy was in force. An insured who was unable to continue making premium payments simply sacrificed all interest in the policy. This led to the practice of insureds selling their policies to speculators who, as owners, named themselves the beneficiary and continued premium payments until the death of the insured. If such purchasers could not collect policy proceeds when the insured died because they lacked an insurable interest in his or her life at the time of his or her death, they would be unwilling to buy the policy. Its marketability was assured by requiring an insurable interest only at the inception of the policy. Any subsequent policy owner did not need to

---

2. The statement that a person has an unlimited insurable interest in his own life is literally incorrect although it describes the way life insurance companies operate. That is, a life insurer acts as if a person has an unlimited insurable interest in his own life by never raising the question. Although a person who dies suffers a loss, he or she cannot be indemnified. Because the purpose of the principle of insurable interest is to implement the doctrine of indemnity, it has no application in the case of a person insuring his or her own life. Such a contract cannot be one of indemnity.

3. The person whose death requires the insurer to pay the proceeds of a life insurance policy is usually listed in the policy as the *insured*. He or she is also known as the *cestui que vie* and the subject. The beneficiary is the person (or other entity) entitled to the proceeds of the policy upon the death of the subject. The owner of the policy is the person (or other entity) who has the authority to exercise all of the rights of the policy, such as designating the beneficiary, taking a policy loan, and so on.

be concerned about the matter of insurable interest. With the advent of cash surrender values in life insurance policies, the practice of selling them in order to avoid forfeiture was discontinued.

Because the legal concept of requiring an insurable interest only at the inception of the life insurance contract has continued, it is possible to collect on a policy where such interest has ceased. For example, if the life of a valuable key person in a firm is insured, in whose life the firm has an insurable interest because his or her death would cause a loss to the firm, the policy may be continued in force by the firm even after the person leaves its employ, and the proceeds may be collected when he or she dies.

Limits payment in property insurance. In the case of property insurance, not only must an insurable interest exist at the time of the loss, but the amount the insured is paid is limited by the extent of such interest. For example, if you have a one-half interest in a building which is worth $100,000 at the time it is destroyed by fire, you cannot collect more than $50,000 from the insurance company regardless of how much insurance was purchased. If more than the value of an insurable interest could be collected, then a person would make a profit on the fire. This would violate the principle of indemnity.

Life payment usually not limited by insurable interest. In contrast with property insurance, all life—and some health—insurance contracts are considered to be valued policies.[4] That is, they are contracts to pay a stated sum upon the occurrence of the event insured against rather than to indemnify for loss sustained. For example, a life insurance contract provides that the insurer will pay a specified sum to the beneficiary upon receipt of proof of death of the person whose life is the subject of the insurance. The beneficiary does not have to establish that any loss has been suffered. Some health insurance policies provide that when the insured is hospitalized, the insurance company will pay a specified number of dollars per day. Such policies are not indemnity contracts. Although an insurable interest must exist at the inception of the contract in order to make it enforceable, the amount of payment is usually not limited by the extent of such insurable interest. The amount of life insurance collectible at the death of an insured is limited only by the amount underwriters are willing to issue[5] and the insured's premium-paying ability. However, the amount of the proceeds of a life

---

4. Some property insurance policies are written on a valued basis but precautions are taken to assure that values agreed upon are realistic, thus adhering to the principle of indemnity.

5. Life and health insurance companies have learned, however, that over-insurance may lead to poor underwriting experience. Because the loss caused by death or illness cannot be measured precisely, defining over-insurance is difficult. It may be said to exist when the amount of insurance is clearly in excess of the economic loss which may be suffered. Extreme cases, such as the individual whose earned income is $100 per week but who may receive $150 per week from an insurance company while he is ill, are easy to identify.

insurance policy which may be collected by a creditor-beneficiary is generally limited to the amount of the debt and the premiums paid by the creditor, plus interest.[6]

comp. sues on your behalf

Subrogation. The principle of indemnity is also supported by the right of subrogation. This right gives the insurance company whatever claim against third parties the insured may have as a result of the loss for which the insurer paid. If your house is burned because a neighbor set fire to leaves in his or her yard and negligently permitted the fire to get out of control, you have a right to collect damages from the negligent neighbor because a negligent wrongdoer is responsible to others for the damage or injury he or she causes.[7] If the house is insured against loss by fire, however, you cannot collect from both the insurance company and the negligent party who caused the damage. The insurance company will pay for the damage and is then subrogated to your rights to the extent of the amount of such payment. The insurer may then sue the negligent party and collect from him or her. This prevents you from profiting by collecting twice for the same loss. The right of subrogation is a common-law right which the insurer would have without a contractual agreement but it is specifically stated in the policy so that you will be aware of it and refrain from releasing the party who is responsible for the loss.[8]

Actual Cash Value. This clause, which is included in many property insurance policies, was illustrated in the earlier discussion of a contract of indemnity. The reason an insured does not receive an amount greater than the actual loss suffered is because the policy limits payment to actual cash value. A typical fire insurance policy says, for example, that the company insures "to the extent of actual cash value . . . but not exceeding the amount which it would cost to repair or replace . . . nor in any event for more than the interest of the insured." Actual cash value means replacement cost less depreciation. If the roof on a house has an expected life of 20 years, half its value is gone at the end of 10 years. If it is damaged by an insured peril at that time, the insurer will pay the cost of replacing the damaged portion, less depreciation. The insured must bear the burden of the balance.

Some property insurance is written on a replacement cost basis, in which case payment is made without deduction for depreciation. This, of course, conflicts with the principle of indemnity.

---

6. This is an area which is difficult to generalize; the statement made above is approximately correct. The point is that the creditor-debtor relationship is an exception to the statement that an insurable interest need not exist at the time of the death of the insured and that the amount of payment is not limited to the insurable interest which existed at the inception of the contract. For further discussion, see S. S. Huebner and Kenneth Black, Jr., *Life Insurance* (9th ed.; Englewood Cliffs, New Jersey: Prentice-Hall, 1976), pp. 121-122.

7. See Chapter 15 for a discussion of the concept of negligence liability.

8. For a complete discussion of subrogation, see Ronald C. Horn, *Subrogation In Insurance Theory and Practice* (Homewood, Illinois: Richard D. Irwin, Inc., 1964).

Other Insurance.   There are a number of other insurance clauses, but one example will show how they function to assure that the principle of indemnity is not violated. If you carry more than one policy on the same building, there is a possibility that by collecting on all policies you may profit from a loss. The pro rata liability clause of the contract prevents this by providing that each insurer will contribute to the loss in proportion to the amount that its policy bears to the total amount of insurance carried. Thus, if there are two $5,000 fire insurance policies and a $5,000 loss is sustained, instead of collecting $5,000 from each insurer and making a profit on the fire, you will be paid $2,500 by each insurer. Payment will not exceed the amount of the loss.

Information Given the Insurer

When the insurer is considering accepting a risk it must have accurate information in order to make a reasonable decision. Should it assume the risk and, if so, under what terms and conditions? The person who makes these decisions is an underwriter, and the decision-making process is known as *underwriting.*

Warranties.   In the early days of marine insurance, most of the information concerning the risk came from the insured. In many cases, he was the only person who knew the facts. The ship to be insured might be unavailable for inspection by the insurer. This led to the practice of including in the agreement the information provided by the insured and referring to his statements as "warranties." The ship would be warranted seaworthy, for example. Once put into the contract, warranties had to be strictly true, not approximately so. This placed the burden of absolute accuracy upon the insured.

This practice is still followed today in some lines of insurance. If the insured, for example, warrants that a watchman will be on duty at all times when the plant is not operating, this warranty must be strictly complied with if the insurance protection is to be maintained. If a fire starts during a time when the plant is not in operation and there is no watchman on duty, the insurer will not have to pay the loss as the warranty has been breached. The insurer does not have to prove that the absence of the watchman had a material effect on the risk. So far as the contract is concerned, warranties are assumed to be material.

PROIR TO ACTUAL CONTRACT

Representations.   When you are negotiating with the insurer for coverage, you make statements concerning the risk. These statements are called *representations* and are made for the purpose of inducing the insurer to enter into the contract. If you misrepresent a material fact, the insurer can void the contract.

Note that "material fact" has been specified. Thus, if the underwriter relies on the facts you give when entering into a contract, the insurer must prove that the fact misrepresented was material if it wants to void the contract; that is, it was so important that if the truth had been known, the underwriter either would not have made the contract or would have done so only on different terms. If you stated that you were born on Friday, March 2 in applying for life insurance when, in fact, you were born on Thursday, March 2, such a misrepresentation would not be material. The exact truth would not alter the underwriter's decision with regard to the application. On the other hand, if the applicant for automobile insurance stated that on one in the family under age 18 would drive the insured vehicle when, in fact, a 17-year-old son drove it frequently, such a misrepresentation would be considered material.

Concealment. Concealment occurs when an applicant for insurance fails to reveal material facts about the risk which only he or she knows. For example, if you apply for fire insurance on your home at a time when the neighbor's house is on fire and fail to reveal this fact, you have concealed it. The characteristics of an insurance contract, which are discussed later, are such that it is essential that both parties to the bargain have equal knowledge concerning its subject matter. When the underwriter relies on you to give all material facts, you must do so. You cannot hold the insurer to the contract if you concealed important information. No insured, however, is expected to be an insurance expert. If the insurance company requires the completion of a long and detailed application for insurance, an insured who fails to provide information the insurer neglected to ask about cannot be proven guilty of concealment.

Agency

Because the insurance business is conducted by agents, a word about agency is appropriate. Agency involves three parties: the principal, the agent, and a third party. The principal creates an agency relationship with a second party by authorizing him or her to make contracts with third parties on the principal's behalf. The source of the agent's authority is the principal. Such authority may be either express or implied. When an agent is appointed, the principal expressly indicates the extent of his or her authority. The agent will also have, by implication, whatever authority is needed to fulfill the purposes of the agency. By entering into the relationship, the principal implies that the agent has the authority to fulfill the principal's responsibilities. From the public point of view, the agent's authority is whatever it appears to be. This is sometimes referred to as "apparent authority." If the principal treats a second party as if the person were an agent, then an agency is created. Agency law and the doctrines of waiver and estoppel have serious implications in the insurance business.

Waiver and Estoppel. The doctrines of waiver and estoppel affect the power of the agent as well as an insurer's position with regard to concealment and misrepresentation.

Waiver is the intentional relinquishment of a known right. In order to waive a right, a person must know he or she has it and give it up intentionally. If a risk is undesirable at the time the agent assumes it on behalf of the company and he or she knows it, the agent will have waived the right to refuse coverage. This situation arises when an agent insures a risk which the company has specifically prohibited. Suppose, in the case just discussed, the agent knew the applicant's 17-year-old son drove the car and also knew the company did not accept such risks. If he or she issues the policy, the right to refuse coverage will have been waived.

Estoppel prevents a person from alleging or denying a fact when through either words or acts he or she has previously admitted the contrary. A company cannot waive a right and then assert it later. Once the agent waives the right to refuse coverage to the applicant for auto insurance, the company is estopped from denying liability for losses that occur while the contract is in force.

Agency by estoppel. An agency relationship may be created when the conduct of the principal implies that an agency exists—an agency by estoppel. In such a case, the principal will be estopped from denying the existence of the agency. This situation may arise when the company suspends an agent but he or she retains possession of blank policies. People who are not agents of a company do not have blank policies in their possession. By leaving them with the agent, the company is acting as if he or she is its agent. If such policies are issued by the agent, the company is estopped from denying that he or she is its agent and will be bound by the policy. If an agent who has been suspended sends business to the company which it accepts, his or her agency relationship will be ratified by such action and the company will be estopped from denying its existence. The company has the right to refuse such business when it is presented, but it waives the right when the business is accepted.

REQUIREMENTS OF A CONTRACT

As noted earlier, the relationship between the insured and the insurer is spelled out in an insurance policy which is a contract between the two parties. A contract is an agreement enforceable at law. If an agreement is to be considered a valid and enforceable contract, it must meet the following requirements: (1) the purpose must be legal, (2) there must be an offer and an acceptance, (3) there must be consideration, and (4) the parties to the contract must be competent.

Legal Purpose

A contract must have a legal purpose. If it does not, it would be contrary to public policy to enforce it. A contract by a government employee to sell secret information to an agent of an enemy country, for example, would not have a legal purpose and would be unenforceable. For the same reason, a contract of insurance to cover the expense of traffic violation fines would be illegal, contrary to public policy, and unenforceable.

Offer and Acceptance

A second requirement of a contract is concerned with the creation of the agreement. There must be an offer and an acceptance. An agreement is reached when one party makes an offer and the other party accepts it. If the party to whom the offer was made requests a change in its terms, he or she has made a counteroffer which releases the first offeror from his or her offer. In the making of insurance contracts, usually the buyer offers to buy and the acceptance is made by the insurer. When you call an insurance agent for insurance on your new automobile and he or she says, "You are covered," you have made an offer to buy and the agent has accepted on behalf of his or her company. Your offer may be verbal, as in this case, or it may be in the form of a written application. Offer and acceptance are essential to the creation of an agreement. They are the mechanism for arriving at a meeting of the minds on the subject matter of the contract by the parties involved.

Consideration $

A third requisite for a contract is consideration. It is the price which the offeror demands for agreeing to carry out his or her part of the contract. The value of the consideration is usually unimportant, but lack of consideration will cause the contract to be unenforceable. In many cases, insurance contracts stipulate that the consideration which induces the insurer to make promises to the insured is the premium *and* certain conditions which are specified in the policy. The insurer's consideration is its promise to pay losses.

Competent Parties

A final essential element for a contract is that the parties to the contract must be competent. Most people are competent to contract, but there are exceptions. Insane or intoxicated persons are not competent. Infants may enter into contracts but such contracts may be voided by the infant. Upon reaching majority (age 18 in some states, age 21 in others), he or she may ratify or reject the contract. If ratified, it would then have the same status as a contract entered into originally by competent parties. A minor who enters into an insurance contract may void it during infancy or ratify it when he or she reaches majority. Some states have laws which give infants the power to enter into binding life insurance contracts on their own lives as young as age fourteen.

Reality of Consent

Contract Defined

The essential elements of a contract are contained in the following definition: A contract is an agreement between two or more competent parties, supported by a consideration, and having for its purpose a legal object.

CHARACTERISTICS OF THE INSURANCE CONTRACT

Insurance contracts must contain the essential elements of a contract which were discussed above. Insurance contracts have several distinguishing characteristics with which we must be familiar in order to understand their creation, execution, and interpretation. They include:

(1) aleatory, (2) conditional, (3) unilateral, (4) personal, (5) adhesion, and (6) utmost good faith.

Aleatory

Insurance contracts are *aleatory*, which means that performance is conditioned upon an event which may or may not happen. The values given up by each party are unequal. The insurer may pay a claim which is much larger than the premium it received. On the other hand, it may pay nothing. In this respect, the insurance contract is like a wager—one party or the other may give up far more than he or she receives. Insurance is not gambling, however, because the contract does not create the risk but instead transfers it. Betting, on the other hand, creates a risk.

Because the insurance contract is aleatory, one might conclude that you receive nothing in return for the premium unless you have a claim. When the contract is one of indemnity, you are as well off not to sustain a loss as to have one. All the insurance will do is restore your original financial condition.

What you do receive for the premium, whether there is a loss or not, is freedom from worry. A person who says, "I have paid fire insurance premiums for five years and never got anything out of it," does not realize that the peace of mind and freedom from worry have been well worth the premium. The purpose of insurance is to reduce uncertainty, which is the cause of worry.

Conditional

An insurance contract is *conditional*. The insurer is obligated to perform only if the conditions set forth in the contract are met. You, in turn, do not promise to meet the conditions but you cannot force the insurer to perform unless you do so. A typical condition is that you must report losses covered by the insurance policy within either a stipulated or a reasonable period of time. You are not compelled to do so, but the insurer need not keep its part of the bargain unless this condition is met. Because of this characteristic of the contract, you must comply with the conditions of the policy if you are to receive its protection.

Unilateral

An insurance contract is usually *unilateral;* only the insurer makes promises. After paying the premium you do not promise anything. You must fulfill the conditions if you expect the insurer to pay, but you do not promise to do so. In contrast, a bilateral contract is one in which both parties make enforceable promises and either party may force the other to perform or pay damages for lack of performance.

Personal

Insurance contracts are *personal*. This means that it is loss to a person, not the property, that is insured. A person says that his or her car is insured. Actually, one is insured against financial loss caused by something happening to the car. If the car is sold, the insurance does not automatically pass to the new owner. The insurance may be assigned to him or her, but only with the consent of the insurer. Because it is people who are insured and they affect the hazard, insurance companies are as concerned about the insured person as they are about the nature of the property which is the subject of insurance. The character, reputation, and conduct of the owner of insured property are significant considerations in underwriting.

Adhesion

NO BARTERING

The insurance contract is a contract of *adhesion*. Unlike contracts that are formulated by a process of bargaining, an insurance contract is prepared by the insurer and accepted or rejected by the buyer of insurance.[9]

This practice has considerable significance with regard to the manner in which the courts interpret insurance contracts in the event of a dispute. When the terms of the policy have more than one meaning, that which favors the insured is held to be the intention of the parties to the agreement, on the assumption that the insurer which writes the contract should know what it wants to say and how to state it clearly. In some cases, favoring the insured has been carried to extremes. In response, insurers have added restrictive and complicated clauses to some contracts to make their meaning clear. When the meaning of the terms is obvious and unambiguous, however, the court will not change the contract to favor the insured.

Utmost Good Faith

Insurance contracts are based on *utmost good faith*—a higher than usual standard of candor and honesty is expected of the parties involved than that expected in the negotiation of other contracts. In the case of contracts other than those dealing with insurance, it is generally assumed that each party has equal knowledge and access to the facts. In contrast with this, early day ocean marine insurance contracts were negotiated under circumstances which forced underwriters to rely on information provided by the insured because they could not get it firsthand. A ship being insured, for example, might be unavailable for inspection because it was on the other side of the world. Was the ship seaworthy? The underwriter could not inspect it, so he required the insured to warrant that it was. If the warranty was not strictly true, the contract was voidable. The penalty for departing from utmost good faith was no coverage when a loss occurred.

Today, the applicant for insurance is required to make representations and refrain from concealment. Where will the automobile be garaged? Who will drive it? Will it be used for business? It is not feasible for the insurer to check on all the information provided by the appli-

---

9. There are some cases in which the insured writes his or her own contract and then places it in the insurance market, but these are in the minority.

cant, but if the insured has misrepresented or concealed any material facts the policy is voidable. The penalty for departing from utmost good faith is still no coverage when a loss occurs. If you misrepresent who drives your car or where it is garaged in order to pay a lower premium for auto insurance, you may have no insurance when you need it most.

Consumer Applications
Identifying Your Firm's Insurance Problems

As a part-time bookkeeper for High Country, Inc., a small manufacturing firm, you mention to Mr. Langdon, your boss and owner of the firm, that you are taking this course. A day or two later, he says to you, "Drop the bookkeeping for a week and look over our insurance. I think we're paying too much premium and I'm not sure we need all the insurance we have."

The thought that you have become an insurance consultant after reading five chapters of this book is gratifying. The thought that you may lay an egg on this assignment makes you feel acutely uncomfortable. You may be able to respond with "I don't know" when your professor asks you a question about the material in this week's assignment, but your boss is accustomed to a great deal more than that. He is a hard-headed businessman who makes lots of money, hates to pay taxes, and believes that insurance is a necessary evil. He thinks you are a bright young person who could go a long way in this business and you would like to preserve that illusion. What can you do?

First, you can recognize that, as bookkeeper, you know more about the business than you might think. Second, you can adopt a goal. Let's say you decide to write a report entitled, "Some aspects of our insurance program you ought to know about." Third, you can go back through this chapter and look for some signals that may lead to the discovery of problems. You put together some prospective signals as follows:

1. Insurable interest
2. Actual cash value
3. Other insurance
4. Warranties

Insurable Interest

In examining the various fire insurance policies the firm has, you find that the insured's name and address for all the buildings is High Country, Inc. This seems reasonable until you recall that the company pays rent for some premises every month. In checking, you find that one goes to Mr. Langdon's son and one to his daughter, both of whom are away at college.

This puzzles you, so you talk to Mrs. Davison, who has been Mr. Langdon's secretary since the day he started the business 27 years ago. She says, "Mr. Langdon gave Building #3 to Jack, Jr. and Building #5 to Denise a long time ago so he could pay them rent instead of an allowance. That way, the money sent to them is a deductible expense for income tax purposes and Mr. Langdon does not have to put them through school with money he has paid taxes on."

Armed with this bit of intelligence, you go back through the insurance policies and find that you were right the first time. The named insured for all buildings, including #3 and #5, is High Country, Inc.

Query: Does High Country, Inc. have an insurable interest in buildings owned by Jack Langdon, Jr. and Denise Langdon? If not, can it collect on the insurance if there is a loss? Can Jack or Denise? You now have one item for your report.

Actual Cash Value

In examining the fire insurance on High Country's buildings you find that the amount of insurance has been increased every year in order to keep it equal to the actual cash value. As the bookkeeper, you are aware that this means replacement cost minus depreciation. Some of the buildings are quite old but in good repair. Building #2, for example, is 25 years old but still suitable for its use as a warehouse. The amount of insurance on it is $200,000. How much would it cost to replace it? When you ask Mr. Bronson, the plant superintendent who is responsible for construction and maintenance, he estimates at least $400,000. If the building is totally destroyed by fire, High Country will be paid $200,000 by the insurance company but it will cost $400,000 to replace it.

Query: Does High Country have $200,000 readily available? Should we try to get the insurance policies changed to a replacement cost basis? You have another item for your report.

Other Insurance

When you checked the insurance on Building #2, you found two policies, each in the amount of $100,000. One was issued by Pacific Fire Insurance Company and the other by Square Deal Insurance, a company owned by Mrs. Langdon's second cousin. When you ask Mrs. Davison about this, she tells you, "The company is pretty small, but Mr. Langdon wanted to help Mrs. Langdon's cousin get started."

Query: What happens when there is a loss? The other insurance provision of both policies says that each company will pay its share. If Square Deal is defunct when High Country has a loss, Pacific Fire will pay its share but who will pay Square Deal's share? If your state has an insolvency fund, the fund will pay. But how quickly? Under the best of circumstances, settling a loss with more than one company can be more time consuming than settling with only one company. If one company is unable to pay its share, you have a real problem. Perhaps High Country should have insurance with only one (strong) company. Another item for your report.

Warranties

In studying the fire insurance policies High Country has, you run across a provision that says, "It is warranted that a watchman will be on duty at all times when the plant is not operating." You are aware that the plant operates two shifts (8 to 4 and 4 to midnight) five days per week. You are also aware that you have seen Joe Luger, the night watchman, in your favorite beer joint well after midnight.

Query: Is it possible that High Country does not have a watchman on duty at all times when it is not in operation? What happens if a fire starts when Joe is supposed to be on duty but is at the Cross-Eyed Owl having a few beers? Another item for your report.

Your Report

Because I don't know enough about insurance to analyze costs, I don't know if we are paying too much premium for our insurance program. I have, however, discovered some problems that should be brought to your attention. They are:

1. High Country does not have an insurable interest in Buildings #3 and #5 because they are owned by your chil-

dren, not the firm. Our insurance agent should issue policies to them and they will have to pay the premium.

2. The insurance on Building #2 is enough to pay for its actual cash value but only half enough to replace it. We should ask our agent about replacement cost insurance on it and our other buildings.

3. There are two insurers on Building #2 and one of them is pretty weak. We would be far better off to have all our fire insurance with one strong company. Under the present arrangement, each company is required to pay only half of each loss. If the weak company becomes insolvent, we would be paid for only half of a loss and it could be inconvenient collecting from the state insolvency fund. Even under the best of circumstances, it is easier to settle claims with one company than with two.

4. According to our policies, there must be a watchman on duty whenever the plant is not operating. If there is not, our coverage is suspended. If we had a fire at such a time, the insurer(s) would pay us nothing. We need some system to assure that watchmen will be on duty when they are required.

Discussion Questions

1. Under what circumstances might a firm have an insurable interest in the life of the president of the United States?

2. Your employer can buy an insurance policy on your life and collect the proceeds even if you are no longer with the firm at the time of your death. Clearly, if you leave the firm, your employer no longer has an insurable interest in your life and would gain by your death. Would this situation make you uncomfortable? What if you learned that your former employer was in financial difficulty? Do you think the law should permit a situation of this kind? Please explain.

3. Can a person who has an insurable interest in your life (e.g., your spouse) buy a policy on your life without your knowledge and consent? Why or why not?

4. You cannot assign your auto policy to a purchaser without the insurer's consent, but you can assign your life insurance policy without the insurer's approval. Is this difference really necessary? Why or why not?

5. Because most insurance contracts are unilateral, only the insurer makes promises—not the buyer. But the contract is conditional and the insured cannot force the insurer to perform unless he or she fulfills the conditions. As a practical matter, therefore, what is the significance of the fact that the contract is unilateral?

6. May the fact that an insurance policy is a contract of adhesion make it difficult for insurers to write it in simple, easy to understand terms? Please explain.

7. Fire insurance policies are designed to pay for no more than the actual loss suffered, but we still have a great deal of arson for profit. How do you account for this?

8. If your house is destroyed by fire because of your neighbor's negligence, your insurer may recover from him or her what it pays you under its right of subrogation. This prevents you from collecting twice for the same loss. But the insurer collects premiums to pay losses and then recovers from negligent persons who cause them. Isn't that double recovery? Please explain.

9. If you have $100,000 insurance on your house but it is worth only $80,000 at the time it is destroyed by fire, your insurer will pay you only $80,000. You paid for $100,000 of insurance but you get only $80,000. Aren't you being cheated? Please explain.

10. "An insurable interest in the life of another may be based on love and affection, such as that of the parent for the child . . ." What about unwanted children who are abused, battered, or neglected? Does the parent suffer a loss when such a child dies? Do you think the requirements for insurable interest in life insurance should be re-examined? What do you suggest?

Cases

5-1 Jack Blitz recently noticed that his health insurance policy states that if he has additional health insurance with another company his policy would combine its settlement coverage with the other policies for a total combined settlement of no more than the maximum stated coverage in either policy. Jack thought this was definitely unfair as he had to pay the full premium for each policy. Why couldn't he collect the stated amount payable on each and make some money on his illness, or at least be refunded part of each policy's premium?

1. What insurance principle is involved here?

2. Explain to Jack the principle behind the concepts involved in determining the probable occurrence of an event and setting equitable rates by the insurance company.

5-2 Walter Brown owns a warehouse in Chicago. The building would cost $400,000 to replace at today's prices, and Walter wants to be sure that he's properly insured. He feels that he'll be better off to have two $250,000 fire insurance policies on the warehouse, because "then I'll know if one of the insurers is giving me the run-around. Anyhow, you have to get a few extra dollars to cover expenses if there's a fire—and I can't get that from one company."

1. If the building is totally destroyed by fire, how much may Walter collect without violating the concept of indemnity?

2. What is Walter's insurable interest? Does it exceed the value of the building?

5-3 Since the insurance contract is one of adhesion, ambiguous terms will be interpreted in favor of the insured. For example, in the Louisiana case of *Albritton vs. Fireman's Fund,* 70 Sou. (2nd) 111 (1953), the state supreme court held that the impact of a car losing its wheel and striking the road surface was a collision.

1. How can such interpretations by the courts help the consumers who buy insurance?

2. Are there any negative effects that these decisions might have?

5-4 The insurance contract is a conditional contract, and the insurer under the personal automobile insurance policy must comply with certain conditions before it may cancel the insured's policy.

1. Discuss three logical reasons why an insurer might be allowed to cancel an insured's auto policy.

2. Turn to Appendix B and look up the allowable reasons for cancellation by the insurer as set forth in the Personal Automobile Policy. How do these reasons compare with those that you suggested?

Chapter Six:
INSURANCE CONTRACTS

INTRODUCTION

The purpose of insurance is to reduce uncertainty. You buy insurance to protect yourself from financial loss so you won't have to worry about it. How do you know you have nothing to worry about unless you know what is in the contract? Most people don't read the insurance policies they buy, but instead rely on their insurance agent to provide them with the coverage they need. Those who do read their insurance contracts have difficulty understanding them.

This chapter deals with this problem by examining the various components of insurance contracts, including the following:

1. Declarations   *BINDING AUTHORITY*
2. Insuring Clauses
3. Exclusions
4. Conditions
5. Endorsements or Riders.

Familiarity with these components will help you find answers to many important questions. A checklist is shown in Figure 6-1 in the Consumer Applications section of this chapter.

DECLARATIONS

The declarations are statements you make which identify you, give information about the risk, and provide the basis upon which the contract

is issued and the premium determined. This information may be obtained orally or it may be in the form of a signed application.

Applications

Although much insurance is sold rather than bought, you are required to make an application, which is an offer to buy. The function of the agent is to induce you to make an offer. As a practical matter, he or she also fills out the application for you and then asks you to read and sign it. The application identifies you in more or less detail, depending upon the type of insurance. It also provides information about the risk involved. For example, in the automobile policy you identify yourself, describe the automobile to be insured, indicate the use of the automobile, where it will be garaged, who will drive it, and so on. Some applications for automobile insurance also require considerable information about your driving and claim experience as well as others who may use the car. In many cases, such as life insurance, the written application becomes a part of the policy. An example is included in Appendix C.

Binders

In some cases, property insurance coverage may be provided while the application is being processed. This is done through the use of a *binder*, which is a temporary contract to provide coverage until the policy is issued by the agent or his or her company.

An agent who has binding authority can create a contract between the insurance company and the insured. Two factors influence the granting of such authority. First, some companies prefer to have underwriting decisions made by specialists in the underwriting department and, therefore, do not grant binding authority to the agent. Second, some policies are cancellable; others are not. The underwriting errors of an agent with binding authority may be corrected by cancellation if the policy is cancellable. Even with cancellable policies, the insurer is responsible for losses which occur prior to cancellation. If it is not cancellable, the insurer is obligated for the term of the contract.

The binder may be written or oral. When you telephone the agent and ask to have your house insured against loss by fire, the agent will ask for the necessary information, give a brief statement about the contract—such as the coverage and the premium cost—and then say, "You are covered." At this point, you have made an oral application and the agent has accepted the offer by creating an oral binder. In some cases the agent may send you a written binder to serve as evidence of the contract until the policy is received. In other cases, the agent merely makes a mental or written note to the effect that the risk has been bound. The written binder shows who is insured, for what perils, the amount of the insurance, and the company in which it is placed.

While an oral binder is as legal as one that is written, in case of a dispute it may be difficult to prove its terms. Suppose your house burns after the oral binder has been made but prior to the issuance of a policy and the agent denies the existence of the contract. How could you prove there was a contract? Or, suppose the agent binds the risk, a fire occurs, and the agent dies before the policy is issued. Unless there is evidence in writing, how can you prove the existence of a contract? Suppose the agent does not die and does not deny the existence of the contract but has no evidence in writing. If he or she represents only one company, the agent may assert that the company was bound and the insured can collect for the loss. But what if the agent represents more than one company? Which one is bound? In one case where the agent assigned business to his companies in rotation, the court held that the company whose turn it was could not deny that it was bound.[1] In a similar case, the court divided the loss among all the companies issuing such policies represented by the agent. While it may be heartening to win such cases in court, legal action is both expensive and uncertain and can be avoided by insisting upon a written binder.

Binding Receipts

Somewhat similar to the binder in property insurance is the conditional or binding receipt. It is issued by the life insurance agent at the time of taking an application if the applicant pays the first premium at that time. The conditional receipt usually does not bind the risk at the time it is issued, but it does put the coverage into effect retroactive to the time of application if the applicant proves to be acceptable. If an applicant meets all the requirements of insurability as of the date of the application, a claim for benefits because of death (or disability) prior to the issuance of the policy will be honored. The binding receipt binds the company on the condition that the risk was acceptable on the date of application.

Period of Coverage

All insurance policies specify the period during which the coverage applies. Life and health policies may cover for the whole life, a specified period of years, or to a specified age. Health policies often cover for a year at a time. Most fire insurance policies are for a term of from one date to another; usually for one or three years. Perpetual policies remain in force until cancelled by you or the insurer. Liability policies may be for a three-month or six-month period, but most are for a year or three years. Some forms of automobile insurance may be written on a continuous basis, with premiums payable at specified intervals. Such policies remain in force as long as premiums are paid or until they are cancelled. Whatever the term for which any policy is to be in force, it will be very carefully spelled out in the contract.

Limitations of Liability

All insurance policies have clauses which limit the liability of the insurer. Life policies promise to pay the face amount of the policy. Health policies limit payment to a specified amount per week, a specified amount for total medical expenses, or on a schedule basis such as so much for board and room and so much for various kinds of surgery.

---

1. *Croft v. Hanover Fire Insurance Co.*, 40 W. Va. 508, 21 S.E. 854 (1895).

Property insurance policies specify actual cash value, cost to repair or replace, and the face amount of insurance, as limits. Liability policies have no limit on the cost of defending you against a claim, but have limits on the claims they will pay on your behalf.

INSURING CLAUSES

All-risks Versus Named-perils

A policy may be written on an all-risks or a named-peril basis. A named-perils policy provides protection against loss caused by the perils listed. An all-risks policy provides protection against all fortuitous loss except that caused by perils which are excluded. All-risks does not mean "all-loss"—there must be a fortuitous event involved. Policies written on a named-perils basis cannot cover all possible chances of loss because of the "unknown hazard." That is, there is always the possibility of loss being caused by a peril which was not known to exist. For this reason, all-risks policies cover many perils not included in named-perils policies. This broader coverage typically requires a higher premium than a named-perils policy.

Very few policies are all-risks in the sense of covering every conceivable peril. Probably the closest approach to this in the property insurance field is the comprehensive glass policy which insures against all glass breakage except that caused by fire, war, and the nuclear peril. Most life insurance policies are all-risks except for suicide during the first year or the first two years. The term "all-risks" actually means "all-perils."

Variation in Insuring Clauses

Some policies have relatively simple insuring clauses, such as that in a life insurance policy. One policy, for example, says, "The Company will pay the face amount of this policy to the beneficiary immediately upon receipt of due written proof of the death of the Insured occurring while this policy is in full force." Other policies have several insuring clauses, each accompanied by definitions, exclusions, and conditions. An example of this type is the Personal Automobile Policy.

Meaning of Terms

When the policy specifies the peril insured against, the meaning of the peril listed and the losses to be indemnified are of major significance. The same is true of perils and losses which are excluded. What a word means may be a matter of how the courts interpret it or how the policy defines it. The meaning of the terms "direct loss" and "fire" as used in the fire insurance policy illustrate how court interpretations determine the scope of insuring clauses.

Direct loss. The fire policy insures against "direct loss by fire . . ." What does this include? "Direct loss" means the value of the property, not the value of its use. The insurer is liable for damage or destruction of the physical property caused by an insured peril but not the loss resulting from the income lost as a result of the physical damage to the property. The latter is a consequential loss which may be insured separately but is not included in the coverage provided by the Standard Fire Insurance Policy.

Proximate cause. Another question which arises in connection with the phrase "direct loss by fire" is the extent to which the damage to insured property must be caused directly by an insured peril. Suppose the water used to extinguish a fire on the second floor leaks through the ceiling and causes damage to the floor below. Does the fire insurance policy cover such damage? Or, suppose the walls of a building damaged by fire are so weakened that they collapse several days after the fire has been extinguished, causing damage to the building next door. Does the fire insurance policy on the building thus damaged cover this loss? Questions of this kind are settled by reference to the *doctrine of proximate cause.*

The proximate cause is the one that is actually responsible for the loss. If there is a chain of intermediate circumstances that led to a result, the proximate cause is that which set the intervening agencies in motion. Thus, in the first case above, fire caused the use of water to suppress the fire and the water, in turn, caused damage to the floor below. The fire policy will cover this loss because fire was the proximate cause. In the second case, the wall fell over because it was weakened by fire. Thus, fire was the proximate cause of the damage to the building next door when the wall fell on it and the fire policy on that building will cover the loss. If an insured peril is the proximate cause of loss, either directly or through intervening agencies, the policy covers the loss.

Fire. "Fire" means oxidation which is so rapid that it produces either a flame or a glow. Combustion may cause damage but unless it produces a flame or a glow, it is not a fire. While the fire policy does not so specify, the fire which causes the direct loss insured against must be a hostile fire. A hostile fire is one which has escaped from the bounds within which it was intended to burn, while a friendly fire is one that stays where it belongs. A fire burning in a fireplace is a friendly fire. If a spark flies out and sets fire to the sofa, the fire is hostile. These meanings have been established through court decisions which provide the basis for resolving most differences of opinion as they arise. In any case which cannot be settled by reference to past decisions, of course, the question may be settled by resort to the court where the jury is the ultimate authority in deciding the distinction between a friendly fire and a hostile fire.

Policy may define terms. In some cases, terms are defined in the policy. The purpose of such definitions is to clarify in advance any question as to the meaning of terms instead of leaving them to be interpreted by the insured or the claims adjuster or the courts after a loss has occurred. The insurer wants to state the terms of the contract clearly so misunderstanding will be avoided.

For example, one burglary policy defines burglary as "the felonious abstraction of insured property from within the premises by a person making felonious entry by actual force and violence." Robbery, on the other hand, is "a felonious or forcible taking of property from the insured's premises by violence inflicted on a person having care or custody of the property or rightful access thereto, by putting such person or persons in fear of violence or by other felonious acts committed in the presence of the person and with the person's knowledge." The Personal Auto Policy defines collision to mean the "upset, or collision with another object of your covered auto." A health insurance policy may define total disability as "complete inability of the insured to perform any and every duty pertaining to his occupation" or "complete inability of the insured to engage in any reasonably gainful occupation for which he is or may become fitted by education, training or experience."

EXCLUSIONS

Whether the policy is all-risks or named-perils, the coverage it provides cannot be ascertained without examining the exclusions. You don't know what the policy covers until you know what it does not cover. The policy may exclude specified perils, property, or losses.

Excluded Perils

Some perils are excluded because they can be covered by other policies. This is the reason for the fire exclusion in the comprehensive glass policy. Others are excluded because they require separate rating. Thus, elevator liability is not covered by the Owners', Landlords', and Tenants' policy unless the elevator is declared and an additional premium is paid, as it must be rated separately. Some perils, such as those associated with war, are excluded because they are considered to be uninsurable. Nuclear energy perils such as radiation are excluded from most policies and must be separately insured. Losses to homeowners caused by the Three Mile Island incident in 1979, for example, were not covered by their homeowners insurance.

Excluded Property

Some property is excluded because it is insurable under other policies. Homeowners policies, for example, exclude automobiles because they are insured under automobile policies. Other property is excluded because the coverage is not needed by the average insured who would, therefore, not want to pay for it. For example, most "floater" policies exclude property on exhibition because of the extra hazard but such coverage is available for an additional premium[2]. Liability policies usually exclude liability for damage to or loss of property of others in the care, custody, or control of the insured because other insurance contracts provide protection for the owner, or because the risk is

2. Floater policies cover property wherever it may be rather than at only specified locations.

viewed as a "business risk" involving the craftsmanship of the insured, such as that of a contractor or processor, which the insurer does not wish to assume.

Excluded Losses

Transportation policies usually exclude marring and scratching of the property insured as this is partially or wholly within the control of the insured, who may be careless if such losses are covered. Losses due to wear and tear are excluded because they are inevitable rather than accidental and thus not insurable. Similarly, inherent vice, which refers to losses caused by characteristics of the insured property, is excluded. Certain products, such as tires and various kinds of raw materials for example, deteriorate with the passage of time. Such losses are not accidental and are, therefore, uninsurable. Losses caused intentionally by the insured are excluded. Liability policies, for example, exclude responsibility for assault and battery by or at the direction of the insured. For the same reason, life insurance contracts exclude death by suicide during the first year (or two years) the policy is in force by providing for a return of premiums paid rather than payment of the face amount of the policy. In order to reduce adverse selection, many health insurance policies exclude pre-existing conditions—medical problems that existed prior to the inception date of the policy.

CONDITIONS

Conditions enumerate the duties of the parties to the contract and, in some cases, define the terms used. Because insurance policies are conditional contracts, it is essential to be aware of the conditions. You cannot expect the insurer to fulfill its part of the contract unless you fulfill the conditions. Failure to do so may release the insurer from its obligations. Many conditions found in insurance contracts are common to all. Others are characteristic of only certain types of contracts. Some examples follow.

Notice

So the insurer can determine the facts and protect itself, all policies require that the insurer be notified when the event, occurrence, accident, or loss insured against takes place. The time within which this notice must be filed and the manner of making it vary with different contracts, but all require notice. The fire policy specifies that "the insured shall give immediate written notice to this Company of any loss . . ." A typical life insurance policy says that payment will be made "immediately upon receipt of due written proof . . ." A health policy requires that "written proof of loss must be furnished to the Company . . ." The automobile policy requires written notice to the company "as soon as practicable."

In some cases, if such notice is not made within a reasonable time after the loss or accident, the insurer is relieved of all liability under the contract. A driver whose automobile struck the hand of a policeman who was directing traffic in St. Petersburg, Florida, did not report the incident to his insurer until over a year later because the policeman assured him that the injury was minor. When it developed a year later that the injury was serious, however, the insured notified his insurer. The insurer was upheld by the court in its refusal to defend the suit. The court said that "a difference of weeks, and sometimes even days, in notification to an insurer of an accident may well determine the success and ability of the insurer in ascertaining the facts surrounding the accident." The insurer is entitled to timely notice. Insureds who fail to fulfill this condition may find themselves without protection when they need it most—after a loss.

Payment of Claims

Most policies require that the insurer must pay claims and in other ways fulfill its obligations under the policy either within a reasonable or a specified period of time. The insurer, however, has no liability until notice is filed by the insured.

Suspension of Coverage

Because there are some risks the insurer wants to avoid, all insurance policies provide that certain conditions suspend the coverage or release the insurer from liability. Some life and health policies have special clauses which suspend coverage for those in military service during wartime. Protection under a Personal Automobile Policy is suspended while the vehicle is used as a taxicab for hire. Fire policies provide that coverage is suspended while the hazard is increased by any means within the control or knowledge of the insured.[3]

Cooperation of the Insured

Some provisions are characteristic of only certain types of policies. While all policies involve the cooperation of the insured in the sense that he or she must fulfill certain conditions before the insurer will pay, liability policies have a specific provision concerning the cooperation of the insured which must be complied with if the insured is to receive the protection of the contract. This is because the investigation of an accident and defense of a suit against the insured are well-nigh impossible unless he or she will cooperate. If the insured fails to do so, the insurer will be released from its obligations under the contract.

Protection of Property after Loss

Most property insurance policies contain provisions requiring the insured to protect the property after a loss in order to reduce the loss as much as possible. An insured who wrecks his or her automobile, for example, has the responsibility for having it towed to the garage for safe-keeping. In the case of a fire loss, the insured is expected to protect un-

---

3. If the neighbor's house catches on fire, the hazard is surely increased for the insured next door. Does this suspend coverage? No, it does not. The clause is designed to protect the insurer from changes in hazard over which the insured has control, such as storing inflammable fluids or explosives in the house. The purpose of suspension clauses is to avoid risks which the insurer is unwilling or unable to bear, not to penalize honest and careful insureds.

damaged property from the weather and other perils in order to reduce the loss. You cannot be careless and irresponsible just because you have insurance.

Examination

A provision peculiar to many health policies is that which gives the insurer the right to have its physician examine the insured during the time he or she receives benefits under the policy. This right cannot be used to harass the claimant, but the insurer is entitled to check occasionally to see if he or she should continue to receive benefits. Property insurance policies have a provision which requires the claimant to submit to examination under oath as well as make records and property available for examination by representatives of the insurance company.

ENDORSEMENTS AND RIDERS

Riders and endorsements are two terms with the same meaning. Riders are used with life and health policies while endorsements are used with property and liability policies. A rider or endorsement makes a change in the contract to which it is attached. It may increase or decrease the coverage, change the premium, make a correction, or make any number of other changes. The Extended Coverage Endorsement, for example, increases the coverage of the fire policy to which it is attached by adding several perils to those in the basic policy. A disability income rider increases the benefits of a life insurance policy by providing for income payments if the insured becomes totally disabled.

PACKAGE POLICIES *Briefly*

At one time, legal restrictions prohibited combining property and liability insurance in one policy. Moreover, there was a tendency to create separate policies for different kinds of risks. For example, personal property in the home was insured by a fire insurance policy, but personal property that was moved about instead of staying in one place was insured by a floater policy. As a result of these practices, families and firms wanting complete insurance protection for property and liability risks had to buy a number of different policies.

The combining of these separate policies into one policy was accomplished by the creation of the Homeowner's Policy for the family and the Special Multiperil Program (SMP) and Businessowner's Policy (BOP) for firms. These policies are called *package policies.*

Package policies have a number of advantages. They provide broad coverage for less premium than buying the same protection with separate policies. Costs are reduced because one policy is processed instead of several. Adverse selection is reduced by requiring that most risks usual to the class of insured for which the package is designed must be insured. This prevents people from insuring only their most hazardous risks. Most package policies automatically increase the amount of insurance needed to keep pace with inflation, thus preventing inadequate limits.

Consumer Applications
Examining the Insurance Transaction

Let's look at the chronology of an insurance experience to see how we can apply what we have discussed in this chapter. The sequence of events is about as follows:

1. You call the agent or the agent calls you about insurance.
2. You apply for a policy.
3. You receive the policy.
4. You pay premiums.
5. You have, or do not have, a loss.

The Application

If the transaction is made by telephone, the agent fills out the application and, if it needs your signature, asks you to stop by the office and sign it. If you get together in person, the agent asks you questions, fills out the application, and asks you to sign it. The application includes a description of what you want and the information the insurer needs. It is similar to ordering a car. Before you get around to the written application (order), you have discussed what you want and the terms of the purchase. The application reduces what you have discussed to writing. Remember, in this whole process you are negotiating a contract. The application should indicate what you want and what it will cost. If it does not have all this information, get it in writing separately.

Read the application carefully before you sign it. This sounds trite, but many of us have a tendency to skip the reading because we as-sume that what we have said is what the agent put in the application. But the agent could have misunderstood. Or, he or she could have edited what you said. That is improbable, but it has happened. Because an insurance contract is one of utmost good faith, you must be sure you don't conceal or misrepresent anything.

Get a Binder

If you apply for property or liability insurance, get a written binder from the agent. It is proof of what you ordered and provides coverage now. Oral binders are as binding as written binders but it can be difficult to establish their existence and their terms. A binder is a temporary contract and, for your own protection, you should insist on a written contract.

Get a Conditional Receipt

Most life insurance agents will ask you to pay the first premium when you sign the application. By getting the first premium now, they avoid having to collect it from you when they deliver the policy. Don't let this fact obscure the benefit for you. Remember that the application will be processed and, if you qualify, a policy will be issued regardless of what happens to you in the meantime if you pay the premium now. By getting a conditional receipt, you are assuring life insurance protection at the earliest possible moment.

Receipt of Policy

When you take delivery on your new car, what do you do? Most people examine the car carefully to be sure that everything they ordered has been delivered. Is it the color you ordered? Does it have the options you ordered? You may overlook something but you surely make an effort to see that you are getting what you ordered because you know you will have to pay for it.

When your insurance policy is delivered, what do you do? Stick it in a drawer? If your agent delivers the policy, you should go over it with him or her carefully to assure that it is what you ordered and you understand what you are getting. Refer to the policy checklist shown in Figure 6-1 so you won't overlook anything. Remember that the policy you receive is the entire contract between you and the insurance company. Regardless of what you may have been promised in the process of filling out the application and during other discussion, if it isn't in the policy you don't get it.

Premium Payments

You must pay premiums to keep an insurance policy in force, but that isn't all you have to do.

Beware of the conditions! This is not to imply that they are unfair, but to remind you that you have a conditional contract. If you don't fulfill the conditions, the insurer does not have to keep its promises. An insurance policy is a contract which creates a continuing relationship between you and the insurance company. If it is to be successful, you must do your part. In order to do your part, you must know not only your rights but also your obligations.

When You Have a Loss

Many people learn most of what they know about their insurance after they have a loss. This is like learning you're out of beer after the guests arrive. There is a significant difference, however. You may be able to borrow some beer from your neighbor or get a case at the nearest store, but you can't rewrite your insurance contract after you've had a loss. You have to do that ahead of time.

Loss settlement procedures and suggestions for problem solving are discussed in the next chapter.

---

1. Who is insured?
2. What property is covered?
3. What perils are covered?
4. How are coverages limited?
5. What perils, losses, or property are excluded?
6. When is the policy in effect?
7. Where does protection apply?
8. What conditions suspend coverage?
9. What claim settlement alternatives are there?
10. What are my rights and obligations?

FIGURE 6-1

Insurance Policy
Checklist

Discussion Questions

1. Comprehensive coverage in the auto policy covers loss caused by falling objects. Would the damage caused to the engine of a car driven through ash that had fallen to the ground after the Mt. St. Helens eruption be covered by the policy? Why or why not?

2. Would the auto insurer pay for paint damage caused by falling ash from Mt. St. Helens? Why or why not? What is the difference between the losses described in questions 1 and 2?

3. A portable electric heater is placed too close to the wood paneling in your study. The result is scorched paneling which must be replaced because of its unsightly appearance. Would this loss be covered by a fire insurance policy? Why or why not?

4. Fire policies suspend coverage while the hazard is increased by any means within the control or knowledge of the insured. On July 4, you have a large fireworks display during which sparks ignite the wood shingles on the roof of your house, causing considerable damage. Will your fire policy cover this loss? Why or why not?

5. Because fireworks cost so much, you decide to make your own in your basement workshop. Unfortunately, some of the materials you use to make the fireworks are ignited by a spark from your electric grindstone. A great deal of damage is caused by the fire. Will your fire policy cover this loss? Why or why not?

6. Your careless driving results in serious injury to Denise Dorlaque, a close personal friend. Because she knows you have liability insurance and the insurer will pay for damages on your behalf, she files suit against you. Wouldn't it be unreasonable for your insurer to expect you to help resist payment of such a well-justified claim? Please explain.

7. When you apply for a life insurance policy, agent John DeLozier says, "If you will give me your check for the first month's premium now, the policy will cover you now if you are insurable." Is this a correct statement or is John just in a hurry to get his commission for selling you the policy? Please explain.

8. In the situation mentioned in question 7, does the agent have binding authority? Please explain.

9. Wouldn't it be much easier for you to understand your insurance policy if the insurer simply used terms in their usual way instead of defining them in detail? After all, you know what robbery is and everybody knows what a collision is. Why do insurers add to the complexity of policies with all these definitions?

10. You learn that a huge forest fire is heading your way. Realizing that the amount of insurance on your home is grossly inadequate, you call agent Jerry Bell and request that the amount be increased from $65,000 to $100,000. Because he lives in the same community, you assume that he is aware of the forest fire so you don't mention it. You are relieved when he says, "I'll bind it now." Will the increased

limits apply if Jerry is unaware of the forest fire at the time you call and it destroys your house the next day? Would your answer be the same if Jerry knew about the forest fire?

Cases

6-1 Leon Bush just replaced his old car with a new one, and he is ready to drive the new car off the lot. He did not have collision insurance on the old car, but he wants some on the new one.

He calls his friend, Carol Carnes, who is an insurance agent. "Give me the works, Carol. I want the best collision coverage you have." Soon after he drives the car away, he is struck by an eighteen-wheeler and the new car is totaled.

Leon then discovers that he has collision insurance with a $250 deductible which he must pay. He is upset because to him "the works" meant insurance for all losses he might have due to collision. Carol had thought that he wanted a more cost-efficient coverage, and had used the deductible to lower the premium.

1. Leon wants to take Carol to court to collect the full value of the auto. What would you advise him?

2. What does this tell you about oral contracts?

6-2 Bill Boggs just applied for life insurance. During the application process, he indicated that he had never had pneumonia, when the exact truth is that he *did* have the disease as a baby. He did fully recover, however, and there were no permanent ill effects. Will this misstatement on the life insurance application be grounds for the insurer to cancel his life insurance after it is issued? Why or why not? If he discovers his error, should he notify the insurer? Will his statements be treated as warranties, or as representations?

1. What if Bill promised that he would not drink or smoke for at least five years after the life insurance was issued? Would this be a warranty or a representation?

2. What if he then smokes during year two, and dies in an automobile accident before the end of the second year? Will his coverage depend on whether he was smoking at the time of the accident?

6-3 J.B. Fox was very excited as he discussed last night's big fire with his friend "Sparky" Jones of the local fire department. One of the largest manufacturing firms in the community burned to the ground and "Sparky" said it had no insurance. J.B. said it was a good thing that he kept his fire insurance right up to date. He noted that if his firm burned, his biggest loss would be covered—that of profits he would not make while his plant was being rebuilt. J.B. felt reasonably certain that this type of loss was covered in his basic fire policy because the policy covered loss caused by the proximate cause—fire. Sparky said he was certainly no insurance expert but he had his doubts about J.B.'s reasoning.

1. Is J.B. correct in his thinking?

2. Would the loss of business profit be covered in a basic fire policy if the fire were the proximate cause of this loss in profit?

6-4 A. J. Jackson was very pleased to hear the life insurance agent say that A.J. was covered the moment he finished completing the application and paid the agent the first month's premium. A.J. had had some health problems previously and really didn't expect to be "covered" until after he had taken his physical and received notice from the company. The agent said that the binding receipt was critical for immediate coverage. "Of course," said the agent, "this coverage is for accidental death until the company either accepts or rejects your application." The agent congratulated A.J. again for his decision. A.J. began to wonder the next morning exactly what kind of coverage, if any, he had.

1. What kind of coverage did A.J. have?

2. Did his submission to the agent of the first month's premium have any impact on his coverage? Why?

3. If you were the agent, how would you have explained this coverage to A.J.?

Chapter Seven:
BUYING INSURANCE

INTRODUCTION

When the decision to buy insurance has been made, you, as risk manager, become purchasing agent for your family or firm. In that capacity, you need to know the following if premium dollars are to be used to the greatest advantage:

1. Insurance buying principles

2. How insurance is marketed

3. How to select an insurance agent or broker

4. How to select a company or companies

5. How to select insurance coverages and compare costs

6. How losses are settled.

INSURANCE BUYING PRINCIPLES

Many people spend enough for insurance to provide an adequate program of protection but fail to achieve this objective because their premium dollars are improperly allocated. They spend too much for some parts of their insurance program and too little for others. You can make the best use of premium dollars by adhering to the following two fundamental buying principles:

1. The large-loss principle

2. Avoid first-dollar coverage.

Large-Loss Principle

According to the large-loss principle, the possible size of loss is a better measure of the significance of a risk than the probability that a loss will occur. The fact that there is a low probability that you will die this year may be comforting, but it has little significance for purposes of making plans. Either you will or will not die this year. The significant factor for planning purposes is that your dependents may suffer a *large loss* if you die. The liability risk is similar. There is a low probability that you will become liable to pay damages because of your negligence. But there is a possibility that you could become liable for damages of thousands or even hundreds of thousands of dollars as a result of your negligence.

Possible large losses which have a low probability are ideally suited to the insurance device. At the same time, the large loss is the one which you cannot bear and for which you cannot prepare other than through the use of insurance.

On the other hand, the more probable small losses are, the easier it is for you to handle them without resorting to insurance. If they are small, you can stand the strain on your budget. If they are frequent, perhaps they can be avoided or prevented. If not, they may be budgetable. Because of the expense involved in operating an insurance company, it is more economical to budget for small, frequent losses than to insure against them.

Avoid First-Dollar Coverage *(DEDUCTIBLES)*

Insurance dollars should not be used to protect against that part of possible losses which you can bear.

Small losses cost the insurer far more than the amount of your claim because of adjustment and overhead costs. In many cases, the amount you receive is less than the cost of processing and adjusting the claim. Because insurance companies must charge premiums high enough to cover all costs of doing business, "first-dollar" coverage is the most expensive. Table 7-1 illustrates this point.

Note that for comprehensive coverage, which pays for damage to the automobile other than that caused by collision or upset, full coverage costs twice as much as with a $50 deductible for a Chevrolet Chevette garaged in an Atlanta suburb. Full-coverage—i.e., no deductible—comprehensive insurance requires the insurer to pay *all* the costs of damage caused by vandalism and other perils except collision and upset. Thus, every time such damage occurs, regardless of how slight, the insurer has to pay for the repairs and the insured pays nothing. By bearing the burden of the first $50 of such losses, the insured can reduce the premium for comprehensive coverage by 50 percent.

For the same kind of automobile in the same location, $100 deductible collision insurance costs almost 17 percent more per year than $200 deductible. A $200 deductible exposes the insured to the risk of paying $100 more of a collision loss than with a $100 deductible, but reduces the cost of insurance. A person who cannot bear such a loss

	FULL COVERAGE	$50 DEDUCTIBLE	TABLE 7-1
Comprehensive	$46.00	$21.00	*Annual Insurance Premiums for Chevrolet Chevette**
	$100 DEDUCTIBLE	**$200 DEDUCTIBLE**	
Collision	$71.00	$59.00	

*Garaged in an Atlanta suburb.

Source: Seibels-Bruce Group.

may be better off to pay the extra premium for $100 deductible. But, if it is bearable, he or she should buy the coverage with a $200 deductible because paying $12 per year to protect yourself against a $100 loss is expensive protection. When a possible loss is bearable, it does not pay to buy insurance to cover the risk.

Waiting period.   This same principle is found in the rating of many types of insurance policies. In health insurance, for example, the maximum duration of benefits can be markedly increased for the same premium if the insured will accept a policy with a waiting period. The waiting period is similar to a deductible: benefits do not commence until the insured has been ill or incapacitated for a specified period of time. Many workers' compensation laws recognize the value of this by specifying a waiting period prior to payment of income benefits.

THE INSURANCE MARKET

Before you start using the buying principles just discussed, you need to know something about the insurance market. Insurance may be bought through agents or brokers or, in some cases, directly from the insurer by mail order. An agent represents the company, whereas a broker represents the buyer; both are compensated by the insurer.

Because life insurance and property-liability insurance developed separately in the United States, somewhat different marketing systems evolved. We will therefore discuss them separately.

Life Insurance Marketing

Most life and health insurance is sold through agents who are compensated on a commission basis. Some is sold by salaried representatives and some by mail. In the latter two arrangements, the buyer deals directly with the company rather than through an intermediary.

Some companies represented by an agent compensated by commission insist that he or she represent them exclusively, while others permit their agents to sell for other companies. In such a case, the agent usually has a primary affiliation with one company and devotes most of his or her efforts to selling its policies.

✓Life insurance companies that sell through commission agents use either a general agency or branch office (managerial) type of field organization.

General agency system. A general agent is an independent businessperson rather than an employee of the company. The general agent's contract with the company authorizes him or her to sell insurance in a specified territory and to appoint subagents. Subagents are his or her agents, not agents of the company. They sell insurance for the general agent who, in turn, places it with the company. The general agent receives a commission on all business generated by the agency, pays part of it to the subagents, and keeps the balance for expenses and profit.

In most cases, the general agent has an exclusive franchise and cannot be transferred from his or her territory unless such action is provided for in the contract. The selection, supervision, and compensation of subagents is entirely up to the general agent.

Branch office (managerial) system. A branch office is an extension of the home office into the field. The manager is an employee of the company who is compensated by a salary and a bonus related to the productivity of the office to which he or she is assigned. As an employee, the manager is subject to control by the company and may be transferred from one office to another.

The branch manager employs agents for the company, but the agency contract is between the company and these agents. The agent derives his or her authority directly from the company rather than from the manager. Although a general agent can employ anyone he or she wishes, the manager cannot employ an agent without the consent of the company. Compensation plans for agents are determined by the company. All expenses of maintaining the office are paid by the company, which has complete control over the details of its operation.

Property-Liability Insurance Marketing

Like life and health insurance, most property-liability insurance is sold through agents or brokers who are compensated on a commission basis, but some is sold by salaried representatives or by mail. Because they account for the bulk of insurance sales, we will discuss the American agency system, salaried representatives, and the exclusive agency system.

American or independent agency system. The most distinguishing characteristics of this system are the independence of the agent, his or her bargaining position with the insurers he or she represents, and the fact that those who purchase insurance through him or her are considered by both insurers and agents to be the agent's customers rather than those of the insurer. The agent is an independent businessperson who represents several companies, pays all agency expenses, is compensated on a commission basis, and makes all decisions concerning how the agency operates.

Because there is competition among companies for the services of agents who produce good quality business, an independent agent who can do so has an excellent bargaining position with the companies he or she represents. In a sense, the agent sells them business. Because those who buy insurance from the independent agent are his or her customers, the company cannot deal directly with them. He or she is their insurance agent. Legally, these agents represent the company, but as a practical matter they represent the customer.

Salaried representatives. Some property insurance companies, called *direct writers*, place business through representatives who are employees of the company.[1] Compensation for such employees may be a salary and/or a commission or bonus related to the amount of business they secure for the company. Regardless of the nature of the compensation arrangement, however, they are employees rather than agents. Such representatives pay none of the expenses connected with securing or servicing business. In many cases, they are specialists who provide engineering and inspection service and devote only part of their time to soliciting business.

Exclusive agency. Several companies in the property-liability field market insurance through exclusive or "captive" agents who are permitted to represent only their company or a company in their group.[2] This system is used by Nationwide, State Farm, and Allstate Insurance companies. They compensate the agent through commissions but the customers are considered to be theirs rather than the agent's. Allstate agents are provided office space at no expense, while State Farm and Nationwide agents pay their own expenses. In either case, the agent has

---

1. The term "direct writer" is frequently used to refer to all property insurers that do not use the American Agency System of distribution, but some observers think there are differences among such companies. It appears to this writer that there are at least the two types discussed in this and the next section.

2. A group is a number of separate companies operating under common ownership and management.

little of the independence of agents who operate under the American agency system.

Brokers

A considerable amount of insurance and reinsurance is placed through brokers. A broker solicits business from the insured just as does an agent, but acts as the insured's agent when the business is placed with a company. Some brokers merely place the insurance with a company and then rely on the company to provide whatever engineering and loss-prevention services are needed. Others have a staff of engineers to perform such services for clients. When it appears desirable, a broker may write a special policy for his or her client and then place it in the market.

Many life insurance agents broker business with companies other than the one with which they are primarily identified, particularly when the business is not acceptable to their own company. Such business is known as "substandard" and there are brokers who specialize in placing it for agents.

Brokers are a more significant part of the marketing mechanism in property, liability, and marine insurance than in life and health insurance. They are most active in metropolitan areas and among large insureds, where their knowledge of specialized coverages and the market for them is important. Some brokerage firms operate on a local or regional basis, while others are national or international in their operations.

Mail Order Distribution

As noted earlier, some insurance is sold by mail. A forerunner of Allstate Insurance Company experimented with selling life insurance by mail. At one time, most insurance sold by mail was in the health insurance field, but a number of insurers are now selling life insurance and automobile and home insurance by this method. Sales are created through advertising in newspapers, magazines, television and radio, as well as by direct mail. Some companies operating a mail order business are licensed in only one or two states; insureds who live in a state in which they are not licensed may be at a serious disadvantage in the event of a dispute with the company.[3]

In many cases, you can save money buying insurance by mail. But, mail order insurers cannot provide the help you may receive from a good agent. Few agents are willing to help you with your risk management program unless you buy enough insurance through them to compensate adequately for such service. Whether this is a crucial matter depends upon how much you know about risk, insurance, and the insurance market. The insurance distribution system is summarized in Figure 7-1.

---

3.   You can call the State Insurance Department and ask if the company is licensed in your state, or call the reference desk of your city or state library.

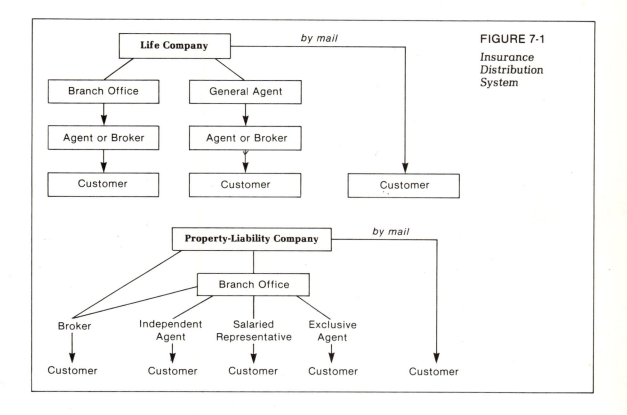

FIGURE 7-1

Insurance Distribution System

SELECTING AN AGENT

Many agents merely sell insurance. Others render valuable service in addition to selling; they act as advisors as well as motivators. The range in quality of insurance agents is enormous—some are awful, and many are mediocre. But there are many top quality agents. Since the premium for insurance includes the agent's compensation, it costs no more to buy through a superior agent than the poorest one. This is one case where it is literally true that "the best costs no more." In fact, it may cost less because a superior agent can help you devise your risk management program and implement it by getting the most for your insurance dollar.

A superior agent is familiar with the risks confronting you, the proper insurance coverages to seek, and the market in which coverage is available at the right price. His or her interest goes beyond the sales commission.

Superior agents will help identify and evaluate your risks and recommend the proper coverage. They will also explain what the policy covers and what it does not cover, as well as what it costs. They will attempt to reduce costs and keep the coverage up to date by reviewing both it and the insured property at regular intervals. Superior agents have good working relationships with their companies. This enables them to get the best deal for you, both in placing the insurance and in settling claims for losses. This does not mean that they will cheat the company for your benefit, but rather that they will take a responsible attitude toward the best interests of both you and company. An agent who will cheat a company may do the same to you.

Superior agents will represent one or more good insurers; if they represent poor companies they are not superior. For the most part, once you have chosen the agent with whom you wish to do business, you will have selected the company or companies with which your insurance will be placed. Thus, your agent must know something about evaluating a company, which is discussed later in this chapter.

SELECTING A COMPANY OR COMPANIES

Most people don't know the name of the company they bought their insurance from unless they have it with an exclusive agency company which advertises extensively, such as Allstate or State Farm. They have relied on their agent to place their insurance in the right company. This is like letting someone else select your bank for you. It may be satisfactory but it isn't necessary to leave the matter of company selection entirely in the agent's hands. He or she can help but you should participate.

In order to make an informed choice, you need to know the things listed in Figure 7-2.

FIGURE 7-2

*Company
Checklist*

1. Is it licensed in my state?
2. Is it financially strong?
3. Does it charge reasonable prices?
4. Are its claims practices fair?
5. What is its cancellation policy?   *Loss Reserve*
6. Does it have adequate capacity?
7. What engineering and loss prevention services does it provide?

Licensed in State

If a company is not licensed in your state, cross it off your list and go on to the next company. Also, get another agent; it is illegal for an agent to represent an unlicensed company, and you should not do business with one who does. If you do business with a company licensed in your state, the state insurance commissioner's office may be able to help you in the event of difficulties with the company. If the company is not licensed in your state, the regulatory authorities are in no position to help you.

There are hundreds of companies licensed in every state, so avoiding one that is not licensed does not greatly restrict the market for the insurance you may need.

As is frequently the case, there are exceptions to what has been said here. Occasionally, and in the case of large firms more than occasionally, the coverage needed is not available from a company licensed in the state. In such a case, the agent may place the insurance in what is called the *surplus lines market*. This market includes unlicensed insurers who are contacted by specially licensed agents called surplus lines agents. Because Lloyd's of London is licensed in only Illinois and Kentucky, most of their American business is placed through surplus lines agents.

Financial Strength

When you buy insurance, you are buying a promise which will be kept in the future. Will the company be able to keep its promises? Clearly, financial strength and stability are of prime importance to the insurance buyer. Information may be obtained in many libraries from *Best's Life Reports* and *Best's Insurance Reports*, as well as other sources.[4]

Best's publishes a General Policyholders' Rating (shown in Figure 7-3) for both life insurance and property-liability companies. Some companies are not rated, either because they have not been in business long enough, or because they did not provide Best's with adequate information on which to base a rating.

A + and A	Excellent	**FIGURE 7-3**
B +	Very Good	
B	Good	*Best's Insurance*
C +	Fairly Good	*Company Ratings*
C	Fair	

In using Best's ratings to judge a company's financial strength and stability, you should consider the rating for not just one but several years. A downward trend is a danger signal. One authority says that A + for six years justifies confidence in the company's financial strength.[5]

Prices

Price is not the sole consideration in buying insurance, but it is a major consideration. Other things equal, why buy insurance from a company whose prices are consistently higher than its competitors? The notion that "you get what you pay for" has long since fallen into disrepute.

---

4. *Best's Fire and Casualty Aggregates and Averages, Best's Insurance Guide with Key Ratings, Moody's Bank & Finance Manual,* and *National Underwriter Life Reports.*

5. Denenberg, Herbert S., "Is 'A-Plus' Really a Passing Grade?" *The Journal of Risk and Insurance,* (September 1967).

Claims Practices

It is unreasonable to expect an insurer to be overly generous in paying claims or honoring claims which should not be paid at all, but you should avoid a company which makes a practice of resisting claims. Even when claims are paid promptly and fairly, a loss is unpleasant and inconvenient. When the company balks and you have to fight for your rights, the whole process is frustrating, time consuming, and you may wind up accepting less than you are entitled to just to get a settlement. Unfortunately, none of the reference books previously cited provides information on company claims practices.

You do, however, have several sources of information. First, you can ask the state insurance department's complaint section if any of the companies you are considering have generated an excessive number of complaints. Not all complaints are justified, but a company which generates more than the average for the amount of business it does should be avoided. Second, you can be on the alert for articles in the press concerning insurer claims practices. Third, you can ask the agent what experience other insureds have had. A top quality agent will not represent a company which has bad claims practices, but he or she knows which companies are the best in this respect. Finally, you can ask your friends and business associates about how their insurers treat them. This provides a small sample, it is true, but some information is better than none. By making these inquiries, you increase the probability that you can at least avoid doing business with the chiselers.

Cancellation Policy

The company's cancellation policy is important. Will it drop you the first time you have a loss? Most companies do not do this but some do. You can get some information by talking with people who have had insurance with the company for some time. You may also be able to depend upon what insurance agents say about the company; a superior agent will not represent a company which cancels too readily. Many insurers now limit their cancellation right by policy provision, especially in automobile and health insurance. Also, some states have legislation which restricts the right to cancel. The extent to which such extra protection is provided should be evaluated when a company is being selected.

Underwriting Capacity

In many cases, the amount of protection needed exceeds the amount an insurance company is financially able to provide. As discussed earlier, reinsurance facilities are used to enable a carrier to issue a policy with higher limits than it is able or willing to retain. This does not mean, however, that reinsurance makes it possible for every insurer to offer the same amount of coverage. Firms differ not only in size but also in the amount of reinsurance they can obtain. Thus, there is considerable variation in capacity. This is an important consideration for the risk manager who wants to avoid having several insurance policies issued by as many different companies to cover one risk.

Engineering and Loss Prevention

In the long run, a business or industrial firm will pay for its own losses plus its share of the cost of operating the insurance companies with which it does business. In addition, it will bear the cost of direct and indirect losses which are not insured. The prevention of loss whenever the efforts required are economically feasible is, therefore, of major significance to the firm. Much of the engineering and loss prevention activity may be carried on by the insurer or under its direction. The facilities the insurer has to devote to such efforts and the degree to which they are successful is an important element to consider in selecting an insurance company—part of the risk manager's success depends upon this element.

SELECTING COVERAGES AND COMPARING COSTS

You can select appropriate coverages if you know exactly what you want and follow the buying principles discussed in this chapter. Knowing exactly what you want involves, first, knowing which risks you want to transfer to an insurer, and second, which insurance policy or policies will cover them. In later chapters, we will discuss the risks to which you are exposed and how to select the insurance most appropriate for you. Because there are significant differences in prices charged by various insurers for similar policies, we will also discuss how to compare costs.

HOW LOSSES ARE SETTLED

If you buy insurance through an agent, you usually notify him or her when you have a loss. If you do not buy through an agent or if you are away from home when a loss occurs, you may notify the insurance company directly. In either case, it is worthwhile to know something about how losses are settled. There is one system in property insurance and another in life insurance.

Property Insurance

In property insurance, the process of paying claims for loss payment is known as *adjustment*. In most cases, the person who represents the insurer in negotiating with the insured about the amount to be paid is called an *adjuster*. Several different types of adjusters are used by insurance companies: the agent, company adjusters, and independent adjusters.

Some agents have the authority to pay for small property losses directly to the insured and make recommendations concerning payment for larger losses. Company adjusters are employees who work out of the home office or branch office of the insurer and devote full time to loss settlement. Independent adjusters, on the other hand, are not insurer employees but work on a contract basis for several insurance companies. In contrast with these people, a *public adjuster* represents the insured rather than the insurance company. He or she generally charges a percentage of the amount received from the insurance company as a fee for service.

When you notify the insurer that you have had a loss, the function of the adjuster is to determine if the loss is covered by your policy and, if so, the amount of the loss. As we shall see when we discuss some of the details of various insurance policies, determining the amount of a loss and whether or not it is covered can be simple in some cases and complicated in others.

Life Insurance

Benefits payable under life insurance contracts are not adjusted; they are paid. The process is much simpler than in property insurance because there are no partial losses; a claim is paid in full or not at all. When proof of the death of the insured is received by the claims department of the insurer, records are checked to determine that the policy was in force at the time of death and that the person who is requesting payment is the one who is entitled to receive payment. Situations in which complications may develop will be pointed out when we discuss policy provisions in Chapter 10.

Consumer Applications

Finding a Superior Agent
and Settling a Claim

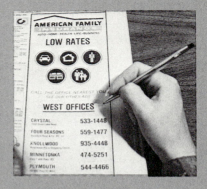

You know what a superior agent can do for you, but how do you locate one? We discussed how losses are settled, but what if you have a problem? These practical questions confront every insurance consumer; so let's discuss them.

How to Find a Superior Agent

Insurance agents are not hard to find. Just look in the Yellow Pages. Or, sit still and one will find you. But how do you identify a superior agent? There is no surefire method to identify a superior agent any more than there is for identifying a superior attorney or superior physician. The questions listed in Figure 7-4 may, however, help you identify those most likely to be superior. Let's discuss them.

stitute for Property and Liability Underwriters to those who meet similar requirements and pass similar examinations in property and liability insurance. Agents who have these designations have demonstrated that they are well-informed career insurance men and women. A life and health agent who is not a CLU, or a property and liability agent who is not a CPCU may be just as well-informed and have just as much ability, but he or she has not demonstrated these characteristics in a way that can be easily identified.

Freedom refers to an agent's ability to shop the market. Some agents represent only one company or group of companies and cannot place business with others. There is nothing wrong with this arrangement, but you

---

1. Is he or she a CLU or CPCU?
2. How much freedom does he or she have?
3. How long has he or she been in the insurance business?
4. Is he or she a full-time agent?
5. Does he or she keep up in the field?
6. Does he or she render service to clients?

FIGURE 7-4

Superior Agent Checklist

The CLU (Chartered Life Underwriter) designation is granted by The American College to those who meet experience, character, and educational requirements. They must also pass a series of rather demanding examinations on life and health insurance. The CPCU (Chartered Property and Casualty Underwriter) designation is granted by The American In-

should be aware of it so you will know what to expect. A captive agent will offer only the insurance provided by his or her companies in the same way a Cadillac dealer typically sells only new Cadillacs and will not suggest that you buy a Lincoln. This is all right if you don't need a Lincoln. The way to find out how much freedom an agent has is to ask him or her.

How long has the agent been in the insurance business? Ask. At least five years is preferable. Education and training prepare an agent to render the service a buyer needs, but there is no substitute for experience. Why do business with a beginner when your family's or firm's financial well-being is at stake? For the same reason, a full-time agent is preferable to a part-time agent. Even full-time agents find it difficult to keep abreast of developments in insurance; it is impossible for a part-time agent to do so. You can find out if an agent is full-time by asking him or her and then verifying the answer by visiting the agency with which he or she is connected.

Does the agent keep up in the insurance field? How can your agent help you if he or she is out of date? Ask your agent what he or she does to keep up. Be specific: What do you read? What insurance seminars have you attended during the last two years? Figure 7-5 shows some good answers.

Does the agent render service? Ask him or her for the names and telephone numbers of several people who buy insurance from the agent. Ask them the questions listed in Figure 7-6.

Handling Your Claim Problem

If you have a problem settling a claim, ask your agent for help. If a superior agent cannot get what you want it is a good idea to recognize that you may be wrong. It is time consuming and an emotional drain for you to fight with the adjuster, who is (usually) well-informed and experienced. It is particularly distressing to do battle and then learn that the adjuster was right. So be sure of the facts. Your conviction that the insurer is wrong should be based on careful consideration of all relevant information. Once that is established, you are ready to proceed. Figure 7-7 suggests questions to ask yourself.

FIGURE 7-5	**READS**	**ATTENDS**

Things the Superior Agent Might Do to Stay Current	CLU Journal
	CPCU Journal
	Best's Review
	Rough Notes
	Wall Street Journal
	Business Insurance
	Risk Management
	National Underwriter
	Weekly Underwriter
		CLU Seminars
		CPCU Seminars
		Risk Management Seminars
		Agents' Association
		    Seminars
		Estate Planning Seminars
		State Bar Association
		    Seminars on Insurance and
		    Legal Issues
		Industry-Sponsored Seminars

FIGURE 7-6	
Agent Service	1. What has the agent done for you lately? 2. What did he or she do when you had a loss? 3. When was the last time you called him or her? 4. When was the last time he or she communicated with you by telephone, mail, or in person? 5. Are you reluctant to ask him or her for service? Why?

---

1. Have I fulfilled all the conditions of the policy?
2. Have I done all the policy requires of me?
3. What does the policy cover?
4. What values are involved?
5. Is the amount of money worth fighting about or is this a matter of principle?
6. What is the problem from the insurer's point of view?

FIGURE 7-7

Questions:

What to Do

Claim negotiations are usually conducted orally, but it is wise to reduce them to writing as soon as possible after each conversation to provide some evidence of what was said. Once you realize that you may have to fight for your rights, it is well to communicate in writing and request that the adjuster do the same. Written statements tend to be conservative; they are created with more care than oral statements. An unreasonable position may not be as obvious when expressed orally as it will when reduced to writing—and this statement applies equally to both sides of any controversy.

You should resist the temptation to be in a hurry about settling. You need the money, it is true, but insurance company management does not like to have resisted claims on the books for an extended period. Disputed claims usually cost more than those settled promptly. Moreover, insurance regulators become concerned about a company that has an excessive number of claims pending.

If a disputed claim involves both personal injury and other losses, you may be able to apply a little leverage by holding back on settlement. For example, suppose physical damage to your automobile is caused by the negligence of an insured driver and the insurer is attempting to chisel you on the repairs and rental of another vehicle while yours is being repaired.

Questions: Did you suffer any injury in the accident? Does your neck hurt? Does your back hurt? Did you go to the doctor? If so, let the adjuster know about it. I am not advocating false claims but I do subscribe to the view that sometimes it is necessary to fight fire with fire.

Sources of Help

It may be worthwhile to write to the state insurance department for help with a claim payment problem.[6] Insurance commissioners do not want to become claims adjusters but they can use moral suasion if they are consumer-oriented and think an insured is being treated unfairly. It is insurance company policy to "get along" with commissioners, especially those who are respected by insurer executives. They may or may not be helpful, but it is worthwhile to make the request.

Another approach is to write to the insurance company president and explain the problem.[7] He or she may or may not be helpful, but many top executives are concerned about their company's image and alert to the consumer's problems. In many cases, they are not familiar with the treatment given their insureds and appreciate hearing from them.

---

6. See Appendix F for addresses of state insurance departments.

7. You can get his or her name and address from your agent or from the state insurance department.

Finally, if all else fails, get a public adjuster or a lawyer. He or she will tell you if you are right or wrong and if it is worthwhile to engage his or her services. In many cases, a company that has ignored your pleading for decent treatment will unbend upon receiving a letter from an attorney or public adjuster. If such is not the case, it may be necessary to take legal action. It is better to negotiate than to fight, but negotiation is most effective when it is based on strength perceived by the insurer. Consult the Claim Negotiation Checklist! (Figure 7-8).

FIGURE 7-8

Claim
Negotiation
Checklist

1. Written record of conversations.
2. Communicate in writing.
3. Take your time.
4. Use leverage.
5. Contact state insurance department.
6. Write the company president.
7. Get a public adjuster or lawyer.

Discussion Questions

1. A friend of yours says, "I know insurance costs more with a small deductible or none at all, but when I have a loss I want the insurance company to take care of *all* of it." How would you respond to this statement?

2. Your friend also says, "I don't bother insuring against losses that probably won't happen. If the insurance company can be guided by probability, why can't I?" How would you respond to this statement?

3. Many people say, "I don't have to be concerned about the financial strength of my insurance company because we have an insolvency fund and, furthermore, a weak company could not get a license in this state." Do you agree? Why or why not?

4. I once said to a life insurance company general agent, "It is usually best to buy life insurance from a person who has been in the business at least five years." This upset him and he said rather vehemently, "How do you think we could recruit an agency force if everybody took your advice?" How would you have answered that question?

5. It is sometimes asserted that you should avoid small insurance companies and always buy from the largest one you can find. Bigger is better! Do you agree with this advice? Why or why not?

6. Some insurers that do business by mail state in prominent type, "No agent will call on you." Is this really an advantage to you or is it their way of making a virtue out of a shortcoming? Please explain.

7. Which do you prefer to do business with, an agent or a broker? Why?

8. Advertising by the Independent Insurance Agents of America extolls the unique features of the American Agency System and the Independent Agent whose logo is the "Big I." Does this advertising influence your choice of an agent? Do you prefer one type of agent to others? If so, why?

9. Under what circumstances would you advise an insured who has suffered a loss to hire a public adjuster?

10. Why do insurance companies engage in loss prevention activities? After all, they merely pay for losses and the fewer losses there are, the lower premiums will be.

Cases

7-1 Your acquaintance, Nancy Barns, recently commented to you that she and Dick, her husband, wanted to reevaluate their homeowners insurance. Nancy said that it seemed the only time they ever had any contact with their present insurance agency was when a premium was due. Nancy asked if you knew of a good agency. She also asked what the term CPCU meant.

  1. Help Nancy to set up standards to evaluate and choose a "good" agency.

  2. Review with her the standards of education and experience required of an agent with the CPCU designation.

7-2 Fred A. Juster recently wrote you indicating that his company would consider settling your insurance claim for approximately one-half of what you believe you should receive. This was Mr. Juster's final offer, according to his letter to you. Bill, your neighbor, suggested you should discuss this matter with the insurance commissioner. Jack, your other neighbor, said as far as he knows, the state insurance commissioner's office didn't settle claim settlement disputes.

  1. In a case of this type what position does your state's office of insurance take?

  2. In what way can the state department of insurance affect disputes between an individual and the insurance company?

  3. What other alternatives could you pursue to seek a fair claim settlement?

7-3 Ms. Judy Maxwell, a 22-year-old single woman beginning her career in real estate sales, recently asked you to help with a perplexing decision. Judy said she must soon make a decision to purchase some health coverage for herself. Her budget will not allow her to buy both "first dollar" coverage and major medical. She likes the idea of health insurance that pays part of the bills common to everyday types of ailments. What she doesn't like is that this coverage is rather expensive and pays up to a rather low maximum amount, then pays no more. Judy realizes that major medical appears to be just the opposite. For the type of major medical Judy would choose, she would have to pay the first $1,000 and then the policy would pay 80% of the bills up to $100,000. She does have some savings in an ordinary life policy. She admits she finds this decision hard to make. It is confusing.

1. Make a recommendation for Judy.

2. What rule of thumb applies in a case such as this?

7-4 You are reading the Sunday newspaper when you notice a health insurance advertisement. Upon reading the ad, you note that you can get the first month's coverage for one dollar, and that the insurance seems to be a real bargain.

1. Are there any problems which you should be aware of when buying insurance through the mail? List them, and explain how you could cope with them if you did purchase coverage in this manner.

Chapter Eight:
LIFE INSURANCE

INTRODUCTION

Life insurance provides protection for two major contingencies. First, an income earner may die prior to the end of his or her income-earning years. This stops income and creates the expenses of death, such as estate taxes and legal fees. Second, he or she may live beyond those years but have no income.

How can an individual or a family cope with these risks? Neither can be avoided. Good health maintenance programs can reduce the probability of death. A savings and investment program may help provide income during retirement. Skillful estate planning may help reduce death taxes as well as the cost of probate.[1]

The probability of death cannot be reduced to zero, however, and many people have so little knowledge and skill in the field of finance that success in creating a retirement program on a do-it-yourself basis is the exception rather than the rule. The risk is too significant to be simply ignored and self-insurance is not feasible because the number of exposure units is too small. While the family may retain part of these life risks, a major portion must be transferred or the family may suffer catastrophic losses. Life insurance can be used to protect against loss of income caused by death as well as the additional expenses which result. It may also help preserve the estate by providing funds with which to pay debts and taxes. Further, life insurance can serve as a vehicle for providing income during retirement.

---

1. Estate planning is discussed in Chapter 13. The term "death taxes" refers to both state inheritance taxes and federal estate taxes.

In this chapter, we discuss the following:

1. How life insurance works.
2. Basic types of life insurance contracts.

HOW LIFE INSURANCE WORKS

Pooling Concept in Life Insurance

Life insurance is based on the concepts of pooling the risks of many into a group, accumulating a fund by contributions from the members of the group, and paying from this fund the losses of the few who suffer loss. The simplest illustration is provided by one-year term life insurance. If an insurer promises to pay $1,000 at the death of the insured during the year, it must collect enough money from the group to pay the claims. If past experience indicates that one percent of the group will die during the year in question, ten deaths may be expected for every 1,000 persons in the group. If a group of 1,000,000 is insured, a total of $10,000,000, or $10 from each person, must be collected in order to pay expected death claims. If actual experience is the same as past experience, $10,000,000 will be collected and 10,000 claims of $1,000 each will be paid.

Predictions based on past experience.   The prediction for the coming year is based on past observations. If it is to be accurate, the group insured must be similar to that which was observed. Moreover, it is necessary to insure a large number of people so that actual experience will approximate the underlying probabilities. The smaller the number insured, the greater may be the deviations from the average. Pooling will work satisfactorily only if large numbers are involved.

Insurer performs two functions.   The insurance company has two primary functions to perform in this insurance scheme. The first is *management.* That is, the members of the group must be selected, premiums calculated and collected, and claims paid. The second function of the company is to *guarantee payment* of claims, whether calculations and predictions have been accurate or not. The company must accumulate funds to meet unexpected deviations from the average. When you pay a premium and join the group, you must be certain that the insurer will keep its promise to pay if you die. If you cannot be *sure,* it is not insurance.

Probability of Death

Characteristics.   In the example of pooling above, it was assumed that ten people out of each 1,000 in the group insured would die during the year. This figure is known as the "death rate" and may be expressed in terms of the number of deaths per 1,000, or as a fraction in which the numerator is the number of deaths and the denominator is the number in the group, or it may be expressed as a decimal or a percentage. Thus, the death rate, which is also referred to as the "mortality rate," may be expressed as 10 per 1,000, or 1/100, or 0.01, or one percent. The death or mortality rate is a measure of the probability of occurrence of death during a given year.

The probability of death has two important characteristics which influence greatly insurer practices and the nature of the contracts they issue. The first of these characteristics is that the probability of death rises with age. The second is that the probability eventually becomes a certainty. An understanding and appreciation of these characteristics will provide the basis for much of our later discussion. They can be illustrated with the mortality curve.

Mortality curve. If we plot the probability of death by age as in Figure 8-1, we have a mortality curve which illustrates the relationship between age and the probability of death. This curve shows that the death rate is relatively high at age zero but declines until age 10. Thereafter, it rises continuously. The rise is rather slow until middle age, at which point it begins to accelerate. In the more advanced years, it rises very rapidly. Although a few people live to age 100, for life insurance purposes it is assumed that by age 99 the death rate equals 1. That is, death during that year is considered to be a certainty.

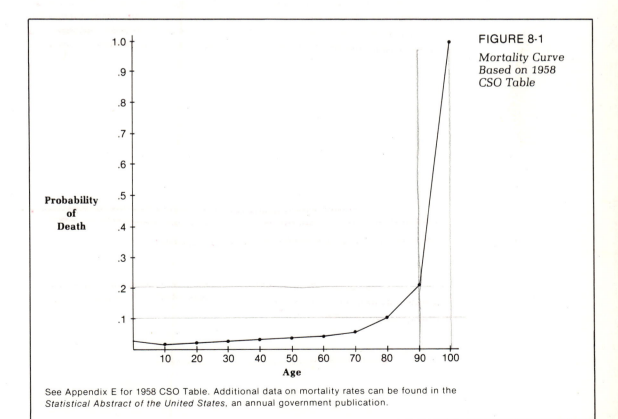

FIGURE 8-1

Mortality Curve Based on 1958 CSO Table

See Appendix E for 1958 CSO Table. Additional data on mortality rates can be found in the *Statistical Abstract of the United States*, an annual government publication.

The mortality curve shows why life insurance for a term of one year costs so little for young people. The probability that payment will be made is very low.

The mortality curve also indicates why the cost of life insurance for one year becomes prohibitive beyond the middle years and at advanced ages. The theory of insurance is that the losses of the few can be paid for by relatively small contributions from the many. If, however, most or all of those in the group suffer losses, the burden becomes too great and the system breaks down.

Level Premium Plan

Nature.   The mortality curve shows that provision of life insurance on a year-to-year basis is feasible only for the relatively young and for limited periods of time. The cost for older insureds becomes prohibitive and leads to a situation in which the insurer is left with a group of insureds whose mortality is even higher than that anticipated. For life insurance protection over a long period or for the entire life span, some system of spreading the cost not only among members of the group but throughout the period is necessary. This is the function of level premium plan life insurance.

A level premium is one which remains constant throughout the premium-paying period instead of rising from year to year. The premium is higher than necessary to pay claims on a year-to-year basis during the early years of the contract but insufficient during the later years.

As Figure 8-2 shows, the level premium for an ordinary life policy (which provides lifetime protection, issued at age 25) is greater during the early years than a one-year renewable term policy for the same period. The difference during the early years makes possible the accumulation of funds which, together with the interest they earn and premiums currently collected, are available for the payment of claims as they occur. It is this accumulation of funds which makes possible a premium which remains level even though the probability of death rises as the insured grows older.

Effect.   The level premium plan does two things. First, it makes possible the insuring of lives for the whole of life at a premium cost which remains constant rather than rising as age advances. Thus, a person who purchases life insurance prior to old age is able to have protection all his or her life at a premium which will not become prohibitive.

The second result of the level premium plan is the creation of life insurance policies which are made up of two elements: (1) reserve or investment, and (2) protection.

While the periodic premium payments exceed death benefits for an insured group during the early years of the policy, they fall short during later years. A reserve is accumulated to offset this deficiency. When an insured dies, the insurer is obligated to pay the beneficiary the face amount of the policy. Part of this payment is an amount equal to the reserve or investment element. The difference between the reserve at any point in time and the face amount of the policy is known as the *pro-*

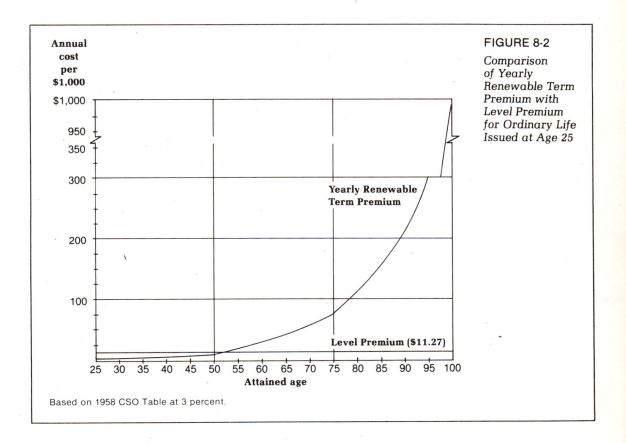

FIGURE 8-2

*Comparison
of Yearly
Renewable Term
Premium with
Level Premium
for Ordinary Life
Issued at Age 25*

Based on 1958 CSO Table at 3 percent.

tection element. As Figure 8-3 illustrates, the protection element declines as each year passes because the reserve increases. All level premium policies have this combination of reserve and protection. The policyowner's right to the investment element is called the *cash value.* It may be obtained by surrendering the policy to the insurance company.

TYPES OF LIFE INSURANCE CONTRACTS

Insurance companies issue four basic contracts that offer protection for the risks of death and old age. They are:

1. Term

2. Whole life

3. Endowment

4. Annuities.

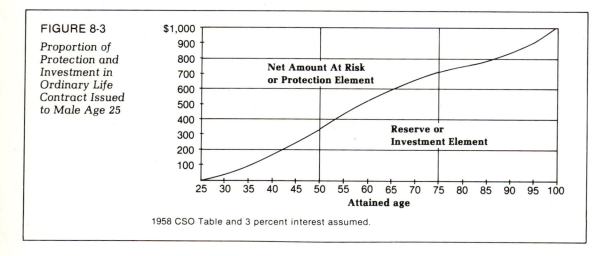

FIGURE 8-3

*Proportion of
Protection and
Investment in
Ordinary Life
Contract Issued
to Male Age 25*

1958 CSO Table and 3 percent interest assumed.

In addition to these basic policies, a number of combination contracts are available.

The function of the first three types is to create a principal sum or an estate. They provide a sum of money upon the occurrence of a specified event. In the case of term or whole life, that event is death. Endowment insurance provides for payment of proceeds upon death prior to a specified age or upon attainment of such age. The purpose of death proceeds is to replace part or all of the potential estate which would otherwise be lost, while the endowment is primarily a savings plan coupled with death protection.

The function of an annuity, on the other hand, is to liquidate a principal sum. The sum to be liquidated may be the proceeds available from a life insurance policy or it may be from some other source, such as savings or investments. Annuities will be discussed in detail in the next chapter.

Term Insurance

Nature of term insurance. Term life insurance is protection for a specified period. When a company issues a one-year term life policy on your life, it promises that it will pay the face amount of the policy *if* you die during the one-year term.

In this respect, a term life insurance contract is similar to fire insurance. In a fire insurance contract, the insurer promises that it will pay if the insured property is damaged or destroyed by fire during the term of the policy. If nothing happens to the property during that time, there is no payment. If a loss occurs after the contract has expired, the insurer has no obligation. With both fire insurance and term life insurance, the event insured against must occur during the term of the policy; otherwise, the insurer makes no payment.

Short term life policies involve virtually no investment element. Long term contracts with a level premium accumulate some investment in the early years but it is depleted at the end of the term because the cost of mortality greatly exceeds the level premium in the later years of the contract. The length of the term varies from one year to policies which are effective to age 65 or 70. The usual terms, however, are five, ten, fifteen, and twenty years.

Renewability.   If you buy a one-year or five-year term policy you may want to continue protection for another term. Unless the policy contains an option giving you the right to do so, you must make application to the insurer and provide evidence of insurability. If your health has deteriorated or you are for any other reason considered to be a poor risk, you may be unable to obtain insurance.

This risk may be handled by purchasing term insurance that provides a renewability option. This option gives you the right to renew the policy for a specified number of additional periods of protection, at a predetermined schedule of premium rates, without evidence of insurability. Renewability protects your insurability for the period specified. After that period has elapsed, you must again make application and prove insurability in order to obtain new insurance. Each time the policy is renewed, the premium rises because you are older, and older-age groups experience higher mortality. Because this leads to adverse selection, the renewable feature increases the cost of protection.

Convertibility.   You can buy a term policy with a convertibility option. This option provides the right to convert the term policy to whole life or endowment insurance without proving insurability. If you buy a one-year convertible term policy renewable to age 65 you may renew each year for several years and then decide you prefer insurance on which the premium, though higher than that of the term policy at the age of conversion, will remain the same year after year and can be kept in force indefinitely. The right to convert makes it possible to obtain such insurance regardless of the condition of your health. Because many people become uninsurable at some point in their lives—some at surprisingly low ages—this is an important right. Most term contracts are both renewable and convertible. Some companies issue term policies which are automatically converted to another plan of insurance at a specified date.

Whole Life Insurance

Nature of whole life insurance.   Whole life insurance provides for payment upon your death regardless of when it may occur. As long as the premiums are paid, the policy stays in force. This is why whole life insurance is referred to as *permanent insurance.*

There are two principal types of whole life insurance: (1) ordinary or straight life, and (2) limited-payment life. The difference between these two types is in the arrangements for premium payment. (See Appendix A for a sample policy.)

Ordinary or straight life.   The premium rate for an ordinary life policy is based on the assumption that premiums will be paid throughout your life. In effect, you are buying the policy on an installment basis and the installments are spread over the balance of your lifetime. This provides permanent protection on a level premium basis for the lowest possible outlay.

As shown in Figure 8-3, the level premium results in the policy consisting of a protection element and an investment element which is called the cash value. The options available with regard to this value are discussed in Chapter 10. It may be noted here, however, that you do not *promise* to pay premiums all of your life but have several alternatives available because of the cash value. One of these is to convert the policy to one which is paid-up and requires no further premium payments.

Limited-payment.   Limited-payment life offers protection for your whole life but involves payment of the premium for a specified period of years or to a specified age. After premiums have been paid during the specified period, the policy remains in force for the balance of your life without further premium payment. The policy is called *paid-up.* A 10-pay life policy becomes paid-up after premiums have been paid for ten years, a 20-pay life policy becomes paid-up after premiums have been paid for 20 years, life paid-up at 65 becomes paid-up at that age, and so on. If you die before the end of the premium-paying period, the policy is paid-up.

As illustrated in Table 8-1, for a given amount of insurance issued at a given age, annual premium payments are larger for limited-payment life insurance than for ordinary life. For example, one company charges $13.31 annually for a $1,000 ordinary life policy issued at age 25 and $21.65 annually for a twenty-pay life policy for the same amount issued at the same age. As the premium payment period is shortened, the premium rises. The savings element in limited-payment policies is greater than in ordinary life. At the end of five years, the ordinary life policy quoted above has a cash value of $30.00, while the twenty-pay life policy has a cash value of $67.00. At any given age of issue, the higher the premium for the basic policy is, the larger the investment element (cash value) will be.[2]

Whole life insurance may be bought for a single premium—the ultimate in limited payment. Single premiums are large because no further payment is required. The policy is paid-up. The investment element is maximized and cash values are high compared with policies bought on the installment plan.

---

2. Premium rates and other information concerning several hundred life insurance companies may be found in *Best's Flitcraft Compend,* published annually by A.M. Best Company, Oldwick, New Jersey 08858; or *Life Rates and Data,* published annually by The National Underwriter Company, 420 East Fourth Street, Cincinnati, Ohio.

	5-YEAR TERM	ORDINARY LIFE	20-PAY LIFE	20-YEAR ENDOWMENT	ENDOWMENT AT AGE 65
Annual premium	$4.77	$ 13.31	$ 21.65	$ 43.15	$ 18.15
Fifth year cash value	0.00	30.00	67.00	164.00	59.00
Tenth year cash value	0.00	98.00	180.00	401.00	157.00
Fifteenth year cash value	0.00	177.00	310.00	677.00	273.00
Twentieth year cash value	0.00	255.00	459.00	1,000.00	408.00
Cash value age 60	0.00	504.00	632.00	_____	817.00
Cash value age 65	0.00	584.00	690.00	_____	1,000.00

TABLE 8-1

Annual Premium Per $1,000 and Cash Values for Term, Ordinary Life, 20-Pay Life, 20-Year Endowment, and Endowment at Age 65 Issued at Age 25*

*Current life insurance premium rates may be found in *Best's Flitcraft Compend,* A.M. Best Company, Oldwick, NJ 08858 and in *Life Rates and Data,* The National Underwriter Company, 420 East Fourth Street, Cincinnati, OH 45202.

Dual function. Whole life policies perform a dual function. They provide protection against the loss of income caused by premature death. On the other hand, if you survive to retirement age and death protection is no longer needed, the cash value can provide monthly income payments. You have lifetime protection against income losses with this combination of protection and investment.

Most policies have cash values after they have been in force for one year (sometimes two). They may be used at any time you want, by either surrendering the policy or making a policy loan.[3]

Endowment Insurance

Nature of endowment insurance. Endowment insurance provides for payment of the face amount of the policy in the event of your death dur-

---

3. If the policy is surrendered, both protection and premium payments cease. If a policy loan is made, premium payments continue, interest is paid on the loan, and protection continues, but the unpaid balance of the loan is deducted from the proceeds at the death of the insured.

ing a specified period or for payment of the full face amount at the end of such period *if* you are still living. Thus, the insurer makes two promises: (1) to pay for death during the endowment period, and (2) to pay for survival to a specified date.

There are two ways of looking at endowment insurance; one is mathematical and the other is economic.

The mathematical view is that the policy consists of two parts: term insurance and pure endowment. The term insurance part provides for payment of the face amount of the policy only if you die during the term. The pure endowment portion pays only in the event that you are living at the end of the period specified.

The economic concept views endowment insurance as a combination of increasing investment and decreasing term insurance. At the inception of the contract, the term insurance part equals the face amount of the policy. As each year passes, however, the investment element grows and the term protection is decreased. For a $1,000 endowment insurance policy, the term life insurance begins at $1,000 and declines to zero while the investment element begins at zero and increases to $1,000 at the end of the endowment period. If you die before the endowment date, the beneficiary receives the investment and the term insurance which together equal the face amount of the policy. Actually, this is essentially the case with any policy which has an investment element. A whole life policy may be considered an endowment at age 100. The investment in the policy equals the face amount at that age because premiums are calculated on the assumption that no insured will survive to age 100. Customarily, one who does is offered the face amount of the policy because at that juncture the face amount and the cash value of the policy are the same.

Because endowment insurance provides for payment of the face amount of the policy in the event of either death or survival, payment is a certainty. The shorter the endowment period is, the higher the premium must be in order to accumulate the required funds. In a sense, endowment insurance is a scheduled savings program, the completion of which is guaranteed whether you live or die.

As Table 8-1 shows, premiums are high compared with term, ordinary life and limited-payment life, especially for short-term endowments at younger ages.

Length of term. Some endowment policies mature at a specified age, such as 55, 60, or 65. Others are written for a specified period of years, such as ten, fifteen, or twenty. As a rule, premiums are payable throughout the term of the contract. When the term is very long, however, limited-payment plans are sometimes used. For example, an endowment at age 65 issued to a relatively young person could be written on a 20-year basis. After payments had been made for 20 years, the policy would be paid up but the face amount would not be payable until death or the attainment of age 65, whichever occurred first.

Term is cheaper in the short run and you can buy a larger amount per dollar of premium. On the other hand, whole life is preferable to term if it is kept in force for a long period of time because the premium is level. The term life premium is lower than the whole life premium initially, but eventually becomes larger (see Figure 8-2 on page 135) and ultimately rises to prohibitive levels.

Which is better, ordinary life or limited-payment? If you want the same amount of life insurance both before and after retirement, ordinary life requires premium payments for life. Limited-payment, such as life paid-up at 65, does not have this drawback. You can convert ordinary life to a paid-up form at any time, but the death benefit will be reduced. For a given annual outlay, such as $300 per year, you can buy more ordinary life than life paid-up at 65, but you will have a smaller amount of insurance in force if you stop premium payments upon retirement. Note in Table 8-3 that a male age 25 could have 15 percent more insurance until age 65 by purchasing ordinary life instead of life paid-up at 65. If he wanted to stop paying premiums then, he would have about 6 percent less paid-up insurance than with paid-up at 65. Which would you prefer for the same premium outlay, $3,077 more insurance to age 65 and $1,146 less thereafter, or the same amount of insurance all your life? Note that one other difference between the policies is that the life paid-up at 65 policy has almost $900 more cash value than the ordinary life policy at age 65.

POLICY TYPE	PREMIUM RATE PER $1,000	FACE AMOUNT OF INSURANCE	CASH VALUE AT 65	PAID-UP INSURANCE AT 65
Level Term to Age 65	$ 8.20	$36,585	$ 0	$ 0
Ordinary Whole Life	13.00	23,077	14,031	18,854
Life Paid-up at 65	15.00	20,000	14,900	20,000
Endowment at Age 65	18.50	16,216	16,216	0*

*When the cash value of a policy equals its face amount, there is no insurance.

TABLE 8-3

Amount of Insurance, Cash Value, and Paid-up Insurance at Age 65 for $300 Annual Premium, Male Age 25

Uses of Endowment Insurance

There are two popular uses for endowment insurance:

1. Accumulation of education funds.
2. Accumulation of retirement funds.

Endowment insurance is sometimes called "an insured savings plan" because you will get the money if you survive to the maturity date of the endowment, and your beneficiary will get it if you die prior to that date. The ex-tent to which the emphasis on savings affects the death benefit and the savings element can be seen in Table 8-4. Note that term to 65 provides 126 percent more death benefit but no savings. Life paid-up at 65 provides 23 percent more death benefit but only 8 percent less savings, while ordinary life provides 42 percent more death benefit and 13 percent less savings. If your family has *any* need for protection, it seems clear that there are better choices than endowment insurance.

TYPE	PROTECTION	CASH VALUE AT 65	TABLE 8-4
			Other Types of Life Insurance Compared with Endowment Insurance
Term to 65	$20,369 more	$16,216 less	
Ordinary Life	6,861 more	2,185 less	
Life Paid-up @ 65	3,784 more	1,316 less	

Based on Table 8-3.

Discussion Questions

1. Some people will not buy a straight life policy because they don't want to pay premiums all their lives. Is this a valid objection? Please explain.

2. Do you think it is wise to buy life insurance on a limited-payment basis during a period of inflation? Why or why not?

3. If you buy a whole life policy to provide protection against loss of income caused by your premature death, does it make sense to use the cash value by making a policy loan? Why or why not?

4. Is buying an endowment policy a good way to accumulate savings? Why or why not?

5. Most individually purchased life insurance is whole life whereas most bought on a group basis is term. How do you account for this?

6. When you die, the face amount of your life insurance policy is paid to your beneficiary. If the policy has accumulated a cash value, what becomes of it?

7. Figure 8-3 shows that the reserve or investment element of an ordinary life policy issued at age 25 is equal to the face amount of the policy at age 100. What is the difference between this and an endowment at age 100?

8. Why is the cash value of a 20-payment life policy larger than that of an ordinary life policy at the end of 20 years? Does this mean it is a better policy?

9. An assessment society provided death benefits by requiring a contribution from all members whenever one died. What problems would you expect with such an arrangement?

10. Why would you expect one-year term insurance which is renewable and convertible to require a higher premium than one-year term insurance without these features?

Cases

8-1 George and Mary Keys are very excited over the news that they are to be parents. Since their graduation from college three years ago, they have purchased a new house and a new car. George is rapidly moving up within the company in his job as special projects engineer. In anticipation of the new arrival(s) George is considering the purchase of some more life insurance. He feels that he needs at least $100,000 in coverage, but his budget for life insurance is somewhat limited.

   1. As George's agent, advise him as to the type(s) of life insurance that seems most appropriate for his situation.

   2. George indicates to you that his financial situation will change in five years when he receives a large payment from his uncle's estate. In what way would this situation affect the type of life insurance you recommend to George?

8-2 Your wealthy aunt Mable recently talked to you, her life insurance agent, regarding her desire to see that her great niece has the funds to attend college. Aunt Mable is in very good health and expects to live for many years to come. She does not know if she should put aside money in a savings account at the bank, buy more insurance on herself, or choose some other plan of action. She simply knows that her great niece will need at least $40,000 to finish college.

   1. What type of investment and/or insurance program would you recommend for her? Why?

8-3 Phil Pratt has decided that the lowest-premium form of life insurance is definitely the best buy. Consequently, he has purchased a $250,000, yearly renewable term life insurance policy. Explain why you might agree or disagree with Phil's philosophy. Will his decision have any possible adverse effects in later years? Are there any realistic alternatives available to him without making premiums too high at a young age?

8-4 Betty Bick is considering the purchase of a whole life insurance policy which would be paid-up at her age 60. She plans to work until then and does not wish to pay any premiums after she retires; but she definitely wants whole life insurance protection.

1. Explain to her any alternatives which she has which would meet the criteria she has established.

2. Why do you think that her choice is a good (or bad) one?

Chapter Nine:
ANNUITIES AND SPECIAL LIFE INSURANCE CONTRACTS

INTRODUCTION

This chapter is concerned with annuities and special types of life insurance contracts designed to provide income protection. Some special contracts are created by combining term and whole life insurance into one policy. Others cover more than one life in the same policy, modify the level premium plan, or provide variable rather than fixed-dollar benefits.

In this chapter we discuss the following topics:

1. Annuities.

2. Special life contracts.

3. Sources of life insurance and annuities.

ANNUITIES

An annuity is a periodic payment that commences at a stated or contingent date and continues throughout a fixed period and/or for the duration of a life or lives. If the duration depends upon a life or lives, the contract is known as a life annuity. The person who receives payments is known as the annuitant. An annuity in which benefit payments cease, and the premium is considered fully earned upon the death of the annuitant, is known as a pure, or straight life, annuity.

The names of the various annuities reflect their duration. A temporary annuity, for example, makes payments for a specified period, such as 20 years. A single life (also called whole life or straight life) annuity makes payments until a designated person dies. With a joint annu-

ity, two or more people are named and payments stop when one of them dies. In contrast, a joint-and-survivor annuity continues payments as long as any of the persons lives. A temporary life annuity is a combination of a temporary annuity and a single life annuity. Payments stop at the end of a specified period or the death of a designated individual, whichever comes first.

Annuities may be classified as either immediate or deferred. An immediate annuity begins payments now while deferred annuities begin payments sometime in the future. Immediate annuities require a single premium, whereas deferred annuities may be bought on the installment plan. The time during which premiums are being paid is called the accumulation period. Figure 9-1 summarizes the ways life annuities may be classified.

FIGURE 9-1

*Classification of
Life Annuities*

1. **Number of Lives**
   A. Single life
   B. Multiple life
      1. Joint
      2. Joint-and-survivor

2. **Method of Premium Payment**
   A. Single premium
   B. Installment premiums

3. **Time Payments Commence**
   A. Immediate
   B. Deferred

4. **Nature of Insurer's Obligation**
   A. Pure—no refund
   B. Refund
      1. Period certain
      2. Premium refund

5. **Units in Which Benefits Expressed**
   A. Fixed dollar
   B. Variable dollar

GuARANteed

Refund Annuities

A refund annuity is one which has some arrangement guaranteeing that the purchaser, or his or her beneficiary, will receive all or part of the purchase price. Because a pure annuity promises benefit payments only during the lifetime of the annuitant, it provides the maximum income per dollar of premium. Many people, however, do not like the idea that they might die shortly after beginning to receive benefit payments from an annuity in which they have made a large investment and thereby lose the bulk of such investment. Insurers have, therefore, made available refund annuities. There are two general forms of refund provisions: (1) payments certain, and (2) premium refund.

Payments certain. This form of refund provision guarantees a certain number of annuity payments whether the annuitant lives or dies. Thus, you can purchase a life annuity with five years certain, ten years certain, or some other period certain. Whether you live or die, payments continue for at least the period specified. If you die prior to the end of the period certain, the payments are made to your beneficiary for the balance of the period. If you outlive the period certain, payments cease at your death.

Premium refund. This form of refund provision promises to refund all or a portion of the purchase price of the annuity if you die before receiving the amount guaranteed.

A cash refund annuity provides for a lump-sum payment to the beneficiary if you die before the whole amount has been paid out. An installment refund annuity, on the other hand, simply continues payments to the beneficiary until the total amount has been paid out. Both arrangements assure full recovery of the purchase price either for you or your beneficiary.

There are variations of this arrangement to suit the demands of the purchaser. Some annuitants want a full refund guarantee while others are satisfied with a 50 percent refund. The effect of such guarantees is to reduce the monthly installments that can be purchased with any given sum of money. The cash refund annuity provides the smallest monthly payment and the straight life annuity provides the largest monthly payment for any given premium. Which is better depends upon your viewpoint. As an annuitant, you might enjoy the larger payments of a straight life annuity. Your beneficiary, however, might enjoy the prospect of getting a refund and, therefore, prefer the refund type.

Deferred Annuities

Most people who buy a deferred annuity pay for it on the installment plan. If they buy a pure deferred annuity there is no refund if they die before the insurer starts making payments to them. Most deferred annuities sold to individuals, however, promise to return all premiums, with or without interest, in the event the purchaser dies prior to the time he or she begins to receive payments.

When you buy a deferred annuity on the installment plan you are engaging in a savings program. There is no protection element involved, any more than would be the case if you made monthly deposits in your savings account at the bank. The advantage of the annuity program, however, is that premium notices motivate people to save. In addition, the interest earned during the accumulation period is tax-sheltered. Moreover, you are guaranteed a specified amount of income upon your retirement some years hence. This could be much more favorable than the lump-sum purchase of an immediate annuity at retirement if interest and/or mortality rates have declined in the interim because such a change would increase the cost of the annuity.

Retirement annuity.   The retirement annuity is the most popular form of deferred annuity. You make periodic installment payments during your working years to assure an income upon retirement. If you die prior to entering on the annuity, the premiums or the cash value, whichever is larger, are returned to your beneficiary. If you want, you can have the income commence at an earlier or later date than that originally specified. Upon retirement, you have several options: (1) cash instead of the annuity, or (2) a pure annuity, with five, ten, fifteen, or twenty years certain, or (3) an installment or cash refund annuity.

Retirement income contract.   The retirement income contract is similar to the retirement annuity except that it provides a death benefit of $1,000 for each $10 unit of monthly life income, or the cash value, whichever is larger. As Figure 9-2 shows, this benefit is a combination of the investment element in the contract and decreasing term insurance. As the investment portion increases, the term portion decreases. Although there is a protection element in the retirement income contract, the major purpose is to provide income payments during retirement.

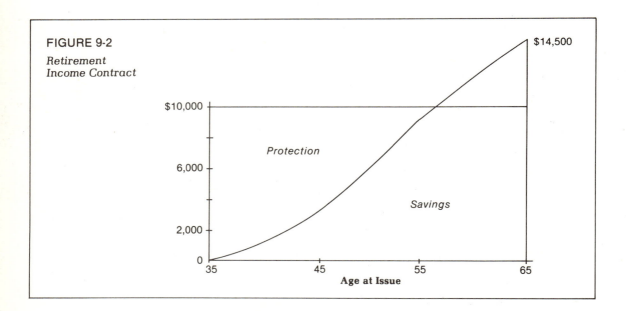

FIGURE 9-2

Retirement
Income Contract

Variable Annuities

All of the life insurance and annuity policies which have been discussed thus far have one important element in common—they promise benefits which are payable in fixed dollars. In recent years, serious criticism has been directed at this feature. The purchasing power of the dollar has declined by 50 percent in 10 years. As a storehouse of value and purchasing power, the dollar is unsatisfactory. As a result, people are dissatisfied with old style, fixed-dollar annuities.

Stabilize purchasing power. The variable annuity was introduced to meet this criticism. When people think of future income needs, they think of them in terms of dollars. What they really need, however, is not a certain number of dollars but the purchasing power that those dollars have now. And they need it at some future date. The objective of a variable annuity is to provide this. The contract is expressed in terms of units rather than dollars. Two types of units are employed: accumulation units and annuity units. Instead of investing in fixed-dollar assets such as bonds, the annuity company invests in variable dollar assets such as common stocks.

How it works. When you pay the monthly premium in dollars you are credited with a number of accumulation units, the amount to be determined by the current value of one unit of investment. For example, if the monthly premium is $50.00 and the current value of a unit is $10.00, you are credited with five units. If the current value of a unit is $9.52 when you pay your next $50.00 premium, you are credited with 5 1/4 units. If the value of a unit is $10.42 when you pay the premium, you are credited with 4 4/5 units. As you pay the premium month after month and year after year, you accumulate units of investment rather than dollars, as would be the case with a conventional annuity.

When you reach retirement age, annuity units are substituted for accumulation units. The number of annuity units payable under the contract is calculated in the same way as would the number of dollars in an ordinary annuity contract. For example, $12,000 accumulated under a conventional annuity will pay a man aged 65 a life annuity of $100 per month. If instead of $12,000 you have accumulated 12,000 units of investment, you can receive a life annuity of 100 units per month.

When you reach retirement age, two factors determine your dollar income: (1) the number of units to which you are entitled, and (2) the dollar value of each unit. If the price of the stocks purchased by the annuity company rises, the income you receive will rise. If stock values decline, your income will decline. If you want, you can elect to buy a fixed-dollar annuity with your accumulation units when you retire. In such a case, the number of dollars you receive per month will remain constant for life and will be determined by the total value of your accumulation units at the time of your retirement.

Theory of variable annuity. The theory of the variable annuity is that the prices of the stock purchased by the annuity company will rise as fast as, and concurrently with, increases in the level of prices for consumer goods. It is assumed that the forces in the economy causing the one will also cause the other. Furthermore, it is said that such investments will share in the growth of the economy, so that the annuitant will benefit not only by storing purchasing power but by accumulating it more rapidly than is possible with traditional methods of saving.

A word of caution. It is clear that fixed-dollar annuities are unsatisfactory during periods when the dollar is depreciating in value, but there is some doubt about the variable annuity as a solution. One basic assumption is that stock prices and other prices march along together. A glance at Figure 9-3 will show how far off this can be over a decade or more. It shows the value of one College Retirement Equities Fund accumulation unit from 1967 through 1979. While the value of the unit occasionally went in the same direction as the CPI, it was worth less at the end of 1979 than it was in 1967.[1] The CPI, on the other hand, more than doubled during the same period. Success in accumulating purchasing power is far from automatic, whether one invests in stock or dollars.

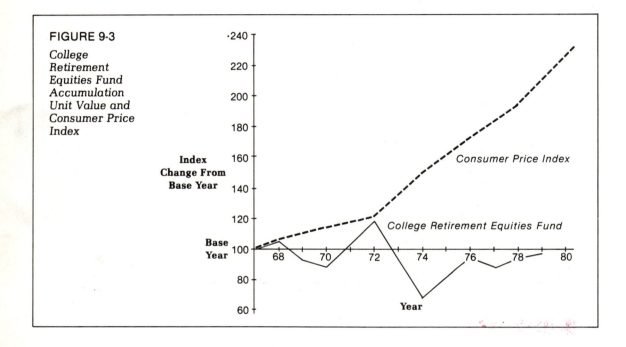

FIGURE 9-3

*College
Retirement
Equities Fund
Accumulation
Unit Value and
Consumer Price
Index*

SPECIAL LIFE CONTRACTS

Variable Life Policies

Fixed-dollar life insurance policies suffer from the same defect as fixed-dollar annuities. What may have been an adequate amount of insurance ten years ago is no longer adequate because the purchasing power of the dollar has declined. One approach to this problem is simply to buy more life insurance—and a great deal of it has been sold on that basis as incomes and the ability to pay premiums have risen. A major defect with this approach is that the person who needs to increase the amount of his or her life insurance may be uninsurable or insurable only at very

---

1. Dividend income added to the accumulation unit was more than the 1967 value of the unit, but the compound rate of accumulation was only about 6 percent annually.

high premium rates. This risk can be shifted to the insurer by buying a policy with a Guaranteed Insurability Option (GIO) which is discussed in more detail in the next chapter. It provides that specified amounts of additional insurance (usually $10,000 or the face of the policy, whichever is smaller) may be purchased at stated intervals (usually three years) without evidence of insurability. Typically, the last opportunity to increase the amount of insurance is at age 40. This option can help solve the problem to that age but, unfortunately, the ravages of inflation may continue long after the insured reaches age 40.

If life insurance is to perform the income replacement function meaningfully, death benefits must be stable in terms of purchasing power. The policy must provide a death benefit which is the same in terms of goods and services whether death occurs the day after the policy is issued or several decades later.

Two approaches are being followed in the development of such a policy. One relates the benefits of the policy to a consumer price index and the other relates them to the stock market. Their problems and the doubts about them are similar to those just discussed concerning variable annuities.

Combination Contracts

In an attempt to serve the public as well as differentiate their product from that of competitors, life insurance companies have developed a bewildering array of contracts created by combining two or more basic types of life insurance into one policy. It is not feasible to list, much less discuss, all the packages which have been placed on the market, but several have been selected to provide a sample. The following policies are discussed: (1) family income, (2) family maintenance, (3) family plan, (4) modified life, and (5) multiple protection.

Family income. The family income policy provides that in the event of your death within a specified period, usually 10, 15, or 20 years from the inception of the policy, monthly payments equal to one percent of the face amount of the policy will be paid to the beneficiary for the balance of the specified period and the face amount of the policy paid to the beneficiary when income payments cease. If you die after the expiration of the specified period, only the face amount of the policy is payable. As shown in Figure 9-4, this contract is a combination of whole life insurance and decreasing term insurance. The whole life is the basic part of the contract and the decreasing term is added on to contribute to the income payments during the specified period. The income payments are made up of interest earned on the proceeds of the basic policy and an annuity liquidation of the proceeds of the decreasing term policy. Typically, the premium for this combination policy is level during the period the term insurance is in force and decreases to the level premium for the basic policy when the term portion expires. The result is maximum protection at a relatively low cost when it is needed; namely, prior to the time when the children have matured and are able to support themselves.

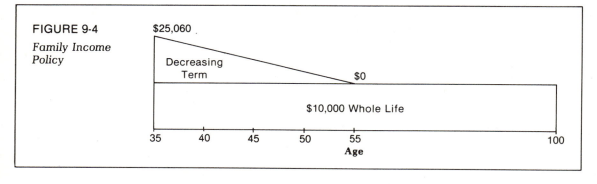

FIGURE 9-4

Family Income
Policy

Family maintenance. . This contract differs from the family income policy in only one respect. That is, the period during which income payments are to be paid commences with your death if it occurs during a specified period commencing with the inception of the policy. Income may be provided for a period of 10, 15, or 20 years from the date of your death. As Figure 9-5 illustrates, the policy is a combination of *level* term and whole life insurance.

If the term portion is for 10 years, income payments are provided for a period of 10 years subsequent to your death if you die within 10 years from the inception of the contract. Longer periods of coverage by the term portion are combined with longer periods of income payment. As the benefit payment period selected increases, the amount of term insurance is also increased. Because this arrangement may result in you having more term insurance than you need as your children grow older, some companies permit a reduction in the income period—and the amount of term insurance—in order to reduce the premium. When this is done, the term portion is reduced in blocks and the contract becomes difficult to distinguish from the family income policy.

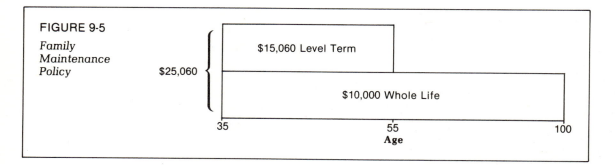

FIGURE 9-5

Family
Maintenance
Policy

Family plan. Sometimes called the family life insurance policy, this is a plan to provide life insurance on the life of every member of the family with one policy. The policy provides insurance in predetermined proportions on all members of the family including children born or adopted after the policy is issued. A typical policy, as shown in Figure 9-6, provides $5,000 of insurance on the life of the husband, $1,000 on his wife, and $1,000 on each child. Insurance on the husband is usually ordinary life while that on the wife is term to the husband's age 65. Insurance on the children is usually term to age 18, 21, or 25. The term insurance provided is convertible upon expiration and the children may convert to permanent insurance in an amount which is some multiple of their term insurance, such as $5,000 of permanent for each $1,000 of term. Some family policies provide for a multiple of the face amount of insurance on the husband's life to be paid in the event that he and his wife both die within a specified period after being involved in the same accident. Generally, the premium rate for the family life insurance policy depends entirely upon the age of the husband, and the number of children in the family does not affect it. For a large family, it may be a bargain.

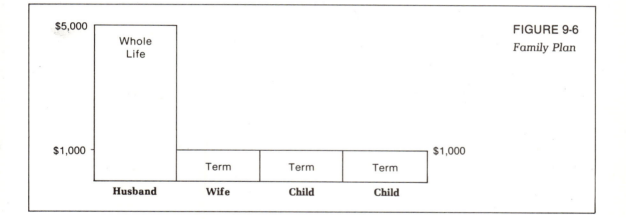

FIGURE 9-6

Family Plan

Modified life. Modified life policies are whole life contracts for which the premium is lower during the first few years of the policy than subsequently, although the amount of insurance remains constant. They were designed to cope with the sales resistance of persons who need whole life insurance but cannot (or will not) pay the regular premium initially. One approach to this problem is the use of term insurance for the first few years (say, five) which is automatically converted to whole life at the expiration of the initial period. The premium for the first five years would be at the term rate and after conversion it would rise to the whole life rate at the attained age of the insured. In order to avoid the sudden and relatively large increase in premium involved in this arrangement, some modified life contracts combine decreasing term insurance with increasing increments of whole life. This results in a premium rise each year but makes the shift from term to whole life gradual. Moreover, the ultimate level premium for whole life after the transition has been completed is somewhat lower than when the first five years of protection have been provided entirely with term insurance.

Another approach to modified life does not involve a combination of contracts but simply reduces the whole life level premium during the initial period of the contract. The reduced premium is greater than that for convertible term insurance but less than the regular premium. At the end of the preliminary period, which is usually five years, the level premium is increased to an amount which is greater than the level premium for whole life at the insured's age upon the inception of the contract but lower than the level premium for whole life at his or her attained age. Thus, he or she pays more for insurance during the initial period than for a modified life policy which used term insurance, but the level premium at the end of the initial period is lower.

Modified life may be better for the seller than for the buyer. The buyer's reluctance to buy whole life may reflect a need for protection but limited resources, in which case term is the better choice. Or, a family income or family maintenance policy which protects income at a lower cost than whole life may be preferable.

Multiple protection.   A multiple protection policy pays a multiple of the face amount if you die within a specified period and the face amount only if you die after the expiration of the period, as shown in Figure 9-7.

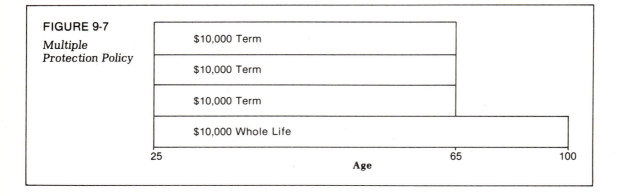

FIGURE 9-7

*Multiple
Protection Policy*

$10,000 Term

$10,000 Term

$10,000 Term

$10,000 Whole Life

25   65   100

Age

The period of multiple protection may be for a specified number of years, such as 10, 15, or 20, or it may be to a specified age, such as 60 or 65. The death benefit during the period is usually two or three times the face amount of the policy. Such a policy may be a combination of term insurance and modified whole life. At the expiration of the term insurance, the entire premium is applied to the basic whole life policy. On the other hand, the policy may combine term insurance with regular whole life, in which case the premium may be level throughout the premium-paying period of the basic policy or it may be reduced at the expiration of the term insurance portion. This may be an economical way to buy term insurance as it stretches the cost over a period of time longer than the term.

SOURCES OF LIFE INSURANCE AND ANNUITIES

Most life insurance and annuities of the types discussed in this and the preceding chapter is sold by life insurance companies. It is bought on either an individual or group basis.

Individual

Life insurance bought by individuals may be classified as either ordinary or industrial although the distinction between these two categories may become somewhat obscure in particular instances. A salesperson who sells in only one of these markets is said to be an "ordinary agent" or an "industrial agent" as the case may be, while an agent who sells in both markets is called a "combination agent."[2]

Ordinary. In the preceding chapter, ordinary life was defined as a whole life policy which was paid for on the installment plan through payment of premiums throughout the life of the insured. The same term is also used to identify a method of marketing life insurance. Used in this sense, ordinary life refers to all types of policies, other than industrial life and credit life, sold to individuals.

Ordinary life is sold to individuals in amounts not less than $1,000. After an agent has sold you on the idea of buying life insurance, you complete an application with the aid of the agent, in many cases take a medical examination, and pay the premium monthly, quarterly, semiannually, or annually, directly to the insurer. Typically, your only contact with the agent is at the time of completing the application, when the policy applied for is delivered, and when the agent makes an attempt to sell you more insurance. If, however, you have selected a superior life insurance agent, the agent will help you evaluate your life insurance program at regular intervals whether or not you need more insurance.

Industrial. Industrial life insurance has several characteristics which distinguish it from ordinary. The premium, which is higher than for ordinary insurance because of the marketing system, may be paid weekly or monthly. The maximum amount of insurance per policy or per person is $1,000. Originally, industrial insurance was sold on the basis of the premium rather than the face amount of the policy. That is, the policy had a face amount equal to whatever 5 cents (or 10 cents, or a quarter, up to a $1 maximum) per week would buy. This method has been abandoned to some extent in recent years, especially for larger policies.

Industrial insurance is generally written on all members of the family from birth to age 65. A medical examination is usually not required although it may be under some circumstances. The agent comes to the door every week or every month and collects the premium for all

2. Generally, an ordinary agent is merely referred to as a life insurance agent. Only those who are not ordinary agents are identified specifically. This practice is the result of the way insurance marketing developed. At one time, it was all individual ordinary. Industrial, combination, and group developed after the ordinary category was well established.

policies the family has in force. Because of the nature of the accounting system employed, the area of the city to which he or she is assigned is called a "debit" and the person is known as a "debit agent." In some cases, the agent may sell ordinary insurance as well as industrial; he or she is then referred to as a "combination agent."

Fading distinctions.   Many of the major differences between ordinary and industrial insurance are gradually disappearing although the remaining differences are greater than the similarities. When life insurance was first developed, the bulk of the policies were short term insurance sold on a single-premium basis. As terms lengthened, policy amounts became larger, and whole life insurance developed, the single-premium became so large that it hindered sales. This led to installment plans involving annual premiums. Even annual premiums, however, were too large for many people and this situation led to weekly premium, or industrial, insurance. Now that both ordinary and industrial life insurance can be purchased on a monthly premium basis, this difference between the two is disappearing.

At one time, all applicants for ordinary insurance were required to take a medical examination while industrial insurance was sold on a non-medical basis. Now, many companies issue ordinary insurance without a medical examination to people in certain categories. In recent years, industrial life insurance and monthly debit ordinary have come to be known as home service life insurance. Both of these types of policies are individual insurance serviced by agents who call at the policyholder's home to collect premiums and sell insurance to members of the household.

Group

Group life insurance is a nearly universal employee benefit in the United States. You acquire it by being a member of a group, such as an employee of a firm, member of a labor union, a trade association, a professional association, and similar groups. Generally, it is term insurance, and the employer pays part or all of the premium.

Instead of a policy, you receive a certificate from the employer (or union or association) which indicates that you are a participant, the amount for which you are insured, and the name of your beneficiary. Insurance is usually available without a medical examination or other evidence of insurability. Almost half of all life insurance in force in this country is on a group basis.

A modification of group life insurance is the development of franchise plans. A *franchise* is an arrangement for selling individual insurance to employees of a firm and having the premiums paid through the employer on a payroll deduction basis. Each insured must establish insurability and each receives his or her own policy. In this respect, the franchise is similar to individual insurance. On the other hand, it is similar to group in that the insurer receives the premiums for all the separate policies from the employer in one payment rather than from each individual policyholder.

Consumer Applications
Adjusting Life Insurance for Inflation

You buy life insurance so that your dependents will have income in spite of your death. The income is stated in terms of dollars but what your family needs is goods and services. So, as the purchasing power of the dollar declines, you need a larger amount of life insurance to assure an adequate amount of income. What are your choices?

Buy More Life Insurance

As long as you are insurable, you can buy more life insurance. What if you become uninsurable? As noted earlier, you can protect yourself against that by buying a policy with a Guaranteed Insurability Option. It has three disadvantages. First, the option is limited to a specified age, such as 40, and you may need more insurance after that age. Second, you must buy the same kind of insurance as the policy you have and the premium will be much higher. For example, one company which offers guaranteed cost whole life for $12.00 per thousand at age 25 charges $21.00 per thousand at age 40. Third, the opportunities to buy additional insurance are not related to the rate of inflation. On the other hand, unlike other arrangements discussed below, you don't lose the next option if you fail to exercise one.

Another alternative is the Inflation Rider Option or Cost-of-living rider, which automatically increases the amount of insurance as the Consumer Price Index rises. It provides term insurance as an addition to the face amount of your permanent policy. If, for example, you have a $100,000 whole life policy and the CPI goes up 5 percent this year, $5,000 of one-year term insurance is automatically written for next year at the premium rate for your age. You are billed for it along with the premium notice for your basic policy. No evidence of insurability is required. You do not have to accept (and pay for) the additional insurance if you don't want it. If you refuse to exercise the option, however, it is no longer available. In other words, you can't say, "I'm short of funds this year, but I will exercise the option next year." Table 9-1 illustrates how the Inflation Rider Option would affect your total amount of insurance if you had bought a $100,000 whole life policy in 1980 and the inflation rate was 5 percent every year.

Buy a Variable Life Policy

Instead of simply buying more life insurance to offset inflation, you may buy a policy which is designed so that the face amount of insurance will increase as the purchasing power of the dollar declines. You may buy an index-linked or an equity-linked policy.

Index-Linked Policies
A typical index-linked policy would be a level-premium $100,000 whole life contract for which the face amount would increase as the CPI goes up, not to exceed 5 percent in any one

TABLE 9-1.

*Amount of
Insurance
Provided by
Inflation Rider
Option at
5 Percent
Inflation Rate*

YEAR	CONSUMER PRICE INDEX	BASIC INSURANCE AMOUNT	OPTION AMOUNT	TOTAL DEATH BENEFIT
1980	100.000	$100,000	———	$100,000
1981	105.000	100,000	$ 5,000	105,000
1982	110.250	100,000	10,250	110,250
1983	115.763	100,000	15,763	115,763
1984	121.551	100,000	21,551	121,551
1985	127.628	100,000	27,628	127,628
1986	134.010	100,000	34,010	134,010
1987	140.710	100,000	40,710	140,710
1988	147.746	100,000	47,746	147,746
1989	155.133	100,000	55,133	155,133
1990	162.889	100,000	62,889	162,889
1991	171.034	100,000	71,034	171,034
1992	179.586	100,000	79,586	179,586
1993	188.565	100,000	88,565	188,565
1994	197.993	100,000	97,993	197,993
1995	207.893	100,000	107,893	207,893
1996	218.287	100,000	118,287	218,287
1997	229.202	100,000	129,202	229,202
1998	240.662	100,000	140,662	240,662
1999	252.659	100,000	152,659	252,659
2000	265.330	100,000	165,330	265,330

year and a maximum total increase of 100 percent. At an annual inflation rate of 5 percent or more, the face amount of insurance would double in 15 years. Because the inflation risk is borne by the insurer, the annual premium is higher than for a fixed-amount policy. For example, at issue age 25 (male) it could be $18 per thousand rather than $12 per thousand for a fixed-amount policy. Table 9-2 shows what an $1,800 annual premium would buy for a 25-year-old male. Note that the fixed-amount policy provides more protection for the first eight years and less protection from the ninth year on. At a lower inflation rate, however, the fixed-amount policy would be larger than the variable policy for a longer period of time. Which policy should you buy? If you prefer more protection now, buy the fixed-amount policy. If you think inflation will continue and if you are willing to accept less protection now in exchange for more protection later, buy the variable policy.

AGE	FIXED AMOUNT POLICY	VARIABLE POLICY
25	$150,000	$100,000
26	150,000	105,000
27	150,000	110,250
28	150,000	115,763
29	150,000	121,551
30	150,000	127,628
31	150,000	134,010
32	150,000	140,710
33	150,000	147,746
34	150,000	155,133
35	150,000	162,889
36	150,000	171,034
37	150,000	179,586
38	150,000	188,565
39	150,000	197,993
40	150,000	200,000

Equity-Linked Policies

The face amount of equity-linked policies fluctuates with the investment performance of the savings element invested in common stocks. The theory is the same as that of the variable annuity; namely, gains in equity investments will offset increases in the Consumer Price Index. The premium may be fixed or variable. With a variable premium policy, face amounts and premiums vary in the same proportion. If, for example, the face amount of insurance doubles, then the premium doubles. With a fixed premium policy, the face amount increases with favorable investment experience but the premium does not change. The practical effect of these differences is that favorable investment experience has more impact on the face amount of insurance than it does with a fixed premium policy.

If you buy either type equity-linked variable life policy, you assume the risk that the stock market may be going down at the same time that the CPI is going up. Figure 9-8 illustrates such an occurrence. When it happens, you could be worse off with a variable life policy than with a fixed amount policy. With a variable premium policy, you also take the risk that the premium you have to pay will increase. Increasing the premium helps increase the face amount of insurance, but it may have a bad effect on your budget.

Should you buy an equity-linked variable life policy? If so, should you buy fixed premium or variable premium? The answer depends on you. How much risk are you willing to take in coping with inflation?

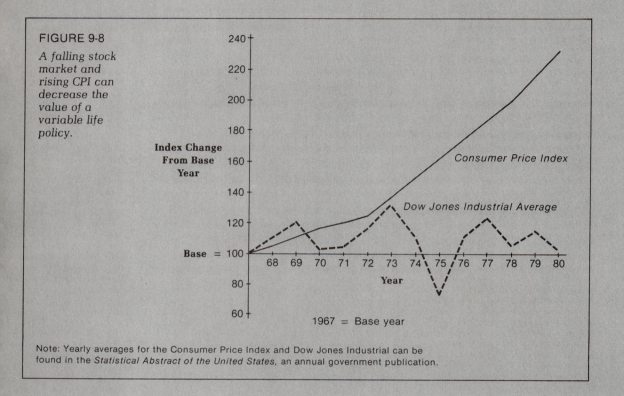

FIGURE 9-8

A falling stock market and rising CPI can decrease the value of a variable life policy.

Index Change From Base Year

Consumer Price Index

Dow Jones Industrial Average

Base = 100

Year

1967 = Base year

Note: Yearly averages for the Consumer Price Index and Dow Jones Industrial can be found in the *Statistical Abstract of the United States*, an annual government publication.

Discussion Questions

1. Why would a decline in interest rates or mortality rates increase the cost of annuities? How can you protect yourself against this possibility?

2. People buy variable annuities because of inflation. Do you think there would be a market for them if inflation stopped? Why or why not?

3. The purpose of insurance is to reduce uncertainty. Do you think the insurance industry has done an adequate job of reducing the uncertainty caused by inflation? Please explain.

4. For any given amount of money, a joint-and-survivor annuity yields less monthly income than a single life annuity. Therefore, some life insurance salespeople suggest choosing the latter, and providing income for the survivor through life insurance on the annuitant. Is this a good suggestion? Why or why not?

5. Under what circumstances would a joint life annuity be suitable?

6. Under what circumstances might a risk-averse person buy a pure life annuity?

7. Why do you suppose the retirement annuity is the most popular form of deferred annuity?

8. Home service life insurance agents call at your home to collect premiums for your policy. Would you prefer this arrangement to mailing the premium to the insurance company? Are there people for whom agent collection of premiums is advantageous? Please explain.

9. When the value of your home rises in terms of dollars because of inflation, there is no problem in increasing the amount of insurance on it. Why is there a problem when the value of your life increases? What is the difference between insuring your home and insuring your life?

10. What is the difference between the family life insurance policy and the industrial life insurance practice of insuring all members of the family? Which system do you think is preferable? Why?

Cases

9-1 Mrs. Abigail Dozer recently indicated to you that she was at that stage in her life when she wanted to seriously consider her retirement from the directorship of Dozer Tractor Company, Inc. She knows how important it is to have a dependable income for the rest of her life. Mrs. Dozer also wants to leave a substantial sum of money to her alma mater upon her death. Her accountant has suggested that this dual task can be accomplished easily, which was surprising to Mrs. Dozer.

1. Suggest two ways this task could be accomplished.

2. If Mrs. Dozer's health is suspect, how will this affect her ability to accomplish her goals?

9-2 Your neighbor, Walt, recently approached you as you were on your way to work as an agent of Lotze Life Insurance Company. He said, "Say—you know what bothers me about that ordinary/savings type of policy your company sells? It's a bad deal. If I die tomorrow your company pays the face amount but you keep all the savings that belong to me now! I don't think that is fair!" Your response was, "Walt, there are other ways to look at that. Let's make an appointment for tomorrow, and I'll show you how to have your cake and eat it too."

1. What did Walt mean by his first question?

2. What solution(s) did you have in mind?

9-3 Joe Kimbell is considering the purchase of a deferred life annuity for his retirement at age 65. He is married and has two children. He would pay premiums monthly until age 65.

1. What factors should Joe consider before deciding to purchase this annuity?

2. What features should it have?

3. If he needs life insurance, how might he combine his life insurance program with his desire for retirement income security?

9-4 Karen Kirk, who is selling life insurance to college seniors, has approached you as a prospective customer. The policy requires only 10% of the first year's premium and you sign a note for the balance. The loan is immediately repayable if you miss an annual premium payment during the first five years of the policy. If you pay each of the next five annual premiums on time, however, the loan will be automatically repaid by a "fifth year special dividend."

1. Should you borrow money to buy life insurance? Why or why not?

2. What alternatives do you have?

Chapter Ten:
LIFE INSURANCE POLICY PROVISIONS

INTRODUCTION

A life insurance policy is written evidence of the intent of the parties to the agreement. The policy and application attached to it constitute the entire contract. Oral statements have no effect unless included in the written contract. This means that anything the agent told you while he or she was selling you on the idea of applying for the policy is not part of the contract unless it is included in the policy. If the agent said or implied, for example, that you could borrow on the policy at a 6 percent rate of interest but the policy says 8 percent, then 8 percent is what you will pay.

While some agents may misrepresent something occasionally as they get carried away with their sales pitch, most are both honest and careful. Anyone can make a mistake, however, and even the better agents are not infallible. And neither are you. It is easy to become confused if you talk with several agents about several different policies. Therefore, you should read your policy carefully when you receive it so you will know what you have bought. If there is something in it you don't understand, contact the agent or company and ask for an explanation.

No standard life insurance contracts are required by law, but some provisions are required while others are optional.[1] The purpose of this

---

1. A typical standard provision law for life insurance, for example, includes the grace period, incontestable clause, and so on. Standard provisions must be included word for word as set forth in the statute or, if different wording is used, the clause must be equal to or better than the one prescribed by statute. Some provisions are optional but must meet the requirements of the law if used.

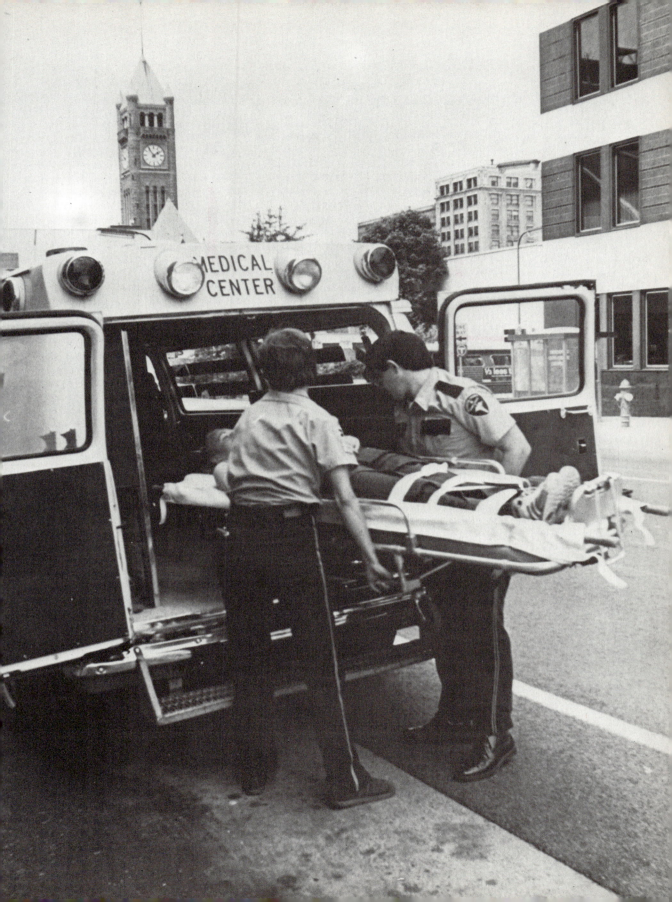

chapter is to help you understand your policy by explaining the major provisions listed in Figure 10-1, as well as other provisions, riders, and provisions peculiar to industrial life insurance. All the provisions shown in Figure 10-1 are in the sample whole life insurance policy in Appendix A.

FIGURE 10-1

*Major Life
Insurance Policy
Provisions*

1. Beneficiary
2. Ownership
3. Dividends
4. Grace period
5. Settlement options
6. Incontestable
7. Misstatement of age

8. Suicide
9. Assignment
10. Policy loans
11. Nonforfeiture values and options
12. Reinstatement

MAJOR PROVISIONS

Beneficiary Clause

The purpose of the beneficiary clause is to enable you to designate to whom the proceeds shall be paid when the policy matures. If no beneficiary is named, the proceeds will go to your estate. There are no legal or contractual restrictions on whom you may designate. Designations may be revocable or irrevocable. Those which are revocable may be changed by the policyholder alone. Irrevocable designations, on the other hand, can be changed only with the consent of the beneficiary.

A beneficiary must survive the insured in order to be entitled to the proceeds of the policy at the death of the insured. It is customary, therefore, to name a beneficiary who is entitled to the proceeds in the event that the first-named beneficiary does not survive the insured. These are known as contingent or secondary, tertiary, and so on, beneficiaries. Such beneficiaries are named and listed in the order of their priority.

If the insured and the primary beneficiary die in the same accident and there is no evidence to show who died first, there is a question as to whether the proceeds shall be paid to the estate of the primary beneficiary or to a contingent beneficiary. Where the Uniform Simultaneous Death Act has been enacted, the proceeds of the policy are distributed as if the insured had survived the beneficiary. Where this act is not in effect, the courts have usually reached the same conclusion. If no contingent beneficiary has been named, the proceeds go to the estate of the insured, thus subjecting them to taxes, probate costs, and the claims of creditors.

A similar problem arises when the primary beneficiary survives the insured by only a short period. In such a case, the proceeds may be depleted by going through the estate of the beneficiary or by virtue of the fact that an annuity-type settlement option had been selected.

This problem can be solved by adding a *common disaster* clause which provides that the beneficiary must survive the insured by a specified period of time or must be alive at the time of payment in order to be entitled to the proceeds. If neither of these conditions is fulfilled, the proceeds go to a contingent beneficiary or the estate of the insured if a contingent beneficiary has not been named.

Beneficiaries should be designated very specifically in order to avoid disputes. The wife should be designated by her given and maiden name along with her husband's last name. For example, Helen Bowery Lomen. To avoid excluding any children, they may be designated as "children who survive the insured." This would include children of all the insured's marriages as well as adopted children. In designating children as beneficiaries, it should be kept in mind that a minor is not competent to receive payment. In the event of the death of the insured prior to the maturity of a child who is a beneficiary, a guardian may have to be appointed to receive the proceeds on behalf of the child.[2]

Ownership

Ownership refers to rights. When you say, "I own this car," you mean you have the right to use it, sell it, lend it, and so on. The owner of a life insurance policy also has rights, such as to assign the policy to someone else, designate the beneficiary, or surrender it for its cash value. When you fill out the application for a policy, one item is concerned with ownership, although it may simply be labelled "rights." At that point, you indicate to whom the rights belong. Typically, you mark the square entitled "insured."

You can, however, name a trust or another person, such as your spouse. In any case, you are designating the owner of the policy. If you select yourself to be owner and later decide to transfer ownership to a trust or another person, you may do so either by making an absolute assignment or by executing an ownership form which may be obtained from the insurance company.

Dividends

Life insurance can be bought on a participating or nonparticipating (guaranteed cost) basis. Participating policies share in the savings the insurer makes because of lower than anticipated expenses and mortality, as well as greater than expected interest earnings on investment. This refund is called a *dividend*.[3] Nonparticipating insurance does not share in this way.

You have the following options with regard to dividends: *only one choose one*

1. Paid in cash

2. Applied toward payment of the premium

4 3. Left with the insurer to accumulate at interest

---

2. This statement is a gross oversimplification designed to call attention to the problem. For further information, see S.S. Huebner and Kenneth Black, Jr., *Life Insurance* (9th ed.; Englewood Cliffs, N.J.; Prentice-Hall, 1976), p. 156.

3. The term "dividend" usually refers to the portion of profits distributed to stockholders. Insurance company dividends to policyholders are considered to be a refund of premiums rather than a part of profits.

NO TAX!

3. 4. Used to buy paid-up additional insurance

5. Used to buy one-year term insurance (some companies).

Grace Period

The cost of the policy is stated in terms of an annual premium, but installments may be paid on a monthly, quarterly, semiannual, or annual basis. The first premium must be paid in advance while you are in good health, and all subsequent premiums are payable in advance. You do not promise to pay them, but payment is a condition precedent to continuance of the insurance. As a matter of practice, insurance companies send a notice to you indicating when the premium is due, but the contract does not require them to do so.

The law requires that the contract must contain a provision that you are entitled to a grace period of not less than thirty days (some say twenty-eight or thirty-one), within which time payment of any premium after the first may be made. In spite of the fact that the premium is past due during this period, the policy remains in force. If you die during this period before the premium is paid, the face amount of the policy minus the amount of the premium past due will be paid to the beneficiary. If the premium is not paid during the grace period, protection ceases and a claim for benefits because of death after that date will not be paid. The purpose of the grace period is to prevent unintentional lapses.[4] If it were not for this provision, an insured whose premium was paid one day late would have to prove his or her insurability in order to have the policy reinstated.

Settlement Options

Life insurance is designed to create a sum of money which can be used to offset economic loss when the insured dies. At one time, the only form in which the death proceeds or cash value of a policy could be paid was in a lump sum. Because lump-sum payment has a number of disadvantages, several additional modes of settlement have been developed and are now included in most policies.

You may select the option you prefer or leave the choice to the beneficiary. You may change the option you select. The settlement options for death proceeds usually are (1) cash or lump-sum, (2) interest option, (3) fixed period option, (4) fixed amount option, and (5) life income options. These options may be used separately or in combination.

Cash or Lump Sum. In a sense, cash settlement is not an option because it is the manner in which proceeds are usually paid if no other arrangement is requested. Because other methods of payment are available, however, cash or lump-sum payment may be considered an option. When proceeds are payable in cash, most companies will permit a beneficiary to place them under one of the settlement options listed in

---

4. The automatic premium loan discussed later in this chapter is also designed to deal with this problem.

the contract. In spite of this, however, the lump-sum option has a number of disadvantages.

First, the beneficiary may fail to exercise the privilege of selecting another option when to do so would be advantageous. Second, the beneficiary's need is usually for income rather than capital; the beneficiary who receives a large sum as life insurance proceeds also acquires a financial management problem for which he or she may be unprepared. Third, the lump-sum option provides no opportunity to protect the proceeds from creditors of the beneficiary. This protection may be arranged only by the insured in connection with other options, as discussed below.

Interest Option. When the proceeds are left at interest, the policyholder may provide that the principal may not be depleted by the primary beneficiary but must be kept intact for payment to another beneficiary upon the death of the first. On the other hand, the beneficiary may be given not only the right to interest earnings but also the right to make withdrawals from the principal. A maximum limit per year may be placed on such withdrawals or there may be no limitation. In the latter case, the interest option is practically the same as having money in a savings account. The difference is that the insurance company guarantees a specified rate of interest and may pay more if its investment earnings are high enough, while there are no long-term guarantees concerning the interest rates paid on savings accounts.

The beneficiary may also be given the right to change to another settlement option, or provision may be made for automatic change at a specified date or upon the occurrence of a specified event, such as the beneficiary entering college. The beneficiary may be given the right to designate the recipient of the proceeds upon the beneficiary's death. Finally, the proceeds being held by the insurer may be protected from creditors of the beneficiary through a spendthrift trust clause which is discussed later.

Fixed Period Option. Under this settlement option, the proceeds are paid out in equal installments over a specified period. Payments may be made monthly, quarterly, semiannually, or annually. They continue to the end of the period whether the beneficiary lives or dies. In the event of the death of the beneficiary prior to the end of the period, the remaining payments may be made to the beneficiary's estate or to a secondary beneficiary, depending upon the desires of the owner or the beneficiary. The fixed period option is a temporary annuity and does not involve life contingencies. The size of each installment is determined by the amount of proceeds, the length of the period during which installment payments are to be made, the guaranteed rate of interest, and the frequency of payments.

If interest in excess of that guaranteed is earned, the size of the installment is increased. Most insurers permit the owner to give the beneficiary the right to commute all remaining installments at any time and receive a lump sum. Some companies will permit the beneficiary to select the date when payments are to begin. Because the size of installments is influenced by the amount of proceeds available, they are reduced if a policy loan is deducted from the death benefit. Similarly, they are increased by dividend accumulations and paid-up additions to the policy. The primary disadvantage of the fixed-period option is that it is inflexible.

Fixed Amount Option. Installments for a fixed amount provide for equal monthly, quarterly, semiannual, or annual payments to be made to the beneficiary until the proceeds are exhausted. The length of the period for which payments are made depends upon the proceeds available, the interest rate guaranteed, and the size payment selected. Interest earnings above those guaranteed as well as dividend accumulations and paid-up additions increase the period of time during which installment payments are made rather than their size. Conversely, a policy loan would decrease the proceeds available and decrease the number of installments.

The fixed amount option is much more flexible than the fixed period option because most insurers permit the policyholder to specify different amounts of income at different times. The beneficiary may also be given the right to make withdrawals from time to time, with or without limitation. The commencement of payments can be deferred by holding the proceeds under the interest option until needed. Many companies will permit the beneficiary to change from the fixed amount option to a life income option.

Life Income Options. These settlement options are immediate annuities. The straight life income, or pure annuity, provides installment payments only so long as the primary beneficiary lives. Refund life income options, on the other hand, guarantee payment of an amount no less than the principal sum by either a cash refund annuity or an installment refund annuity.

The most widely used life income option is the life income with period certain. This provides payments to the beneficiary for life with payments to be made for a specified number of months or years in any event. Some companies also offer a joint-and-survivorship life income option which provides for continued payments to a secondary beneficiary if the primary beneficiary dies. The size of payments under life income options depends upon the type of life income selected, the amount of the proceeds, the rate of interest assumed, the age of the beneficiary when the income commences, and the sex of the beneficiary. Women live longer than men; therefore, a given amount of money provides a larger income for a man than a woman the same age. Similarly, life insurance costs less for women than for men the same age.

Incontestable Clause

Most contracts are contestable until they have been executed. Either party may take legal action in an attempt to have the contract voided, which would make it unenforceable. At one time, life insurance contracts could be contested at any time. This meant that a widow claiming benefits for the death of her husband on a policy bought twenty years previously might find that the insurer would refuse to pay on the grounds that some misstatement of the insured made it possible for the insurer to void the contract.

In this situation, no insured could ever be sure that a claim would be paid promptly, if at all. Since the person who made application would be unavailable for questioning, the claimant would be in a difficult situation. This detracted from the value of life insurance by creating an element of uncertainty and resulted in bad publicity for the life insurance industry when claims were contested on the basis of technicalities. As early as 1864, therefore, insurance companies began to incorporate an incontestable clause in the contract on a voluntary basis; today, such a clause is generally required by statute.

A typical clause makes the contract incontestable after it has been in force two years during your lifetime. If you die prior to the end of the two years, the policy never becomes incontestable. If you live beyond the period, the policy cannot be contested, even for fraud. If the insurer is going to contest the policy, it must do so within the two-year period. If you, the applicant, make misstatements about your health, habits, or other vital information which, if the truth were known, would prove you to be uninsurable,[5] the insurance company must contest the policy within the contestable period if it wishes to void the contract. It cannot plead in court that the knowledge was not available until three years later. While the incontestable clause may force the insurer to do considerably more investigating initially than would otherwise be the case, and perhaps does result in some claims being paid that should not, it is a great boon to the honest policyholder who wants to be *sure*.

Misstatement of Age

Your age when you apply for life insurance has a direct bearing on its cost. It is, therefore, a material fact and its misstatement would ordinarily be expected to provide grounds for voiding the contract. Rather than permit voidance, however, most state laws require that all policies include a provision that if your age has been misstated, the amount of the insurance will be adjusted to that which the premium paid would purchase at the correct age.

For example, if a male age 26 purchases an ordinary life policy in the amount of $10,000 and states that he is age 25, the premium in Company X would be quoted as $123.20 per year. Upon learning the insured's correct age, the Company can reduce the amount of insurance to $9,693.15, which is the amount that $123.20 per year will buy at a rate of $12.71 per thousand at age 26 in Company X. On the other hand, if the insured finds that he has overstated his age, he is entitled to an up-

---

5. Or, would cause the insurer to be willing to issue a policy only on a different basis; e.g., at a higher premium rate or with special restrictions, such as a war clause or aviation clause. These clauses are discussed later in this chapter.

ward adjustment in the amount of insurance. Because the adjustment for misstatement of age is not a contest of the policy but merely the operation of a policy provision, it is not affected by the incontestable clause. Thus, this adjustment can be made at any time prior to the payment of a claim.

Suicide Clause

The suicide clause provides that if you commit suicide, whether sane or insane, within (usually) two years from the date the policy was issued, the sole obligation of the insurer is to return the premiums. This clause is a compromise between two conflicting theories. One is that, since insurance operates on the basis of chance occurrences, it is unfair to expect the company to bear the burden of what is not a matter of chance. Paying such claims is like paying a policyholder on a fire policy who burns his or her own house down. On the other hand, the purpose of life insurance is to provide for the beneficiary, who, in many cases, was dependent upon the insured. The loss to the beneficiary is just as great whether the cause of death was suicide, accident, or natural.

The period of time during which payment for suicide is excluded will, presumably, protect the company from being defrauded by those contemplating suicide when they purchase the insurance. At the same time, restricting the exclusion to this period offers protection to the beneficiary when no fraud is involved. At least, it is felt that very few people would plan suicide for as much as two years ahead.

If the company wishes to deny a claim on the grounds that death was caused by suicide during the period of exclusion, it must prove conclusively that the death was suicide. Because there is a strong presumption against suicide on the grounds that everyone has an instinct for self-preservation, proving suicide can be very difficult.[6]

Assignment

As the owner of a life insurance policy you can transfer part or all of your rights to someone else. The assignment clause provides, however, that the company will not be bound by any assignment until it has received notice, that any indebtedness to the company shall have priority over any assignment, and that the company is not responsible for the validity of any assignment. This provision helps the company avoid litigation about who is entitled to policy benefits.

If I assign my policy to you and die before the insurer has been notified, the company may pay the death benefit to the beneficiary I had named. You may try to force the company to pay you on the grounds that

---

6. The following case is illustrative: A young man was found in his room with a bullet wound in his head. A revolver which had one empty shell in its chamber was found lying near his right hand. The presumption against suicide was not overcome by testimony stating that the insured had been despondent and that the gun, because of a safety device, could not have been accidentally discharged. The court felt that the insured might have intentionally pulled the trigger thinking the gun was unloaded, thus making the shooting an accident. *Lewis v. New York Life Insurance Company,* 113 Mont. 151, 124 P 2nd 579 (1942).

you are the owner and, as such, are entitled to the benefits. But the clause will prevent you from collecting because it provides that the company is not bound by the assignment until it receives notice. If it had received notice, it would not have paid the proceeds to the beneficiary.

Furthermore, after the company receives notice of my assignment of the policy to you, the company can subtract the amount of any loan I have made against the policy before it pays you any benefit.

Policy Loan

In addition to nonforfeiture options, you have the right to borrow an amount equal to the surrender value from the insurer at a rate of interest specified in the policy (usually 7 or 8 percent). Interest is payable in advance on the anniversary date of the policy. When you die, however, the proceeds of the policy are reduced by loans and interest due. For example, a policy with a face value of $10,000 and loans and interest equal to $2,000 would require a payment of $8,000 to the beneficiary. While the loan right is a valuable one, its abuse can at least partially defeat the purpose of the insurance program.

In many cases, you can request an automatic premium loan clause in the policy. It provides that if you fail to pay the premium, a loan in the amount of the premium due will automatically be made, if there is enough unencumbered surrender value to cover the loan and the interest for one year. This is a valuable provision which you should request when you buy life insurance as it is easy to overlook payment of a premium. The automatic premium loan will prevent the policy from lapsing.

Nonforfeiture Values and Options

We pointed out in Chapter 8 that the level premium plan results in the accumulation of a reserve or investment element in the policy which increases as each year passes. At one time, it was customary for the insurer to keep this investment element if the insured stopped paying the premium. It was said that the insured forfeited the value. Eventually, some life insurance companies voluntarily adopted the policy of refunding the cash value to an insured who surrendered (returned) the policy to the company. This practice is now required by the Standard Nonforfeiture Law.

When you stop making premium payments, several options are available:

1. Take the surrender (cash) value in cash.

2. Continue the policy in force with a smaller face amount that is paid-up.

3. Continue the policy in force as extended term insurance.

These amounts are listed in the policy in a Table of Cash, Loan, and Other Values. An example is shown in Table 10-1.

TABLE 10-1

*Guaranteed
Values for
$10,000 Whole
Life Policy For
Male Age 35*

END OF POLICY YEAR	CASH OR LOAN VALUE	PAID-UP INSURANCE	EXTENDED TERM INSURANCE YEARS	DAYS
1	$ 14	$ 30	0	152
2	174	450	4	182
3	338	860	8	65
4	506	1,250	10	344
5	676	1,640	12	360
6	879	2,070	14	335
7	1,084	2,500	16	147
8	1,293	2,910	17	207
9	1,504	3,300	18	177
10	1,719	3,690	19	78
11	1,908	4,000	19	209
12	2,099	4,300	19	306
13	2,294	4,590	20	8
14	2,490	4,870	20	47
15	2,690	5,140	20	65
16	2,891	5,410	20	66
17	3,095	5,660	20	52
18	3,301	5,910	20	27
19	3,508	6,150	19	358
20	3,718	6,390	19	317
Age 60	4,620	7,200	18	111
Age 65	5,504	7,860	16	147

Reinstatement

The reinstatement clause provides that, unless the policy has been surrendered for cash or unless it has been continued as extended term insurance and the full period has expired, it may be reinstated at any time within three (in some cases, five) years after default. Payment of all overdue premiums on the policy and other indebtedness to the insurer plus interest on these items is required in addition to payment of the current premium. You must also provide evidence of insurability satisfactory to the insurer.

Evidence of insurability is the same in the case of reinstatement as it is for obtaining new life insurance. This means that the company is concerned about your health, occupation, hobbies, and any other factor that may affect the probability of death.

Why would you apply for reinstatement instead of new insurance, considering the fact that you must prove that you are insurable and, therefore, could get a new policy just as easily as having the old one reinstated? The explanation is that there may be features in the old policy that are preferable to those currently available. Settlement options, for example, may be more liberal because they are based on mortality and interest assumptions more favorable than those used currently. Or, you may be interested in building up cash values by a lump-sum payment of back premiums, or the premium rate effective when you were younger may be more attractive to you than the rate at your present age if you bought a new policy.

In pointing out the advantages of reinstatement, it is sometimes said that reinstatement is preferable to the purchase of a new policy because a new policy involves heavy front-end costs, primarily commissions to the selling agent, the burden of which is passed on to the insured. You can avoid this by reinstating your old policy, on which you have already paid all or part of such costs, rather than purchasing another policy. This is true but not compelling. A new policy may or may not cost more than reinstating the old one. The only way to find out is to make cost comparisons. If a new policy costs less than reinstating an old one, you are better off to buy the new policy and do not need to worry about the manner in which the insurer recovers the cost of issuing it.

OTHER PROVISIONS

Spendthrift Clause

Many states have statutes that protect the cash value and proceeds of a life insurance policy from creditors of the insured, except for the claims of federal tax authorities. A number of states also have statutes which provide protection against claims of creditors of the beneficiary. The most common statutes concerning protection of proceeds against creditors of the beneficiary, however, are those which authorize inclusion of a spendthrift clause in life insurance policies.

The effect of a spendthrift clause is to deny access to the proceeds by creditors of a beneficiary prior to the time such proceeds are in his or her possession. The clause provides that benefits payable to any beneficiary cannot be assigned or transferred and are not subject to commutation or encumbrance or any legal process, execution, garnishment, or attachment proceeding.

Spendthrift clauses are not automatically included in the policy and cannot be added by the beneficiary after the insured's death. The policyholder can, however, request that it be included in the installment provisions of the policy. Note that the clause protects only funds being held by the insurance company, not those which have been received by the beneficiary.

Aviation and War Clauses

Two restrictive clauses found in some policies are aviation clauses and war clauses. The aviation clauses are becoming less restrictive than in the early days of aviation. Some exclude all aviation deaths except those of fare-paying passengers on scheduled airlines. Such an exclusion is usually found in double indemnity provisions. Other clauses exclude only death in military aircraft; this is a common exclusion. Some exclude death which occurs when the insured is acting as a pilot or a student pilot. Most, but not all, aviation restrictions can be eliminated by payment of extra premium.

The purpose of war clauses is to control adverse selection by those who buy life insurance. Persons entering military service during wartime may be more inclined to buy life insurance—and buy it in larger amounts—than those not likely to be exposed to the perils associated with war. Two types of war clauses have been used to cope with this problem: (1) the status clause, and (2) the result clause.

The status clause excludes any claims for death while the insured is in military service, regardless of the cause. The result clause is less restrictive in that it excludes only death which is the result of war. In both cases, the insurer's only obligation is to refund premiums paid or pay an amount equal to the policy reserve. War clauses usually appear in policies written during a war or a period of impending war— especially in policies issued to young men of draft age. They are usually cancelled at the end of the hostilities.

LIFE INSURANCE RIDERS

Through the use of riders, life insurance policies may be modified to provide special benefits in the event of total disability. These benefits are waiver of premium and disability income. In order to qualify for such benefits your disability must be total, permanent, and occur prior to a specified age, usually 55 although some companies specify age 60. Disability may be caused by either accidental injury or sickness; no distinction is made. For the first two years of benefit payments, you are considered to be totally disabled whenever, because of injury or disease, you are unable to perform the duties of your regular occupation. Beyond two years, benefits continue only if you are unable to perform the duties of any occupation for which you are qualified by reason of education, training, and experience. Most riders define blindness or loss of both hands, both feet, or one hand and one foot as total disability. Typically, disability longer than six months is considered to be permanent.

Other benefits that may be added by rider or a special clause in the policy are the accidental death benefit and the guaranteed insurability option.

Waiver of Premium

This benefit is offered by all life insurance companies and is included in about half the policies sold. Some companies provide it automatically. It provides that life insurance premiums due after commencement of total disability shall be waived. If you paid a premium after such disability began and before the expiration of the six-month period which establishes permanency of the disability, the premium is refunded. Premiums are waived as long as you remain totally disabled. If the contract is endowment insurance, premiums discontinue at maturity. If it is a term contract, however, most companies continue protection for the balance of your life if you remain totally disabled.

Waiver of premium has no effect on any other provision of the policy. Your rights and benefits continue just as they would if you continued making premium payments. The waiver of premium benefit does not increase family income but it releases premium dollars for other uses and keeps insurance protection in force. Cash values continue to increase and dividends (if the policy is participating) continue to be paid.

Disability Income *FAMILY INCOME*

This rider provides an income benefit of $10 per month per $1,000 of face amount of life insurance while total disability continues after the first six months of such disability, provided it commences prior to age 55. Some companies provide $5 per month per $1,000, while others offer as much as $20 per month. At one time, payments were made for the balance of the insured's life so long as total disability continued, but most contracts today limit payment to age 65. At that age, the policy matures as an endowment, which is less favorable than a continuation of income benefits because the insured cannot buy an annuity equal to the income benefit with the policy proceeds. Other benefits of the policy, such as dividends and cash values, are unaffected by the operation of the disability income rider.

NOT TRUE

Accidental Death Benefit Rider

This rider is sometimes called double indemnity. It provides that double the face amount of the policy will be paid if your death is caused by accident and triple the face amount if you were riding as a paying passenger in a public conveyance. Because it does not add greatly to premium and *appears* to double the protection of the policy, it is very popular. The loss of income resulting from death, however, is usually unrelated to its cause. It is just as great whether you die of natural causes or by accident. The drawback with this rider is that many insureds tend to think of their protection in terms of the double indemnity benefit and forget that it is payable only in the event of death caused by accident. Thus, they think they have twice as much protection as is actually the case. The rider, however, has great sales appeal.

Many people advocate the purchase of double indemnity because accidents claim more lives than all other causes of death combined for youths age 15 to 24. They forget that the possible size of a loss is more important than the probability of the loss occurring. If one is guided by probability, however, in spite of what has been said earlier, it is worthwhile noting that only 22 percent of deaths in the group age 25–44 are caused by accidents.

A typical double indemnity clause includes the following definition of accidental death: "Death resulting from bodily injury effected solely

FIGURE 10-2

*Accidental Death
Benefit Rider*

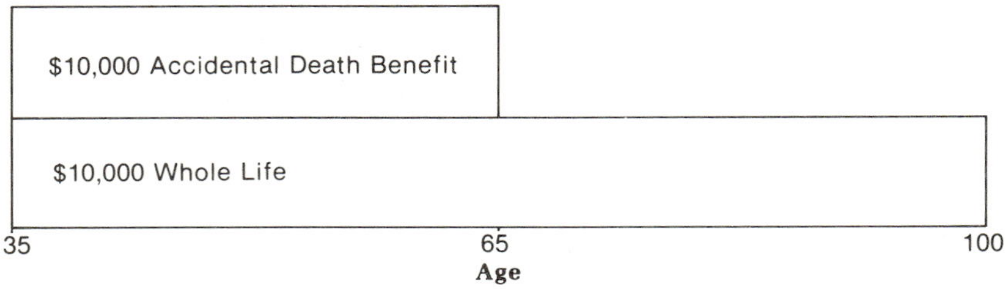

$10,000 Accidental Death Benefit

$10,000 Whole Life

35   65   100

Age

through external, violent, and accidental means independently and exclusively of all other causes and within ninety days after such injury.'' ''Accidental means'' is somewhat more restrictive than ''accident.'' It requires that both the cause and the result must be unintended. Jack decided to prove his skill with a pistol by shooting an apple off Bill's head. Bill moved his head at the wrong time and lost it. The court denied a plea by Bill's widow for double indemnity because the means was not accidental. The phrase ''solely through external, violent, and accidental means'' is designed to avoid paying double for the insured whose death is really caused by disease, such as the victim of a heart attack who dies in an automobile accident which is caused by the attack.

Certain causes of death are excluded by the double indemnity provision. Typically, suicide, violations of the law, gas or poison, war, and certain aviation activities other than as a passenger on a scheduled airline are excluded. This rider is usually in effect to the insured's age 60 or 65.

Guaranteed Insurability Option

Many insurers will add this rider to whole life or endowment policies for an additional premium. It gives you the right to buy additional amounts of insurance at 3-year intervals up to a specified age without proof of insurability. The usual maximum age is 40. The amount of each additional purchase is usually equal to or less than the face amount of the original policy. If you buy a $10,000 ordinary life policy with the GIO rider at age 21, you can buy an additional $10,000 every three years thereafter to age 40 whether or not you have become uninsurable. By age 40, you would have a total of $70,000 ordinary life. The new insurance is issued at standard rates on the basis of your attained age when the option is exercised.

The details of this rider vary depending on the insurer, but they all follow the same general pattern. If the original policy has a waiver of premium provision and/or accidental death benefit, the new policies will have the same provisions if you want them. If premiums on your original policy are being waived, many insurers provide for the waiver of premium benefit automatically on additional insurance. Some insurers, however, offer a less liberal guaranteed insurability option with regard to waiver of premium. They may, for example, include waiver of premium in additional insurance only if premiums are not being waived for the original policy at the option date. Clearly, not all GIO's are the same; you must look before you buy.

INDUSTRIAL LIFE INSURANCE PROVISIONS

Many of the provisions in industrial policies are the same as those found in ordinary insurance which have been discussed above. There are some differences, however. Loan values are usually not provided because policy size and cash values are small. Assignment is prohibited except to banks as collateral for a loan. Death benefits are paid only in a lump sum because the face amount of the policy is small. Usually there are no dividend options, but dividends are automatically credited against future premiums or used to buy paid-up additions to the policy. The incontestable clause is usually for one year, rather than two, and there is no suicide clause. Provision is made for changing the plan from a weekly premium to a monthly premium, and some companies permit conversion to ordinary insurance.

Facility of Payment Clause

This clause provides for payment of the proceeds if the beneficiary named in the policy does not submit a claim within a specified period after the death of the insured, or if the beneficiary is the estate of the insured, or pre-deceases the insured, or is not legally competent. Payment may be made to the executor or administrator of the insured, or to a named beneficiary, or to any relative of the insured appearing to the company to be equitably entitled to the proceeds. The facility of payment clause makes possible a fair settlement without undue expense or delay which would not be justified by the relatively small amount of money usually involved.

Other Clauses

Industrial life insurance policies automatically include double indemnity for death by accidental means as well as a dismemberment provision similar to an accident policy. You may take the policy "on approval" for two weeks. If you do not want to keep it, your premium will be refunded in full.

Consumer Applications

Choosing Options
In a Life Insurance Policy

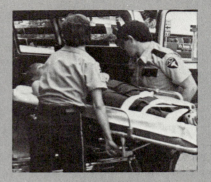

Three important choices you make when you buy a life insurance policy are:

1. Who should own the policy?
2. Which dividend option should you select?
3. Which settlement option should you choose?

Let's see how to make these decisions.

Who Should Own Your Policy?

When you buy a car or house, you give careful consideration to the matter of ownership. Should you own it? Should your spouse own it? Or should you own it jointly? In contrast, most people who buy life insurance almost automatically name themselves as policyowner. As we shall see when we discuss estate planning in Chapter 13, there may be situations in which consideration should be given to having someone other than yourself owner of the policy on your life.

One such situation is when you want to reduce the size of your taxable estate in order to reduce the burden of estate taxes. If you are the owner of life insurance in the amount of $100,000, when you die the proceeds of the policy go to your beneficiary but are considered part of your estate for purposes of determining the size of your taxable estate. On the other hand, if you are not the owner, the proceeds are not part of your estate for tax purposes. The difference this can make in your estate tax can be calculated by reference to Table 10-2. If your taxable estate without the insurance is zero, the tax is zero. But with the insurance proceeds included for tax purposes, the tax would be $18,200.

In most states, having your spouse be the owner of insurance on your life will accomplish this. In community property states, however, it will not affect your estate tax because you are both held to have a one-half interest in each other's property. (These states are listed in Figure 10-3). You need the help of your attorney to decide who should own the insurance on your life, but you should make the decision consciously rather than automatically.

Which Dividend Option?

If you have budget problems, you may be tempted to take policy dividends in cash. Before you make that choice, you should consider applying them toward payment of the premium, especially if you are paying premiums on a monthly basis. Why? Suppose the monthly premium is $19.13. Twelve payments equals $229.56. But, if you paid annually, the premium would be $216.83, a saving of $12.73 or 5½ percent. If your dividend is $141.38, the cash required to pay the annual premium is $75.45. If you can save $12.73 by paying out $75.45 annually, that's a return of almost 17 percent. Because dividends increase every year, your cash outlay will go down every year.

TABLE 10-2

*Federal Estate
Tax Rate
Schedule*

If the Amount Subject to Tax is:	The Tax* is:
Not over $10,000	18% of such amount
From $10,000 to $20,000	$1,800 plus 20% of amount over $10,000
From $20,000 to $40,000	$3,800 plus 22% of amount over $20,000
From $40,000 to $60,000	$8,200 plus 24% of amount over $40,000
From $60,000 to $80,000	$13,000 plus 26% of amount over $60,000
From $80,000 to $100,000	$18,200 plus 28% of amount over $80,000
From $100,000 to $150,000	$23,800 plus 30% of amount over $100,000
From $150,000 to $250,000	$38,800 plus 32% of amount over $150,000
From $250,000 to $500,000	$70,800 plus 34% of amount over $250,000
From $500,000 to $750,000	$155,800 plus 37% of amount over $500,000
From $750,000 to $1,000,000	$248,300 plus 39% of amount over $750,000
From $1,000,000 to $1,250,000	$345,800 plus 41% of amount over $1,000,000
From $1,250,000 to $1,500,000	$448,300 plus 43% of amount over $1,250,000
From $1,500,000 to $2,000,000	$555,800 plus 45% of amount over $1,500,000
From $2,000,000 to $2,500,000	$780,800 plus 49% of amount over $2,000,000
From $2,500,000 to $3,000,000	$1,025,800 plus 53% of amount over $2,500,000
From $3,000,000 to $3,500,000	$1,290,800 plus 57% of amount over $3,000,000
From $3,500,000 to $4,000,000	$1,575,800 plus 61% of amount over $3,500,000
From $4,000,000 to $4,500,000	$1,880,800 plus 65% of amount over $4,000,000
From $4,500,000 to $5,000,000	$2,205,800 plus 69% of amount over $4,500,000
Over $5,000,000	$2,550,800 plus 70% of amount over $5,000,000

*This amount is reduced by taxes paid on gifts made after 1976.

Source: Publication 448, *A Guide to Federal Estate and Gift Taxation 1979 Edition*, p. 26. Washington, DC: Department of the Treasury, Internal Revenue Service.

Arizona	Nebraska
California	New Mexico
Idaho	Texas
Louisiana	Washington

FIGURE 10-3

*Community
Property States*

Suppose you don't need the cash. Should you leave dividends to accumulate at interest? That depends on the interest rate the insurer pays on such deposits and your alternatives. If the insurer pays 3 percent on deposits and your savings bank pays 5 percent, don't leave money with the insurer. One advantage of leaving it with the insurer, of course, is the simple fact that if you don't see it, you won't spend it. You may, however, pay dearly for your lack of willpower.

Unless you have more life insurance than

you need or have a serious budget problem, you are probably better off to use the dividends to buy paid-up additions or one-year term. The better choice between the two depends on your situation. If you need protection *now*, buy one-year term. If you need it over a long period of time, buy paid-up additions. If you die soon, your spouse will be grateful if you bought term. If you live to a ripe old age, you will be pleased if you bought paid-up additions.

Which Settlement Option?

As noted earlier, most companies will permit a beneficiary to place cash proceeds under one of the other settlement options. Considering the circumstances in which cash life insurance proceeds may become available, however, it may be in the best interest of your dependents to select some other option and specify that it can be changed by the beneficiary. If you don't know what other choice to make, specify the interest option along with the right to make withdrawals, or change to another option. This avoids a situation in which a large sum of money is handed to someone unprepared to manage it.

Should the proceeds be left at interest? That depends upon the needs of the beneficiary and the interest rate paid. Your policy specifies the minimum rate to be paid but the current rate may be considerably higher. Therefore, when a comparison with alterna-

tives is made, it is necessary to find out what the insurer is currently paying. If the insurer pays 5 percent on deposits when 7 percent is readily available at no more risk, it would pay to move the money.

Should the proceeds be used to provide monthly income? Here again, the settlement options listed in your policy show the minimum income provided. If you are trying to help a friend make the choice, find out what is offered currently. Then compare it with alternatives.

What monthly income does the company offer the beneficiary? If the beneficiary is a female age 25, the minimum provided for each $1,000 of proceeds by one company for zero years certain (a pure annuity) is $2.89 per month. That is a rate of return of 3½ percent per annum. The same company provides a minimum of $5.02 per month for a female age 60, a rate of return of 6 percent. How do these returns compare with what can be obtained elsewhere?

When you look at alternatives, be sure they are truly comparable with the safety and service provided by the insurer. Remember that money left with the insurer is protected from creditors of the beneficiary. Moreover, the risk of losing the money is close to zero. This does not mean that large differences between what the insurer offers and what is available elsewhere should be disregarded. It does mean, however, that you should not risk a lot for a little, especially in a situation where a steady and certain income is at stake.

Discussion Questions

1. The premium on Bill Brown's policy was due September 1. On September 15, he mailed a check to the insurance company. On September 26, he died. When the insurance company presented the check to the bank for collection, it was re-

turned because there were insufficient funds in Bill's account. Does the company have to pay the claim presented by Bill's beneficiary? Why or why not?

2. Clancy knew he could not meet the physical requirements for insurability, so he had his twin brother, Clarence, take the physical examination in his place. A policy was issued, and three years later, Clancy died. The insurance company claim department manager learned that Clancy's twin took the examination in his place, and refused to pay the claim. Clancy's beneficiary sued the company for the proceeds, claiming that the contestable period had expired. Did the company have to pay? Why or why not?

3. If you name your spouse beneficiary of your life insurance irrevocably, you cannot change the designation without his or her consent. Should you get yourself into that situation? Please explain.

4. In view of the fact that you pay the premiums on a policy insuring your life, why would you name someone else the owner? What are the drawbacks with this arrangement?

5. In order to keep money in her savings account as long as possible, Lena L'Amour pays all her bills at the last possible moment. When you call the grace period in her life insurance policy to her attention, she decides to take advantage of it by paying the monthly premium two days prior to the end of the grace period every month. Do you think this is a good idea? Why or why not?

6. If you burn your house down, the fire insurance company will refuse to pay for it. If you commit suicide after your life insurance policy has been in force for two years, however, the insurer will pay the face amount to your beneficiary. Isn't this a departure from the concept that insurance is to pay for fortuitous losses? Please explain.

7. Many people think it is ridiculous to buy a life insurance policy without the waiver of premium rider. Do you agree? Why or why not?

8. People buy life insurance because they don't know when they may die or what may cause their death. In spite of the fact that accidental death benefits are paid only when death is caused by accident, however, the accidental death benefit rider has great sales appeal. How do you account for this apparent inconsistency in the way people make decisions?

9. If you don't need life insurance now but realize you may need it sometime in the future, would you be interested in buying a Guaranteed Insurability Option, if it was available, without buying a policy now? Please explain.

10. Some life insurance agents urge young people to buy a policy now even if they don't need it because, "you may not be able to buy it later and, even if you can, it will cost more." Is this reasoning valid? Why or why not?

Cases

10-1 An agent from Horizontal Life Insurance Company, a company with the slogan, "For level-headed protection—see us," recently contacted you for an appointment. During this appointment, Mr. Keen Been, the agent, introduced you to a feature of their ordinary life contract, that, if you chose now, would automatically increase your life insurance protection each year no matter what your physical condition. Mr. Been indicated that this was not the case with his competitor's policy from "that nonparticipating stock company." You find this a strong selling point for Mr. Been's company.

1. What is Mr. Been describing?

2. Is this feature unique to his company?

3. Is what Mr. Been said about his competitor's nonparticipating policy true?

10-2 Your friend recently purchased a life insurance policy with a "triple indemnity" clause. She was very happy with this purchase as she noted to you when she said, "This policy is really great! I have three times as much insurance with this policy as I would have with a regular policy with just a little extra premium. The policy has a 'savings' plan and is paid up in twenty years. If I die due to an accident while a paying passenger on an airplane, bus, train, or ship it will pay three times the face amount. If some other type of accident takes my life, it pays twice the face amount. This is good insurance for me as I need all the protection I can get for my five children."

1. What do you think of her decision to purchase this type of life insurance?

2. Is this coverage unique?

10-3 Therese Thomas misstated her age on her application for life insurance, saying that she was 25 when she really was 28. After three years, she died of injuries from a fall when riding a horse. When her sister, the beneficiary, submitted proof of death to the insurer, the insurer denied coverage, but offered to return all premiums paid in, plus interest. The sister is considering bringing suit against the insurer, contending that the incontestable clause prevents the insurer from denying liability.

1. Is the sister right? Explain.

2. Is the insurer right? Explain.

3. How much should the beneficiary receive?

10-4 The insured has an accidental death benefit rider on his life insurance policy. Discuss why you think this rider will or will not pay his beneficiary in each of the following situations.

1. The insured dies from a fall through a dormitory window on the tenth floor. His room is locked from the inside, and the window has no ledge outside the frame. There is no suicide note.

2. The insured dies in a single-car automobile accident, on a clear day and with no apparent mechanical malfunction in the vehicle. He has been very depressed about his job and has undergone therapy with a counselor, during which he discussed suicide; however, there is no note.

3. The insured contracts pneumonia after he is hospitalized from injuries received from a fall from a ladder while rescuing Mrs. Thames' cat from a tree. He dies of the pneumonia thirty days after the fall.

Chapter Eleven:
HEALTH INSURANCE

INTRODUCTION

The health risk is like the life risk in that neither can be avoided. Good health maintenance programs reduce the probability of poor health but do not eliminate the risk. Poor health has a twofold financial impact on the individual or family: it increases expenses and reduces (or stops) earned income. Health insurance provides protection against the risks of unplanned medical expense and loss of income.

The following aspects of health insurance are discussed in this chapter:

1. Medical expense coverages

2. Income coverages

3. Limited contracts

4. Health insurance policy provisions.

MEDICAL EXPENSE COVERAGES

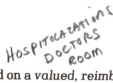

Medical expense benefits may be provided on a *valued, reimbursement,* or *service* basis.

On a valued basis, the insurer agrees to pay a specified amount of money upon the occurrence of a specified event, such as $100 per week while you are confined to a hospital. Whether you use the money to pay the hospital or replace lost income is not specified.

The reimbursement basis applies the principle of indemnity by providing payment for loss, such as hospital expense, within specified

limits and for specified causes. You would receive, for example, up to but not exceeding $100 per day while confined to a hospital to pay for your hospital room and board. If the cost was $76 per day, the insurer would pay $76 per day. If it was $150 per day, the insurer would pay only $100 per day.

On the other hand, with a policy providing service benefits the insurer arranges for specified services rather than the payment of money. If you pay for part of these services, they are referred to as partial service benefits. If you pay no additional charge beyond the premium, they are called service benefits.

Blue Cross plans provide service benefits. The coverage you select is a matter of the type of service you want; i.e., ward, semi-private room, or private room. If you enter a nonmember hospital,[1] a stated dollar allowance is payable toward the cost for room and board.

The basic forms of medical expense protection are hospital, surgical, and medical insurance. They are limited in terms of the types of services (or expenditure reimbursement) provided as well as the dollar limits of protection. As Figure 11-1 shows, these forms provide first-dollar coverage instead of protection against large losses. Major medical and comprehensive insurance deal with this risk.

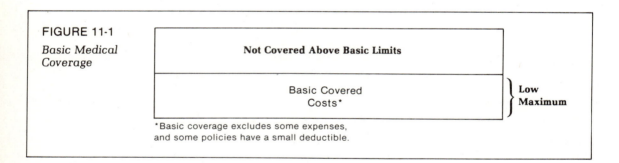

FIGURE 11-1

*Basic Medical
Coverage*

Not Covered Above Basic Limits

Basic Covered
Costs*

} Low
Maximum

*Basic coverage excludes some expenses,
and some policies have a small deductible.

Hospital Insurance

The basic hospital policy covers you, your spouse, and unmarried children (to age 18 or 21). It provides for room and board, some nursing service, and hospital extras. Private nurse expense can be covered for additional premium.

Hospital extras are the extra charges incurred while in the hospital which are not included in board and room, such as use of the operating room, anesthetics, x-rays, drugs, laboratory charges, and physiotherapy. These charges may be covered on a schedule basis, such as $25 for x-rays, and so on, or on a blanket basis with a maximum limit for all such charges. The blanket basis is more liberal than a schedule of amounts for each item. Some policies specify a limit within which full reimbursement is provided and a second higher limit within which there is partial reimbursement.

---

1. One which does not belong to a Blue Cross plan.

Maternity coverage requires additional premium. It is expressed as a flat amount or a multiple of the daily room and board benefit. Blue Cross plans, on the other hand, make full-service maternity benefits available, some for a limited number of days, some without limit, and others on a reimbursement basis up to a stated maximum amount.

Exclusions specify the circumstances under which benefits are not provided. Typically, in order to avoid duplication, coverage is not provided when workers' compensation benefits are received. Aviation injuries are excluded unless sustained as a fare-paying passenger on a scheduled airline. Injuries sustained in attempted suicide while sane are excluded. Expense related to pregnancy is excluded unless maternity benefits have been purchased. Mental disorders are not covered, nor are a series of such ailments as appendicitis, heart disease, and so on, unless they occur at least 90 days after the inception of the policy. An insured is not covered while on military duty, and benefits are not payable to anyone eligible for services provided by a hospital owned or operated by the federal government. Injury caused by war or enemy action is excluded.

Many policies have a small deductible, such as $25 or $50, in order to reduce claims and premiums.

Surgical Insurance

Benefits under this form of insurance are usually paid according to a schedule of surgical procedures. The policy lists the maximum benefit for each type of operation covered. Sometimes the benefit is stated as reimbursement up to the "usual and customary" surgical charges in the region where the operation is performed. Usually offered in combination with a hospital expense policy, this coverage applies whether surgery is performed in a hospital or in a doctor's office. It usually excludes occupational injury and disease to the extent that benefits are provided by workers' compensation.

Medical Insurance

This insurance covers all or part of doctors' fees for hospital, office, or home visits other than for surgical services. *Benefit payments are made on three bases:* (1) in-hospital, (2) total disability, or (3) non-disability.

In-hospital medical provides payment for visits by a physician only while you are confined to a hospital as an in-patient. Some policies have an over-all limit of a daily rate multiplied by the number of days in the hospital while others simply have a daily limit or a limit per visit.

Total disability medical covers physicians' charges whether or not you are in the hospital so long as you are totally disabled. It is usually written only for employed persons because of the problem of determining whether or not a person who is not employed is totally disabled. Some policies apply a deductible of one or more visits when you are not hospitalized.

Non-disability medical pays physicians' fees for home, office, or hospital visits. It commonly has a deductible. Most medical insurance policies pay benefits on a reimbursement basis up to the limit provided.

Common exclusions from medical insurance coverage are pregnancy, childbirth, dental work, eye examinations, x-rays, drugs, and so on, as well as treatment in or from a government hospital for which no charge is made. Group medical insurance usually excludes injury for which workers' compensation benefits are payable.

Non-disability medical pays physicians' fees whenever you need medical services. In contrast, in-hospital and total disability medical provide protection only under specified circumstances. But, if you are injured or ill, you may need a doctor even if you are not hospitalized or totally disabled. Unless you have non-disability medical coverage, you cannot be sure that unplanned medical costs will be covered.

MAJOR MEDICAL AND COMPREHENSIVE INSURANCE

The hospital, surgical, and medical expense insurance policies discussed above are basic contracts in the sense that they provide for many of the expenses caused by poor health but on a somewhat selective basis and within rather narrow limits. They are weak in the breadth of their coverage as well as their maximum benefit limits. Two approaches have been made to correct this weakness: (1) major medical insurance, and (2) comprehensive medical insurance.

Major Medical Insurance

This insurance covers almost all medical expense. It provides for virtually all charges made by both hospital and doctor, including the benefits of hospital, surgical, and medical insurance and in addition such expenses as drugs, medicines, blood, plasma, and similar items. Some policies require hospital admission at some time during the course of treatment in order for coverage to apply but others cover whatever is ordered by a physician regardless of where performed. Common exclusions are expenses covered by other insurance, pregnancy, childbirth, dental expenses, injuries or sickness covered by workers' compensation, mental illness,[2] war and military service, self-inflicted injuries, and so on.

Major medical policies have four fundamental features:

1. High maximum limits

2. A large deductible

3. Broad coverage

4. Percentage participation. *80/20 PERCENT*

Maximum limits vary upward from $10,000 per person. In some cases they are unlimited. The limit applies to the total amount the insurer may pay. It may apply to each injury or illness separately, or to a policy year, a benefit year, a calendar year, or to the total of all payments to a claimant during his or her lifetime.[3]

---

2. Many group contracts cover mental illness but with internal limits.

3. A policy year is from one anniversary date of the policy to the next. A benefit year begins at the inception of a disability and runs for the succeeding twelve months.

As Figure 11-2 shows, the deductible is large, ranging from $300 to $750. Its purpose is to eliminate small claims, thus making possible high limits and broad coverage at a reasonable premium rate. Amounts paid by basic policies are counted toward the deductible.[4]

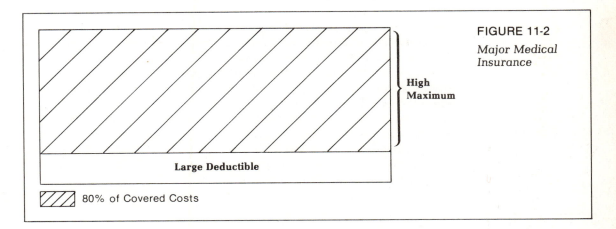

FIGURE 11-2

Major Medical Insurance

High Maximum

Large Deductible

80% of Covered Costs

The percentage participation clause requires you to pay some portion of expense in excess of the deductible. It may vary from 10 to 30 percent; 20 percent is common. Its function is to encourage you to keep expenses as low as possible by making you bear part of the burden.[5]

If you are covered by a major medical policy with a $300 deductible, a 20 percent participation clause, and a $50,000 limit, hospital and medical expense of $2,300 would be allocated as follows:

Total bill	$2,300
Deductible	300
Balance	$2,000
Insurer pays 80% of excess over deductible	$1,600
You pay 20% of excess over deductible	$ 400
You pay deductible	$ 300
Total you pay	$ 700

4. Group major medical contracts may have a smaller deductible known as a "corridor deductible" under which basic contract benefits may not be counted toward the deductible. You have to pay the deductible after your basic contract benefits are exhausted before the major medical begins to pay.

5. Because you have little or no control over some medical expenses, this statement may seem ridiculous. Studies have shown, however, that such cost-sharing reduces the utilization of health care services.

Premiums for major medical are influenced by family size, the size of the deductible, the maximum limit, and the percentage of participation. If you can bear the burden of smaller hospital and medical bills or a part of larger bills, major medical provides excellent protection against a financial catastrophe caused by illness or injury.

Comprehensive Insurance

As the example of allocation of expense under a major medical policy illustrates, most of the burden is borne by the insurer but that which remains with you may be sizeable. As illustrated in Figure 11-3, comprehensive insurance deals with this problem by providing a smaller deductible and lesser participation (or none at all) while retaining the other features of major medical. Some comprehensive policies reduce the deductible to $25 or $50 with a 20 percent participation and a maximum of $10,000 or more. Others eliminate the deductible and provide for participation only on that portion of the expense of a disability in excess of a specified amount, such as $250.

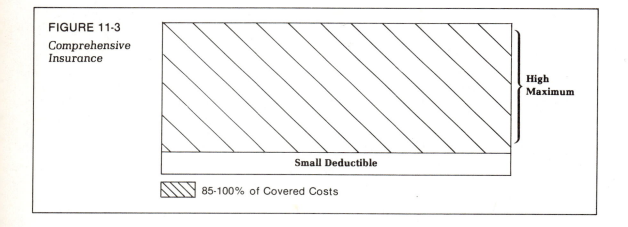

FIGURE 11-3
*Comprehensive
Insurance*

High Maximum

Small Deductible

85-100% of Covered Costs

Comprehensive coverage is more expensive than major medical and is usually sold on a group basis. It is compared with major medical in Table 11-1.

DENTAL INSURANCE *omit*

Except for fractures or dislocations of the jaw or injuries to natural teeth which qualify as an eligible expense under major medical policies, the medical expense policies just discussed do not cover dental expenses. Dental coverage, however, is available through insurance company group plans, prepayment plans, and dental service corporations.

Dental insurance pays for normal diagnostic, preventive, restorative, and orthodontic service as well as that required because of accidents. Some employee group plans pay all costs on a first-dollar basis,

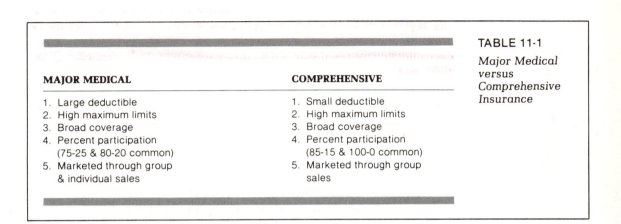

MAJOR MEDICAL	COMPREHENSIVE	TABLE 11-1
1. Large deductible	1. Small deductible	*Major Medical versus Comprehensive Insurance*
2. High maximum limits	2. High maximum limits	
3. Broad coverage	3. Broad coverage	
4. Percent participation (75-25 & 80-20 common)	4. Percent participation (85-15 & 100-0 common)	
5. Marketed through group & individual sales	5. Marketed through group sales	

but the bulk of such insurance involves a deductible and participation. Deductibles are generally $25 to $50 and participation ranges from 20 to 25 percent except for orthodontic service, which may be written on a 50/50 basis. Maximum payments for each person covered are specified on an annual and lifetime basis, such as $1,000 in any one year and $50,000 in any lifetime. There is, however, considerable variation in the way maximum payment is specified. Usual exclusions are dental services for purely cosmetic purposes and losses caused by war and occupational injuries or sickness.

DISABILITY INCOME COVERAGES

Insurance to protect against income loss is provided by the life insurance riders discussed in Chapter 10 and separate disability income contracts. In addition to this protection, persons whose disability arises out of and in the course of employment receive income benefits through the workers' compensation law of the state where they are employed. Workers in five states and one territory receive income benefits provided by compulsory nonoccupational disability insurance programs.[6] The Social Security program includes income for disabled workers who meet the eligibility requirements.[7]

---

6. California, Hawaii, New Jersey, New York, Rhode Island and Puerto Rico.

7. Workers' Compensation and Social Security are discussed in Chapters 19 and 12, respectively.

Disability income contracts provide income while you are totally or, in some policies, partially disabled. They vary with regard to the definition of disability, the cause of disability, the amount of income provided, the benefit duration, and the waiting period.

Disability Defined

Total disability may be defined as "complete inability of the insured to perform any and every duty pertaining to his occupation" or "complete inability of the insured to engage in any reasonably gainful occupation for which he is or may become fitted by education, training or experience." The first definition is, of course, more liberal than the second because it refers to *his* occupation rather than to *any* occupation. Some policies combine the two definitions, using the first to satisfy the requirement for total disability during an initial specified period (e.g., two years) of disability and defining total disability in terms of the second thereafter.

Generally, total and irrecoverable loss of sight of both eyes or loss of two or more limbs establishes total disability.

When sickness benefits for total disability are payable for an extended period, some policies define total disability in terms of confinement to the home or, in some cases, to the hospital.[8]

Partial disability is even more difficult to define than total disability. It is usually measured in terms of your inability to perform some of the important duties of your job. One policy defines it as "the inability of the insured to perform one or more, but not all, the important daily duties pertaining to his occupation."

Cause of Disability

Some contracts provide income benefits for disability caused by accident only; others for both accident and sickness. In either case, whether a disabling injury qualifies you for accident benefits depends upon how injury is defined in the policy. Two definitions are used:

1. Accidental bodily injury

2. Bodily injury by accidental means.

The first definition is broad; only the result need be accidental. The second, in contrast, requires that both result and means be accidental. You may strain your back lifting a heavy object. The injury is accidental but the means is not. You did just what you intended to do. Another case: while lifting a heavy object you slip on a wet floor and that causes a strained back. Both result (back strain) and means (slip on wet floor) are accidental.

Because of the difference in benefits, it is necessary to distinguish between losses caused by accident and those caused by sickness. One approach to this is the provision that losses resulting from injuries must start within 90 days after the injury. Loss resulting from injuries which

---

8. Definitions of total disability vary more among health insurance policies than they do among life insurance policies.

begin after the 90-day period are deemed to have resulted from sickness.

Moreover, a loss is not considered to be caused by accident unless it results "directly and independently of all other causes." This provision is designed to eliminate from the definition of accidental bodily injury those which are actually caused by illness or disease. For example, a person who suffers a heart attack and is injured when he or she falls to the ground would not qualify for accident benefits but would qualify for sickness benefits.

Pre-existing conditions are excluded from individual policies[9] by the statement that insurance is provided for "loss resulting from sickness contracted and first treated by a physician while this policy is in force..." In some policies, a *probationary period* is included by referring to "sickness contracted and causing loss commencing after the first fourteen days from the date of this policy." The purpose of these clauses is to avoid paying sickness benefits to a person who was sick before buying the insurance.

Amount of Benefit

Some contracts state the amount of the benefit in terms of dollars per week or month, while others (especially group coverage) state it as a percentage of your basic salary. In either case, the insurer is wary of having the benefit equal to anything approaching 100 percent of your salary. Typically, the amount is limited to around two-thirds of earned income. The purpose of this limitation is to reduce moral hazard. If insureds received a benefit equal to 90 or 100 percent of their weekly or monthly earnings, some of them may be inclined to fake disability. This would, of course, result in benefit payments in excess of those expected by the insurer.

Benefits for sickness are not as generous as those for accident. For example, a policy may provide benefit payments for five years if disability is caused by accident, but only two years if caused by sickness. Some long-term policies pay to age 65 for sickness but for life when the cause of disability is accident.

Some policies pay no benefits if the sickness or accident is work connected and you receive workers' compensation benefits. Such policies are called *nonoccupational*. Benefits for partial disability are usually paid only for disability caused by accident and, in some policies, only following a period of total disability.

The *average earnings* or *coordination of benefits* clause is designed to deal with the problem of overinsurance which may occur when a person has more than one policy. For example, a person whose salary is $1,000 per month may have two disability income policies, each of which provides $600 per month income benefits. In the event of total disability, he or she would lose $1,000 per month salary but receive $1,200 per month insurance benefits. Such a situation may lead to bene-

---

9. But not from group policies.

fit payments greater than those anticipated when the premium rate was established.

The average earnings clause provides for a reduction in benefit payments if the total amount of income payments under all insurance policies covering the loss exceeds your earnings at the time disability commenced or your average earnings for two years preceding disability, whichever is greater. The amount of the reduction is the proportion by which all benefits would have to be reduced in order to prevent total benefits from exceeding average earned income. In the illustration above, for example, total insurance exceeded income by one-fifth, in which case the benefits of each policy containing an average earnings clause would be reduced by one-sixth. A reduction of the payment provided by each policy from $600 to $500 per month would eliminate the excess.

If you have several policies, some of which do not have an average earnings clause, you may still receive income benefits in excess of your average earnings. Even if all policies have such a clause, you may receive benefit payments equal to your average earnings and find it profitable to be disabled. Benefit payments escape some or all taxes and you avoid expenses connected with your job, such as transportation, while you are not working. Nevertheless, the average earnings clause is a step in the direction of solving the problem of overinsurance.

Benefit Duration

Short-term policies are those with benefits payable up to two years; long-term plans have benefits payable for longer periods, such as 5 years, 10 years, or to retirement age. Some short-term policies have benefit periods as short as 13 weeks. Because most disabilities are of relatively short duration, long-term benefits do not cost proportionately more than short-term. From your point of view, the longer term policy is preferable because it protects you against an unbearable risk.

Waiting Period

Benefit payments start a specified length of time after you become disabled. This prevents "first-dollar" coverage and puts the burden of small losses on you. It also reduces the number of claims and, therefore, the cost of the coverage. In short-term contracts, the waiting period may be from a few days to two weeks. For long-term contracts, it varies from 30 to as long as 180 days. In some contracts, the waiting period applies only when disability is caused by sickness; benefits for disability caused by accident begin immediately.[10]

---

10. Why should the time benefits start depend upon the cause of your disability? Because it is easier to determine if you are injured than if you are sick. If you say, "I am disabled because of a broken leg," the insurer can have a doctor examine you and determine if your leg is broken. If you say, "I am disabled because I am sick," there is no way to determine objectively if you are. But, if you are confined to bed at home or in a hospital and under a doctor's care for 30 days (or whatever the waiting period is) the insurer has some evidence that you are disabled by sickness.

The health insurance contracts discussed so far do not cover all possible causes of disability and many leave serious gaps in protection. They are generally rather broad, however, in the sense that the benefits provided become available when you are disabled by injury as a result of any cause not excluded or sickness of whatever nature. Thus, all perils not excluded are covered and, for the most part, the exclusions are not numerous. Limited contracts, on the other hand, provide benefits only for specified illness or injury and, in the case of the latter, only when the injury resulted from specified causes and/or under specified circumstances. Benefits may be on a reimbursement basis for medical expense, or disability income, or a lump-sum payment.

The variety of limited contracts is the one aspect of such contracts which seems to be the least limited. A brief description of a few of them may illustrate their general nature.

The dread disease policy, which originated as the polio policy prior to the development of an effective vaccine for polio, provides for reimbursement of a broad range of medical expenses to a high limit if you contract one of the diseases listed. The diseases included are low in frequency but high in severity, such as cancer. The sale of cancer policies has increased rapidly in recent years.

Other limited contracts provide lump-sum payments or disability income for accidental injury or death under specified circumstances. The aviation ticket policy, for example, provides benefits for accidental death, dismemberment, or loss of sight; plus medical expense reimbursement, if death or injury is caused by an aviation accident during a specified trip. A ticket accident policy covers all types of travel accidents for a specified period of time—usually short. Automobile accident policies provide benefits for accidental injury related to riding in or operating an automobile. Some insurers issue annual travel accident contracts which provide protection against accidental injury or death during travel for a year at a time, thus eliminating purchase of coverage for each separate trip. They may cover all travel, or automobile or aviation travel.

Limited accident contracts require what appear to be relatively low premiums but provide highly specialized coverage. If the right kind of injury results from the right cause at the right time, benefits are payable. The needs of the family for expense reimbursement and income replacement are the same, however, regardless of the exact nature and timing of the cause of disability. Limited contracts may lead to a false sense of security if you do not appreciate their limitations. They are not a substitute for more expensive but broader protection such as that discussed earlier.

HEALTH INSURANCE POLICY PROVISIONS

Some of the provisions in health insurance policies were discussed in this chapter. Several others are similar to those in life insurance policies, such as the grace period, incontestable,[11] reinstatement, and assignment clauses, which were discussed in Chapter 10. Three provisions which have not been discussed previously are the exclusions, the change of occupation clause, and the continuance provisions.

Exclusions

Most group policies and some individual policies, such as the more liberal disability income, have very few exclusions. Exclusions vary from one policy to another depending upon the nature of the benefits and the circumstances under which they are to be provided. The following are typical: war or act of war, military service, intentionally self-inflicted injury, certain aviation activities, and disability for which workers' compensation benefits are payable. Some limited policies have such a lengthy list of exclusions that it is sometimes rather difficult to imagine a situation under which benefits are payable.

Change of Occupation

This clause is commonly included in contracts designed for sale to persons whose occupations are generally not hazardous. It provides that if you change to a more hazardous occupation than the one you had at the time you applied for insurance, the benefits are reduced to those which the premium you are paying would provide. The clause is similar in effect to the operation of the misstatement of age clause in a life insurance policy. If you change to a less hazardous occupation, however, benefits are not increased but the premium is reduced.

Continuation Provisions

You do not have to pay the next premium due on your health insurance policy but it will not continue in force unless you do. If you decide it is not the best policy for you, all you have to do is ignore the premium notice. But, suppose you are satisfied with the policy and are willing to pay the premium. What guarantee do you have that it can be kept in force? The answer depends on the continuance provision.

Individual health insurance policies (including both medical and income coverages) handle continuance in six different ways:

1. No provision.

2. Cancellable by the insurer at any time.

3. Cancellable only on an anniversary date or date on which the premium is due.

4. Conditionally renewable.

5. Guaranteed renewable.

6. Noncancellable.

---

11. In health insurance policies, the incontestable clause is labelled "time limit on certain defenses."

No provision. The policy simply terminates upon expiration of its term. This is like a five-year term life insurance policy. After it has been in force for five years, it expires. If you want more coverage, you have to buy another policy.

Cancellable by the insurer at any time. With this provision, the policy does not have a term. It simply remains in force as long as you are willing to pay the premium and the insurer is willing to accept it. You don't know from one day to the next if you will have coverage.

Cancellable only on an anniversary date or date on which the premium is due. If the anniversary date is January 1 and premiums are paid annually, you can be sure of having coverage for one year. If premiums are paid monthly, however, you can be sure for only a month at a time. If they are paid weekly, you can be sure for only a week at a time. If they were paid daily . . . Well, you get the idea.

Conditionally renewable. The insurer can terminate the policy only on an anniversary date and only under circumstances specified in the policy. The policy may provide, for example, that the insurer can terminate coverage when you retire. Or, it can refuse to renew all policies of the kind you have in the state. This means the company can't pick on you as an individual but it can eliminate you and all the rest of the insureds who have a policy the same as yours. If you have too many claims, the only way the insurer can get rid of you is to terminate all insureds with your type of policy in the state.

On the other hand, even if you have never filed a claim but loss experience with the rest of the policyholders who have policies like yours has been bad, you may be dumped with all the rest. "Misery likes company," but you will still have to find another health insurance policy to replace the one that was terminated. If you are old or ill, that may be difficult.

Guaranteed renewable. The insurer agrees that you have the right to continue the policy in force for a substantial period of time—to age 65, for example. The insurer has no right to make any changes *except* in the premium rate for a class of insureds. The insurer can change the premium rate for all insureds of a certain age, or in a certain territory, or a particular policy form. It cannot change your premium and leave unchanged all others in your classification. It cannot, in other words, pick on individuals. Whatever happens to the class will happen to you. No more. No less.

Noncancellable. You have the right to continue your policy in force for a substantial period of time—to age 65, for example—by paying premiums when due. The insurer has no right to make any changes. The premium may be level or it may increase according to a schedule included in the policy. Thus, the policy may be like level premium term life insurance to age 65 or it may be like annual renewable term life insurance to age 65. This is the best continuance provision and it is the most expensive. The purpose of insurance is to reduce uncertainty and this provision eliminates any uncertainty about your power to keep the coverage in force.

Consumer Applications
Buying Medical Expense Insurance

You may buy basic hospital-medical expense insurance or major medical. Or, you may buy both. But, there are hundreds of such policies on the market. How do you make a choice?

Buying Basic Hospital-Medical Insurance

Buying hospital-medical insurance is about like buying a car. If you simply look at a number of policies, you will be confused about how to compare their benefits and cost. While no checklist can cover every conceivable aspect of an insurance contract, even a simple one can be helpful. It will help you identify features of major importance so you can look at them first. After you evaluate them, you can look at other provisions to see if they are comparable with other contracts.

Figure 11-4 provides some guidelines for you to follow in evaluating proposals for a basic policy. The daily hospital benefit usually refers to the maximum payable for a semi-private room. You can determine the amount you need by calling a local hospital or the state hospital association for rates in your area. If a policy does not indicate a semi-private room, ask the agent to specify in writing what type of room is being quoted. The maximum benefit period can be as little as 30 days or as much as two years. The longer the maximum stay, the higher the premium, but the increase is not proportional. Miscellaneous hospital expense is usually a specified sum multiplied by the number of days you stay in the hospital.

Surgical expense is subject to maximum limits listed in a schedule of surgical procedures, not exceeding usual and customary charges. If the limit you select is too low to cover usual and customary charges, you will have to pay the difference. Amounts listed for

1. Daily hospital benefit . . . . Maximum per day	$ _____	FIGURE 11-4
(Maximum benefit period _____ days)		*Basic Hospital-*
2. Miscellaneous hospital expense . . . . Maximum	$ _____	*Medical*
3. Surgical expense . . . . Schedule max.	$ _____	*Insurance*
4. Inpatient medical expense . . . . Per day	$ _____	*Checklist*
5. Outpatient medical expense . . . . Maximum	$ _____	
6. Deductible	$ _____	
7. Supplemental benefits premium	$ _____	
8. Covered persons?	$ _____	
9. Continuation provision?	$ _____	
10. Total Annual Premium	$ _____	

inpatient and outpatient medical expense provide benefits equal to the charges for service, not exceeding usual and customary charges. The number of days for which inpatient medical expense is paid may be less than the maximum number of days hospital benefit provided.

You may want supplemental benefits added to the basic policy, depending upon what is excluded. For example, the policy may exclude pregnancy benefits, private nursing benefits, or other benefits you want. If such is the case, you want to know how much will be added to the annual premium.

Three other items are of crucial importance. First, how much is the deductible? Does it apply to different benefits separately or as a group? Second, who is covered? If you have dependents, you may want benefits for them. Third, what is the continuance provision? Is the policy guaranteed renewable with premium rates subject to change? Or, is it non-cancellable? If the latter, is the annual premium level or will it increase according to a schedule?

A checklist helps you to decide what you should have. It can also be used to evaluate the policies an agent shows you. Unless the various policies provide similar kinds and amounts of coverages, however, it is very difficult to compare cost. Instead of attempting that, you are better off to create simple specifications based on the checklist. Then shop for policies that meet those specifications just as you do when you shop for a car. The following is a sample specification:

Daily hospital benefit (semi-private)	$100
Maximum benefit period	365 days
Miscellaneous hospital expense	$500
Surgical expense	$750 maximum
Inpatient medical expense per day	$ 25
Outpatient medical expense	$100
Deductible	$100
Guaranteed annual renewable	

If you go to your agent, broker, or company office and say, "This is what I want," some of them will show you policies they think are better than what you want but don't fit your specifications. Others, however, will respond to your request as best they can. The result will be several policies similar enough so you can compare costs. Cost isn't everything, but if you want to compare several policies that have most of the features you want, it's a good place to start. After you identify the policies that fit your needs and your budget, you can compare some of the details of the benefits in arriving at a choice. If you follow this procedure, you will come closer to getting what you need than you will if you try to shop without a checklist.

Buying Major Medical Insurance

An ideal major medical policy has the following features:

1. High maximum limits
2. Large deductible
3. Percentage participation
4. Broad coverage.

When you read this list, you think a major medical policy would cover virtually any medical expense. Some policies, however, reduce coverage with internal limits and exclusions (sometimes called exceptions). A classic example of internal limits is a surgical schedule like the one in a basic policy. It places dollar limits on surgical procedures and further limits payment by requiring that charges be "usual and customary." Another method to limit coverage is to list "eligible medical expenses." This restricts payment to items listed, which is the opposite of what you think of as broad coverage. So when you shop for a major medical policy, beware of limitations on the coverage.

When you find a policy that provides truly broad coverage, it is worthwhile to determine the price of the policy with various maximum benefit amounts and various deductible-participation combinations. Then select the combination which offers you adequate maximum benefits, broad coverage, and a reasonable cost-retention tradeoff. The format shown in Figure 11-5 may help you to compare policies. Simply use a copy of the form for each policy and each maximum benefit per person (or family, if that's the way the maximum applies.)

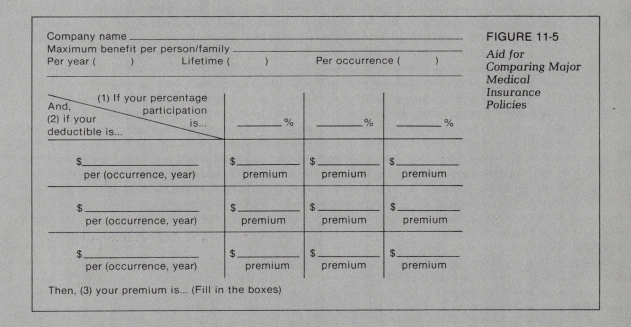

FIGURE 11-5

*Aid for
Comparing Major
Medical
Insurance
Policies*

Discussion Questions

1. Moral hazard is a much greater problem in health insurance than in life insurance. Why?

2. How have health insurers attempted to cope with moral hazard? Do these efforts add to the complexity of health insurance policies? Should they be restricted? Please explain.

3. When you buy health insurance, the greater the benefits the higher the premium. And the better the continuation provision, the greater the cost. If you can't afford the best coverage *and* the best continuation provision, should you choose less coverage or a less desirable continuation provision? Please explain.

4. Common exclusions in dental insurance are dental services for purely cosmetic purposes and losses caused by war and occupational injuries or sickness. How can these exclusions be justified?

5. Which do you prefer, the valued, reimbursement, or service basis for providing medical expense benefits? Why?

6. What is meant by the statement: "The benefits of a disability income policy are no better than the definition of disability"?

7. Do you think it is fair to have a more restrictive definition of total disability for sickness in a disability income policy than for disability caused by accident? After all, if you are disabled and can't work, you need income replacement regardless of the cause of your disability. Please explain.

8. Blue Cross-Blue Shield plans provide benefits on a service basis but many plans pay only the "usual and customary" fee for a doctor's services. If the doctor charges more than the "usual and customary" fee, you have to pay the difference. Do you think this is fair? Please explain.

9. The "change of occupation" clause in a health insurance policy is similar in effect to the "misstatement of age" clause in a life insurance policy. What is the purpose of these clauses? Are they fair? Explain.

10. Measured by the portion of the premium paid out in benefits to policyholders, many cancer insurance policies are a terrible rip-off. Nevertheless, the sale of cancer insurance has grown rapidly in recent years. How do you account for this? Do you think the sale of such policies should be prohibited or restricted in any way? Please explain.

Cases

11-1 Carl Stack, your friend from high school, is trying to decide what is the best health insurance policy to buy. He has offers for a cancer policy for a low premium each year, a major medical policy for a higher premium, and a hospital policy for a premium which falls midway between the premiums for the other two. All policies are noncancellable until his age 65.

   1. Discuss the major features which will affect Carl's decision. Explain what you would look for, and why.

   2. Which product would you choose, if you were to buy only one and had a limited—but adequate—budget to work with?

11-2 Bob Watson has a long-term disability income health insurance contract, and he is disabled. After the 60-day waiting period, Bob begins receiving the $600 per month in benefits. Although this is less than his pre-disability income of $900 per month, he is able to get along quite nicely.

After two years, the insurer tells him that it is stopping payment under the contract.

1. Why might the insurer stop payments after two years?

2. What might Bob do to receive payments again?

11-3 Jane has the following medical expense insurance: (1) a policy she purchased when she was a single college student, (2) a policy covering her as a member of the group where she is employed, and (3) a policy covering her husband and his family, under his employer's group insurance contract.

1. How might you expect these policies to coordinate her medical expense benefits, if all of them have a coordination of benefits provision?

2. What would happen if the policy she purchased as a student has no coordination of benefits provision?

3. Is there a danger of violation of the concept of indemnity here?

11-4 Joanne's group disability income policy has a coordination of benefits provision which offsets, dollar-for-dollar, all benefits for disability which she receives from any governmental or group-related insurance contract. This policy would pay two-thirds of her predisability pay, or $800 per month—since she makes $1,200 per month—before any offset. Jane also has an individual disability income policy which pays $200 per month in the event she is disabled.

1. If she is disabled on the job so that she is eligible to receive $400 per month from workers' compensation and $300 per month from social security, how much will she receive from the group disability income contract? Will this be the total she receives? If not, what will the total be?

2. How would this change if she were earning $1,800 per month, with two-thirds of that the group benefit, but with none of the other figures changed?

Chapter Twelve:

LIFE AND HEALTH INSURANCE PROVIDED BY SOCIAL SECURITY

INTRODUCTION

Thus far we have identified and evaluated the major life and health risks to which a family is exposed and examined the voluntary methods available for handling the economic losses caused by death, disability, and old age. In the next chapter, we will show how the technique of risk management can be used to analyze the needs created by premature death, disability, or old age and establish a framework within which to protect the family against these risks. Prior to the discussion of managing life and health risks, however, it will be helpful to become familiar with Social Security, our largest involuntary life and health insurance program.

Social Security provides income continuation in the event of death, disability, or retirement. It also provides medical expense benefits for disabled or retired persons and specified dependents. We discuss the following aspects of the program in this chapter:

1. What "Social Security" means

2. Who is covered

3. Persons eligible for benefits

4. Types of benefits

5. Amount of benefits

6. How benefits are financed

7. How Social Security is administered.

WHAT "SOCIAL SECURITY" MEANS

Communication problems often develop because our language is replete with terms that have more than one meaning. "Social Security" provides a good example. It is a generic term applied to all governmental measures designed to provide economic security. For a program to be included in this category, it must (1) be organized and undertaken by the government, and (2) have the broad social purpose of preventing want and destitution. Social insurance falls within this definition and is, thus, a form of social security.

Social insurance programs, however, are only part of the total social security efforts of the government. In addition to the program discussed in this chapter, the Social Security system includes such programs as public assistance, aid to dependent children and the blind, aid to mothers, medical care for veterans, and so on. These programs are *not* insurance.

The public assistance program for the aged, for example, is financed by both federal and state funds which come from the general revenue. Benefits are paid to the aged who are found to be in need and without resources, not on the basis of any contributions which have been made by them or on their behalf. Such a plan does not involve the application of insurance principles to measure the risk insured against or to spread the cost of losses. Instead, it is a welfare plan for a specified group of people.

Within the Social Security system there is a social insurance program known by millions of people simply as "Social Security." This program, which is discussed in this chapter, is really only one of many parts of the over-all social security program. Reference to this part by the same name as the whole program is sometimes a source of confusion, but it is understandable in the light of its historical development.

When the social security program was created in 1935, an important segment of the total program was the compulsory pension plan known as "Old-Age Insurance" or OAI. Later, survivors benefits were added, and the program was referred to as "Old-Age and Survivors Insurance" or OASI. When disability benefits were added, it became "Old-Age, Survivors, and Disability Insurance" or OASDI. Now that hospital and medical benefits are included, the program is referred to as OASDHI. The Social Security Administration now refers to the program as Social Security in its publications.[1]

COVERAGE

Most employees in private industry, most self-employed persons, and members of the armed forces are covered by Social Security. Nearly

---

1. One of the most complete sources of information concerning the Social Security program is the *Social Security Handbook,* which is revised frequently by the Social Security Administration and available from the U.S. Government Printing Office, Washington, D.C. A considerably smaller but very useful paperback book is the *Social Security Manual* published by The National Underwriter Company of Cincinnati, Ohio.

one out of every seven persons in this country receives monthly social security checks.

Coverage is compulsory for most workers. The major exclusions from the program are railroad workers who are covered by the Railroad Retirement Act and federal government employees who are covered by other programs.[2] State and local government employees are covered on an elective basis as a group; i.e., if two-thirds of the firemen employed by a city elect to be covered by Social Security, the whole group must participate. Employees of nonprofit organizations are included if the organization waives its exemption. Ministers are covered automatically unless they request a waiver on religious grounds. Members of religious sects whose beliefs prohibit acceptance of benefits are exempt.

ELIGIBILITY

In order for you and your family to be eligible for benefits, you must achieve insured status. You may be either fully insured or currently insured, depending upon your work history. Most types of benefits are payable if you are *fully insured*. Some are payable if you are either fully or *currently insured*. The amount of work required to become insured is measured in quarters of coverage, which correspond to the quarters of the year. A calendar quarter is each three-month period beginning January 1, April 1, July 1, or October 1.

In 1981, an employee received one quarter of coverage for each $310 of earnings, up to a maximum of four quarters each year. This measure of earnings is adjusted every year to take account of increases in average wages.

A self-employed person or farm worker receives a quarter of coverage on the same basis but must have annual earnings of at least $400 before any quarters of coverage are credited.

You are *fully insured* when you have 40 quarters of coverage, or when you have at least six quarters of coverage and at least as many quarters of coverage as there are years elapsing after 1950 (or, if later, after age 21).

You are *currently insured* if you have at least six quarters of coverage in the 13-quarter period ending with the quarter in which you die.

BENEFITS

Social Security provides the following benefits: (1) survivor's, (2) retirement, (3) disability, and (4) Medicare. The insured status needed for these benefits is outlined in Tables 12-1 through 12-4.

---

2. A person who is employed by a railroad temporarily and then changes to other employment is covered by Social Security for both types of employment rather than under both programs. Coverage credits earned while working for a railroad are transferred to his or her Social Security employment record.

TABLE 12-1

*Who Gets
Monthly Benefits
if Worker Fully
Insured?*

1. Retired worker (at age 62 or over)
2. Wife of retired worker (at age 62 or over)
3. Wife of retired worker (at any age if caring for a child)
4. Child of retired worker
5. Husband of retired worker (at age 62 or over)
6. Widow of worker (at age 60 or over)
7. Widower of worker (at age 60 or over)
8. Disabled widower or worker (at age 50 or over)
9. Dependent parent of deceased worker

TABLE 12-2

*Who Gets
Monthly Benefits
if Worker Fully
or Currently
Insured?*

1. Child of deceased worker
2. Widow or widower of worker any age if caring for a child

Note: Survivors also receive lump-sum death benefit.

Survivor's Benefits

The surviving spouse of a fully or currently insured deceased worker is entitled to benefits if caring for a child who is under age 18 or disabled by a disability that began before age 22. A child of a fully or currently insured deceased worker is entitled to benefits if: (1) he or she is under age 18, disabled by a disability that began before age 18, or between ages 18 and 22 and a full-time student, (2) the child was dependent on the deceased worker, and (3) the child is not married.

A widow or widower of a fully insured deceased worker is qualified for benefits at age 50 if disabled, otherwise at age 60. A parent of a fully insured deceased worker is entitled to benefits if he or she: (1) is at least age 62, (2) was receiving at least half support from the child,[3] (3) has not remarried since the child's death, and (4) is not entitled to a retirement or disability benefit equal to or larger than the parent's benefit.

In addition to these benefits, a lump-sum death payment is made upon the death of a worker who is fully or currently insured. It is paid to

---

3. At the time of the child's death, or at the beginning of a disability that lasted until the child's death, or when the child became eligible for retirement or disability benefits.

the widow or widower if she or he was living in the same household with the worker at the time of death. If there is no eligible widow or widower, it is paid to the funeral home for burial expense or to the person who paid the burial expense.

Retirement Benefits

A fully insured worker can elect to receive full retirement benefits at age 65 or reduced benefits as early as age 62.[4] A wife of a retired worker is entitled to a monthly benefit if she is (1) at least age 62, or (2) caring for at least one child (under age 18 or disabled and disability began before age 22) of the retired worker. A child of a retired worker who is (1) under age 18, or (2) a full-time student between 18 and 22, or (3) disabled if disability began before age 22, is also entitled to a benefit.

Disability Benefits

A disabled worker who meets the eligibility requirements shown in Table 12-3 is entitled to a monthly disability benefit after a waiting period of five months if he or she is under age 65 and has been disabled for 12 months, or is expected to be disabled for at least 12 months, or has a disability which is expected to result in death. A wife, child, or husband of a disabled worker is entitled to a monthly benefit upon meeting the same qualifications as those listed above in connection with retirement benefits.

---

1. Disabled worker
2. Child of disabled worker
3. Wife of disabled worker (if caring for child)
4. Wife of disabled worker (at least age 62)

Note: If disability began at or after age 31, must have worked in covered employment half of last 10 years. If disability began before age 31, must have worked in covered employment half of quarters between age 21 and onset of disability (but not less than six quarters).

TABLE 12-3

Who Gets Monthly Benefits if Fully Insured Worker Disabled?

Medicare Benefits

Medicare consists of two parts: (1) the basic hospital insurance benefits plan, and (2) the voluntary supplementary medical benefits plan. Eligibility requirements are shown in Table 12-4.

Basic hospital benefits. Hospital insurance is automatically effective for those qualified, without payment of premium. Others who are age 65

---

4. The retirement benefit is reduced for a retired worker under age 72 whose annual earned income exceeds a specified amount.

TABLE 12-4

*Who Is Eligible
for Medicare?*

Person age 65 who is entitled to monthly social security or railroad retirement benefits.

Person under age 65 who has been entitled to disability benefits for at least 24 months.

Widow age 50 or older who is entitled to both a mother's benefit and disability benefits.

Note: Persons 65 and over but not eligible for hospital insurance can get it by enrolling and paying a monthly premium if they also enroll for medical insurance.

---

and over may enroll and have the insurance by paying a premium if they also enroll for the supplementary medical benefits plan. The basic hospital insurance plan provides:

1. Inpatient hospital services for up to 90 days in each "spell of illness,"[5] subject to a deductible during the first 60 days and participation during the next 30 days. At present benefits levels, you would pay the first $204 of hospital charges and Medicare would pay the rest for up to 60 days. For the next 30 days, you would pay $51 a day and Medicare would pay the rest.

2. Posthospital extended care in a skilled nursing facility for up to 100 days in each "spell of illness." After the first 20 days, you pay $25.50 a day and Medicare pays the rest.

3. Posthospital home health services for up to 100 visits.

Supplementary medical benefits. Anyone eligible for the basic hospital benefits plan and anyone age 65 and over who is either a citizen or a lawfully admitted alien with at least five years residence in the United States is eligible for this plan. Those who are receiving social security or railroad retirement benefits are enrolled automatically unless they

---

5. A "spell of illness" begins the day a patient is admitted to a hospital. It ends when the patient has been in neither a hospital nor a facility primarily furnishing skilled nursing or rehabilitative services for 60 days. There is no limit on the number of 90-day benefit periods a person can have.

elect not to be covered. Each person who enrolls pays a monthly premium. [6]

You pay the first $60 of covered medical expenses each year. After that, Medicare pays for 80 percent of standard charges for such expenses. Table 12-5 shows the expenses covered by the medical benefits part of Medicare.

TABLE 12-5

Medical Expenses Covered by Medicare

1. Doctors' services, including house calls, office visits, services in the hospital, and other institutions.
2. Hospital diagnostic studies on an outpatient basis.
3. Services and supplies relating to a physician's services to outpatients.
4. Outpatient physical therapy and speech pathology furnished by specified agencies.
5. Dentists' bills for bone surgery.
6. Outpatient psychiatric treatment, not to exceed $250 per year.
7. Home health services up to 100 visits per year.
8. Diagnostic tests.
9. Radiation therapy.
10. Surgical dressings and similar items.
11. Ambulance service under certain circumstances.

AMOUNT OF BENEFITS

As just noted, medicare benefits are stated in terms of services paid for directly to the purveyor or on a reimbursement basis to the insured. The amount paid is the same for all persons enrolled. In contrast, the amount of the survivor's disability and retirement benefits is not the same for everyone but is, instead, based on the insured's covered earnings since 1950 or after the year the insured reached age 21, if later.

Primary Insurance Amount

The Primary Insurance Amount (PIA) is the basic unit used to determine the amount of various monthly benefits. Before 1978, you could calculate your average monthly earnings by a fairly simple method and determine your PIA from a table which showed the PIA for various levels of average monthly earnings. Because this method penalized workers with a long work history which included the lower wages of 10 or 15 years ago, the PIA is now based on average *indexed* monthly earn-

---

6. Premium rates may increase but increases are limited to not more than the percentage by which Social Security cash benefits have been increased since the last premium adjustment.

TABLE 12-6
Social Security Benefits

Average Indexed Monthly Earnings	BENEFITS FOR LIVING WORKERS AND THEIR DEPENDENTS						BENEFITS FOR SURVIVORS OF DECEASED WORKERS						
	Retirement Benefit		Disability Benefit	Benefits for Dependents				Spouse not caring for child					
	Age 65	Age 62		Spouse not caring for child		Child or Spouse Caring for Child	Age 65	Age 60	Age 50 & Disabled	Child or Spouse Caring for Child	One Parent	Spouse and one Child or two Parents	Maximum Family Benefit
				Age 65	Age 62								
% of P.I.A.	100%	80%	100%	50%	37.5%	50%	100%	71.5%	50%	75%	82.5%	150%	
500	264	212	264	132	99	132	264	189	132	198	218	397	437
600	296	237	296	148	111	148	296	212	148	222	245	445	525
700	328	263	328	164	123	164	328	235	164	246	271	493	612
800	360	288	360	180	135	180	360	258	180	270	297	541	660
900	392	314	392	196	147	196	392	281	196	294	324	589	703
1,000	424	340	424	212	159	212	424	303	212	318	350	637	746
1,100	454	363	454	227	170	227	454	325	227	340	374	681	795
1,200	468	375	468	234	176	234	468	335	234	352	387	703	819
1,300	484	387	484	242	181	242	484	346	242	363	399	726	847
1,400	498	399	498	249	187	249	498	357	249	374	412	748	872

Source: Detlefs, Dale R., *1979 Guide to Social Security* (Louisville, Kentucky: Meidinger and Associates, 1978), pp. 28-29.

Reprinted with permission of Meidinger, Inc. 1980.

ings. Earnings for prior years are adjusted to what they would have been if wage levels in earlier years had been the same as they are currently.

As a result, there is no easy way to make an estimate of your PIA. You can't just calculate a simple average of your wages and consult a table. The Social Security Administration has computerized wage histories for all workers and the PIA calculation is made by the computer when an application for benefits is processed. Unless you apply for benefits, the only way you can obtain an estimate of your PIA is to calculate it yourself. Later in this chapter, we will show you how.

If your covered work experience is less than seven years, you can simply calculate your average monthly earnings during the best two years and refer to Table 12-6 for a rough estimate of your benefits. Because benefits are adjusted for inflation every year, you should contact the local Social Security office if you want current benefit levels.

HOW BENEFITS ARE FINANCED

Disability, survivors, retirement, and hospital benefits provided by Social Security are financed through payroll taxes paid by the employer and the employee and by a special tax on earnings paid by the self-employed. Supplementary medical benefits are financed by collection of monthly premiums from persons enrolled in the program, matched by amounts appropriated from general revenue of the federal government.

The combined OASDI and Hospital Insurance tax rates for employers, employees and self-employed persons, and the maximum annual wages or earnings subject to tax are shown in Table 12-7.

YEAR	EMPLOYER EMPLOYEE	SELF-EMPLOYED	MAXIMUM WAGE OR EARNINGS BASE
1980	6.13%	8.10%	$25,900
1981	6.65%	9.30%	29,700
1982-84	6.70%	9.35%	29,700*
1985	7.05%	9.90%	29,700*
1986-89	7.15%	10.00%	29,700*

TABLE 12-7

Social Security Tax Rates and Maximum Wage or Earnings Base for Employers, Employees and Self-Employed

*Maximum wage base and maximum earnings base subject to automatic adjustment in 1982 and thereafter based on changes in wage levels.

Source: Detlefs, Dale R., *1979 Guide to Social Security* (Louisville, Kentucky: Meidinger and Associates, 1978).

Reprinted with permission of Meidinger, Inc. 1980.

ADMINISTRATION

The Social Security program is administered by the Social Security Administration, an agency of the United States Department of Health, Education, and Welfare. Local service is provided by offices located in the principal cities and towns of the 50 states and Puerto Rico. Applications for social security numbers and the various benefits as well as enrollment for the medical insurance plan are processed by the district office. Disability determination, the decision as to whether or not an applicant for disability benefits is disabled as defined in the law, is made by a state agency (usually the vocational rehabilitation agency) under agreements between the State and the Secretary of the Department of Health, Education, and Welfare. Qualification for hospital and medical benefits is determined by the district office, but claims for such benefits are processed through private insurer intermediaries under contract with the Social Security Administration.

The first decision concerning a person's qualification for benefits under the various parts of the program is made at the local level. Simple and effective procedures exist for appeal by any applicant for whom the decision is unsatisfactory. There is no charge for such appeals and the claimant receives courteous assistance from Social Security personnel.

Consumer Applications
*Estimating Your Benefits
and Covering Medicare Gaps*

In order to estimate your Social Security benefits, you must know how to calculate your average indexed earnings. Because Medicare does not cover all hospital and medical expenses, many people need insurance to fill in the gaps. How are these problems handled?

Your Average Indexed Earnings

To estimate your benefits from Social Security publications, you must calculate your average indexed yearly and monthly earnings. Here is how to do it.

1. Enter your actual yearly earnings in Column 1 of worksheet in Figure 12-1.

2. Ask the local Social Security office if the figures in Column 2 are correct; if not, make the necessary correction. Also, ask them for the indexing factor for every year you have earnings.
3. Multiply the lesser of Column 1 or Column 2 by the indexing factor. Enter that sum in Column 4.
4. Cross out up to five of the years for which indexed earnings are the lowest, but leave at least two years.
5. Total the indexed earnings that remain.
6. Divide that sum by the number of year's earnings in the total. The result is your average indexed yearly earnings. Divide by 12 to convert to a monthly basis.

| | THE LESSER OF: | | | | | |
Year	COLUMN 1 Your Actual Earnings	OR	COLUMN 2 Social Security Taxable Wage Base	COLUMN 3 × Indexing Factor =	COLUMN 4 Indexed Earnings For Year	
1976	_____		15,300	_____	_____	
1977	_____		16,500	_____	_____	
1978	_____		17,700	_____	_____	
1979	_____		22,900	_____	_____	
1980	_____		25,900	_____	_____	
1981	_____		29,700	_____	_____	
1982	_____		31,800	_____	_____	
1983	_____		33,900	_____	_____	
1984	_____		36,000	_____	_____	
1985	_____		38,100	_____	_____	
				Total	_____	

FIGURE 12-1
*Social Security
Indexed Earnings
Worksheet*

If you started working in covered employment in 1976 and calculated your average indexed yearly earnings in 1980, you would have the following in Table 12-8:

health insurance policies but inadequate coverage. What would you advise an older person who is worried about the gaps in medicare? Tell him or her the following:

TABLE 12-8

*Example of
Completed Social
Security Indexed
Earnings
Worksheet*

YEAR	COLUMN 1*	COLUMN 2	COLUMN 3**	COLUMN 4
1976	$ 6,800	$15,300	1.144	$ 7,779.20
1977	12,000	16,500	1.079	12,948.00
1978	17,900	17,700	1.000	17,700.00
1979	24,000	22,900	1.000	22,900.00
			Total 1978 & 1979	$40,600.00
			Average Indexed Yearly Earnings	20,300.00

*Assumed earnings.
**1980 index factor.

You must leave at least two years, so you can cross out only two. Because they are lowest, you cross out indexed earnings for 1976 and 1977. The sum of the years remaining is $40,600. You divide that by the number of years represented (2) and find that your average indexed yearly earnings is $20,300.

Medicare and Medigap Insurance

Many older people live alone or associate only with other older people who have similar problems. Most have limited incomes. They must handle their savings with care because it's too late in life to replace anything they lose. They are grateful for Social Security checks and medicare but worry about what it doesn't cover—the gaps. As a result, they are very susceptible to a smooth sales pitch and scare tactics. Many wind up burdened with several

1. When an agent calls on you to "talk about the high cost of health care," or some other sales pitch, don't be taken in by the fact that he or she is a good Christian who quotes from the Bible, is clean-cut, interested in the problems of older people, and so on. Think about hanging onto your money. Ask for a written proposal that shows what medicare covers, what you would have to pay if you did not have a medigap policy, and what part of that the policy you are looking at will pay. Tell him or her you promised your son-in-law, who is a professor of insurance, that you would send all proposals to him before you bought any insurance. That will get rid of the crooks.

2. Don't buy a cancer policy or a "dread disease" policy. They promise to give

large benefits for what appears to be a small premium but the coverage is extremely narrow. What if you have a disabling stroke instead of cancer?

3. Don't assume that a high-cost policy is best. Cost is not necessarily a good indicator of benefits. A New York study revealed that some lower-priced policies provided more benefits than others that cost more.

4. Ask the agent what the company's anticipated loss ratio is for this policy. The loss ratio is the percentage of the premium paid to, or on behalf of, the policyholder. If it is less than 60 percent, don't buy from that company. You'll be paying too much. On the other hand, 70 or 75 percent is good.

5. Buy only one policy. That's all you need to cover the gaps left by medicare. Read the policy carefully as soon as you get it. You should be able to return it in ten days and get your money back if you don't want it. See if the policy dovetails with medicare. Some medigap policies are written on a "carve-out" basis. They

in effect say, "We cover all health care expenses up to a specified (high) limit except those covered by medicare."

6. Ask yourself these questions about the policy:
   a. Does it pay for your part of the hospital bill after the first 60 days of your stay?
   b. Does it cover your hospital bill after 90 days of your stay?
   c. Does it pay the posthospital extended care deductible after the first 20 days?
   d. Does it pay for posthospital extended care after 100 days?
   e. Does it pay your share of the medical bill after you pay the deductible?

7. If there is anything in the policy you don't understand, ask the agent to explain it. When he gets through, tell him or her your memory is bad and you want the explanation in writing so you can keep it with the policy for future reference. Tell the agent that what he or she says is easier to understand than the policy.

Discussion Questions

1. Social Security benefits are financed through payroll taxes. Up to the maximum earnings base, the more you earn, the more tax you pay. Income benefits, however, favor lower income workers. You may earn twice as much as I do and pay twice as much tax, but you will not be entitled to twice as much income benefit. Do you think this is fair? If not, should it be changed? How?

2. Do you think Social Security coverage should be voluntary? Why or why not?

3. Supplementary medical benefits are financed partly from general revenue of the federal government. Do you think payroll taxes should be eliminated and all benefits financed from general revenue? Why or why not?

4. Social Security income benefits are adjusted annually for inflation. Why don't all public and private plans do the same?

5. In recent years, insurance regulatory authorities have exerted pressure on private insurers to issue insurance policies that can be easily understood by the average person so they will know what benefits are provided. The Social Security Administration does not have to do this. Do you think it should? Why or why not?

6. It has been suggested that Civil Service employees should be covered by Social Security instead of having a separate retirement system. Do you agree? Why or why not? Why do federal employees oppose it?

7. One way to establish national health insurance would be to expand Medicare to cover everyone without regard to age or work history. Do you favor this? Why or why not?

8. Why does Medicare have deductibles and participation provisions as well as limitations on benefits? Considering the fact that many older people worry about what is *not* covered and wind up paying too much for insurance to cover the gaps in Medicare, don't you think such gaps should be eliminated?

9. From time to time, one hears the statement that Social Security is in financial trouble and we may not receive the benefits we expect. Do you think this is true? If it is true, what should be done about it?

10. "Social Security benefits are a matter of law, not contract. Therefore, Social Security cannot be compared with private insurance." Do you agree with this statement? Why or why not?

Cases

12-1 Mr. C.J. Abbott worked hard all his life and built up a successful business. His daily routine involved helping with management decisions in the business even though the majority of it was now owned and managed by his sons. He continued to draw a salary from the company sufficient to cover his expenses each month. C.J. was fully insured under Social Security, yet he did not presently receive, nor had he ever received, Social Security benefits. He celebrated his 70th birthday last May. His close friend, George Simms, noted that C.J. was really making a big mistake by working. He said, "You are really working for peanuts." C.J. replied, "How do you figure that?"

1. What did George mean?

2. Why do you think C.J. continued to work?

3. What is the logic behind this reduction of Social Security retirement benefits?

12-2 One day your professor was expounding upon the idea that the Industrial Revolution certainly had a significant impact upon the business of insurance. She said that prior to the Industrial Revolution, families stayed together but the Industrial Revolution tended to scatter the younger members of the family far from home. She next indicated that because of this change in the family new forms of insurance were created by private industry. Then in the 1930's our Federal Government became involved in the insurance/annuity field.

1. Why do you think the Federal Government got involved with insurance related tasks?

2. Is this development consistent with the recent suggestion that all private employers should be required to provide retirement benefits for all employees?

12-3 Your father-in-law was employed by a state agency for 40 years prior to his retirement last year. He was not covered by Social Security on his state job. During the last three years of his career with state government, however, you employed him on a part-time basis to do some surveying work on a housing development for which you had an engineering contract. You paid both the employer's and employee's Social Security tax, deducting the latter from his wages during the time you employed him.

When he retired, he applied for Social Security retirement benefits. Several months later, he was notified that he was not entitled to benefits because the work he did for you was "in the family," and not bona fide employment. The implication in the notice he received was that the job you gave him was really designed to qualify him for Social Security benefits rather than "real" employment.

1. What should your father-in-law do?

2. How can you help him?

Chapter Thirteen:
MANAGING LIFE AND HEALTH RISKS

INTRODUCTION

Now that we have examined life and health insurance and the benefits provided by Social Security, we can take another look at the life and health risks confronting the family. In this chapter, we discuss the following:

1. How to assure income continuation in case of disability, premature death, or retirement of the family income earner(s)

2. Estate planning

3. Business uses of life and health insurance.

LIFE AND HEALTH RISKS

In evaluating life and health risks, you must determine what will happen to cash flow and assets if any of the following occur:

1. Death of an income producer—either father or mother

2. Disability of father or mother

3. Disability or death of non-income producer

4. Retirement of income producer(s)

5. Unusual medical expense.

Either the death or disability of a father or mother will stop the income they produce, whether cash flow or services. Death will also sub-

ject the family to estate settlement costs, including administration expenses and taxes. These can reduce family assets. Resources may also be decreased if the need for cash forces asset liquidation under unfavorable circumstances.

Disability of the father or mother stops their income production and increases expenses. Disability or death of non-income producers increases expenses. Retirement of a cash income producer stops cash flow. When cash flow is reduced or stops or unexpected expenses are incurred, family assets may be diminished.

Handling the Risks

How can the family handle these risks? There are several alternatives. First, some losses are so regular that they may be budgeted. A few years of experience will show how many visits to the doctor and dentist, for example, may be expected. Second, an emergency fund can bear the burden of unexpected small losses that cannot be handled through the regular family budget. Such a fund should be large enough to cover first-dollar losses such as small medical and hospital expenses. It should also provide funds to take the place of income that may be lost because of short-term disability.

But what about the risk of large expenses and/or loss of income because of death or long-term disability? Clearly, these risks cannot be borne by the family even if it does have an emergency fund—possible losses are simply too large and unpredictable. Unless they are already covered by group life and health insurance, they must be insured on an individual basis.

Procedure

In order to determine how much life and health insurance your family may need, you must:

1. Identify and evaluate the family's needs in the event of disability, premature death, or retirement of the family income producer

2. Assess the resources available to fill such needs

3. Evaluate the disparity between family resources and family needs

4. Estimate the amount of insurance required to fill the gap between resources and needs.

We will demonstrate this procedure with a simple case.

THE MORAN CASE

In looking at this case, we will give our attention to the family's general situation, its income needs, and its resources. Then we will look at the income it would have in the event of Gary's disability, death, or retirement.

Family Situation

The Moran family has three members:

1. Gary, born 1950

2. Lori, born 1953

3. Daughter Liz, born 1978

Gary is a sales manager whose income in 1980 was $36,000 annually. Lori was employed in marketing research from 1973 to 1978, at which time her salary was $12,000 annually.

The family's assets are:

Home bought in 1973	$80,000
Two automobiles	10,000
Furniture and other personal property	30,000
Checking account	1,000
Savings account	5,000

Their liabilities are:

Balance on home mortgage	$50,000
Current bills	1,000
Balance on automobiles	5,000

Income Needs

Based on their present income, Gary and Lori think that the family needs an income of $2,100 per month in the event of Gary's death. Should Gary be totally disabled, they estimate that they would need another $200 per month for his care. In determining disability income needs, this difference is important. Under normal circumstances, it might be feasible to plan for a reduction following a readjustment period in the event of Gary's death. With inflation, however, Lori's real income will decline as time goes on. So, they plan for a level dollar income as far into the future as possible.

Resources

The family has three types of basic resources in addition to the assets just listed:

1. Those provided by Social Security

2. Those provided by Gary's employer

3. Those provided by their individual insurance.

Social Security benefits. Based on Gary's present salary, let us assume a maximum PIA of $650. In the event of his total disability in 1980, the family would be entitled to $1,140 per month—the maximum family benefit—after a waiting period of five months. In the event of his death, Lori would be entitled to $487.50 (75% of PIA) for a widow's benefit until Liz reached age 18. She would also be entitled to the same amount on behalf of Liz until Liz reached age 18 (or age 22 if a full-time student).

Employee benefits.   Gary's employer provides him and his family the following benefits:

1. Group life insurance in the amount of 2 times his annual salary

2. Paid sick leave equal to his income for 30 days

3. Long-term disability income to age 65 equal to 2/3 of annual salary, minus total Social Security benefit; 30 day waiting period

4. Group major medical
    $300 annual family deductible
      10 percent participation
    $500,000 aggregate lifetime limit

5. Dental coverage
    $50 per person annual deductible
    $1,000 per person per year limit
    $50,000 aggregate family lifetime limit

6. Pension at age 65 equal to 2/3 of Gary's final three years average salary, minus 1/2 of his Social Security retirement benefit.

Individual coverage.   Lori has a $15,000 ordinary life policy and Gary has a $25,000 ordinary life policy. He also has a decreasing term policy in an amount equal to the balance on their home mortgage. They do not have credit life insurance in connection with their other debts.

Income in the Event of Disability, Death, Retirement

Disability income.   In the event Gary became totally disabled, his present salary would continue for 30 days. Then, for the next four months, his group LTD plan would pay $2,000 per month. At that time, the family would become entitled to Social Security disability income benefits of $1,140 per month and his group plan benefit would be reduced to $860 per month. Thus, the total disability income benefits would remain at $2,000 per month. This is $300 per month less than they need. When Liz reaches age 18, hers and Lori's Social Security benefits would stop, but that would simply reduce the offset. Total disability income would remain at $2,000 per month until Gary reached age 65.

Income if Gary dies.   If Gary dies, Lori and Liz would be entitled to $975 per month Social Security benefits until Liz reached age 18 (or 22 if a full-time student). The mortgage on their home would be paid by the decreasing term insurance. Lori would receive $72,000 proceeds from Gary's group life insurance and $25,000 from his ordinary life policy.

She could either select an income settlement option, or leave the proceeds at interest, or take the proceeds in cash and invest them in either certificates of deposit or a no-load commercial paper fund.

The choice would depend on the level of interest rates. When rates are high, an annuity type settlement option is not the best choice if it yields less income than interest bearing investments. The way to find out is to ask the insurance company what they are paying currently on the interest only option and various other options and then compare the monthly income with other alternatives. If the current rate on treasury bills, certificates of deposit, or a commercial paper fund is 10 percent, Lori can earn $9,700 annually ($808 per month) on the proceeds of Gary's life insurance. With that and $975 from Social Security, her monthly income would be $1,783, which is $317 less than the $2,100 per month needed.

When Liz reaches age 18 (or 22 if in school), Social Security benefits cease. Although we could argue that income needs will decrease—since Liz leaves the household—we'll leave them unchanged to allow for the effects of inflation. From then until Lori reaches age 60—a period commonly called the Social Security "Blackout Period"—she will have only the interest on Gary's life insurance proceeds. If she continues to earn 10 percent, that would be $808 per month. If the interest rate dropped to 5 percent, she would receive $404 per month. She could buy a 5 percent, 27-year fixed period annuity of $552 per month. But that would be only $148 per month more than just the interest she could earn at 5 percent, and it would liquidate the fund.

At age 60, Lori would be entitled to a Social Security widow's benefit of $465 per month. If she still had the proceeds of Gary's life insurance at that time, she could buy a straight life annuity of $623 per month or simply earn interest on the proceeds. The best alternative for her depends upon the rate of interest she could earn. If rates are high, interest on the proceeds is the best choice. If they are low, however, an annuity may be best. Even if she could make 10 percent ($808 per month) interest, that plus $465 per month Social Security benefit would be $827 per month short of the $2,100 per month agreed upon as necessary.

When Gary retires. Based on his present salary and the current benefit level, his retirement benefit will be $24,000 annually or $2,000 per month, less half his $650 monthly Social Security benefit. Lori, however, will be entitled to a wife's benefit at age 62 of $325 per month. Their total retirement benefits would then be $2,650 per month as follows: Lori's Social Security benefit of $325, Gary's Social Security benefit of $650; and Gary's company pension of $1,675.

Also, by the time Gary is age 65, the cash value of his and Lori's ordinary life policies will be roughly 55 percent of the face amount. Thus, if they surrendered his $25,000 policy and her $15,000 policy, they would receive $22,000. At 10 percent interest, they could make $183 per month, or at 5 percent interest, they could make $92 per month. On the other hand, they might take the proceeds in the form of a joint-and-two-thirds life annuity which would provide $243 per month for both of them and $162 per month to the survivor. Using the 10 percent assumption of $183 per month, their total retirement income would be $2,833 per month.

Program Review

Let's look at Figures 13-1, 2 and 3 to see what gaps there are. Figure 13-1 reveals that family income in the event of Gary's total disability is short of the $2,300 monthly income objective by $300.

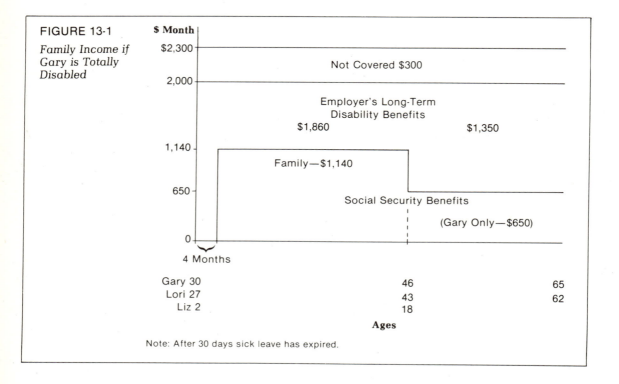

FIGURE 13-1

*Family Income if
Gary is Totally
Disabled*

Figure 13-2 shows three gaps in family income in the event of Gary's death. The first is $317 per month until Liz reaches 18. The second is $1,292 per month during the Social Security "Blackout Period" of 17 years. The third is $827 per month from Lori's age 60 on.

Figure 13-3 reveals no gaps for retirement.

What should Gary do? He might ask his insurer to add a disability income rider to his $25,000 ordinary life policy. If the rider provided $10 per month per thousand dollars of face amount, he would receive $250 per month during total disability, still falling $50 per month short of the family goal of $2,300 per month. Alternatively, he could go to another insurer and purchase a separate, $300 per month disability income policy.

The gaps in coverage for family income in the event of Gary's death cause an even more pressing problem. The amount of income during the blackout period is a bit over one-third of that required. At 10 percent in-

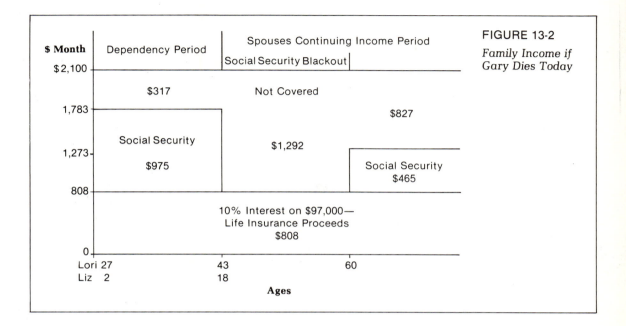

FIGURE 13-2

*Family Income if
Gary Dies Today*

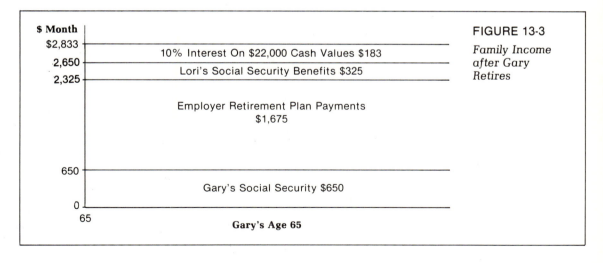

FIGURE 13-3

*Family Income
after Gary
Retires*

terest, it would take a principal sum of $155,000 to fill this gap. Although that amount of life insurance may not seem feasible for this family, it is painfully clear that Gary needs more life insurance. Filling about half the gap would require $75,000.

What should he buy? At age 30, a $75,000 ordinary life policy would cost about $1,000 annually. The first year cost for a yearly renewable term policy would be under $200, and even the 10th year premium would be less than $300. However, the premium will rise rapidly later, exceeding $600 by age 50, and exceeding the ordinary whole life policy's premium after age 55. Probably, Gary would do well to consider renewable and convertible term, which would allow him to convert to whole life if his income later gives him that flexibility.

So far as medical expenses are concerned, the Moran family has excellent coverage. Their program shows no gaps in that area.

We have, however, not dealt with the risk that Lori might die or become disabled. She produces no money income for the family, but she manages the household and takes care of their child. Who will do that in her absence? How much will it cost? How long would the proceeds of her $15,000 ordinary life policy pay for the replacement of her services? Her death or disability would decrease real income, cause extra expense, and create financial strain for the family. The process of determining the protection required to handle this risk is the same as that we have discussed with regard to the risk of Gary's death or disability.

An Alternative

Even the most optimistic author realizes that many family risk managers will not want to go through the process just discussed to determine how much and what kind of life and health insurance they require in order to protect family assets and income. An alternative is to provide a life and health agent with the facts of your family's situation and its objectives and ask him or her to make recommendations. Many insurance companies perform the calculations for their agents as a means of facilitating sales. It may be desirable to obtain recommendations from more than one agent, so that you can see how the recommendations compare with each other and with your own estimates. When this is done, you should remember that different interest rate assumptions lead to different results, so you should ask what the insurer's assumptions were. A higher interest rate assumption will result in a lower amount of life insurance needed, while a lower interest rate assumption will generate a higher amount of life insurance required.

ESTATE PLANNING AND BUSINESS INSURANCE

We have concentrated thus far on the life and health risks faced by a typical family and the insurance required to transfer these risks. Two other situations in which life or health insurance may be needed are in estate planning and business situations.

Estate Planning

The property you own is your estate. Because you can't take it with you when you die, your death results in ownership of your property being transferred to someone else. Who the "someone else" is depends on the terms of your will or the law in your state. The transfer process involves taxes and administrative costs.

The major reason you should have a will is so your estate will be distributed in accordance with your wishes. If you die without a will (intestate), your estate is distributed in accordance with the laws of the state in which you are a resident. Some of the provisions of South Carolina law illustrate what happens. (See Figure 13-4).

A second reason for having a will is that it may be possible to reduce both taxes and administrative costs. For example, if you are married

---

Case 1: Married man or woman with one child
          Distribution: Surviving spouse: one-half
                            Child: one-half

Case 2: Married man or woman with two or more children
          Distribution: Surviving spouse: one-third
                            Children: two-thirds

Case 3: Married man or woman, no children
          Distribution: Surviving spouse: one-half
                            Parents, brothers, sisters:
                                balance equally divided

Case 4: Married man or woman, no children or brothers or sisters
          Distribution: Surviving spouse: one-half
                            Parents only: one-half

FIGURE 13-4

Estate Distribution by Law

---

you may take advantage of the marital deduction to reduce the federal tax on your estate. This deduction provides that any portion of your adjusted gross estate[1]—up to 50 percent or $250,000, whichever is greater—left to your spouse is not included in your estate for federal tax purposes. If you have a $250,000 adjusted gross estate and leave it all to your spouse, your estate would pay no tax. If you leave nothing to your spouse, the estate tax would be more than $70,000.

When you die, taxes, administrative costs, and all your bills must be paid before the remainder of your estate is transferred to your heirs. Sale of the assets in your estate for this purpose reduces the amount available for your heirs. Furthermore, it may be difficult to sell such assets for their true worth, especially if business assets are involved.[2] So in addition to life insurance needed to continue income for your survivors, you may need life insurance to pay taxes, administrative costs, and other indebtedness in order to assure that your survivors receive *all* of your estate rather than just part of it.

Business Uses of Life and Health Insurance

If you own an interest in a business as a sole proprietor, partner in a partnership, or stockholder in a close corporation,[3] it may be difficult to

---

1. When the federal estate tax return is filed, the first step is to arrive at the total value of all assets owned by the deceased. Next, all obligations—including all debts, funeral expenses, estate administration costs, and so on—are deducted to arrive at the adjusted gross estate.

2. This problem is discussed below.

3. A close corporation is owned by very few stockholders. It is said to be "closely held," in contrast with one that is owned by hundreds or thousands of stockholders.

sell your interest for its true value in the event of your death or total, permanent disability. This risk can be handled with a buy-and-sell agreement between you and a prospective purchaser while you are alive and well. Prospective purchasers are the following:

1. For a sole proprietorship: key employees

2. For a partnership: your partners

3. For a close corporation: other stockholders.

Buy-and-sell agreement. In a buy-and-sell agreement, you agree to sell, and the prospective purchaser agrees to buy your interest in the firm in the event of your death or total, permanent disability. The agreement establishes the price for your interest or includes a formula by which the price can be determined at the time of sale. The price may be a lump sum upon your death, or income for life or a specified period in the event of your disability. This agreement assures a market for your business interest in the event of your death or disability. In a partnership or close corporation buy-and-sell agreement, you also make the same agreement with regard to your partners interest or other stockholders interest so that they are protected in the event of death or disability just as you are.

Where does the money come from to fulfill the obligations undertaken in a buy-and-sell agreement? Through life insurance and disability income insurance. In a sole proprietorship, your employee-purchasers buy insurance to pay in the event of your death or disability. In a partnership or close corporation, the partners or stockholders buy insurance on each other. If one of them dies or becomes disabled, you and your other partners or stockholders are able to buy him or her out and continue to control the business. The buy-and-sell agreement assures you, should you become disabled (or your heirs, in the event of your death) of a market for your business interest and assures business associates that they can buy the interest.

Key Person Insurance. As we noted earlier in this chapter, your employer may provide life and health insurance for you in a group plan. It is for your benefit. Another circumstance in which your employer may insure your life is for the benefit of the firm. If you are a key employee whose contribution to the firm is crucial to its success, your death would cause loss to the firm as well as to your family. If, for example, you are an outstanding sales manager, sales and profits may decline significantly for a time in the event of your death. You may be hard to replace. To protect itself against this loss, the firm may insure your life and name itself beneficiary of the policy. Clearly, it has an insurable interest in your life. It must have your consent to do so, but most employees are flattered by such concrete evidence of their value to the firm.

Consumer Applications
Creating Your Own Retirement Plan

With social security benefits and a generous retirement plan provided by Gary's employer, the Moran family will have an adequate income when Gary reaches retirement age. Many Americans, however, are not in such an enviable position. You may find yourself at retirement age without an adequate retirement income for one of the following reasons:

1. You moved from job to job and never qualified for retirement benefits.
2. The plan that covered you provided inadequate benefits.
3. None of your employers had a retirement plan.

What alternatives do you have? If you are to have an adequate income when you retire, you must set aside part of your income as you go along. But if you have to pay taxes on income you save and taxes on the earnings generated by your savings, the process of accumulation may be painfully slow. On the other hand, if you can set aside before-tax dollars, and if the earnings they generate are tax-sheltered, you can accumulate funds for retirement at a much faster pace. This is demonstrated by Table 13-1 which shows that, at a 10 percent earnings rate on savings, sheltered savings will accumulate almost 70 percent more than nonsheltered over a 10-year period. And the longer the accumulation period, the greater the difference.

There are two situations in which you may arrange to accumulate retirement funds on a tax-sheltered basis:

1. You are self-employed
2. You work for an employer who does not have a qualified pension plan.

If you are self-employed, you can establish a Keogh Plan, also known as an HR-10 Plan. If your employer does not have a qualified pension plan, you can establish an individual retirement account or individual retirement annuity plan, usually referred to as an IRA.

The HR-10 or Keogh Plan

Who and How Much?

Keogh plans are for people who earn self-employment income. Even if you have a job with a firm that has a qualified pension plan, you can establish a Keogh plan based on other earned income. For example, you may work for wages or salary during the day but operate your own TV repair shop in the evening and on weekends. Savings from the net earned income from such self-employment is what Keogh is all about.

You can make a tax-deductible contribution to your plan equal to the lesser of $7,500 or 15 percent of your annual earned income up to $100,000. Let's suppose your net income from the TV repair shop is $5,000 this year. You can deposit $750 in your Keogh account and

TABLE 13-1

Sheltered Versus Nonsheltered Savings from $100 Income, Assuming 30% Tax Bracket, 10% Interest

| Year | SHELTERED | | NONSHELTERED | |
	Available for Saving	Amount End of Year	Available for Savings*	Amount End of Year**
1	100	110.00	70	74.90
2	100	231.00	70	155.04
3	100	364.10	70	240.79
4	100	510.51	70	332.54
5	100	671.56	70	430.72
6	100	849.72	70	535.77
7	100	1,043.58	70	648.18
8	100	1,257.94	70	768.45
9	100	1,493.74	70	897.14
10	100	1,753.11	70	1,034.84

*After paying income tax on $100 income. (Uncle Sam comes first).
**After paying income tax on interest earned.

reduce the taxable portion of your self-employment income to $4,250.[4] If you are in the 30 percent income tax bracket, you save $225 in taxes. Furthermore, the investment income earned on money you put into the plan is not taxed currently.

What If You Have Employees?

If you employ others to help you run the TV repair shop, you must include them in your Keogh plan and make deposits on their behalf equal to the same percentage of their salary as you do for yourself. Thus, if your earned income for the year is $50,000 and you deposit 15 percent ($7,500) in the plan for yourself, you must do the same for your employees. Your secretary who earns $10,000 for the year, for example, is entitled to a contribution to the plan of 15 percent, or $1,500. If your secretary is also your spouse, of course, you are tax-sheltering family income.

How About a Defined Benefit?

A Keogh plan may be used to provide a defined benefit, which means that you decide on a specific amount of benefit (e.g., $400 per month) when you retire. The contribution each year depends upon the amount needed to pay for the benefit. This requires actuarial help to determine your contributions and is far more complicated than the arrangement just discussed.

---

4. If your total annual income does not exceed $15,000, you can put up to $750 of your self-employment income into the Keogh plan even if that is 100 percent of such income during the year.

Tax Treatment

If you leave the funds in your Keogh plan until at least age 59½, you receive favorable tax treatment. Deposits are tax deductible and earnings on funds in the plan are not currently taxable. If you take the money out of your plan before you reach age 59½, you not only pay regular income tax on it but are also subjected to a tax penalty of 10 percent on the amount withdrawn, unless you are disabled. On the other hand, you are required to begin to receive benefits from the plan when you reach age 70½. Such benefits are taxed as ordinary income.

The Individual Retirement Account or Annuity (IRA)

Who and How Much?

While an IRA does not allow you to set aside as much as a Keogh plan, it is still very helpful if you work for an employer who doesn't have a qualified pension plan. To start an IRA, you need the help of a savings and loan association, bank, or life insurance company so the money you put into your account or annuity will be managed by someone other than you. The savings and loan association or bank invests the money in a savings account, certificates of deposit, or some similar arrangement. The life insurance company allocates the money toward the purchase of some kind of annuity. You can put up to 15 percent of your annual compensation, not to exceed $1,500, into the account each year.

If your spouse has no earned income, you may set up a *spousal IRA* which increases the contribution limit to $1,750 per year. If your spouse works for a firm that does not have a qualified pension plan, each of you can create an IRA and each deposit up to $1,500 per year.

Like a Keogh plan, contributions made to an IRA reduce your income tax burden. They are made with pretax dollars. Furthermore, you are not required to pay income tax currently on plan investment earnings.

Tax Treatment

Like a Keogh Plan, you receive favorable tax treatment if you leave funds in your IRA until you reach age 59½. If you take any money out of the plan before you reach age 59½, however, you pay regular income tax on it plus a penalty of 10 percent of the money withdrawn. In addition, you are required to begin taking retirement benefits out of the IRA not later than age 70½. If you fail to do so, a 50 percent tax will be levied on the amount you should have taken out. Suppose, for example, the funds in your IRA when you reach age 70½ can provide retirement benefits of $500 per month but you don't need the income. In order to avoid income tax on the benefits, you postpone starting them. When the IRS catches up with you three years later, you will be penalized $9,000, which is 50 percent of $500 for 36 months. If it were not for this penalty, you could leave the funds in your IRA accumulating earnings tax-free until the day you die, whereupon they would be distributed to your heirs as part of your estate.

Discussion Questions

1. In view of the significance of Social Security survivor benefits, would you consider having a child late in life a clever family risk management technique? Please explain.

2. Instead of leaving property in your estate directly to your spouse and children, you can leave it in trust for them to be managed by a trustee. What advantages do you see in this arrangement for your family?

3. Would you prefer to have your best friend act as trustee for your estate or have the trust department of your bank perform that function? Please explain.

4. If you are a sole proprietor, having a buy-and-sell agreement with one or more of your employees assures a market for your business in the event of your death or total and permanent disability. What benefits may you get from this arrangement prior to death or disability?

5. What advantages are there in having a life insurance agent help you create a program to manage the life and health risks for your family? Are there any disadvantages?

6. Suppose both Gary and Lori Moran were chemical engineers, each earning an annual salary of $50,000. Would they still need an income replacement program? Why or why not?

7. Some husbands say, "I don't worry about income for my family if I die. My wife can always go back to her old job and make a good living." What do you think of this attitude?

8. One reason given for buying term life insurance is that "you don't need life insurance after your children have grown up." What exceptions are there to this statement?

9. In 1981, Bob Gray earns $14,000 annual salary at the electric supply store and $1,000 from self-employment repairing electric hot water heaters. If he has a Keogh plan, he can put $750 into it that year, thereby reducing his taxable self-employment income to $250. In 1982, his salary at the store increases to $15,000 and his self-employment income increases to $2,000. That year, however, he can put only $300 (15 percent of $2,000) into his Keogh plan because his total annual income exceeded $15,000. What do you think of this provision in the law? What effect does it have on Bob's ability to save?

10. If Bob Gray hires 18-year-old Kevin Segillo to help him repair hot water heaters, Gray will have to include him in the Keogh plan and make deposits equal to the same percentage of Kevin's salary as he does for himself. Do you think this requirement is fair? Do you think it might discourage Bob from hiring Kevin?

Cases

13-1 After discussing the mechanics of determining life and health needs with Jim, your neighbor, you both begin to reflect on your individual situations. You determine that in the case of your death your family would need an additional

$200.00/month. Your solution is to purchase the necessary amount of life insurance, with the type to be determined by your budget limitations.

After some thought, Jim responds that after considering his situation and budget, his solution is rather simple. If he were to die prematurely, his family would be hard pressed for only so long as it took his wife to find a new husband, preferably one with money. To Jim, these were the facts of life. After all, his wife is young and attractive, and she cannot stay in mourning all her life.

1. What percent of the population do you think has an adequate funding program for their families in case of their untimely death?

2. Are there any problems with Jim's approach? What are they? How can they be solved?

13-2 The manager of the local Social Security office discussed the benefits of the program with your wife's karate club. That evening after dinner she said to you, "Did you ever stop to think what it would cost for you to buy enough insurance coverage in the private sector to duplicate the coverage of Social Security?" You indicated you had not, but it did seem to be worth considering.

1. If you were 30 years old, fully insured for OASDHI, and had a wife of 28 with one child 2 years old, what would you estimate the replacement cost of the OASDHI coverage to be?

2. What if you were 40, with a 37-year-old wife, and children ages 5, 7, 8, 10, 12, 13, 15 and 17? Estimate the life insurance coverage needed to duplicate coverage for this family.

13-3 Bill Masters, age 50, has accumulated a sizable estate. Included are a $150,000 home, with only $20,000 in unpaid mortgage balance; his personally-owned business, which has assets of four million dollars and liabilities of 2.5 million; and a stock portfolio worth over a million dollars. He has a wife, Jane, age 48, and three children, all of whom are married college graduates.

1. Why should Bill plan his estate?

2. Is there any reason to consider life insurance in this plan?

3. If it were included, what type of life insurance would you recommend?

13-4 Harriet is a single worker, covered by group medical expense insurance provided by her employer. She was in the hospital for a week last month, and has now received statements from her insurer. The statements confuse her.

"I thought that I had full coverage above my deductible, but there are some strange things happening. Most of my expenses were paid, but the insurer refused a part of my room charges each day, and they paid only a part of the surgeon's bill, even though the operation is listed in the contract. On top of that, they refused to pay for the last day, even though my doctor plainly told me that I could stay if I didn't feel like going home."

1. Can you explain to Harriet some of the complications which she is encountering here?

2. Do you have any recommendations as to how this coverage may be improved or supplemented by personally-purchased coverage?

Chapter Fourteen:
BUYING LIFE INSURANCE[1]

INTRODUCTION

Most people don't buy life insurance in the usual sense. That is, they don't decide on their own that they need life insurance and then go shopping for it. Rather, someone sells it to them. Once they are sold on the idea of applying for a life insurance policy, they don't shop—they buy. In many cases, they assume that "life insurance costs pretty much the same regardless of where you buy it."

Actually, there are big differences in the cost of similar policies. And the difference between a high cost policy and a low cost policy can amount to thousands of dollars during your lifetime. So if you are to get the most for your money and buy the policy that fills your needs best, you must shop for life insurance just as you do for other major purchases. In order to do that, you must know how to compare costs.

In this chapter, we discuss the following:

1. Traditional Net Cost Method

2. Interest Adjusted Cost Method

3. Net Payment Cost Index

4. Choosing between Term and Whole Life

---

1. Much of the discussion in this chapter is adapted from James L. Athearn, IT PAYS TO SHOP FOR LIFE INSURANCE (Indianapolis: The National Underwriter Company, 1977).

TRADITIONAL NET COST METHOD

Traditionally, life insurance salespeople demonstrated the cost of a policy over a period of years simply by adding up all the premiums paid and subtracting from that total the dividends received and any cash value at the end of the period. This assumed that the policyowner surrendered the policy for cash at that time. As the example in Table 14-1 shows, the annual net cost calculated by this method is startlingly low compared with the annual premium. In fact, the net cost for the participating policy is negative at the end of 20 years, which implies that you can have life insurance protection for 20 years and make a profit on the transaction when you surrender the policy.

TABLE 14-1

*20-Year Net Cost
Per $1,000 for
$10,000 Straight
Life Policy Issued
to Male Age 35*

	GUARANTEED COST	PARTICIPATING
Annual premium per $1,000	$ 18.89	$ 22.91
20 years premiums	377.80	458.20
*Total dividends	0.00	161.25
Cash value end of 20 years	362.00	362.00
Net cost	15.80	−65.05
Average cost per year	.79	−3.25

*Projected dividends are:

YEAR	DIVIDEND	YEAR	DIVIDEND	YEAR	DIVIDEND
1	$2.14	8	$ 6.73	15	$11.30
2	2.78	9	7.39	16	11.56
3	3.44	10	8.05	17	11.82
4	4.09	11	8.70	18	12.08
5	4.75	12	9.35	19	12.34
6	5.41	13	10.00	20	12.60
7	6.07	14	10.65		

The impression that life insurance can be costless or even profitable stems from the fact that this method of cost calculation ignores interest foregone by the policyowner. It is like saying, "If you will give me a million dollars for a year, I will let you live in my house free for the year and give the million dollars back to you at the end of the year. It will cost you nothing to live in the house." Clearly, use of the house is not free because giving up the use of a million dollars for a year involves a sacrifice. If you could earn 5 percent interest per annum after taxes, the opportunity cost of living in the house would be $50,000 for the year. And so it is with the premium dollars you give up to have a life insurance policy in force for 20 years.

The interest adjusted (I-A) method takes into consideration the interest you could earn on the money you use for premium payments. As Table 14-2 shows, premiums are accumulated at interest just as they would be if you invested the money. Note that the 20-year interest adjusted surrender cost for the guaranteed cost policy is $293.84 rather than the $15.80 shown in Table 14-1 because premium payments are accumulated at interest for 20 years instead of simply multiplied by 20. This is the amount you sacrifice.

	GUARANTEED COST	PARTICIPATING
Annual premium per $1,000	$ 18.89	$ 22.91
Accumulated premiums (at 5%)	655.84	795.41
Less accumulated dividends	0.00	235.21
Less cash surrender value	362.00	362.00
I-A surrender cost for 20 years	293.84	198.20
Surrender cost index per year	8.46	5.71

Note: 20-year conversion factor (at 5%) is 34.719.

TABLE 14-2

20-Year Interest-Adjusted Surrender Cost Per $1,000 for Straight Life Policy Issued to Male Age 35

For the participating policy, both premiums and dividends are accumulated at interest. The premium accumulation is larger than in Table 14-1 because interest is considered, but so is the dividend accumulation. On the one hand, you are measuring the sacrifice involved in paying premiums, but on the other hand, you are measuring the benefits of accumulating dividends at interest. The net result is an interest adjusted surrender cost of $198.20 for the 20-year period as opposed to a profit of $65.05 when interest is ignored.

In Table 14-1, the average cost per year for the two policies was calculated by simply dividing the net cost figure by 20. In Table 14-2, however, the I-A cost for 20 years is annualized by dividing it by a conversion factor of 34.719 to arrive at the surrender cost index per year.[2] The surrender cost index is not simply an average for the 20-year period but a measure of the annual cost assuming an interest rate of 5 percent. It is the amount of money required annually to accumulate at 5 percent interest the total I-A surrender cost for the 20-year period the policy was in force.

---

2. One dollar per annum accumulated at 5 percent per year = $34.19.

If you invested $8.46 every year at a net return of 5 percent per annum, you would have $293.84 at the end of 20 years. If you invested $5.71 every year at a net return of 5 percent per annum, you would have $198.20 at the end of 20 years.

Therefore the $8.46 and $5.71 cost indexes represent the annual sacrifice you have made in order to have the policies in force for 20 years.

NET PAYMENT COST INDEX

Both the traditional net cost method and the I-A surrender cost index method are designed to measure the cost of a policy when you surrender it for cash after having paid premiums for a number of years. The assumption is that you will live for a specified number of years and then surrender the policy for its cash value. They measure cost from the "if I live" point of view.

The net payment cost index, on the other hand, measures the cost if you keep the policy in force until the day you die. This is the "if I die and the beneficiary gets the policy proceeds" point of view. Table 14-3 shows how this cost is calculated.

TABLE 14-3

20-Year Interest-Adjusted Net Payment Cost Per $1,000 for Straight Life Policy Issued to Male Age 35

	GUARANTEED COST	PARTICIPATING
Annual premium per $1,000	$ 18.89	$ 22.91
Accumulated premiums (at 5%)	655.84	795.41
Less accumulated dividends	0.00	235.21
I-A net payment cost for 20 years	655.84	560.20
Net payment cost index per year*	18.89	16.14

*Conversion factor is 34.719.

When we divide $655.84 by the conversion factor, we find that the net payment cost index per year is $18.89, which is the same as the annual premium. Now we know that when we compare level premium guaranteed cost policies on a net payments basis, all we have to do is compare the annual premium for one policy with the annual premium for another.

But the net payment cost index for the participating policy is less than the annual premium because dividends are paid. Thus, the I-A net payment cost for a par policy is not the same as the annual premium. If dividends were the same every year, all we would have to do to compare the net payments index with another policy is subtract the dividend from the annual premium. But dividends are not the same every year so we have to follow the procedure outlined in Table 14-3.[3]

TWO INDEXES TO COMPARE

There are two indexes to compare when you shop for life insurance. One is the surrender cost index which looks at cost from the "if I live" point of view. The other is the net payment cost index, which looks at cost from the "if I die" point of view. Which index is more important for you? Who can say? Will you live 20 years (or some other period of time) and then surrender the policy? Or will you keep the policy until you die? No one knows when you will die. But if you are *sure* you are not going to surrender the policy, then the net payment cost index is more significant to you than the surrender cost index. On the other hand, if you think you may surrender the policy sometime, the reverse is true. You have to decide which is better for you. No one can tell you.

ONLY

TERM OR WHOLE LIFE

Which should you buy, term insurance or whole life? That depends on answers to the following questions:

1. How much premium can you pay?

2. How long will you need the insurance?

If you need a large amount of life insurance but are unable to pay the premium for whole life insurance, you should buy term. Your family is better off if you have an adequate amount of term insurance than an inadequate amount of whole life, regardless of which policy may be better in the long run.

If you need life insurance for only a short time, term costs less than whole life. The longer you need life insurance, however, the more favorably the cost of whole life compares with term. If at age 25 you buy two $10,000 policies, one an annual renewable term policy for a first year premium of $48.60 and the other a whole life policy for an annual premium of $113.00, it is clear that the term policy is cheaper if you die the first year. If you accumulate the annual cost for both policies at 5 percent interest, eventually the sacrifice for the term policy will exceed that for the whole life policy, but "eventually" is a long time, as shown in Table 14-4. If you keep both policies and die at or before age 77, the whole life policy will cost more than the term policy. But if you die any time after age 77, the reverse is true.

---

3. An alternative is to accumulate the dividends and divide the total by the conversion factor (34.719 at 5%) to calculate the Equivalent Level Dividend, which can be subtracted from the annual premium to arrive at the net payment cost index. In this case, accumulated dividends ($235.21) divided by 34.719 equals $6.77. In turn $22.91 minus $6.77 = $16.14.

TABLE 14-4

*Premiums for
Annual
Renewable Term
Life Insurance
and Whole Life
Insurance, Both
Issued at Age 25,
Accumulated at
5 Percent.
Policy Amount:
$10,000*

POLICY	AGE 77	AGE 78
Annual renewable term	$28,818	$31,229
Whole life	29,128	30,703

But suppose you keep the policies for several years and then drop them. The cash value of the whole life policy reduces the cost when you surrender it but the term policy has no cash value. At what point in time is the sacrifice for the whole life policy less than that for the term policy on a surrender basis? This is shown in Table 14-5.

TABLE 14-5.

*Net Cost for
Annual
Renewable Term
Life Insurance
and Whole Life
Insurance,
Issued Age 25,
Accumulated at
5 Percent.
Policy Amount:
$10,000*

Policy	Premiums	Cash Value	Net Cost
END OF 6 YEARS			
Annual renewable term	$351	—0—	$351
Whole life	$807	$450	$357
END OF 7 YEARS			
Annual renewable term	$422	—0—	$422
Whole life	$996	$590	$406

If you keep both policies for at least seven years and then stop paying premiums on them at that time or later, the whole life policy costs less than the term life policy. But if you drop both policies prior to the seventh year, the term policy is cheaper.

Most people are not sure they will keep a policy in force until the day they die, nor are they sure they will die early enough so that term is the best choice. One thing they can be certain of, however, is that at older ages the annual premium for term becomes almost prohibitive. For example, the annual premium at age 77 for the term policy in our example is over $800, more than seven times the annual premium for the whole life policy. The annual premiums for both policies are equal at age 51; from then on, the annual premium for the term policy increases rapidly.

Assuming a higher or lower interest rate and comparing policies with higher or lower premiums will yield results different from those shown in our examples, but the implication for decision-making purposes will be similar. Term life insurance is preferable in the short run, but whole life may be better in the long run. Because so much depends on how long you keep your policy and when you die, it is wrong to say that term is better or whole life is better. Life insurance is like medicine. What is best depends on your needs and your premium-paying ability. Suggestion: be wary of anyone who tells you that term is always best or that whole life is always best. What is best depends on your circumstances.

Consumer Applications
Comparing Policy Costs

To compare policy costs, you need to know where to get cost information, whether the index number you find is high or low, and the significance of apparently small differences in index numbers. You also need to know how to compare one participating policy with another, how to compare a participating with a guaranteed cost policy, and how to use index numbers to compare term and whole life policies.

Where to Get Cost Information

If you want to shop for life insurance, you need cost information. Where can you get it? First, ask a life insurance agent or call a life insurance company. Second, look in *Consumer Reports.* It publishes periodic reports on life insurance costs which include premium rates, cost indexes, and other information for several hundred companies. Third, look in the most recent *Interest-Adjusted Index,* which is published by The National Underwriter Company. If your library does not have the latest edition, call life insurance agencies, agents, and companies listed in the Yellow Pages. Or buy a copy.[4] You can save the price many times over by staying away from high cost life insurance policies.

Is that Index High or Low?

Clearly, an index number by itself is meaningless. Whether it is high or low depends upon other index numbers. You can get some notion about this by comparing index numbers for similar policies at the age nearest yours listed in the *Interest-Adjusted Index.* Unfortunately, that publication does not include an array of indexes which would enable you to determine easily what is high or low. *Consumer Reports* does, however, show which policies are highest and which are lowest, by company, for certain policies. Table 14-6 illustrates the range of surrender cost indexes revealed by another study for an ordinary life policy in the amount of $100,000 for males age 25.

Caution: Do not use the indexes shown as a standard against which to compare those quoted by an agent or company. Prices and costs for life insurance change constantly and you must use the most recent information available. Would you judge the cost of a pound of coffee today on the basis of an advertisement in a year-old newspaper?

---

4. Write to: The National Underwriter Company, 420 East Fourth Street, Cincinnati, Ohio 45202.

	LOW	MEDIAN	HIGH	TABLE 14-6
Guaranteed Cost	1.10	3.29	5.79	
Participating	0.54	2.07	4.77	

TABLE 14-6

*20-Year
Surrender Cost
Indexes for
$100,000
Ordinary Life
Policy for Males
Age 25*

What's the Difference?

Because the index numbers in Table 14-6 are small and the differences among them seem even smaller, it is easy to underestimate the significance of the differences. Let's take a look at Table 14-7, which shows the 20-year cost of the $100,000 policy, using the indexes to make the calculation.[5]

If you bought the lowest cost guaranteed cost policy and I bought the highest cost, my total sacrifice over a 20-year period would be more than five times as much as yours.[6] Or, if I bought the lowest cost participating policy

	GUARANTEED COST	PARTICIPATING	TABLE 14-7
Low	$ 3,819.00	$ 1,875.00	
Median	11,423.00	7,187.00	
High	20,102.00	16,561.00	

TABLE 14-7

*20-Year
Surrender Cost
for $100,000
Ordinary Life
Policy Issued to
Male Age 25*

5. When we calculated the surrender cost index as shown in Table 14-2, we accumulated the annual premiums at interest, subtracted the surrender value to arrive at the surrender cost for 20 years, and then divided by the conversion factor to get the surrender cost index per year. When you start with the index number, you calculate the total surrender cost for the period by multiplying the index number by the conversion factor and the result by the number of thousands face amount of the policy. For example, let's use the low guaranteed cost index of $1.10.

$$\$1.10 \times 34.719 \times 100 = \$3,819.00$$

6. I'm assuming here that we're both age 25, a fantastic assumption for me to make but so pleasant that I don't mind being on the short end of the deal. Note that I win with the participating policy.

and you bought the highest cost, your sacrifice over a 20-year period would be almost nine times as much as mine. Does it pay to shop for life insurance?

Comparing Participating Policies

Suppose you are considering the purchase of a $100,000 participating whole life policy. The two lowest cost policies you find both have a surrender cost index of 1.05. Both companies have an A+ rating in Best's and you can find no reason to prefer one over the other. What can you do? Two things: (1) compare the net payment index and, (2) compare the equivalent level dividend. If one has a smaller net payment index than the other, that's a plus.

The reason is simple: if you keep the policy until you die, the one with the lower net payment index will require less sacrifice. If it also has a smaller equivalent level annual dividend, that's another plus. The smaller the ELD, the less dependent the surrender and net payment indexes are on dividends. Dividends are not guaranteed; they are projected. A smaller dividend projection is more conservative than a larger dividend projection, so you may have more confidence in it.

Comparing Par and Guaranteed Cost Policies

Some people say that comparing a par policy with a guaranteed cost policy is like comparing apples with oranges. The implication is that it cannot, should not, be done. Well, if you don't have money enough to buy both apples and oranges, you may have to make a choice—and that involves comparing them. Whether or not you are supposed to, you will compare par and guaranteed cost policies. And you can use the indexes to do it. Look at the two policies in Table 14-8.

The surrender cost index for the par policy is much lower than for the guaranteed cost policy and there is little difference between the net payment indexes. But the indexes for the par policy are quite dependent on the dividend projection. By what margin can actual dividends be less than those projected without having the par policy surrender cost be more than the guaranteed cost policy? If actual dividends were 88 cents instead of $3.36, the two policies would have the same surrender index. But that would be a decrease of almost 74 percent. What is the probability that actual dividends during the next 20 years will be 74 percent less than those projected? Various studies of dividend histories justify the belief that such a large difference between projected and actual dividends has a rather low probability. So if surrender cost is more important to you than net payment cost, buy the par policy. On the other hand, if the reverse is true, you may prefer the guaranteed cost policy because its cost does not depend on dividends.

TABLE 14-8

Participating and Guaranteed Cost Policy Comparison

	Surrender Cost Index	Equivalent Level Dividend	Net Payment Index
Participating	1.05	3.36	7.20
Guaranteed Cost	1.93	0.00	7.11

Term Versus Whole Life

Earlier in this chapter, we showed how to compare term and whole life policies. For a quick approximation, use of published indexes is easier than the method we illustrated. For example, suppose you want to compare a guaranteed cost, whole life policy issued at age 20, with an annual renewable term to age 99 for a 20-year period.

One such policy we looked at has a 20-year surrender cost index of $1.93. An annual renewable term policy offered by another company has a surrender cost index of $1.94. What does this mean? It means that if you buy both policies, keep them in force for 20 years and then drop them, the term policy will have cost you a penny more per thousand per year than the whole life policy.

But suppose you die at the end of 20 years and the policies are still in force. The whole life policy has a net payments index of $7.11, while the net payments index for the term policy is the same as the surrender cost index.[7] So on a surrender cost index basis, one policy is as good as another. On a net payments index basis, the term policy is a far better buy.

Caveats for the Life Insurance Shopper

1. Cost is important, but other things matter.
2. Published data may be out of date.
3. Some companies are low cost on certain policies, high cost on others.
4. Some policies are low-cost at one age or amount, but a poor buy at another.
5. "Other things" may not be equal.

The purpose of shopping is to get a general idea of the range of cost so you can distinguish between high, low, and medium. But buying life insurance is like buying a car. The base price of two cars may be identical but the cost including all the options you want differs widely. Some policies, for example, include waiver of premium at no extra charge; others require additional premium. Some companies quote premium rates for your age on your nearest birthday (ANB), while others are for your age last birthday (ALB). During a given year, you may be 20 for one company and 21 for another; the rate quoted by both companies for age 20 would not be comparable. Cost is lower for females than for males but the difference from policy to policy or from company to company is not uniform.

Some policies are for nonsmokers or nondrinkers or for teachers or residents of certain states. Two policies with identical premium rates on an annual basis may be quite different if you pay premiums by the month.[8] Most companies sell a number of similar but not identical policies. In a few cases, a company is competitive for all policies, ages and amounts. Usually, a company is competitive for certain policies, at some ages and at some amounts, but not for all policies at all ages and amounts. You must shop for the policy you want in the amount you want and at your age. Another important consideration is the agent or broker. Some are helpful, others are not.[9]

You can get comparable proposals by asking an agent, broker, or company to complete a form like the one in Figure 14-1.

---

7. Why? Because the term policy has no cash value.

8. A 1978 study of the annual percentage rate for the added cost of paying premiums on other than an annual basis revealed a cost range of 4.9 percent to 29.3 percent.

9. See Chapter 7.

FIGURE 14-1

*Life Insurance
Proposal per
Thousand Dollars*

Date _____

Your Name _____ Date of Birth _____

Agents Name _____ Company Name _____

Policy Type_____ Policy Name_____ W.P. Yes No

Participating   Yes   No   Guaranteed Cost   Yes   No   ANB _____   ALB _____

Face Amount _____ Annual Premium _____ Monthly Premium _____

Note: Indexes based on monthly premium payment.

Year	End of Year Cash Value	End of Year Dividend	Equivalent Level Div.	Net Payment	Surrender Cost
1					
2					
3					
4					
5					
6					
7					
8					
9					
10					
11					
12					
13					
14					
15					
16					
17					
18					
19					
20					

Source: James L. Athearn, *It Pays To Shop For Life Insurance.*

Reprinted with permission of The National Underwriter Co., Cincinnati, OH.

Discussion Questions

1. Considering the fact that most adults need life insurance, why don't they just go out and buy it? Why do they wait for someone to sell it to them?

2. Many people will move their savings from one account to another in order to make ¼ of 1 percent more interest annually. They shop around for the best deal. Why don't they shop for life insurance?

3. Using the traditional net cost method, an agent is frequently able to show that the cost of having a life insurance policy in force for 10 or 20 years is negative. Why do you suppose anyone would believe that? Do you consider such illustrations dishonest? Comment.

4. If you were going to make your own life insurance cost calculations, how would you decide the interest rate to use?

5. Until we experienced interest rates so high that many people could not qualify for home purchase financing, the average borrower was more interested in the total monthly payment required than the interest rate charged. How do you account for this attitude?

6. In order to simplify the consumer brochure for life insurance buyers, the Wisconsin Insurance Commissioner decided not to include the net payment cost index. A number of life insurance companies objected strongly. Why?

7. J. Edwin Logan says, "I am never going to surrender the straight life insurance policy I buy. Therefore, all I am going to use for cost comparison purposes is the net payment cost index." Do you share this veiw? Why or why not?

8. Would whole life insurance be cheaper if such policies had no cash surrender values? Please explain.

9. A model regulation concerning life insurance cost disclosure created by the National Association of Insurance Commissioners was adopted by a number of states during the late seventies. An advisory committee was appointed to determine its effectiveness. How could that be measured?

10. One authority on life insurance has suggested that guaranteed cost policies are an anachronism that should be eliminated from the marketplace. What could be the basis for this suggestion? Do you agree with it? Why or why not?

Cases

14-1 Joe, age 35, has been presented with two life insurance policies. Both are whole life, but one—policy A—is a nonparticipating contract with an annual premium of $190, while the other—policy B—is a participating contract with gross premiums of $220 per year. Both policies are for $10,000. The projected dividends for the par policy are as follows:

> $15 per year for years 1–5
> $20 per year for years 6–10
> $30 per year for years 11–15
> $40 per year for years 16–20
> $50 per year for the remaining years up to age 100

  1. What factors should Joe consider in choosing the policy he will buy?

  2. Can you calculate for him which is the better buy?

14-2 Betty, age 35, has just heard a sales presentation by an agent who told her that all cash-value life insurance gives very poor returns on her investment. The agent told her that she should buy term life insurance only, and invest the difference between the term insurance premiums and whole life premiums in a mutual fund which she sells. Betty has owned a $25,000 whole life insurance policy since she was 23. She is considering cashing it in in order to pay the first premium for an equal amount of yearly renewable term life insurance, and invest the remaining cash value in the mutual fund.

1. What factors should Betty consider before making this decision?

2. Can you tell her what to do? Explain.

14-3 Martha is not happy with the life insurance cost comparisons which she has read in various magazines. "They just don't use realistic interest rates," she says. "There is no way that I would be happy with anything less than 20 percent, and none of them even comes close!"

1. What advice could you give Martha?

2. How would you explain the interest rate assumptions to her?

Chapter Fifteen:
THE LIABILITY RISK

INTRODUCTION

From an economic point of view, the risks of death and disability are the most important for many households. Perhaps the next most serious risk is that of liability. While liability losses are infrequent and less obvious to the casual observer than death and disability, they can reach catastrophic proportions. Although suits for damages are becoming more common and receive much more publicity than in the past, many people are either unaware of the risk or do not understand it. The purpose of this chapter is to discuss the following:

1. The nature of the liability risk
2. The significance of liability
3. The sources of the liability risk.

NATURE OF THE LIABILITY RISK   3ᴿᴰ PARTY CLAIM

The risks of death, disability, loss by fire and flood, and so on, are in a sense natural risks. That is, the losses which occur are the result of natural or physical causes. Liability, on the other hand, is a risk of another sort. It is purely a creation of the law. It may be defined as the possibility that a person or those for whom he or she is responsible will be required to pay certain sums in discharge of a responsibility imposed by law.

Two elements of this definition merit additional comment. First, "certain sums" means a certain amount of money decided upon by the court. From the point of view of the person who may become liable, this

is a matter of considerable uncertainty. Moreover, the potential loss is open-end in that it may be for any amount. This is in contrast with the risk of loss to property, where the most that can be lost is the value of the property itself plus loss of use while it is being repaired or replaced. Second, "imposed by law" refers to laws created by our society. Thus, the law is whatever the courts and legislatures have decided upon. It may vary from one jurisdiction to another and from time to time.

Basis

As shown in Figure 15-1, the liability risk may arise out of either statutory or common law. Statutory law is the body of written law created by legislative bodies. Common law, on the other hand, is based on custom and court decisions. In evolving common law, the courts are guided by the doctrine of *stare decisis.* Under this doctrine, once a principle of law is found applicable to a given set of facts, the courts will adhere to the established principle and apply it to future cases involving similar facts. This practice provides enough continuity of decision making so that many disputes can be settled by referring to previous decisions concerning similar situations instead of taking the matter to court.

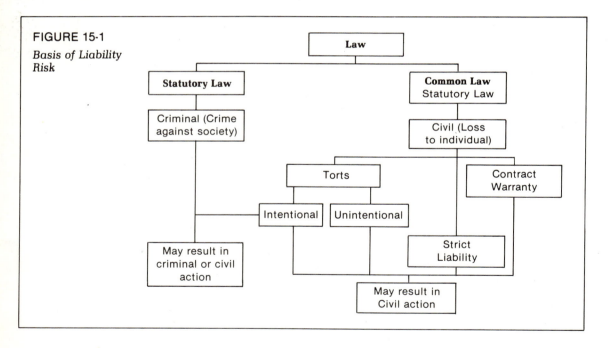

FIGURE 15-1

*Basis of Liability
Risk*

The field of law includes criminal law and civil law. Criminal law is concerned with acts that are contrary to public policy; i.e., crimes. Civil law, in contrast, deals with acts that are not against society as a whole but which cause injury or loss to an individual. Civil law has two branches, one concerned with the law of contracts and the other with the law of torts. Liability may stem from either contracts or torts.

A tort is "a wrongful act or omission arising in the course of social relationships other than contracts, which violates a person's legally protected right, and for which the law provides a remedy in the form of action for damage."[1] The person who commits a tort is known as the *tort feasor*. A tort may be intentional in that it is for the purpose of injuring another person or his property or it may be unintentional. The latter are called negligence torts, and they are the basis for most liability.[2]

If you are negligent and someone suffers bodily injury or property damage as a result of it, you may be liable for damages. Negligence refers to conduct or behavior. It may be a matter of doing something you should not do, or failing to do something you should do. It has been defined as "the omission to do something which a reasonable man, guided by those considerations which ordinarily regulate the conduct of human affairs would do, or doing something which a reasonable and prudent man would not do."[3]

Liability may also be based on a contract or a warranty. When you sign a rental agreement for tools, for example, the agreement may provide that the tools will be returned to the owner in good condition, ordinary wear and tear excepted. If they are stolen or damaged, you are liable for the loss. If you offer your car for sale and assure the buyer that it is in perfect condition, you have made a warranty. If the car is not in perfect condition, you may be liable for damages because of a breech of warranty. This is why some sellers offer goods for sale on an "as is" basis; they want to be sure there is no warranty.

Liability may be absolute rather than based on negligence, contract, or warranty. If you have property that is dangerous to others or you engage in an activity that may cause harm to others, you may be liable without regard to fault. In some states, for example, the law holds owners or operators of aircraft absolutely liable with respect to damage caused to persons or property on the ground. Similarly, if you dam a creek on your property to build a lake, you will be absolutely liable for injury or damage caused if the dam collapses and floods the area below.

In some jurisdictions, the owner of a dangerous animal is liable for any harm or damage caused by the animal. Such liability is a matter of law. If you own a pet lion, you may become liable for damages regardless of how careful you are. The responsibility your employer has to you in the event you are injured or contract an occupational disease is based on the same principle of liability without fault.[4]

Finally, liability may be vicarious. The liability of one person may be

---

1. J. A. Donaldson, *Casualty Claim Practice* (rev. ed.; Homewood, Illinois: Richard D. Irwin, Inc., 1969), p. 17.

2. Liability may also be based on warranty or contract, or it may be absolute and not involve negligence. These aspects of liability are discussed later.

3. C. A. Kulp, *Casualty Insurance* (3rd ed.; New York: The Ronald Press Company, 1956), p. 55.

4. Workers' compensation is discussed in Chapter 19.

based upon the tort of another. As will be shown later, vicarious liability may stem from employer-employee and other relationships.

Responsibility for Damages

The courts have adopted the principle that a person whose conduct is negligent should be held responsible for whatever damage results. In attempting to specify what kind of conduct is considered to be negligent, the courts have developed various concepts of behavior and standards of care, the latter depending upon the circumstances.

As was indicated in the definition of negligence, everyone has a duty to do what reasonable people will do and to refrain from doing what reasonable people will not do. You have a legal duty to exercise reasonable care. If you do something which is unreasonable or imprudent, you are negligent; you failed to live up to your duty to exercise reasonable care. If some innocent party is injured as a result of your conduct, you can be held responsible for damages. If you intended harm to result, you are guilty of a crime. In either event, you can be held responsible for damages resulting from your conduct.

In summary, responsibility for damages based on negligence stems from the following:

1. A duty on the part of one person to another

2. Breech of that duty

3. Damage or injury to the second party

4. A causal connection between the breech of duty and the damage or injury.

SIGNIFICANCE OF THE LIABILITY RISK

The liability risk is significant for several reasons: (1) the possible size of loss, (2) the cost of defense, (3) uncertainty of the outcome of a claim, and (4) increasing frequency of claims.

Possible Size of Loss

While verdicts for property damage are becoming more frequent and growing in size, the largest amounts for damages have been awarded in bodily injury cases. Prior to 1951, the highest bodily injury verdict in the United States was for $260,000. By 1977, the million dollar milestone had been passed at least 56 times.[5]

Concepts of the economic loss caused by bodily injuries have changed drastically during this century. For example, in 1896 a verdict of $1,100 was held adequate for the loss of a leg by a child. About fifty years later, a case involving serious burns and loss of sight to a child was settled out of court for $180,000. In 1902, a federal district court in California awarded $3,000 for the loss of a leg and fractured

---

5. *U.S. News & World Report*, Dec. 4, 1978, p. 53.

ribs. In 1949, the same court thought a similar injury was worth $100,000. Today, such an injury would cost several times that much.

Not all awards are of such size. However, the average size of verdicts for bodily injury has been increasing. Judges have recognized that the cost of living has risen and the decreased purchasing power of the dollar should be reflected in damage suit verdicts. In one case involving a verdict of $150,000, the court said that while the verdict was large, "we would not have the right to shut our eyes wholly to the fact that it is not out of line with what juries more and more generally have been doing under present economic conditions."[6] The effect of inflation, rising income levels, and a greater appreciation of the value of human life is unmistakable.

Cost of Defense

Bodily injury verdicts illustrate the loss potential of the liability risk but a verdict is only part of the story. If someone sues you or threatens to sue you for damages, a great deal of time, effort, and worry are involved in settling the claim. Whether the claim is groundless or not, you must defend yourself in order to avoid having to pay large sums of money. If you ignore the problem the plaintiff may win the case by default. You must hire an attorney to defend you if you want to prevent such a loss. The attorney may, in turn, find it necessary to hire an investigator to determine all the facts of the case. If the attorney thinks that the plaintiff (party suing) may get a judgment against you, he or she may recommend that you attempt to compromise with the plaintiff. This will involve an "out-of-court" settlement.

You may think you are innocent of any negligence or responsibility for damages, but you do not know how the case may come out in court. In one case in which the plaintiff had offered to settle for $2,500 before the trial started, a settlement of $52,500 was made out of court after the trial had gone on for ten days.[7] In another case in which the plaintiff had offered to settle for $15,000 prior to trial, the verdict was for $105,000.[8]

Uncertainty of Outcome

While many cases result in verdicts which favor the defendant, the chance that he or she will lose is cause for considerable worry. Even if an adverse decision can be appealed in order to get the size of the judgment reduced, such action is expensive and the results are uncertain. Thus, the defendant in a suit for damages involving negligence may be faced with a choice between paying too much to get a compromise settlement or spending more money on attorney's fees without any assurance of success. A large verdict may spell financial ruin and further appeals may drain the defendant of resources. Furthermore, regardless of how such negotiations and appeals are finally concluded, they may involve distasteful publicity.

---

6. *Foster v. Pastana*, 177 Pac. (2nd) 54.

7. *Alaimo v. City and County of San Francisco*, Superior Court, San Francisco, No. 382797.

8. *Fuller v. Gonzales*, Superior Court, Santa Clara County, No. 72154.

Increasing Frequency

Claims for damages are increasing in frequency as well as size. More than 7,000,000 lawsuits are filed in this country every year. Children sue their parents, husbands and wives sue each other, Michelle sues Lee[9], and friends sue friends. A young man in Colorado filed suit against his parents, charging that their inhumane and inadequate care when he was a child made it impossible for him to fit into society as an adult. A woman in New Jersey sued her husband for damages. He had accidentally chopped off part of her finger with a hedge trimmer. The California Supreme Court ruled that a person injured by a drunken partygoer can sue not only the drunk but the host of the party as well.

A special report by *U.S. News & World Report* entitled, "Why Everybody Is Suing Everybody" said, "Americans in all walks of life are being buried under an avalanche of lawsuits." One factor contributing to this may be the existence of insurance; people feel that the insurance company is going to pay, not the person they are suing, so why be concerned? Two other factors contributing to this situation are claims consciousness and the attitude of juries.

Claims consciousness.   Publicity given to damage suits has increased awareness of the potential. People see others getting large awards and say, "Why shouldn't I?" Attitudes toward risk have changed as our sense of individual responsibility has declined. People expect to be protected; when they are not, they blame someone else for the loss they suffer. This is illustrated by the California man who, upset at being stood up on a date, unsuccessfully sued his would-be companion for $38 to compensate him for driving 40 miles for nothing.

Attitude of juries.   At the same time, many people who serve on juries have developed a "share the wealth" philosophy which leads them to believe that an opportunity to redistribute some of the wealth owned by rich citizens and insurance companies should not be passed up. In many cases, it is claimed, the judgment is not based on the defendant's negligence, but on the apparent needs of the plaintiff and the financial condition of the defendant, including the amount of insurance he or she has. This philosophy ignores the fact that insurance is a pooling device and the money paid out by insurers is obtained from policyholders. When claim payments increase, premium rates are forced upward.

MAJOR SOURCES OF PERSONAL LIABILITY

Personal liability may stem from your activities, the activities of those for whom you are responsible, and the property you own or control. While automobiles are the major source of liability for most individuals and households, there are many other kinds of activities and property which may involve an individual in suits for damages. Some of these are discussed below before attention is turned to the problem of automobile

---

9. *Marvin v. Marvin*, C-23303, Superior Court, County of Los Angeles, 1979.

liability. While some of the cases mentioned did not result in judgment against the defendant, the defendant was subjected to the worry and expense of defending himself or herself.

Activities

People may be liable for damages caused by their own actions or those of someone else. For example, a man in Chicago sued a fishing companion for $50,000, claiming that a hook cast by his friend was imbedded in his eye and that as a result the eye had to be removed.[10] A golfer drove a ball which struck his caddy in the head; a $10,000 judgment resulted.[11] A member of a deer hunting party saw something move which, in the uncertain light at dusk, he took to be a deer. He fired—and then found that he had shot another member of his party. A substantial judgment resulted.[12]

Minors. Generally, a minor is liable for his or her own torts, but there are circumstances under which damage caused by a child may lead to liability on the part of his or her parents. In some states, the law specifies that parents are liable for damage caused intentionally—such as vandalism—by their children. Thus, there is vicarious liability by statute. The parent becomes liable for the child's tort.

Parents. On the other hand, parents may be held responsible for damages because they were in some respect negligent with regard to their children rather than because of vicarious liability. For example, the parents of a four-year-old child who injured his baby-sitter were required to pay damages. The child had a habit of violently attacking and throwing himself against people. The baby-sitter did not know this and was injured when the child suddenly knocked her to the floor. The court said the parents had a duty to warn the baby-sitter of the risk of which they had knowledge and of which the baby-sitter would not likely be aware. In contrast, they had told the sitter, "Don't worry, he's playful, but not bad."[13]

In another case, the parents of a boy who struck and injured a playmate were held liable because their knowledge of his vicious propensities and failure to restrain him constituted negligence.[14] When a domestic servant was struck by a baseball bat wielded by the eight-year-old son of her employer, the latter was held liable for damages.[15] In all these cases, parents were held liable because of their own negligence rather than vicariously. Whether liability is direct or vicarious, however, the financial burden may be unbearable. Children may or may

---

10. Reported in the Sales Section of the *Fire, Casualty and Surety Bulletins.*

11. *Gardner v. Heldman,* 15 C.C.H. (neg.) 876.

12. *Webster v. Seavy,* 138 Atl. 541.

13. *Ellis v. D'Angelo,* 253 Pac. (2nd) 675.

14. *Condel v. Save,* 11 C.C.H. (Neg.) 238.

15. *Zuckerberg v. Munzer,* 18 C.C.H. (Neg.) 1002.

not be a joy for their parents, but their activities may constitute a serious liability risk.

Property.   You not only have a duty to the public with regard to your activities, but also in connection with real and personal property you own or for which you are responsible. The duty—the degree of care—varies with the circumstances. The owner or tenant of premises, for example, does not owe the same duty to all those who enter upon his or her property. The highest degree of care is owed to invitees, whereas the standard of care is less for licensees and lowest for trespassers.

A *trespasser* is a person who enters the premises of another without either express or implied permission from a person who has the right to give such permission. Generally, the only duty owed to a trespasser is to refrain from taking steps to harm him or her. There are several exceptions to this statement, the most important being concerned with trespassing children. This is discussed below in connection with attractive nuisance.

A *licensee* is a person who enters premises with permission but (1) not for the benefit of the person in possession, or (2) without a reasonable expectation that the premises have been made safe for him or her. If your automobile breaks down and you ask the owner of the nearest house if you can use his or her telephone, the permission you receive to enter the house makes you a licensee. A social guest and guests in an automobile are licensees rather than invitees. Because a licensee is the party who receives the benefit of entering the property, he or she is entitled to a minimum degree of care by the owner or tenant. They must avoid harm to licensees and warn them of any dangerous activity or condition of the property but need not make the place safer than it was before.

An *invitee* is a person who enters the premises with permission but who is entitled to a higher degree of care than a licensee. If the possessor of the property will benefit as a result of the person's presence, the latter is an invitee. Thus, a customer in a store is an invitee and this is the case whether he or she makes a purchase.

For the most part, it is your reasonable expectations that determine your status. If you may reasonably expect that the premises have been made safe for you, you are an invitee. For example, if I invite you to a party at my home, you are an invitee. If you should reasonably expect to accept the premises as is without special effort on the part of the possessor, then you are a licensee. The distinction between a licensee and an invitee is not always clear because it depends on reasonable expectations. What is reasonable?

In any particular case, the liability of the owner to an injured party will depend upon:

1. His or her duty to the injured party

2. His or her failure to fulfill that duty

3. A causal connection between such failure and the injury sustained.

The significance of whether the injured party is a trespasser, a licensee, or an invitee lies in the difference in the duty to which he or she is entitled. Some of the situations which may lead to liability for a homeowner are illustrated in the next section.

Illustrative cases. A guest who fell on a slippery floor was awarded damages against the homeowner. In another case, a visitor fell down steps which were not properly lighted because a servant had failed to turn on a light. While it was the servant who was negligent, the homeowner had to pay because the servant was his representative. Thus, his liability was vicarious; he was not negligent but his employee was. In another case, a homeowner repaired a canopy and then hired a painter to do some painting. When the painter crawled onto the canopy to complete the painting job, the canopy collapsed. The homeowner was held liable for the injuries sustained. When the milkman tripped over a gate stop in the center of the driveway on the premises where he made deliveries, the homeowner was held responsible for his injuries.

Boats and pets. Other property may lead to liability. Boats, for example, may cause damage or injury and the people who own or operate them may be held liable. One case in Michigan resulted in both the owner-operator and his guest being held liable for damages when the boat in which they were riding struck a swimmer. This is a particularly serious problem in congested areas where there are boats, water skiers, and swimmers.

Pets are also a source of liability, especially if it is known that they are vicious. In one case, a mailman collected damages for a dog bite. In another case, an elderly man fell and broke his arm when a dog frightened him. He sued both the present and the former owners of the dog because the dog frequently stayed with the former owners and was at their home at the time the man was injured.

Attractive nuisance. In some cases, small children are attracted by dangerous objects or property. In such circumstances, the owner has a special duty toward the children, especially if they are too young to be entirely responsible. This is called the doctrine of *attractive nuisance.* An attractive nuisance is anything attractive to small children which may harm them. This means, for instance, that those who own power lawnmowers must be especially watchful if there are small children who may be injured through their own curiosity. If you leave your rotary mower running while you go in the house to answer the telephone and there are small children in the neighborhood who may be attracted to it, you are being negligent in not exercising greater care on behalf of such children. The most modern and rapidly growing attractive nuisance is the swimming pool. While some courts have held that those who own swimming pools are not necessarily baby-sitters for the community, it appears that they do have the duty of keeping children out. There have been many cases in which children entered the neighbor's pool without permission and were drowned. The result is a suit for damages and in many cases a verdict for the plaintiff.

Automobile Liability

Significance. Ownership and operation of an automobile is probably the greatest source of liability any individual has. With about 150 million automobiles operating and millions of people driving them, automobile accidents cause an amazing amount of death and destruction.

There are over 17 million automobile accidents every year and the total cost involved is more than $30 billion. One driver out of every eight is involved in an accident during an average year. The property damage that may be caused by an automobile can easily reach $25,000 or $100,000 or even more. In the case of bodily injuries, claims of $100,000 are not unusual. While stories about large damage suits appear in the newspapers almost daily, smaller claims have become so commonplace that they are no longer considered newsworthy. The automobile policy will be discussed in the next chapter, but at this point the problem as it affects you and your family will be outlined.

Responsibility of driver and owner. As the driver of an automobile you are responsible for its careful and safe operation. If you do not operate it in a reasonable and prudent fashion and someone is injured as a result of such lack of care, you may be held liable for damages. If, for example, you carelessly drive through a stop sign and run into another car, you may be liable for the damage done.

Through either direct or vicarious liability, the owner of an automobile may be responsible for the damage it causes when driven by another person. In some states, the "family purpose doctrine" makes the owner of the family car responsible for whatever damage it does regardless of which member of the family may be operating the car at the time of the accident. The theory is that the vehicle is being used for a family purpose and the owner as head of the family is therefore responsible.

If you lend your car to Sid Smith so he can go buy a case of liquor for a party you are having, he will be your agent during the trip and you may be held responsible if he is involved in an accident. Your liability in that case is vicarious; you are responsible for Smith's negligence. On the other hand, if Smith is not a competent driver, you may be held directly liable for putting a dangerous instrument in his hands. In such a case, it is your own negligence you are responsible for.

Parents' responsibility. Many parents assume responsibility for automobile accidents in which their children may become involved without realizing that they are doing so. In some states, minors between the ages of 16 and 18 are issued drivers licenses only if their application is signed by a parent or guardian. What many parents do not realize is that by signing the application they assume responsibility for damage arising out of the child driving any automobile. Ordinarily, a child is responsible for his or her own torts but the parent becomes liable by contract.

Consumer Applications
Becoming Liability Risk Conscious

Like some strange diseases that have un-pronounceable names, the liability risk seems rather remote. Does it affect you? If so, what can you do about it? Let's examine these questions.

Does Liability Risk Affect You?

Not infrequently, students reading about the liability risk for the first time have the feeling that they really don't need to be concerned about it because, "I don't have any assets," or "You can't get blood out of a turnip." Well, you may or may not be judgment proof. And maybe you can't get blood out of a turnip, but not everyone knows that and they may try.

What is a judgment? Webster's says it is "an obligation (as a debt) created by the decree of a court." If the court grants a plaintiff a judgment against you, that person is your creditor and you are his or her debtor. You may not be able to pay the debt, but you are wrong if you think that your inability to pay means you won't be injured. The judgment may, in effect, be a mortgage against your future.

In most states, the party who gets the judgment against you can attach your property, both real and personal. Many states limit a creditor's rights with regard to certain kinds of property, but if you are at all successful in your career, such laws offer little protection. While judgments expire periodically in some states, they are usually renewable. This gives the creditor a continuing right to take property you may acquire in the future. This ongoing threat may not bother you, but many people find it a real psychological burden.

And that isn't all. Many states allow garnishment of part of your wages by your creditor. This is a legal process by which your employer is required to make deductions from your salary to pay your creditor. Having a judgment against you will not enhance your reputation, particularly with your employer. Unhappily, you may not be able to keep it a secret.

What Can You Do?

If it is possible for you to become liable to pay damages to someone and if it is unlikely that you are judgment proof, what can you do? The most important thing you can do is train yourself to be conscious of the liability risk. Remember that every piece of property you have and every activity you engage in involves a possible liability exposure. Look at every situation from this point of view. Unless you identify risks, you don't have an opportunity to do anything about them. A liability checklist may be helpful.

Liability Checklist

It is probably impossible to create a checklist of liability risks that will include every exposure for every individual or family. Table 15-1 may, however, serve as a starting point. As we discuss some of the items it contains, you may think of others.

269

TABLE 15-1

*Possible Sources
of Personal
Liability*

Activities

Home or Work
    occupation
    contracts
    home maintenance

Recreational
    golf
    camping
    archery
        hunting

Social
    club member
    entertain guests

Property

Home
    swimming pool
    lawn mower
    other power tools
    poorly-maintained
        walkways, steps
    pets

Vehicles
    automobile
    motorcycle
    snowmobile
    boat
    airplane
    off-road recreational vehicle

Almost any activity may inadvertently lead to liability because of a momentary lapse in judgment that results in injury or damage. Your hobbies can involve liability exposure. Are you a model airplane enthusiast? Could careless operation of your model airplane cause it to hit someone? Have you signed any contracts lately? Did they have hold-harmless clauses? When you rent tools or equipment, it is not unusual for the contract you sign to provide that you are responsible for any injury caused to anyone, even if the real cause was faulty maintenance by the equipment rental shop. You may assume this risk without realizing it.

Your children may damage a neighbor's property. Kids have been known to build a campfire under the neighbor's porch. You may cause a forest fire if you are careless with your campfire. You may cause your neighbor's home to burn if your trash fire gets out of control through your carelessness.

When your neighbor borrows your chain-saw, what responsibility do you have to him or her? Are you responsible for defects in the saw that may cause injury? Suppose you don't check to see that he or she knows how to handle the saw and is, as a result, injured. Could you be held liable? Suppose you are target shooting and the neighbor's eight-year-old son comes along and asks to "take just one shot." If he accidentally shoots someone, you may be responsible for putting a dangerous instrument into the hands of an incompetent.

Your home is your major asset and also a major source of liability exposure. Your swimming pool may be considered an attractive nuisance, so it's your responsibility to protect the neighbor's children. Every power tool you have involves a similar exposure. Your lawn mower, power saw, electric hedge trimmer, and other tools can cause injury to a curious young child. You may become liable to a person who trips over your child's tricycle or inadvertently steps on an abandoned skate board. Even your dog can cause liability by hurting someone or by damaging a neighbor's property.

What about social activities? You know that you have responsibilities for guests in your home and are aware of the potential for liability. But what about social organizations you belong to? Are you a member of an association? If so, you may have liability in connection with its activities. This means that you may become liable, along with other members of the association, for the actions of a member. That's a real shocker, isn't it? If you belong to a fraternity or sorority or similar organization, is it an association and what are the possible liability risks for you? When you realize that you may become legally liable for the actions of other people, the possible scope of such liability should get your attention.

How to Cope

After you have become liability risk conscious and are able to identify potential sources of loss, how can you cope with them? First, you can avoid some of them. For example, when you sign an equipment rental agreement, read it. Look for hold-harmless clauses. Tell the rental people you don't mind being responsible for the equipment itself, but you have a policy against assuming someone else's liability exposure. Most of the time, they won't know what you're talking about because they use what they call a "standard form," and don't read it themselves. If you persist, however, they will agree to strike out hold-harmless clauses.

Second, be careful. This sounds trite, because most of us think we're always careful. But if we think about each situation from the point of view of potential loss, we are inclined to be more careful. One reason people who work on high-voltage power lines are very, very deliberate in each move they make is because a wrong move may be the last one. You don't have to look at every move you make exactly that way, but you can be more careful than you have been. Example: is your campfire out? Maybe? Or absolutely?

Third, transfer. Does your liability insurance cover you for *this* exposure? Does your employer's liability insurance cover you for liability you may have in connection with your job? Does the association to which you belong have liability insurance to protect itself and its members?

Discussion Questions

1. Your neighbor's small children run wild all day, every day, totally ignored by their parents. You have forcibly ejected them from your swimming pool several times but they return the next day. Your complaints to their parents have had no effect. Do you think it is fair to hold you responsible for the safety of these children simply because your swimming pool is an attractive nuisance? Aren't their parents being negligent? Can you use their negligence in your defense in the event one of the children drowns in your pool and they sue you for damages?

2. Isn't it enough for you to be held responsible for your own actions without being responsible for someone else's? Please comment.

3. If the doctrine of *stare decisis* worked perfectly, wouldn't the number of cases that require court action decline? Why or why not?

4. In some countries, the liability risk is far less significant than it is in the United States. How do you account for this?   *SOCIAL PROGRAMS*

5. In the United States, it is common practice for the compensation of plaintiff's attorneys in liability cases to be a percentage of the damages awarded by the court. In Great Britain, on the other hand, compensation in such cases is on a fee basis. Which system do you prefer? Why?

6. Under the doctrine of absolute liability there are situations in which you may be held liable for damage or injury to someone regardless of how careful you have been. Is this fair? Why or why not?

7. Products liability judgments have increased tremendously in both size and number during the last decade. As a result, manufacturers and sellers of goods have become very safety conscious. This being the case, why do we have a federal Consumer Products Safety Commission?

8. Considering the factors involved in establishing responsibility for damages based on negligence, what do you think is your best defense against such a suit? *PRove Your not Responsisable*

9. Do you think the fact that the owner or tenant of real property owes a different duty to various categories of people who enter the premises may increase the amount of litigation in this area? Please explain.

10. A physician or surgeon may become liable for damages on the basis of contract or negligence. Why is the latter more common than the former? Does your answer to this question tell you something about managing your liability risks? What?

Cases

15-1 Your neighbor's English bulldog, Cedric, is very friendly. But you wouldn't know it by looking at him! Last Monday a rather strange set of circumstances happened at the neighbor's home. The substitute mailman met Cedric as he was approaching the mailbox. Because he is afraid of even small dogs, the sight of Cedric approaching caused the mailman to collapse from fright, fall to the ground, and break his left arm. A motorist, who observed this situation while driving by, rammed the neighbor's parked car. The parked car then proceeded down the street through two fences, finally stopping in Mrs. Smith's living room.

1. Is there a case for litigation involving your neighbor?

2. Where does the motorist's liability fit into this picture?

15-2 In an interesting case in Arizona, *Vanguard Insurance Company vs. Cantrell vs. Allstate Insurance Company,* 1973 C.C.H. (Automobile) 7684, an insurer was held liable for personal injuries inflicted on a storeowner when the insured robbed the store and fired a warning shot to scare the owner. The robber's aim was bad, and he hit the owner. Because he had not intended to harm the owner, the insured convinced the court that the exclusion under a homeowners policy of intentional injury should not apply.

1. What reasoning might the court have applied to reach this decision?

2. Do you agree with this decision, and why?

15-3   Most states have a vicarious liability law dealing with the use of an automobile. For instance, California and New York hold the owner liable for injuries caused by the driver's negligence, while Pennsylvania and Utah make the person furnishing an automobile to a minor liable for that minor's negligence. Ohio, Indiana, Texas, Hawaii, and Rhode Island make the parent or guardian or signer of the minor's application for a license liable for the minor's negligence.

1. Why do these states do this?

2. Do you agree with this approach? Why?

3. If you are a resident of a state which has no such vicarious liability statute, does this mean that you are unaffected by these laws? Why?

15-4   In *Steyer vs. Westvaco Corporation*, 1979, *C.C.H. (Fire & Casualty)* 1229, and in *Grand River Lime Company vs. Ohio Casualty Insurance Company*, 1973 *C.C.H. (Fire & Casualty)* 383, industrial operators were held liable for damages caused by their discharge of pollutants over a period of years, even though they were not aware of the damage they were causing when discharging the pollutants.

1. How might this affect the public at large?

2. What impact will it have on liability insurance?

3. Since the discharge of pollutants was intentional, should this be insurable at all?

Chapter Sixteen:
MANAGING AUTOMOBILE RISKS

INTRODUCTION

As was pointed out in Chapter 15, the automobile is a major source of
liability risk for the family. In addition, it generates a major property
risk because it may be damaged, destroyed, or stolen. It also is a major
focus of personal risk, because its use may cause death or injury to a
guest or member of the family. These losses can increase expenses and
reduce family assets and income. The following points are discussed in
this chapter:

1. The need for automobile insurance

2. Basic automobile insurance coverage

3. The Personal Automobile Policy

4. Differences in coverage.

Why Insurance?

Because of the widespread ownership and use of automobiles, most of
us are affected by these risks. Avoidance is out of the question for most
people because the automobile is an integral part of their daily lives.
Loss prevention and control efforts may reduce the probable frequency
and severity somewhat, but the possibility of loss remains. Most
families can retain and budget for the first-dollar portion of some
losses, such as physical damage to their automobiles, or even the whole
loss if the vehicle is worth only a few hundred dollars. But virtually no

one is financially able to retain all of the risks associated with the automobile.

There are several reasons for this. First, the possible size of liability losses is huge. Second, lenders who finance the purchase of automobiles require borrowers to purchase insurance against loss by collision, fire, theft, and other perils. Third, many states have laws which, directly or indirectly, require the transfer of liability risk to an insurer. Thus, nearly all adults need automobile insurance and its cost is a significant item in the family insurance budget.

Because adequate insurance for and in connection with the automobile is necessary, it is discussed in some detail in this chapter. Also, familiarity with the procedure involved in analyzing automobile coverage is helpful in the interpretation of other property and liability policies.

BASIC AUTOMOBILE INSURANCE COVERAGES

Most automobile insurance coverages have evolved through long usage. Although other, less essential coverages can be added to your automobile policy, the major coverages can be divided into the following basic groupings:

I. Liability Coverages—Third Party *[handwritten: HARM TO someone]*

    A. Bodily Injury Liability *[handwritten: Physical]*

    B. Property Damage Liability *[handwritten: Damage to something]*

II. No-Fault Coverages—First Party

    A. Collision

    B. Non-Collision Automobile Damage—Comprehensive

    C. Health Insurance

        1. Medical Payments

        2. Disability Income

        3. Pain and Suffering or Mental Anguish

III. Uninsured Motorists Coverage—Reverse Third Party

Types of Automobile Insurance Policies

With some variations, these coverages may be found in many standard policy forms, including the Family Automobile Policy (FAP), the Personal Automobile Policy (PAP), the Special Automobile Policy (SAP), and the Standard or Basic Automobile Policy (BAP). The first three are for personal-use vehicles only, while the BAP is designed to insure both commercial-use vehicles and personal-use vehicles, including trucks and motorcycles that may not be covered by the other policy forms.

With the wide variety of automobile insurance policies available, reference to "the automobile policy" is an oversimplification. However, we can divide the various contracts into two major groups: first, those policies emphasizing traditional tort liability concepts, and second, those policies sold in jurisdictions which have attempted to reduce the role of tort liability in automobile accidents. While the second group of policies often is called *no-fault, all forms of automobile insurance contain some liability coverages and some no-fault coverages.*

The major differences in contracts that affect you involve the timing, the breadth, and the conditions for eligibility involved in these liability and no-fault coverages. Some policies emphasize one type of coverage more than others, some cover more perils than others, and some insure persons which others do not insure. *To understand your own policy, you will have to study it carefully.*

In the following discussion, we use the PAP as an example of the fundamental coverages available. This recently developed form is more readable than the other forms and is gaining in popularity; so you are likely to see it in the future. However, *your current policy can—and probably will—differ from the PAP on several points.*

THE PERSONAL AUTOMOBILE POLICY

Like all automobile insurance policies, the PAP is complicated. A copy of the PAP is found in Appendix B, and you may wish to refer to it as you study this chapter. It combines liability insurance, health insurance, and property insurance into one package policy. The persons, perils, and property insured may vary from coverage to coverage, and from one set of circumstances to another. The policy is designed to provide you with a broad range of protection covering your ownership, use of, or injury by an automobile. It is made more complex because the insurer must attempt to clarify the coverages, so that the courts will not determine that the policy covers losses which the insurer has not intended to cover. Therefore, even with the simplified PAP, you may get the feeling as you read the policy that its designers said, "let's write a policy that will protect you and your relatives and those persons to whom you have a moral or legal obligation, against as many risks associated with the automobile as we can, without insuring *everybody* against *everything.*"

There is no way that such a complex policy can be simplified without creating opportunities for misunderstandings. However, we can examine it in light of the basic coverage groupings mentioned above, while we keep in mind the four basic parts of the insurance contract: the declarations, insuring clauses, exclusions, and conditions.

Declarations

The declarations identify you by name and address, show the term of the policy, the premiums charged, the coverages provided, and the limits of liability of the coverages. You—and your spouse, if you are married—are the *named insured(s)*. A description of the automobile(s) covered—by year, name, model, identification or serial number, and date of purchase—is included. The loss payee for physical damage to the automobile is listed to protect the lender who has financed the automobile's purchase, and the garaging address is shown. The latter is an important underwriting factor, as is the statement that the insured has not been cancelled for automobile insurance during the preceding three years.

Liability Coverage (Third Party)

As we discuss the coverages, you will find that the insuring clauses in the PAP are located in various sections of the policy. You should be sure to locate *all* insuring clauses in your own contract. In the PAP, the liability insuring clause says:

> We will pay damages for bodily injury or property damage for which any covered person becomes legally responsible because of an auto accident. We will settle or defend, as we consider appropriate, any claim or suit asking for these damages. Our duty to settle or defend ends when our limit of liability for this coverage has been exhausted.

Who is covered.   Liability coverages provide protection for you, members of your immediate family living in your home, and others while driving your car(s) if they reasonably believe that they have your permission to do so. Also, you and your immediate family are covered while driving another person's car when you reasonably believe that you have the owner's permission.

If claims are brought against you or other covered persons, the liability coverage provides legal defense, the cost not being considered part of the insurer's limit of liability. If you are found liable, the insurer pays on your behalf to the plaintiff(s), up to the limit(s) of liability under the policy.

However, the insurer retains the right to settle claims without your approval, if it finds this expedient. This keeps many cases out of court and reduces insurance claims expenses, but it can cause a rude surprise for you in at least two ways. One, if you want to contest the claim because it seems improper, while the insurer finds it simpler and cheaper to settle, the insurer may settle despite your protests. Two, if you have purchased inadequate liability coverage, the insurer may merely pay its total limit(s) and not provide legal defense. For example, if the insurer's aggregate liability limit is $20,000 and if you are clearly at fault in an accident involving liability far in excess of that limit—say, $40,000—the insurer may choose to pay its full $20,000 limit without contest, thus completely removing itself from the cost of legal defense. In this case, if the insurance coverages had a much higher limit—say, $50,000—the insurer would probably provide defense in order to reduce the judgment it would have to pay.

The "covered auto."   Any automobile listed in the declarations, any automobile replacing an automobile listed in the declarations, or an additional automobile—if you ask the insurer to add it within 30 days of the time you acquire it—will be covered. This includes pickups, panel trucks, and vans, *if they are not used for business purposes.* A trailer you own, if it is designed to be pulled by a passenger automobile, pickup, panel truck, or van, qualifies as a covered auto. Also, any passenger automobile, pickup, panel truck, van—or a trailer they can pull—that is used as a temporary substitute when your own can't be used because of servicing, repairs, damage, or breakdown, becomes a covered auto for liability coverage purposes.

✓ **Single or split limits.** While liability coverage under the PAP usually is subject to a single, aggregate limit, it can be divided into two major sub-parts: bodily injury liability and property damage liability. Bodily injury liability applies when your car kills or injures persons in other vehicles, pedestrians, or passengers in your own car (other than immediate family members residing in your home). Property damage liability coverage applies when your car damages property belonging to others. Although the first thing you probably think about under this coverage is the other person's car—and you're right—this coverage also applies to other types of property. It could cover street signs, fences, bicycles, telephone poles, and houses. Remember, however, that it doesn't apply to your house or to other property you own, because you cannot be legally liable to yourself.

pro = greater than lower limit

If you choose a single limit of liability to cover all liability, including both property damage and bodily injury, then the insurer will pay on your behalf for all losses up to this limit, whether they are property-related or injury-related. The only limit you are concerned with in this case is the aggregate limit. However, once all losses equal this limit, you will have to bear the burden of any further liability.

If you choose a split limit of liability, there will be a set of limits specifically applied to bodily injury, and a single, aggregate limit applied to property damage. For the bodily injury limits, one limit applies per person, per occurrence, and the second, larger limit is the aggregate which the insurer will pay for all persons injured, per occurrence. The limits are usually expressed in $1,000 units. An example of bodily injury liability premium cost factors is found in Table 16-1.

No-Fault Coverages (First Party)

The basic design. First party coverages pay you for covered losses regardless of who is at fault. You are the *first party* while the insurer is the *second party.* It is interested primarily in establishing that a covered loss has occurred and determining the amount of that loss before indemnifying you. This creates a nonadversary atmosphere in which your fault—or the lack of it—does not need to be determined, and thus assures you a speedier claims process. If a *third party* is legally responsible for the loss, the insurer has the right to subrogate against that party after paying you.

Collision. If your car collides with another object or vehicle, or if it is damaged by upset, this coverage pays the actual cash value—or the

TABLE 16-1

*Factors for
Increased Bodily
Injury Liability
Limits*

$BI LIMITS	FACTOR*
$ 10/20	1.0
20/20	1.26
15/30	1.23
20/40	1.38
25/50	1.50
35/35	1.52
50/100	1.80
100/200	2.05
100/300	2.14
250/500	2.33
500/500	2.43
500/1000	2.53
1000/1000	2.72

*The factor is applied to the base rate; e.g., the rate for $20/40 is 1.38 times the rate for $10/20.

Source: Insurance Services Office, *Private Passenger Manual.*

Used with permission © Insurance Services Office, 1980.

cost of repair or replacement, if less—regardless of who caused the loss. Most collision coverage is sold on a deductible basis. Deductibles have been rising as a cost-control device to counteract the effect rising prices of cars and car repairs have had on premiums. Small deductibles cost much more than large ones. For instance, Table 16-2 shows that in Texas, collision with a $100 deductible costs 21 percent more than collision with a $200 deductible.

Damage to your automobile other than collision. This coverage—which is called comprehensive in other automobile policy forms— provides actual cash value coverage against damage to your covered auto caused by a long list of named perils. Included perils are theft, larceny, explosion, earthquake, windstorm, hail, water, flood, vandalism, malicious mischief, riot, civil commotion, glass breakage, missiles, fire, and falling objects. It even covers contact with a bird or animal, which is excluded from the collision coverage. While this coverage is seldom sold without a deductible today, its deductible usually is smaller than the collision deductible.

DEDUCTIBLE*	FACTOR
$ 25	1.36
50	1.31
75	1.26
100	1.21
150	1.10
200	1.00
500	.50
1,000	.30

TABLE 16-2

*Factors for
Collision
Premiums*

*Factors are based on a standard collision deductible of $200, which has a factor of 1.00. Thus, if the collision premium with the $200 deductible is $100, then the premium with a $50 deductible is 1.31 × $100, or $131.

Source: Texas Automobile Insurance Services Office, "Texas Automobile Insurance Rates Effective November 1, 1979," Austin, Texas, p.5.

The Public Records of the Texas State Board of Insurance.

The policy also covers at least part of the transportation expenses you may incur if your car is stolen. It says:

> In addition, we will pay up to $10 per day, to a maximum of $300, for transportation expenses incurred by you because of the total theft of your covered auto. We will pay only transportation expenses incurred during the period beginning 48 hours after the theft and ending when your covered auto is returned to use or we pay for its loss.

Medical payments. This health insurance coverage pays for all reasonable and necessary medical expenses incurred within three years of an accident, up to the policy limit. It includes medical, surgical, X-ray and dental services, plus ambulance, hospital, and professional nursing services. In the event of death, the cost of funeral services is covered. You and your family members are covered while in or on your car, if riding in another car, or if pedestrians struck by a car. Your guests are covered while in or on your car. The limit of liability applies to each person, with no limit on the number of persons covered. The minimum limit is $500 per person. Table 16-3 shows the relative cost for higher limits.

TABLE 16-3

*Factors for
Medical
Payments
Premiums*

COVERAGE LIMIT PER PERSON	FACTOR
$ 500	1.0
1,000	1.2
2,500	1.6
5,000	1.8
10,000	2.3

Note: Factors are based on a standard medical payments coverage limit of $500 per person.

Source: Texas Automobile Insurance Services Office, "Texas Automobile Insurance Rates Effective November 1, 1979," Austin, Texas.

The Public Records of the Texas State Board of Insurance.

Uninsured Motorists Coverage (Reverse Third Party)

This coverage will pay you or a member of your family if a third party driver is legally liable to you for bodily injury caused by an auto accident, if that person has no liability insurance and cannot pay, or if that person is a hit-and-run driver and cannot be found. It also will pay your guests, but only if they are in or on a covered automobile designated in the PAP when injured by the third party. In short, *it works just like bodily injury liability insurance owned by the liable third party, with one major exception: you pay the premiums.* Minimum coverage is that amount required to satisfy your state's automobile financial responsibility law for bodily injury liability.

You can buy more than the basic limit of coverage. This expands the policy to cover you when the other party is insured but has a limit of bodily injury liability coverage less than your state's uninsured motorists limit. In such a case, if your injuries exceed the third party's policy limits, your uninsured motorists coverage will pay the excess of loss over the other policy's limit—not exceeding its own limit—thus becoming *under-insured motorists coverage* for the difference. You can also add property damage liability coverage to your uninsured–motorists coverage if you wish.

Other Major Factors to Consider in the PAP

Conditions.   The PAP calls this part "Duties after an Accident or Loss." It includes such basic requirements as notifying the insurer of loss, submission of proof of loss, forwarding to the insurer notices or legal papers, submission to physical examinations, and allowing the insurer access to pertinent medical reports and records. If your car is damaged, you must take reasonable steps to protect it from further loss and allow the insurer to appraise its damage; if it is stolen, you must notify the police promptly. If a hit-and-run driver causes you injury, you must notify the police and send the insurer legal papers if suit is brought. Remember that the insurer has no obligation to you unless you comply with policy conditions.

General Provisions. The most important general provisions of the policy are the following:

1. You are covered in the United States, its territories or possessions, and in Canada.

2. You cannot assign the policy without the insurer's written consent.

3. You may cancel by returning the policy or by giving advance written notice to the insurer.

4. The insurer may cancel if you fail to pay premiums, or if your drivers license—or the license of another person living with you who usually uses a covered auto—is suspended or revoked.

5. The insurer may refuse to renew the PAP on its policy anniversary.

Exclusions. Each coverage has a list of exclusions. Among those most likely to affect you are the following:

1. *For liability insurance,* you are not covered for intentionally caused losses, for losses arising out of the use of your auto for business purposes, or for motorcycles or other vehicles having less than four wheels.

2. *For medical payments coverage,* you are not covered for injuries while on a motorcycle, while using your car for business purposes, or while living in the car.

3. *For uninsured motorists coverage,* you are not covered for injuries suffered when the other vehicle is owned by you or a family member, while using your car for business purposes, if the other vehicle is owned or operated by a self-insurer or governmental agency, or if the other vehicle is not designed primarily for use on public roads.

4. *For damage to your automobile* (collision and comprehensive), you are not covered for tapes and sound equipment, normal wear and tear, CB equipment, or while using the auto for business purposes.

DIFFERENCES IN COVERAGES YOU MAY ENCOUNTER

The Personal Auto Policy illustrates the major coverages included in most automobile insurance policies. There are, however, several differences in coverage you may encounter if you choose another policy form or if you live in a no-fault state. The most important differences are health insurance benefits provided by adding or expanding one or more of the following coverages:

1. Medical Payments

2. Disability Income

3. Pain and Suffering or Mental Anguish.

Personal Injury Protection (PIP)

Typically, expansions of coverage simply increase the limits available for medical payments. Some, however, add income coverage to replace part of your income if you are disabled in an automobile accident. This benefit may also include payments to replace uncompensated personal services, such as those of the parent who maintains the home. Various combinations of these coverages are usually combined under the heading "Personal Injury Protection." Usually, there is an aggregate limit per person per accident for all benefits provided by the PIP. If the per person limit is $2,500, for example, you could collect a maximum of $2,500 for loss caused by one automobile accident, whether the loss was all medical expense, all income replacement, or some combination.

No-fault Automobile Insurance

In many states where Personal Injury Protection coverage is added to your policy, your right to sue others is limited by law. These states are referred to as *no-fault* states. Usually, the law in a no-fault state provides a loss "threshold" which must be reached before one party can sue another party in connection with loss caused by an automobile accident. After this limit, which may be stated as a specific type of bodily injury or death or a cumulative amount of dollar loss suffered, is reached, an injured party has the right to sue for damages. The purpose of this arrangement is to limit litigation to large losses only.

When Personal Injury Protection is added to your policy, the insurer compensates you directly for economic loss caused by an auto crash, without regard to fault. Economic loss means loss of earnings because of injury or death, medical expenses, and similar measurable losses. Some no-fault laws also provide limited first party payments for pain and suffering, in addition to paying for economic loss.

In states where litigation is limited to large losses only, the no-fault system can speed up the process of compensating automobile accident victims. Moreover, funds formerly used for defense under a fault system can be used for payment of first-party benefits. Where the system works well, it uses a smaller part of the premium dollar for defense and a larger part for compensation.

Consumer Applications
Shopping for Auto Insurance

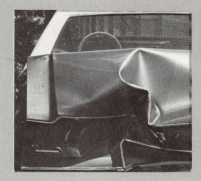

Table 16-4 shows the range of premiums for an auto insurance policy in one territory in one state. The policy included personal injury protection ($15,000), bodily injury liability ($25,000), property damage liability ($10,000), uninsured motorist coverage ($25,000), comprehensive coverage with no deductible, and $100 deductible collision coverage. The car was a year-old mid-size.

How to Shop

First, contact your state insurance department for information on buying auto insurance. Some departments have detailed information about premiums charged by companies licensed in their state. If you have that, you can decide which insurers to avoid.

Second, organize information an insurer

	CLEAN RECORD		THREE MOVING VIOLATIONS	
	Low	High	Low	High
Pleasure	$146	$848	$146	$2,846
To/from work	$168	$962	$168	$2,890

TABLE 16-4

Annual Premium for Identical Auto Insurance for Same Car

Source: *No-fault Insurance*, Motor Vehicle Insurance Division, State Department of Regulatory Agencies, Honolulu, Hawaii 96813.

While the range of prices may not be as great where you live, it is reasonable to believe that there is enough variation to justify your shopping for the best deal. Price isn't the only consideration, of course, but there is no reason you should waste your money. Many excellent companies sell auto insurance at reasonable prices.

will need about you. Figure 16-1 can be used as a guide.

Third, decide what coverages and limits you want. Tell the insurer or agent "I want a quote on a Personal Auto Policy." Figure 16-2 can be used as a guide. You may want to list more than one limit for liability, medical payments, personal injury protection, and

FIGURE 16-1

*Auto Insurance
Information
Checklist*

A. Drivers in Household:

Driver No.	Name	Within Last 3 Years	
		No. of Accidents	No. of Moving Violations
1.			
2.			
3.			
4.			

B. Automobiles to be Insured:

	Make	Model & Year	Uses: Car Most (Driver No.)	Car Used For: (P) Pleasure (T&F) To & From Work (B) Business	Annual Mileage
Car 1					
Car 2					

Source: *No-fault Insurance*, Motor Vehicle Insurance Division, State Department of Regulatory Agencies, Honolulu, Hawaii 96813.

uninsured motorist coverage. You should list several deductibles for collision and comprehensive.

Fourth, if you have done business with an independent agent, ask him or her for quotes from several companies. If you have not done business with an independent agent, find one in the Yellow Pages and ask for several quotes. Next, contact several exclusive agency companies and repeat the process. Finally, ask your friends or the state insurance department for the name of one or more insurance-by-mail companies and contact them for quotes.

Fifth, be sure you give everyone you contact the same information and ask for the same policy. Otherwise, you will wind up with price quotations that cannot be compared because they don't provide the same coverage or are not based on the same information.

Sixth, modify your copy of Figure 16-2 so you can list all quotes on one large sheet of paper. Then you can identify the combination of limits and deductibles offered at the best price for your needs.

How to Reduce Auto Insurance Costs

First, choose the largest deductibles you can bear. The higher the deductibles, the lower your premium.

Second, don't buy collision insurance on an old car. The most the insurer will pay is its actual cash value, regardless of how much repairs would cost. Bear the risk yourself, just as you do with deductibles.

Third, buy a make and model that has good collision loss experience. As Table 16-5 shows, buying the right car can easily save $100 a year on insurance premiums. Call your state insurance department and ask them for information on this.

Fourth, don't buy a "muscle car," sports car, or high performance car. They boost insurance costs.

```
                        Annual Cost                          FIGURE 16-2
_____  _____  _____
(company name)    (company name)    (company name)          Automobile
                                                            Insurance
Liability                                                   Pricing
   Bodily Injury                                            Worksheet
   $/person, $/accident  _____  _____  _____    Personal Auto
   Property Damage                                          Policy
   $/accident            _____  _____  _____
   Single Limit
   $/accident            _____  _____  _____
_____
First-Party
   Collision      $_____ deductible_____  ____  ____
                  $_____ deductible_____  ____  ____
                  $_____ deductible_____  ____  ____
   Comprehensive  $_____ deductible_____  ____  ____
                  $_____ deductible_____  ____  ____
                  $_____ deductible_____  ____  ____
   Medical Payments $_____ per person_____   ____  ____
                  $_____ per person_____   ____  ____
                  $_____ per person_____   ____  ____
   Personal Injury $_____ per person_____   ____  ____
      Protection  $_____ per person_____   ____  ____
                  $_____ per person_____   ____  ____
_____
Uninsured Motorists
   Bodily Injury  $_____ per person,
                  $_____ per accident      ____  ____
   Property Damage $_____ per accident      ____  ____
   Single Limit   $_____ per accident      ____  ____
_____
TOTAL ANNUAL PREMIUM   $_____  $_____  $_____
                       _____  _____  _____
```

Fifth, look for the following discounts:

a. Good student discount
b. Non drinkers discount
c. Non smokers discount
d. Second-car discount
e. Driver-training discount

Sixth, if you have more than one car, don't use both of them to drive to work. "Pleasure use only" is cheaper than "to and from work."

Seventh, don't duplicate insurance. If you have adequate health insurance to protect you against medical expense, why buy medical payments with your auto insurance? Some insurers add accidental death insurance to an auto policy for extra premium. If you need life insurance, buy a policy that provides benefits for death by any cause.

TABLE 16-5

*Auto Insurance
Rates for
Suburban
Cleveland
Drivers, by Car
Model*

	DRIVER A IMPALA	DRIVER B CATALINA	DRIVER C FIREBIRD
$100,000 Liability	$227	$227	$227
$50 Deductible Comprehensive	96	136	163
$200 Deductible Collision	135	162	186
Total	$458	$525	$576

Source: *Journal of American Insurance*, Fall 1979.

Reprinted with permission from the Journal of American Insurance. © 1979.

Discussion Questions

1. Some auto insurance policies are written with a single limit for liability while others have split limits. The Personal Auto Policy can be written either way. Which do you prefer? Why?

2. In recent years, an increasing percentage of cars totally destroyed by fire are "gas guzzlers." How do you account for this? If you were in the insurance business, would you be reluctant to insure such vehicles?

3. David Thompson says, "Buying Uninsured Motorist coverage is an awkward substitute for life and health insurance. Besides that, it protects you only in certain situations. I'd rather spend my money on more and better life and health insurance." Do you agree? Why or why not?

4. Automobile financial responsibility laws require you to have some minimum amount of auto liability insurance. If liability insurance is to protect you from loss caused by your negligence, why should the law force you to buy it? Don't you think this is a decision for you to make? Please explain.

5. You have a Personal Auto Policy with a single liability limit of $300,000. In backing out of a parking space, you scrape the side of the car next to yours, causing $150 in damages. Your insurer sends a check for $100 to the owner with a letter which says, "When you have the damage repaired, send us a copy of the paid bill and we will send you $50. Unless you have the damage repaired, we will make no further payment." Do you think this is fair? Why or why not?

6. The purpose of the financial responsibility law is to assure that innocent third parties will be paid for damage they suffer because of somebody's negligent driving. Your insurance, however, does not apply to damage caused by your car when it is stolen. Do you think it should? Why or why not?

7. The place where your car is garaged is an important underwriting factor; i.e., it influences the premium rate. In view of the fact that Americans drive all over the country, doesn't this seem illogical? Please explain.

8. The deductible for comprehensive coverage is usually smaller than for collision coverage. Does this make sense to you? How do you account for it?

9. Physical damage to your car is paid in full, subject to a deductible, and medical payments coverage pays for reasonable and necessary medical expenses, but the transportation expense allowance is limited to $10 per day after a waiting period. This leaves you bearing most of the cost of car rental. Is this fair? Please explain.

10. Medical payments coverage does not apply to "bodily injury sustained while occupying any vehicle located for use as a residence or premises." Is this a reasonable exclusion? Why or why not?

Cases

16-1 Patty, age 17, has been told repeatedly by her father not to let anyone else drive her car under any circumstances. However, at the local drive-in hamburger emporium, Mack, age 19, persuades her to let him drive the car. While they are driving down the highway, Mack loses control, spins the car around, and broadsides a tree. Is this covered by Patty's father's personal automobile insurance policy? Remember, her father, the named insured, specifically denied her the permission necessary to allow another person to drive the car, so the question of agency might arise here.

16-2 Barney has a PAP with $30,000 in bodily injury liability coverage, $10,000 in property damage coverage, and collision coverage with a $200 deductible. While pulling his boat and trailer to the lake—which are not listed in the policy's declarations—he passes a car, loses control, sideswipes the car he is passing with his trailer, then rams a tree with his car. The losses are as follows:

Barney (medical expenses)		$ 1,300
Barney's girlfriend (medical expenses)		2,450
Driver of other car		
medical expenses	3,500	
mental anguish	20,000	23,500
Barney's car		4,000
Barney's boat		800
Barney's trailer		500
Farmer's tree		300
Other driver's Mercedes		9,800

Using the PAP in Appendix B, explain what will and will not be paid by his insurance contract, and why.

16-3 Sue parks and locks her Corvette while attending classes at her college. When she returns, it is gone. She reports its loss to her insurer and notifies the police immediately. Because she must commute to school and to work, she immediately rents a car for $140 per week or $22 per day for any part of a week. Twenty-three days after it disappeared, her car is recovered. It has been driven over 12,000 miles, its right side has been destroyed in an accident, and the interior has been vandalized.

Sue has a PAP with comprehensive coverage and a $50 deductible. Explain her coverage to her, noting what she can expect to recover from her insurer, and why.

Chapter Seventeen:
MANAGING HOME RISKS

INTRODUCTION

Home is not just a haven, it is also a source of risks for families and individuals. These risks are summarized in Table 17-1.

Most families can retain the risk of small physical–damage losses and the first-dollar portion of large losses, but few can retain all the risks associated with their home. Moreover, most homes are bought on the installment plan and lenders insist upon having insurance against physical damage to homes they finance. The most common method for homeowners or tenants to insure these risks is by buying a Homeowners Policy, a flood insurance policy, and title insurance.

In this chapter we will discuss the following:

1. The different kinds of homeowners policies

2. The Homeowners Special Form

3. Flood insurance

4. Title insurance.

HOMEOWNERS POLICIES

Homeowners Policies are similar to automobile policies in that they combine several coverages into one policy. They are a combination of property and liability insurance with a little health insurance for guests and residence employees. The persons insured vary from coverage to coverage and place to place.

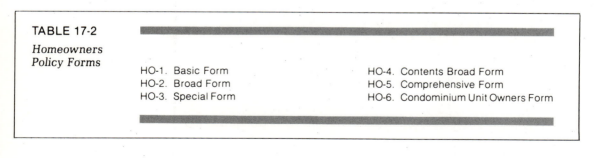

TABLE 17-1

*Risks of
Your Home*

1. Liability
2. Damage to, or destruction of, home
3. Loss of use of the home
4. Loss of, or damage to, personal property
5. Defective title

If the insurer promised *only* you that it would pay for damage *only* to your desk caused *only* by fire and *only* when the desk was at a specified location, the contract would be simple and easy to understand. But when protection is extended to the property at other places, other property, other causes of loss, and to other people under some, but not all, circumstances, the contract becomes complicated. When the insurer adds liability insurance for you and some, but not all, other people, plus medical expense coverage for others but not you, things go from bad to worse so far as complexity is concerned. To say that Homeowners Policies are multidimensional is, indeed, an understatement. But they are well organized and the provisions are stated in simple terms so you can determine who is covered, what is covered, the amount of coverage, and the conditions and exclusions.

First we will look at the different kinds of homeowners policies shown in Table 17-2, then we will examine the Homeowners Special Form in some detail.

TABLE 17-2

*Homeowners
Policy Forms*

HO-1. Basic Form	HO-4. Contents Broad Form
HO-2. Broad Form	HO-5. Comprehensive Form
HO-3. Special Form	HO-6. Condominium Unit Owners Form

Each policy consists of a declarations page (see page 429) and Homeowners Policy jacket to which the form is attached. The same declarations page and policy jacket are used for all forms.

Following the declarations page, the balance of each form is divided into two sections. Section I pertains to the dwelling, other structures, personal property, and loss of use. A $100 deductible, which can be increased, applies to Section I coverages. Section II includes personal liability coverages for you and medical payments to others. Each section lists the coverages provided, the perils insured against, and the exclusions and conditions applicable to that section. Finally, conditions applicable to both sections are listed. This format is shown in Figure 17-1.

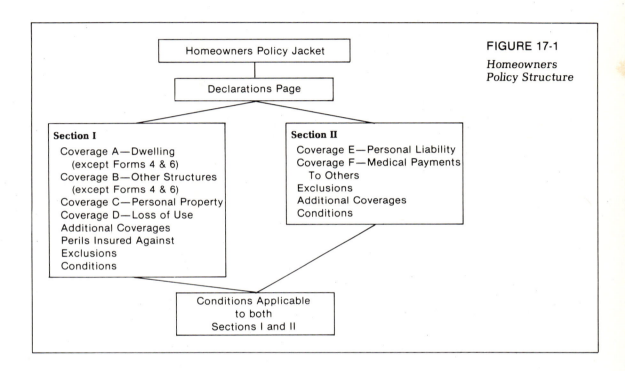

FIGURE 17-1

Homeowners Policy Structure

Table 17-3 outlines the coverages in Section I, amounts of insurance for each coverage, and the perils included for the various forms. Note that the limit for Coverages B, C, and D is a specified percentage of the amount of insurance on the dwelling (Coverage A) in Forms 1, 2, 3, and 5. Thus, when you decide upon the amount of insurance to have on your house, you have automatically selected the amount for other coverages. Forms 4 and 6 do not cover a dwelling or other structures, so the amount for Coverage D is based on that selected for Coverage C (personal property).

The basic amount for Section II (Coverages E and F) is the same for all forms but can be increased for additional premium. The insuring agreements, exclusions, and conditions for Section II are the same for all forms.

The basic differences among the forms are in Section I. Forms 4 and 6 do not include insurance on the dwelling and other structures because 4 is for tenants and 6 is for condominium owners. The latter have an interest in the building in which they live as well as related structures but such property is insured on behalf of all occupants in a separate policy.

TABLE 17-3

Section I Homeowners Coverages

COVERAGE	FORM HO-1	FORM HO-2	FORM HO-3	FORM HO-4	FORM HO-5	FORM HO-6
A	$8,000 min.	Same	Same	Not included	$15,000 min.	Not included
B	10% of A	Same	Same	Not included	Same as HO-1	Not included
C	50% of A	Same	Same	$4,000 min.	Same as HO-1	$4,000 min.
D	10% of A	20% of A	20% of A	20% of C	20% of A	40% of C

Perils Covered Under Section I

FORM HO-1	FORM HO-2	FORM HO-3	FORM HO-4	FORM HO-5	FORM HO-6
Fire or lightning Windstorm or hail Explosion Riot or civil commotion Aircraft Vehicles Smoke Vandalism or malicious mischief Theft Glass Breakage	Same as HO-1 plus Falling objects Weight of ice, snow or sleet Collapse Accidental discharge or overflow of water or steam Bursting of steam or hot water heating system or A-C Freezing plumbing and heating or A-C Artificially generated electricity	All risk on A, B & D Contents same as HO-2 (except glass breakage)	Contents same as HO-2 (except glass breakage)	All risk on A, B, C, & D	Contents same as HO-2

Another basic difference among the forms is the perils covered. Some are named-perils while others are all risks. Form 1, you will note, has a considerably shorter list of perils than other forms written on a named-perils basis.

THE SPECIAL FORM (HO-3)

Because it is representative of the various forms, we will examine this form in some detail. We will, in effect, take a guided tour through the policy, referring to the part we are discussing by page number so you can refer to it for more detail as we go along. Our purpose is to familiarize you with its structure and content so you will know what to look for and how to find it in any Homeowners Policy.

Agreement and Definitions

These two parts of the policy follow the declarations page. They are the same in all homeowners forms. The agreement on page 432 says,

> We will provide the insurance described in this policy in return for the premium and compliance with all applicable provisions of this policy.

Two aspects of this agreement should be noted. First, the portion following the words "in return for" is the consideration that is vital to the contract. Unless you comply with the provisions of the policy, the consideration is incomplete. The insurer is saying, "if you comply with the provisions, we will provide the insurance described in the policy." Second, we must look further in the policy to find out what insurance is described.

Before we can determine what insurance is described, we must know the meaning of the terms used in the policy. They are defined in detail on page 432 under the heading "Definitions." Because they are so important, they are listed separately in Table 17-4.

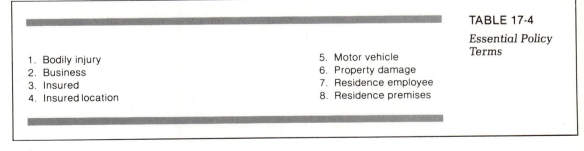

TABLE 17-4

Essential Policy Terms

1. Bodily injury
2. Business
3. Insured
4. Insured location
5. Motor vehicle
6. Property damage
7. Residence employee
8. Residence premises

Armed with the terminology shown in Table 17-4, we are prepared to examine the following parts of Section I:

1. Coverages

2. Perils insured against

3. Exclusions

4. Conditions.

SECTION I—COVERAGES

Coverage A

This covers the dwelling on the *residence premises*, plus structures attached to the dwelling, such as an attached garage. It also covers materials and supplies on or adjacent to the residence premises for use in the construction, alteration, or repair of the dwelling or other structures.

Coverage B

This covers other structures on the residence premises which are separated from the dwelling, such as a detached garage. It does not apply to any structure used for business purposes or rented to any person not a tenant of the dwelling, unless used solely as a private garage. The location of this exclusion and the way it is stated illustrates two important points. First, exclusions are not always called exclusions. They may appear as "we do not cover," or following the word "except." Second, they may appear any place in the policy, not just under the heading "Exclusions."

Coverage C

This part of the policy says,

We cover personal property owned or used by any insured while it is anywhere in the world.

Note that this includes property you own as well as that belonging to others while you are using it. If you borrow your neighbor's lawnmower, it is protected by your insurance as if it were yours.

At your request, this coverage applies to personal property owned by others while it is on the part of the residence premises occupied by any insured. Property usually situated at an insured's residence other than the residence premises is subject to a limit of 10 percent of the Coverage C limit, or $1,000, whichever is greater. If you, as a member of your parent's household, rent a room at school, the personal property you have in the room is subject to this limit.

Two provisions in Coverage C merit careful attention. One is "Special Limits of Liability" and the other is "Property Not Covered." Under the former, dollar limits are placed on some property for loss caused by any peril and on other property for loss caused by theft. The prominent listing of these special limits should call your attention to any gaps in coverage if you have the kind of property listed. You may want to cover it with a Scheduled Personal Property Endorsement added to your policy.

Much of the property not covered is related to conduct of a business and, therefore, not suited for homeowners coverage. It should be noted that tape players and their tapes and citizen band radios and their accessories and antennas are not covered.

Coverage D

This coverage protects you from losses sustained because the premises cannot be lived in as a result of a direct loss to either the premises or neighboring premises. Additional living expense is provided if a loss covered under Section I makes the residence uninhabitable. If a similar loss makes the part of the residence rented to others uninhabitable, the policy pays for its fair rental value. If a civil authority prohibits you from using the premises as a result of direct damage to neighboring premises by a peril insured against in this policy, both additional living expense and fair rental value loss will be paid for a period not exceeding two weeks.

Additional Coverages

At this juncture, you might think that every conceivable source of loss in connection with your home and personal property has either been covered, modified, or excluded. Such is not the case. For example, why debris removal coverage? Because other coverages provide for repair or replacement of damaged property but not the cost of removing the debris which remains after a fire or windstorm. Without this coverage, you would have to pay for hauling away the trash that remains after the insurance company paid for repair or replacement of damaged property.

You are required to protect insured property after a loss, but you will be paid for the cost involved. Moreover, the insurer agrees to pay up to $250 fire department charges incurred to save covered property. All risk coverage is provided for up to 30 days on property removed from premises endangered by a peril covered by the policy. If it were not for this provision, you might be better off to leave personal property in your house while it burned to the ground rather than remove it and risk having it damaged or destroyed by a peril other than those included in the policy.

Protection is also provided for loss to trees, shrubs, and other plants, and loss in connection with credit cards, forgery, and counterfeit money.

SECTION I—PERILS INSURED AGAINST

Coverages A and B—Dwelling and Other Structures

Under this heading, the policy says:

> We insure for all risks of physical loss to the property described in Coverages A and B except . . . .

The most important word is "except." The first exception is all losses excluded under Section I—exclusions which we will discuss later. In addition, there are six other exceptions which are lengthy and detailed. They are listed on page 435. Note that while the coverage is for all risks, it by no means covers all losses under all circumstances.

Coverage C—Personal Property

Under this heading, the policy says (on page 435):

> We insure for direct loss to property described in Coverage C caused by:

This is followed by a list of sixteen perils which includes all those in Table 17-3 except glass breakage. Most of these perils have some explanation of what they include as well as specific exclusions. The theft peril is most elaborate in this respect and some of the exclusions warrant discussion (see page C-6). It does not include loss caused by theft committed by any insured. This sounds absurd until you consider how many people are included in the definition of insured. There may be relatives in the household who would steal from each other. Theft in or from a dwelling under construction or of materials and supplies for use in the construction is excluded because the risk is too great. Theft from any part of a residence rented by an insured to other than an insured is excluded. If you rent a room to an outsider, for example, and he or she steals something from that room, the loss is not covered.

Theft coverage on property away from the residence premises is limited. Note that your property as a student who is an insured under the policy is covered while you are at school *if* you have been there at any time during the 45 days immediately before a theft loss occurs. If you leave some of your personal property in a rented room during vacation and have been gone more than 45 days at the time they are stolen, the loss is not covered.

SECTION I—EXCLUSIONS

We have already noted so many exceptions and exclusions that you would think there wouldn't be much left to exclude. The exclusions listed in the exclusions section are summarized in Table 17-5.

Some of these exclusions deserve comment. The law in your city, for example, may provide that a building which does not comply with the building code is permitted to stand, but if it is damaged by fire or other peril to the extent of (say) 50 percent of its value, it must be demolished.

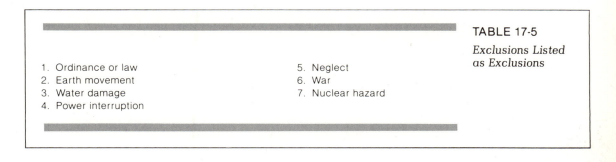

TABLE 17-5

Exclusions Listed as Exclusions

1. Ordinance or law
2. Earth movement
3. Water damage
4. Power interruption

5. Neglect
6. War
7. Nuclear hazard

The first exclusion listed in Table 17-5 says, in effect, "We will pay for the loss caused directly by an insured peril but not one caused by the ordinance." If your garage does not meet building code requirements and is damaged by fire to such an extent that it must be razed, the insurer will pay only for the fire damage. You will bear the rest of the loss.

If earth movement completely demolishes your house, the loss will not be paid. If, however, loss caused by earth movement is less than total, the remaining value is covered against loss caused by certain perils which are listed in the exclusion. If your house is 90 percent destroyed by earth movement and the remainder burns, the insurer will pay for only the value destroyed by fire.[1]

The water damage exclusion is not identical with the earth movement exclusion but works in the same way. That is, it excludes loss caused by specified water damage and then says, "direct loss by fire, explosion or theft resulting from water damage is covered."

Exclusion No. 4 says that a loss suffered when a power interruption off premises causes the food in your freezer to spoil is not covered. If, however, the power interruption off premises shuts down your heating system and the plumbing freezes, that loss is covered. Freezing of plumbing is covered but thawing of frozen food is not. Other exclusions are self-explanatory except for the nuclear hazard exclusion. In that case, you must refer to Condition No. 14 in the conditions section of the policy to determine just what is excluded.[2]

---

1. Earthquake coverage can be added by endorsement for additional premium. It has a deductible of from 2 to 5 percent.

2. It seems that the writers of this policy have difficulty deciding what is a peril and what is a hazard. The existence of a nuclear plant in the community is a hazard. The cause of loss, such as radiation or radioactive contamination, is a peril. In any case, it is painfully clear that the underwriters want to stay as far away as possible from anything nuclear.

SECTION I—CONDITIONS

As we have seen, there are several ways to limit coverages provided by the policy, including:

1. By special limits of liability, as in Coverage C.

2. By listing property not covered, as in Coverage C.

3. By listing losses not covered, as in Additional Coverages and in Perils Insured Against.

Another place where coverages are limited is the Conditions Section. It outlines your duties, the company's duties and options, what happens in the event of a dispute between you and the company about the amount of a loss, and the position of mortgagees and bailees.[3] Table 17-6 lists the conditions in Section I of the policy.

TABLE 17-6

Section I—
Conditions

1. Insurable interest and limit of liability	8. Suit against us
2. Your duties after loss	9. Our option
3. Loss settlement	10. Loss payment
4. Loss to a pair or set	11. Abandonment of property
5. Glass replacement	12. Mortgage clause
6. Appraisal	13. No benefit to bailee
7. Other insurance	14. Nuclear hazard clause

Because this is a conditional contract, you must be familiar with the conditions or your failure to fulfill one may result in a loss not being paid. This point is emphasized by Condition 8 which provides that you cannot bring legal action against the insurer unless you have complied with the policy provisions and the action is started within one year after the occurrence causing loss or damage.[4]

The provision for settling losses (page 438) to buildings is a little confusing, so it warrants some explanation. Here's how it works: If the total amount of coverage equals at least 80 percent of the current replacement cost of your home (at least $80,000 on a $100,000 structure, for ex-

---

3. A mortgagee is the lending agency; when you borrow money to buy a home, you sign a note and a mortgage. You are the mortgagor who executes a mortgage in favor of the mortgagee. A bailee is a person who holds another person's property; the bailor is the person who leaves his or her property with the bailee.

4. If the one-year time limit conflicts with state law, the law prevails. In South Carolina, for example, it is six years.

ample), you are paid the full cost of replacing or repairing the damage up to the policy limits. There is no deduction for depreciation.

On the other hand, if the amount of coverage is less than 80 percent of the replacement cost, the insurer will pay the larger of (1) the actual cash value, which is replacement cost minus depreciation, or (2) that proportion of the cost to repair or replace, without deduction for depreciation, which the total amount of insurance on the building bears to 80 percent of its replacement cost. An example may help clarify what the policy says.

Suppose that at the time of a $20,000 loss it would cost $100,000 to replace your home. And suppose you have $70,000 insurance on it. The loss would be settled as follows:

$$\frac{\text{Amount of insurance carried}}{80\% \text{ of replacement cost}} \times \text{loss} = \text{Payment}$$

$$\frac{\$70,000}{\$80,000} \times \$20,000 = \$17,500$$

If, however, the actual cash value of the loss was greater than $17,500, you would be paid the larger amount. Unless there has been no depreciation at all—an unlikely situation—you will have to bear part of the loss.

Clearly, you are well advised to carry an amount of insurance equal to at least 80 percent of the replacement value of your home. But even if you do, what happens in the event of a total loss? If you have $80,000 insurance on your $100,000 house and it burns to the ground, you will lose $20,000. Furthermore, if you have $80,000 insurance at the beginning of this year, will that be 80 percent of the value of your house later in the year? If the price trend shown in Table 17-7 continues, you should (1) add an Inflation Guard Endorsement to your policy to increase the amount of insurance automatically every year, and (2) increase the amount of insurance to 100 percent of replacement value. That will assure being paid in full for partial losses and provide more complete protection against a total loss.

TABLE 17-7

*Consumer
Price Index*

	CPI		
1967	100	1974	148
1968	104	1975	161
1969	110	1976	170
1970	116	1977	182
1971	121	1978	195
1972	125	1979	217
1973	133	1980	232

SECTION II—LIABILITY COVERAGES

This may be the most important coverage provided by the Homeowners Policy. It complements the coverage provided in your automobile policy by protecting you against liability losses in connection with your home and your personal activities. Coverage E, Personal Liability, says (on page 440):

> If a claim is made or a suit is brought against any insured for damages because of bodily injury or property damage to which this coverage applies, we will: (a) pay up to our limit of liability for the damages for which the insured is legally liable; and (b) provide a defense at our expense by counsel of our choice.

Defense is far more significant than may appear. Its cost is in addition to the limit of liability stated on the declarations page. The obligation to defend you, however, ends when the amount the insurer has paid for damages resulting from an occurrence equals the limit of liability. The basic limit is $25,000 but can be increased significantly for a small additional premium.[5]

Although damage to property rented to you, occupied or used by you, or in your care is excluded from the liability coverage, the exclusion does not apply to property damage caused by fire, smoke, or explosion. Thus, it protects you against the risk that property belonging to others may be damaged by fire through your negligence while in your care. This fire legal liability risk may be important to you if you rent premises or furnishings. Their owner may have fire insurance but the insurer who has to pay for a loss you caused may sue you under its right of subrogation.

SECTION II—NON-LIABILITY COVERAGES

The policy provides two benefits without reference to an insured's liability: (1) medical payments to others, and (2) damage to property of others.

Medical Payments

This coverage is similar to that provided by the Personal Auto Policy. Instead of relating to injuries connected with an automobile, however, it is related to your home and your personal activities. Moreover, benefits are provided for people other than you and members of your household.

---

5. There are two reasons for buying higher limits. First, a judgment for damages resulting from an occurrence may be far greater than $25,000. Second, if the limit is low, there may be a situation in which it is cheaper for the insurer to pay than to defend. This could leave you in a position where you either have to pay for the balance of the damages, for your own defense, or—perish the thought—both. An insurer's interest in a liability claim is directly related to the size of the limit.

It is designed to take care of situations in which you may feel a moral obligation for medical expense incurred by others but for which you are not legally liable.

Damage to Property of Others

This coverage is similar to that provided by medical payments in that it pays for damage you are not legally liable for but feel obligated to pay. The insurer agrees to

> pay up to $250 per occurrence for property damage to property of others caused by any insured.

Even intentional acts of children under age 13 are covered although it seems reasonable to think that repeated acts of destruction by a sub-teen might lead to reluctance to renew the policy at the end of its term.

OTHER PROVISIONS

Exclusions applicable to Section II are concerned primarily with business and professional pursuits of any insured, premises not covered by the policy, and aircraft, motor vehicles, and watercraft of a specified size and/or horsepower. Section II conditions are similar to those in the automobile policy. Conditions applicable to both Sections I and II (see page 443) are simple and straightforward. It should be noted that the policy does not cover any insured who has intentionally concealed or misrepresented any material fact relating to the insurance. If you try to pad a claim, the company may not have to pay you anything. While the policy may be cancelled by either party, the insurer's right to do so is subject to some restriction. It may, however, refuse to renew the policy without any reason.

OTHER RISKS

Two major risks which are too significant to be retained and cannot be avoided are not covered by the insurance discussed thus far in this chapter. They are the possibility of losses by flood or title defect.

The Flood Risk

Homeowners Policies exclude loss caused by flood because of the problem of adverse selection. This major gap in coverage can be filled by having your agent purchase a flood insurance policy from the National Flood Insurance Association if your home is in an area approved for the program. The policy covers losses that result directly from river and stream, coastal and lakeshore flooding. Losses resulting from flood-related erosion and mudslide in those areas, as a result of storm activity, are covered. Sewer back-ups are covered only when they are clearly caused by a general condition of flooding.

Maximum limits available are $70,000 on the dwelling and $20,000 on the contents. The policy has a deductible of $200 or 2 percent of the loss, whichever is greater, applied separately to dwelling loss and contents loss. A loss of $20,000 to the dwelling and $10,000 to its contents would be paid as follows:

	LOSS	DEDUCTIBLE	PAYMENT
Dwelling	$20,000	$- (.02 \times \$20,000) =$	$19,600
Contents	$10,000	$- (.02 \times \$10,000) =$	9,800
		TOTAL	$29,400

The Title Risk

There are two approaches to the risk that you may suffer an unbearable loss when a previously undetected defect in the title to your property is discovered. One is loss prevention by having a competent attorney search the records at the county courthouse to ascertain if a claim against the property exists. In many areas, there are firms which compile records, called abstracts, for property in the area they serve. In such cases, the abstract rather than the county records is examined by an attorney, who then renders an opinion as to the soundness of the title possessed by the seller. The shortcomings of this method of handling the risk are that the records may be incomplete or inaccurate or the attorney who examines them may overlook something. The attorney does not provide a guarantee that the title is clear of defects; he or she merely renders an opinion.

The other approach to handling the title risk is to buy title insurance. A title insurance policy protects you against loss caused by a defect in the title which existed at the time the policy was issued. It does not cover defects which come into existence after the policy is issued. The insurer says, "If anything was wrong with the title to this property at the time this policy was issued, we will defend you and pay for the loss caused when it is discovered, within policy limits."

Before making this promise, the insurer attempts to determine if defects exist. If any are found, they are described in the policy and excluded from coverage or a policy is not issued until they have been removed. A single premium is paid for the policy and it remains in force indefinitely. As a general rule, it cannot be assigned. When title to the property is transferred, the purchaser must buy his or her own title insurance policy if protection is desired.

Consumer Applications

*Shopping for Home Insurance
and Reducing Costs*

Table 17-8 shows the range of annual premiums for a Homeowners Form 3 policy to cover a single family brick dwelling located on the south side of Chicago as revealed in a study by Professor Allen F. Jung. The startling difference between high prices and low prices clearly demonstrates that it pays to shop for home insurance.

As with auto insurance, price isn't the only consideration, but the possibility of saving 40 or 50 percent a year on your home insurance is worth some effort. The range of prices may not be as great where you live, but a good guess is that there is enough variation to justify shopping. Who knows, you may find more variation in prices rather than less.

How to Shop

First, as with auto insurance, contact your state insurance department for information on buying home insurance. They may be able to give you information about premiums charged by companies licensed in your state. It will help you avoid the high-priced companies.

Second, organize information the insurer will need. Figure 17-2 can be used as a guide. Your house is one of the following types of construction:

1. Frame.
2. Brick, stone or masonry veneer.
3. Brick, stone or masonry.
4. Frame with aluminum or plastic siding.

TABLE 17-8

*Annual Premium
for $40,000
H.O. 3 Policy
with $100
Deductible*

	INSURANCE COMPANIES	AGENTS, BROKERS	SAVINGS & LOAN ASSOCIATIONS
High	$248.00	$251.00	$253.00
Low	$117.00	$131.00	$130.00
Median	$167.50	$173.00	$159.50

Source: Allen F. Jung, "Rate Variations Among Suppliers of Homeowners Insurance," *Best's Review*, December 1979, pp. 22-26.

Reprinted with permission of the A.M. Best Co., Oldwick, NJ

FIGURE 17-2

*Home Insurance
Information*

Your name and address

Name and address of mortgagee

Construction type
Number of feet from hydrant
Insurance you want

Form (e.g. HO-3)
Coverage A amount (e.g. $100,000)
Coverage E amount (e.g. $25,000)
Coverage F amount (e.g. $500 per/pers)

Third, decide what insurance you want. You will say to the insurer or agent: "Please give me a quote on a Homeowners Form 3 with the following limits:

Coverage A (Dwelling) $100,000
Coverage B (Liability) $25,000
Coverage F (Medical Payments), $500 per person.

"I would like a quote for the policy with various deductibles, including $100, $250, and $500. I would also like to know what the annual premium would be for higher limits on Coverages E and F."

Fourth, contact several agents, several exclusive agency companies, and one or more insurance-by-mail insurers for quotes.

Fifth, be sure you give everyone you talk to the same information and ask for the same quotes. You won't get exactly comparable quotations from everybody you talk to, but they will be closer to what you want if you are specific.

Sixth, make a form similar to Figure 17-3 and enter the quotes. You will have to make one form for the limits you requested and other forms for increased limits on Coverages E and F. Then you can compare annual premiums for the basic limits and also for increased limits. With that, you can decide which company will provide you with what you want at the best price.

How to Reduce Home Insurance Costs

First, when you buy or build a home, consider insurance costs. It costs more to insure a frame house than one made of brick, stone, or masonry because average losses are higher. You will also find that, in many areas, frame houses cost more to maintain.

FIGURE 17-3

*Home Insurance
Pricing
Worksheet—
Homeowners
Form 3*

ANNUAL PREMIUM

Deductible	Company	Company	Company
$100			
$250			
$500			
Other			

Second, choose the largest deductible you can bear. But be sure you get enough premium reduction to offset the extra burden you will have in the event of a loss. Also, keep in mind that the premium reduction for various deductibles is not the same for all insurers.

Third, price other forms. An HO-2 provides less coverage than an HO-3 but costs less. Remember, however, that you have to bear the burden of uninsured losses. You may sacrifice valuable protection without saving enough in premiums.

Fourth, community factors that affect insurance premium rates may seem beyond your control, but you can help influence them. You can encourage better fire department service, improvements in the water system and building code, and a better police department. These improvements not only lead to reduced insurance premiums but they save property and lives.

Discussion Questions

1. Why is title insurance preferable to loss prevention as a method of handling the title risk? Why can't you simply shift this risk to the attorney whom you pay for checking on the title? If you could do that, would it be as good as insurance? Why or why not?

2. Medical payments coverage in Homeowners Policies provides benefits for people other than you or members of your household. Do you really have an obligation to pay the medical bills for other people who are injured through no fault of your own simply because they are on your premises? Why or why not?

3. What is the significance of the fact that there has never been an earthquake where you live?

4. Why do both auto and homeowners policies exclude tapes and CB equipment?

5. The Personal Auto Policy does not list a dollar amount of coverage for physical damage to your car but specifies actual cash value minus the deductible. If your Homeowners Policy were written the same way, you would not have to worry about having an adequate amount of insurance. Why is it different from the auto policy?

6. Will the Inflation Guard Endorsement alone assure that you have enough insurance on your home? Why or why not?

7. What is the justification for the provision that damage to your home will be paid on a replacement basis if you have coverage equal to 80 percent of replacement cost, but on a less favorable basis if you have a smaller amount of insurance? Do you think this provision is reasonable?

8. The Homeowners Policy in Appendix C provides replacement cost coverage for buildings if you have adequate limits, but personal property losses are paid on an actual cash value basis. How do you account for this difference?

9. Some insurers provide replacement cost coverage on both buildings and personal property. Why is it "some" rather than "all"?

10. Homeowners coverage of damage to property of others is limited to $250 per occurrence. Does purchase of such coverage violate the buying principles discussed in Chapter 7? Why do you suppose it is in the policy?

Cases

17-1 Bill has a Homeowners Policy with the Special Form (HO-3). His home has a replacement value of $80,000, and the contents are worth $45,000 at replacement cost or $35,000 at actual cash value. He has a detached greenhouse with heat and humidity control housing his prized collection of exotic flowers. The flowers are valued at $11,000, and the greenhouse would cost $7,500 to replace at today's prices.

His policy has the following coverages:

Dwelling	$60,000
Unscheduled Personal Property	30,000
Personal Liability, per occurrence	25,000

A property coverage deductible of $250 per occurrence applies.

Analyze each of the following situations in light of the above information. Determine all applicable coverage(s) and limit(s) and explain all factors which might affect the coverage provided by the policy. Use the specimen policy in Appendix C to make your analysis.

1. A windstorm causes $20,000 in repair-cost damages to the house, and subsequent wind-blown rain causes damage to the contents of the house—$18,000 in replacement cost, or $11,000 at actual cash value. The greenhouse is a total loss, as are the exotic plants. Debris removal to satisfy the city's health laws costs $350, and further debris removal to clear the way for repairs costs another $280. Two maple trees valued at $600 each are blown down, and their removal costs another $400. Bill must move his family to a nearby rental home for two months during repairs to the house. Rental costs are $600 per month, utilities at the rental house are $350 per month, and his mortgage payments of $550 per month continue payable. It costs Bill another $80 per month to commute to work and to drive his children to their school. The telephone company charges him $50 to change his telephone to the rental unit and back to his home again.

2. Bill takes the family to the movies the day after they move back into their newly-repaired home. While they are watching the movie, their home is burglarized, with the following losses:

Bill's manuscript for a new book on antiques, which he conservatively values at $20 per hour × 1,000 hours		$20,000
Bill's wife's mink coat		6,500
Bill's coin collection		5,600
His wife's pearl necklace		3,400
His wife's diamond earrings		3,000
One of a matched pair of 1880 flintlock pistols, considered by Bill—and antique dealers—as a "one-of-a-kind" set. Valued at $5,000 for the set, the remaining pistol is worth only $1,500 because of the loss of the first pistol		3,500
Travelers' checks		400

In addition, the burglar causes property
damage to the premises as follows:

Back door	$ 260	
Burn on oriental rug	650	
Broken lamp	80	
Vandalism of cut crystal	2,380	
Vandalism of furniture	3,675	7,045

17-2 In the case of *Arenson vs. National Automobile and Casualty Insurance Company*, 286 Pac. (2nd) 816, the supreme court of California held that the insurer was liable for the insured's liability when the insured's child intentionally damaged the property of others, even though the policy specifically excluded liability for damage caused by an insured intentionally.

1. Can you explain the logic of the court?

2. How might this affect your liability coverage for property damage under a personal liability or a homeowners insurance contract?

Chapter Eighteen:
BUSINESS PROPERTY AND LIABILITY INSURANCE

INTRODUCTION

As we have seen, family risk management is simple in theory but complicated in practice. For the most part, the risks are relatively simple and easy to understand but the insurance designed to deal with them is not. As you might expect, the situation for a typical firm is even more complex, especially with regard to property and liability risks. This chapter will discuss the following:

1. Business property coverage

2. Business liability risks

3. Business liability coverage.

Like the property and liability risks of the family, those faced by a firm may be insured with several different policies. Or, many of them can be covered by a single package policy, such as the Businessowners Policy (BOP), which is designed for the small to medium-size store, office, or apartment. As Figure 18-1 shows, the format of the policy is similar to the Homeowners Policies.

DIRECT LOSS COVERAGES

Buildings and business personal property are covered on a replacement cost basis. Insurance on the building increases by 2 percent automatically every quarter to adjust for inflation.[1] You are required to carry

---

1. A greater rate of increase is available for additional premium.

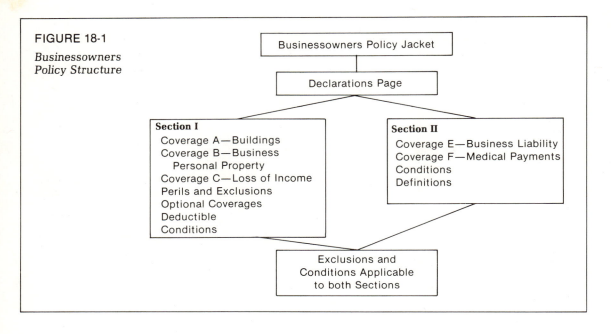

FIGURE 18-1

Businessowners
Policy Structure

100 percent of replacement value on the building but losses are paid on a replacement basis even if this requirement is not met. A $100 deductible applies to most property losses.

Buildings

All buildings on the premises are included under Coverage A. A "building" includes the property listed in Table 18-1. Because the items are all included in the term "building," their replacement value must be considered along with the building itself in determining the amount of insurance for Coverage A.

Business Personal Property

Property insured by Coverage B is shown in Table 18-2. If the amount of insurance under Coverage B is equal to at least 100 percent of the insured's average values during the 12 months prior to a loss, the amount of protection can be increased by 25 percent if needed to cover loss at a peak season. Suppose values during the past 12 months have averaged $40,000 and you have carried that amount of insurance. A loss of as much as $50,000 can be covered. If you have a fluctuating inventory, this is a valuable extension of coverage. It is called the *Seasonal Automatic Increase* agreement.

	TABLE 18-1
	What Is a Building?

1. The building itself.
2. All garages, storage buildings, and appurtenant structures.
3. Fixtures, machinery, and equipment permanently installed.
4. Personal property of the owner relating to service or maintenance of the building.
5. Outdoor furniture and yard fixtures.
6. Other personal property of the owner furnished to tenants.
7. Trees, shrubs, or plants. Limit of $250 per item and $1,000 per loss.

	TABLE 18-2
	Property Insured by Coverage B

1. All business personal property you own usual to your business, and at the described premises.
2. Similar property of others in your care, custody or control.
3. Improvements and betterments you make to premises you rent. Such an investment belongs to the building owner but the tenant has an insurable interest in it.
4. Property other than money and securities temporarily away from the premises, including in transit, up to $1,000 per occurrence.
5. Property at a newly acquired location is automatically covered up to $1,000 for 30 days.

Perils Covered

Two BOP forms are available. The Standard Form pays for loss caused by named perils. The Special Form is written on an all-risks basis. The perils covered and optional coverage available for both forms are shown in Table 18-3. Except for sprinkler leakage and transportation, the perils listed for the Standard Form are the same as those covered by homeowners forms HO-1 and HO-2, shown in Table 17-3 in Chapter 17. Damage caused by earth movement, flood, back-up of sewers and drains, and underground seepage is excluded. Earthquake damage may be added to either form by endorsement, subject to a percentage deductible (usually two percent).

TABLE 18-3

*Businessowners
Policy Covered
Perils*

Standard Form	Special Form
Fire and lightning	All risks
Windstorm or hail	Optional coverages:
Explosion	Employee dishonesty
Riot or civil commotion	Earthquake
Aircraft or vehicles	Boiler and machinery
Smoke	
Vandalism and malicious mischief	
Sprinkler leakage	
Transportation	
Optional coverages:	
Burglary and robbery	
Employee dishonesty	
Earthquake	
Boiler and machinery	

Sprinkler leakage coverage pays for loss caused by leakage or discharge from an automatic sprinkler system or the collapse of a tank forming a part of the system. In addition to the perils listed in Table 18-3, including transportation as a peril broadens the Standard Form to cover loss to property in transit caused by the following:

1. Collision, derailment, or overturn of a transporting conveyance

2. Stranding or sinking of vessels

3. Collapse of bridges, culverts, docks, or wharves.

LOSS OF INCOME

When direct damage is caused by an insured peril to property owned by your firm, the cost of repair or replacement is paid under Coverages A or B. While repair or replacement is going on, however, income may be stopped because the firm cannot continue operations or cannot collect rent for premises that are unusable. Moreover, you may have additional expenses in getting the business going again after repairs have been completed. Such indirect losses can be a greater burden for the firm than the damage to the property itself.

Under Coverage C, the BOP pays for actual business loss sustained and the expenses necessary to resume normal business operations when damage from an insured peril interrupts the business or stops rental income while premises are untenantable. "Actual business loss sustained" is the amount by which earnings and rents are reduced after deducting expenses that do not continue while business is interrupted or premises cannot be occupied. If your apartment building is destroyed by fire, for example, rental income will stop while it is being rebuilt but maintenance expenses will also stop.

There is no dollar limit on the amount of loss that will be paid but there is a time limit. Benefits are paid for the length of time required to rebuild, repair, or replace the damaged property, not to exceed 12 months from the date of the loss. You are required to reduce the business interruption loss to the extent possible by continuing as much of the operation as feasible at the same or another location. If this is not done, the reduction which could have been accomplished is taken into consideration when the loss is settled. This is a crucial point you should remember when a loss occurs. Keeping in touch with the adjuster may help avoid a misunderstanding and an unsatisfactory loss settlement.

BURGLARY, ROBBERY, AND THEFT

The Special BOP protects all insured business personal property against theft losses. Money and securities losses, however, are limited to $10,000 on premises and $2,000 away. Burglary and robbery can be added to the perils covered by the Standard BOP up to 25 percent of the Coverage B limit. Money and securities protection is limited to $5,000 on premises and $2,000 away. Both forms have a $250 deductible.

Theft means any act of stealing while burglary involves forcible entry into or out of the premises. Robbery is taking property by violence or threat of violence. Therefore, the Standard form with burglary and robbery added does not provide as broad coverage as the Special Form. Shoplifting, for example, is theft but it is neither burglary nor robbery.

Neither form pays for loss caused by:

1. Employee dishonesty

2. Mysterious disappearance

3. Inventory shortages

4. Loss suffered when the insured is tricked into parting with property.

EMPLOYEE DISHONESTY

Outsiders are not the only people who steal from the firm. Some of the biggest losses are those caused by employees who steal from their employer. Protection against this risk can be added to both forms of the BOP with the Employee Dishonesty option for additional premium.

This coverage protects your firm against loss of money or other business personal property through dishonest acts of employees, subject to a basic limit of $5,000 per occurrence and a deductible of $250. A series of dishonest acts by one employee or by a group which takes place within a policy period is one occurrence so far as the limit and the deductible are concerned. Because large losses usually take place over a long period during which an employee (or group) takes a little at a time, the basic limit may be too low.

There is no coverage for loss caused by the dishonesty of the insured or any partner, officer, director, or trustee. It does not, for example, protect you from loss if your partner steals from the firm. Moreover, insurance is suspended with respect to an employee from the time the insured, an officer, or a partner first discovers the dishonesty. If you catch Joe stealing, he may apologize and return the loot. You, in turn, may keep him on the job. But employee dishonesty insurance no longer applies to him and you bear the risk that he will steal again (and again and again).

BOILER AND MACHINERY

Neither BOP Form covers loss caused by the explosion of steam boilers, pipes, turbines, and engines owned or controlled by the insured, nor do they cover loss to such objects caused by a condition within the object.[2] They can be covered by adding the Boiler and Machinery option.

This coverage is written on a replacement cost basis to cover loss from an accident to any steam or hot water heating boiler or air conditioning unit.

"Accident" does not include deterioration or wearing out or the breakdown of certain parts named in the coverage. The insurance company has the right to inspect objects but has no obligation to do so. If the inspector discovers a dangerous condition, he or she has the power to suspend the insurance immediately with regard to the defective object.

While the insurer is not obligated to inspect the objects insured, it usually does so on a regular basis. Many firms buy the insurance to obtain inspection service because it makes a significant contribution to their loss prevention and control program.

BUSINESS LIABILITY RISKS

Business firms are exposed to the liability risk in the same way as individuals and families but on a much greater scale. They have more opportunities for liability and the possible size of loss is greater. Huge judgments against firms receive a great deal of publicity, but even those too small to make headlines could put a medium size firm out of business. Several million suits for damages are filed in the United States every year and a considerable portion of the defendants are business firms.

Major sources of liability for the firm are listed in Table 18-4. We will explain them and then examine the liability coverage provided by the BOP.

---

2. Condition within the object means something other than an outside force that causes the breakdown of equipment (object).

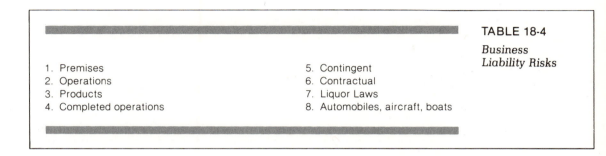

TABLE 18-4

*Business
Liability Risks*

1. Premises
2. Operations
3. Products
4. Completed operations
5. Contingent
6. Contractual
7. Liquor Laws
8. Automobiles, aircraft, boats

Premises

As discussed in Chapter 15, owners and tenants of real property owe a duty to members of the public. Failure to fulfill such duty may result in a suit for damages by an injured party. A customer who is injured in a fall caused by a slippery floor may sue the store owner. Some store managers identify certain customers as being prone to such accidents. As a loss control measure, they follow them throughout the store in an attempt to prevent them from having an accident on the premises. In spite of such efforts, accidents will happen and suits will be filed.

Operations

Contractors perform most of their work away from their premises, so their greatest liability exposure is on the job. Bystanders may be injured by equipment operating on the job, excavations may damage the foundation of adjacent buildings, blasting operations may damage nearby property or injure someone.

Products

Products liability is virtually a growth industry; it is one of the most rapidly growing sources of risk for the firm. As noted in Table 18-5 liability may be based on negligence, breach of warranty, or strict liability in tort.

TABLE 18-5

*Basis for Product
Liability*

1. Negligence
2. Breach of warranty
3. Strict liability in tort

Negligence.   When a firm manufactures and/or sells a commodity inherently dangerous to human life, health, or property, it has a duty to protect those who use it against damage which may result if proper care is not exercised. Failure to fulfill this duty constitutes negligence and may provide the basis for liability. Failure to warn the purchaser that the paint you sell may burn skin unless removed immediately may result in injury to the buyer and a lawsuit against you.

Strict liability.   A firm may be held liable for damage caused by a product even though neither negligence nor breach of warranty is established. The doctrine of strict liability is illustrated by the following decision in a case:

> The plaintiffs must prove that their injury or damage resulted from a *condition* of the product, that the *condition* was an unreasonably dangerous one and that the *condition* existed at the time it left the manufacturer's control.[3]

Completed Operations

Closely related to products liability is that which stems from activities of the firm in installing equipment or doing other jobs for hire off its own premises. Defective workmanship may cause serious injury or property damage for which the firm may be held liable. For example, a roofing company employee was injured in a fall from a fire escape when a cable broke. The court held the fire escape company negligent for using a cable of insufficient size.

Contingent Liability

Generally, a firm that hires an independent contractor to perform work is not liable for damage or injury caused by the contractor. There are, however, a number of exceptions to this general rule. In some situations, the firm may be liable for an independent contractor's negligence if it did not use reasonable care in selecting someone competent. If the activity to be performed by an independent contractor is inherently dangerous, the firm is absolutely liable for damages and cannot shift its liability to the contractor. The fact that the contractor agrees to hold the firm harmless will not relieve it from liability. A firm that hires an independent contractor to do a job and then interferes in the details of the work may find itself liable for the contractor's negligence.

Contractual Liability

It is possible to become liable for someone else's negligence by agreeing to do so. In view of the fact that much of the discussion in this book is concerned with how to avoid risk and how to transfer the financial

---

3. *Suvada v. White Motor Company,* 32 Ill. 2d 614, 210 N.E. 2d 182 (1965).

burden, it may be surprising to learn that assumption of the liability risk is common. An example is the owner of premises shifting the liability risk to a tenant by means of a hold-harmless clause in the lease. A typical clause may read as follows:

> It is agreed the lessor shall not be liable for any damage, either to person or property, sustained by the lessee or by any other person, due to the building or any part thereof, or any appurtenances thereof, becoming out of repair, or due to the happening of any accident in or about said building, or due to any act or neglect of any tenant or occupant of said building, or of any other person.

This assumption of risk may lead to contractual liability, a situation in which a firm becomes liable not through its negligence but someone else's.

Liquor Laws

Many states have laws which impose special liability on anyone engaged in the liquor business in any way. Some apply not only to those who sell liquor but also to the owner of the premises on which it is sold. The laws are concerned with injury, loss of support, and damage to property suffered by third parties who have no direct connection with the store or tavern. If, for example, liquor is served to an intoxicated person or a minor and the person served causes injury or damage to a third party, the person or firm covered by the law may be absolutely liable.

Automobiles, Aircraft, and Boats

Exposure to liability through ownership or operation of automobiles, aircraft, and boats is the same for the firm as it is for an individual. One potential source of loss sometimes overlooked is automobile nonownership liability. This refers to a situation in which an employee uses his or her own automobile on company business and is involved in an accident. The secretary who says, "I'll drop the mail off on my way home," is an agent for the firm during that portion of the trip, and the firm may be liable in the event of an accident. The secretary's Personal Auto Policy covers the employer in such circumstances but may have inadequate limits. Another automobile nonownership exposure concerns vehicles that are rented or leased; a firm's automobile policy may not cover this exposure automatically.

BUSINESSOWNERS LIABILITY COVERAGE

Section II of the Businessowners Policy provides a broad range of liability protection for the firm. The insuring agreement says:

> The company will pay on behalf of the Insured all sums which the Insured
> shall become legally obligated to pay as damages because of bodily injury,
> property damage or personal injury caused by an occurrence to which this
> insurance applies.

If there were no exclusions, all the exposures we have discussed
would be covered. There are, however, a number of exclusions. The
most important are:

1. Automobiles	4. Liquor liability
2. Aircraft	5. Workers' compensation
3. Boats away from the premises	6. Professional liability[4]

As we will see, however, there are exceptions to these exclusions.
Some coverage is therefore provided by an exception to an exclusion
rather than a direct statement. Like the personal liability section of
homeowners policies, the policy has a single limit of liability and provides defense, supplementary payments, and medical payments.
Several aspects of this coverage deserve special attention.

Personal Injury Liability

Most liability policies cover bodily injury and property damage but not
personal injury. Personal injury coverage of the BOP protects the firm
against liability for false arrest, slander, defamation, invasion of privacy, and similar acts.[5] A zealous store employee attempting to reduce
shoplifting losses may expose the firm to a suit for damages by accusing
an innocent customer of stealing something. Some storeowners hire
specially trained people to deal with the shoplifting problem but the personal injury liability risk is still present.

Fire Legal Liability

The policy promises to pay as much as $50,000 on behalf of the insured
for legal obligations resulting from fire or explosion damage to structures which the insured rents or occupies. This covers the risk that your
firm may become liable for damage to premises you rent from others.
The fact that the owner of the premises has them insured does not solve
the problem because the fire insurer has the right of subrogation
against you if loss is caused by your negligence.

---

4. Except for professional liability in connection with pharmacological services of a retail
drug store.

5. Claims stemming from advertising are excluded; Advertiser's Liability insurance must
be bought separately.

Host Liquor Liability

The policy excludes liquor liability coverage for someone in the liquor business and the owner or lessor of premises used in such business. It provides coverage, however, if your firm's only connection with liquor is the serving of alcohol at a function which is incidental to your business and there has been no intentional violation of law in this connection. If your firm has an office party or reception for prospective clients, for example, there is coverage. On the other hand, if the premises are used as a liquor store or saloon, there is no coverage.

Contractual Liability

The BOP covers liability assumed by your firm *if* (1) the assumption is by way of a written contract and (2) it is for damages which would be covered by the policy when claim might be made directly against the insured.

For example, the policy does not cover the firm's liability for owned automobiles, so it will not cover a contractual assumption by the firm of the automobile owner's responsibility. On the other hand, because there is coverage for premises liability, the policy also covers the assumption of the owner's liability.

Nonowned Automobiles

Except for the parking of automobiles, liability arising out of an owned automobile is excluded. This exclusion, however, does not apply to a nonowned private passenger automobile or station wagon used in your business. There is also coverage for occasional *and* infrequent use of a nonowned commercial vehicle (e.g., truck) in the firm's business.

Medical Payments

This coverage is similar to the homeowners policies. Limits are $1,000 per person and $10,000 each accident. Unlike the homeowners medical payments protection, the BOP covers only injuries for which there is bodily injury liability protection. If an incident is covered from the standpoint of liability for bodily injury, it is also covered for medical expenses. Coverage is excluded with regard to nonowned automobiles and products and completed operations hazards.[6] It does not apply to the named insured, employees covered by workers' compensation, or any employee injured in the course of employment.

Umbrella Liability Policy

The basic limit for Section II of the BOP is $300,000. It can be increased to $1,000,000. The single limit applies per occurrence whether the claim is for bodily injury, property damage, personal injury, or a combination. An exception to the application of the limit per occurrence is the Completed Operations and Products coverages. For both of these,

---

6. The policy says "hazard," but it means risk.

singly or combined, the stated limit is also the aggregate limit for all occurrences during the one-year policy period. Thus, payment of a Completed Operations claim of $150,000 and a Products claim of another $150,000 exhausts a $300,000 limit so far as these coverages are concerned for the remainder of the policy period. Limits for other coverages could, of course, be exhausted by a single occurrence.

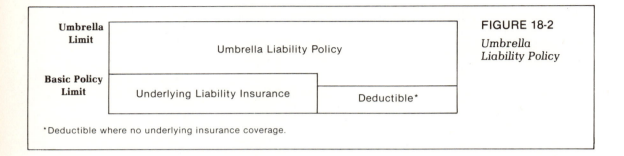

FIGURE 18-2

*Umbrella
Liability Policy*

As Figure 18-2 shows, the Umbrella Liability Policy covers this risk by providing excess coverage over underlying insurance. Except for excluded risks, it also provides excess over a specified amount, such as $25,000, for which there is no underlying coverage. Typically, you are required to have specified amounts of underlying coverage, such as the BOP with a $300,000 limit and automobile insurance with the same limit. When a loss occurs, the basic contracts pay within their limits and then the umbrella policy pays until its limits are exhausted. If there is no underlying coverage for a loss covered by the umbrella, you pay the first $25,000 and the umbrella insurer pays the excess.

OTHER LIABILITY RISKS

What about the liability risks not covered by the BOP? Space limitations prohibit discussing all of them, but several merit some attention: automobile, professional liability, and workers' compensation. The latter is discussed in the next chapter.

Automobile Liability

If the business is a proprietorship and the only vehicles are private passenger automobiles, the Personal Auto Policy or a similar policy will cover the automobile risk. If the business is a partnership or corporation or there are other types of vehicles, other automobile insurance must be purchased. The risks and the coverages are similar to the automobile insurance discussed in Chapter 16.

Professional Liability

Most people have greater respect for professionals than they do for others. Members of a profession claim that they have met very high standards of education and training as well as character and ethical conduct. They are expected to keep up with developments in their field and maintain the high standards established for the profession. As a result, the duty a professional owes to the public is considerably greater than that owed by others. Along with this duty, of course, comes liability for damage caused by failure to fulfill it. We *expect* more from a professional and when we don't get it, we sue for damages.

The risk to which physicians and surgeons are exposed illustrates the position of a professional. In taking cases, doctors represent that they possess—and the law imposes upon them the duty of possessing—the degree of learning and skill that is ordinarily possessed by others in their profession. Doctors must use reasonable care and diligence and their best judgment in exercising their skill and the application of their knowledge to accomplish the purpose for which they are employed.

Some cases illustrate the risk to which medical doctors are exposed. A plastic surgeon who made his patient look worse instead of better had to pay $115,000 for the damage. A court awarded $4.5 million to a girl suffering acute kidney failure as a result of alleged malpractice.

Professional liability insurance (also called medical malpractice insurance) is not only expensive but difficult to obtain in some parts of the country. The insurer promises to pay on behalf of the doctor sums he or she becomes obligated to pay as damages because of

> injury arising out of the rendering of or failure to render . . . professional services . . . or by any person for whose acts or omissions (the doctor) is legally responsible. . . .

The policy also provides defense against alleged malpractice. Although other liability policies permit the insurer to settle claims without the insured's permission, some medical malpractice policies require the insured's permission. This is because compromise settlements may be construed as an admission of fault and be harmful to the doctor's professional reputation. Many policies, however, provide for settlement by arbitration without the insured's consent in order to reduce legal expenses.

Professional liability insurance is also available for accountants, architects, dentists, lawyers, real estate brokers, insurance agents, and other professionals.

Consumer Applications

Cutting the Cost of Business Insurance

Your firm can reduce its insurance costs by controlling losses and buying insurance the way it buys other goods and services. Your insurance business will be sought after if it develops a favorable loss ratio. Nobody in the insurance business wants bad risks, but everybody wants good risks. Therefore, loss control is essential. It reduces not only insurance costs but also uninsured losses. Let's postpone our discussion of loss control, however, and examine how your firm can affect the cost of insurance through its buying practices, assuming that it is a desirable risk.

Buying Insurance for the Firm

Buying insurance for the firm is like buying it for a family or individual, but you may need more help from agents or brokers in determining what you need as well as in shopping for it. What should you do the first time you buy? Before you start shopping you have to decide exactly what you're looking for. Suppose you decide you want a Businessowners Policy, but don't know which form? Do you want the Standard or the Special Form? Get several prices on each so you can compare them.

Ask about Services

But price alone isn't enough. You need service. The most important service for your firm includes:

1. Help in determining insurance needs
2. Help in shopping for coverage
3. Help with loss prevention
4. Help with claim settlement.

If you tell an agent, broker, or company representative that you are concerned about adequate coverage, price, *and* service, he or she will recognize that you are a reasonable, rational buyer. While you cannot be sure ahead of time what quantity and quality of service you will receive, you can request a written statement of what you can expect. This does not mean a brochure extolling the virtues of the selling organization but a specific statement tailored to your needs. Such a statement has two functions:

1. It tells you what to expect.
2. It gives you something to refer to at renewal time.

What to Do at Renewal Time

When a policy anniversary or renewal time rolls around, a quality agent, broker, or company representative will suggest a review of your needs and coverages. In addition to that, you should review the service you have received and check on insurance costs. If your firm is a desirable risk, you have a good bargaining position. Use it—but don't abuse it.

Question the premium at renewal time. Ask the agent to check on it. How does it compare with alternatives? *Caveat:* Although you should ask about cost at renewal time and check with other sources occasionally to see what is available in the insurance market, it is foolish to hop from agent to agent or company to company for a few dollars. People who never question price frequently pay too much, but you should start out with the assumption that your agent or broker will do right by you. If you are too lethargic, you may not get the best deal. But if you are fickle and unreasonably demanding, no one wants your business.

Reduce Cost by Reducing Losses

Loss prevention and control pays off in two ways. First, it saves the firm money it would lose on uninsured losses. Second, it leads to reductions in premium rates. Let's look at a few examples of how losses can be controlled.

Employee Dishonesty
Employee dishonesty losses exceed those caused by burglary, robbery, and theft committed by persons not employed by their victims. They are probably equal to or greater than annual fire losses. Your firm can prevent embezzlement by taking the following steps:

1. *Careful selection of employees.* Check their background so you won't hire a criminal. *Caveat:* Be careful you don't violate federal law in this process. There are limits to what you can ask a prospective employee and an improperly conducted investigation can violate privacy rights.
2. *Awareness of an employee's spending pattern.* Many embezzlers have been discovered through their spending habits. Example: Young man, salary $1,000 per month, owns one automo-

bile, one pickup, just bought new Corvette for himself and three-carat diamond for wife. Did he win big at the dog races or is he stealing from you?
3. *Adequate internal control.* The duties of one employee should serve as a check on the duties of another employee. Don't have one person in charge of ordering, billing, and receiving. Every employee should be required to take a regular annual vacation. Have his or her duties performed by another employee during such absence; don't just let the work stack up until the employee's return.
4. *Report embezzlement to the insurer immediately upon discovery,* but beware of a false accusation that could lead to a personal injury suit. If dishonest employees go scot-free, others may be tempted.
5. *Have outside accountants make frequent and complete audits,* and follow their advice with regard to the improvement of internal controls.

Fire
If you are going to build or remodel a building, ask your insurer for advice while you are in the planning stage. By following such advice, you can reduce fire insurance premium rates markedly. The most important factors are construction, layout (arrangement of space), and protection. From the fire loss point of view, the best construction is fire-resistive while the worst is wood frame. Incorporation of fire walls and fire partitions at the time of construction can reduce the probability of a fire spreading, thereby reducing losses. Protection features such as sprinkler systems and detection and alarm systems also reduce losses.

Some of these insurance premium rate reducing features can be built in only at the time of building or remodeling. Others, such as a sprinkler system, can be added later but only at considerably greater cost. Because the cost of fire insurance (or losses) is, like death and taxes, always with us, you may save considerable money over the long term by considering fire prevention during the planning stage.

Discussion Questions

1. The Businessowners Policy is different from most Homeowners Policies in that it covers both buildings and personal property on a replacement basis. How do you account for this difference?

2. Like the Homeowners Policies, the BOP requires you to carry a specified percentage of replacement value on the building. Unlike the Homeowners Policies, however, you are not penalized when you fail to fulfill this requirement. How do you account for this difference?

3. The Seasonal Automatic Increase agreement in the BOP is significant for some businesses but not for others. Give an example of each category and justify your choice.

4. Many business firms suffer severe losses through employee dishonesty. What kinds of business do you think are least susceptible to such losses? Why?

5. Sometimes settling claims for business interruption losses is time consuming and difficult. Why? Would you recommend hiring a public adjuster for such losses? Why or why not?

6. If you were manager of a supermarket, how would you deal with the problem of shoplifting?

7. To reduce the probability of being sued for malpractice, many doctors practice "defensive medicine." Part of what they do for a patient, such as conduct additional tests, is more to establish that they did everything possible than because they considered it essential for the patient's welfare. What effect does this have on the cost of health care? How can this problem be solved?

8. Why does the BOP exclude losses caused by mysterious disappearance and inventory shortages?

9. The BOP requires you to buy insurance equal to 100 percent of the replacement cost of the building. Is the insurer simply trying to sell more insurance or is there some other explanation for this requirement? Please explain.

10. Corporations A, B, and C are owned by the Larson family. A is in the wholesale business, B in retailing, and C owns premises occupied by A and B. The lease agreements between C and the other two corporations have a hold-harmless clause similar to the one on page 321. Does it create a risk for the Larson family? What function does it perform?

Cases

18-1 In the case of *Keyser Canning Company vs. Klotz Throwing Company* (W. Va.), *118 S.E. 521* (1923), an employer was held liable for fire damages to another business when a fire was started due to the negligence of an employee who was a known smoker, and who threw a cigarette stub into a wastebasket in a room containing highly flammable materials.

1. Why should liability arising from fire on the premises of a business be treated any differently by an insurer than any other form of liability?

2. What could a business occupying a shopping center site leased from another business do to protect itself from legal liability for fire losses to the owner of the building?

3. For its liability to other tenants?

18-2 An interesting case involving dramshop liability arose in the litigation of *Schlein vs. Goldberg, 146 Atl. (2nd) 648*, when the court held that the operator of a tavern was liable for injuries suffered by the plaintiff, to whom the tavern operator sold liquor. After being served, the plaintiff drank the liquor and then was injured in a fight with another person. The court held that the plaintiff's contributory negligence was no defense for the tavern operator, and awarded a judgment to the plaintiff.

In an opposite decision, the supreme court of New Hampshire could find no reason to eliminate the defense of contributory negligence. *Ramsey vs. Anctil, 211 Atl. (2nd) 900* (1965).

1. Why do you think these court decisions are in conflict?

2. What should be the response of the courts in cases like these?

3. What would such a response do to the sellers of alcoholic beverages?

18-3 Smyth Corporation does not own a boat and has made no special provisions for any liability arising from the use of boats. However, Jack Smyth, Jr., a company vice president for sales, takes a customer out for a day on the lake, using his own private boat. The vice president negligently causes a boating accident, injuring the client and persons occupying the other vessel as well.

1. Is the Smyth Corporation liable to the client and/or the persons in the other boat?

2. Will its liability insurance cover this incident?

3. Will the vice president's personal liability insurance protect him?

18-4 Green Company has a fire insurance policy with a business interruption rider. The business occupying the corner lot on their block catches fire, and the fire department must destroy part of Green's building to contain the fire. In addition, the city fire inspector then closes the street for a three-week period due to the fire damage and the danger of building collapse in the neighboring store. This causes Green a loss of sales amounting to $2,500 a day, plus extra advertising expenses of $800 per week.

1. Can Green recover from its insurer?

2. Why or why not?

Chapter Nineteen:
WORKERS' AND UNEMPLOYMENT COMPENSATION

INTRODUCTION

Part of your income loss and health care cost risk is borne by your employer involuntarily. Workers' compensation laws require employers to provide medical and income benefits to employees disabled on the job as well as income to survivors of employees whose death is job related. Unemployment compensation laws require employers to pay for income benefits to employees who become unemployed. The following programs are discussed in this chapter:

1. Workers' compensation laws and benefits

2. Workers' compensation insurance

3. Self-insurance

4. State funds and second-injury funds

5. Unemployment compensation.

WORKERS' COMPENSATION LAWS

Prior to the adoption of workers' compensation laws, a worker had to prove that an injury was the fault of his or her employer in order to recover damages. If fault could not be proven, the employer had no responsibility to the injured employee. This system became unacceptable in an industrial society because some accidents are an inherent aspect of the workplace and it is difficult if not impossible to prove who is at fault. As a result, many injured workers received inadequate com-

pensation or none at all. Moreover, there was little incentive for employers to devote resources to loss prevention and control.

In view of the fact that the burden of industrial injuries stems from industrial activity, it seems reasonable to consider their cost as part of the total cost of production. This is the basic principle of workers' compensation systems. They require employers to pay benefits without reference to fault.

Every state and territory now has a workers' compensation law and there are federal laws applicable to longshoremen and harbor workers, to nongovernment workers in the District of Columbia, and to civilian employees of the federal government. Workers' compensation laws differ from state to state, but they all have the purpose of assuring that injured workers and their dependents will receive benefits without question of fault. The following discussion is concerned with (1) coverage, (2) benefits, (3) how benefits are provided, and (4) the employer's risk.

Coverage

Inclusive or exclusive. Workers' compensation laws are either inclusive or exclusive. Inclusive laws list all the employments which are covered; exclusive laws cover all employments except those which are excluded. Typically, agricultural, domestic service, and casual labor are excluded, although a few states include agricultural labor. Some states limit the coverage of the law to occupations classified as hazardous. Certain injuries are excluded, such as those caused by willful misconduct or intoxication and those deliberately self-inflicted. Occupational disease is covered by most laws, either by a blanket inclusion of all occupational diseases or by a list of those which are covered. Most laws apply to all employers in the employments covered; others apply only to employers who employ more than a specified number of employees, such as three or more.

Compulsory or elective. In most states, the law is compulsory. In a few, either the employer or the employee can elect not to come under the law. If either one elects out, an injured employee must prove the employer was at fault in order to recover damages. When an employer elects out, requirements for proving fault favor the employee somewhat, while the reverse is the case when an employee elects out. Actually, few employers or employees elect out.

Benefits

Two types of benefits are provided for the injured worker—disability income and medical.

Medical. All laws provide unlimited medical and hospital care. Typical cases may not involve great medical expenses, but it is not unusual for medical bills to run into thousands of dollars. About one-third of the total paid out for workers' compensation benefits is for hospital and medical bills.

Income. All workers' compensation laws require that the injured worker be paid cash benefits during temporary or permanent total disability. All laws have a waiting period; i.e., the worker is not compensated for the first few days of his or her disability.

Most benefit payments are related to the wages earned by the employee. For example, workers may receive two-thirds of their average weekly wage but not more than $200 per week nor less than $25 per week (or their weekly wage, if it is less than the minimum). Some laws relate weekly benefits to the size of the family.

In the event of permanent total disability, some laws require income payments for life, while others place a maximum on the number of weeks for which benefits must be paid. (See Table 19-1.) In permanent partial disability cases, the law includes a schedule of lump-sum payments for the loss of various parts of the anatomy which may be paid in lieu of, or in addition to, income benefits. (See Table 19-2.) Some states pay on the former basis, some on the latter. In the event of death caused by an accident on the job, benefits are paid to the surviving spouse and dependent children. (See Table 19-3.)

Rehabilitation. Most people who are disabled by injury or disease make a complete recovery with ordinary medical care and return to work able to resume their former duties. Many workers, however, suffer permanent disability of such a nature that something more than income payments and ordinary medical services is required to restore them to the greatest extent possible to their former economic and social situations. Rehabilitation is the process of accomplishing this objective.

Rehabilitation involves the following: (1) physical-medical attention in an effort to restore workers as nearly as possible to the state of health which existed prior to their injury, (2) vocational training to enable them to perform a new occupational function, and (3) psychological aid to help them adjust to their new situation and be able to perform a useful function for society.

Most workers' compensation laws do not place this responsibility on the employer, but about half the laws require special maintenance benefits to encourage disabled workers to cooperate in a rehabilitation program. Such programs are conducted by both state and federal agencies and also by some of the larger insurance companies.

How Benefits Are Provided

Workers' compensation laws hold the employer responsible for providing benefits to injured employees. Employees do not contribute to this cost. In most states, employers may insure with a private insurance company or qualify as self-insurers. Eighteen jurisdictions have workers' compensation funds. In six of these, the state fund is exclusive; that is, employers are not permitted to buy compensation insurance from a private insurance company but must insure with the state fund.[1] Where the state fund is competitive, employers may choose

---

1. Ohio, Washington, and West Virginia have exclusive funds but permit self-insurance.

TABLE 19-1

Income Benefits for Total Disability

STATE	PERCENT OF WAGES	MAXIMUM WEEKLY PAYMENT	MINIMUM WEEKLY PAYMENT	TIME LIMIT TEMPORARY	TIME LIMIT PERMANENT	AMOUNT LIMIT
Alaska	66 2/3	$650.00	$ 65.00	Duration of disability	Duration of disability	None
California	66 2/3	154.00	49.00	Duration of disability	Life	None
D.C.	66 2/3	426.26	106.57	Duration of disability	Duration of disability	None
Georgia	66 2/3	110.00	25.00	Duration of disability	Duration of disability	None
Illinois	66 2/3	353.19	101.90-132.45*	Duration of disability	Life	None
Kentucky	66 2/3	131.00	44.00	Duration of disability	Duration of disability	None
Maryland	66 2/3	241.00	25.00	208 Weeks	Duration of disability	None
Mississippi	66 2/3	98.00	25.00	450 Weeks	450 Weeks	44,100
Missouri	66 2/3	125.00-120.00**	16.00	400 Weeks	None	50,000***
Ohio	66 2/3-72[1]	258.00	86.00-129.00[2]	200 Weeks	Life	None

*101.90-Temporary; 132.45-Permanent
**125.00-Temporary; 120.00-Permanent
***Temporary

1. 66 2/3 After 12 weeks; 72 first 12 weeks
2. 86.00-Temporary; 129.00 Permanent

Source: United States Chamber of Commerce, *Analysis of Workers' Compensation Laws,* 1980, Chart V.

Copyright 1980, Analysis of Workers' Compensation Laws, Chamber of Commerce of the United States.

TABLE 19-2
Benefits for Scheduled Injuries

STATE	ARM AT SHOULDER	THUMB	THIRD FINGER	LEG AT HIP	ONE EYE	HEARING BOTH EARS
Alaska	$ 43,680	$10,400	$ 3,500	$ 40,320	$22,400	$28,000
California	26,687	3,797	1,260	24,220	8,452	21,770
D.C.	132,993	31,970	10,657	122,763	68,202	85,252
Georgia	24,750	6,600	3,300	24,750	13,750	16,500
Illinois	105,957	24,723	8,830	97,127	56,510	70,638
Kentucky	44,540	11,266	2,882	44,540	19,650	20,436
Maryland	24,300	8,100	2,430	24,300	20,250	20,250
Mississippi	19,600	5,880	1,960	17,150	9,800	14,700
Missouri	20,880	5,400	3,150	18,630	12,600	15,120
Ohio	29,025	7,740	2,580	25,800	16,125	16,125

Source: United States Chamber of Commerce, *Analysis of Workers' Compensation Laws*, 1980. Chart VI.

Copyright 1980, Analysis of Workers' Compensation Laws, Chamber of Commerce of the United States.

TABLE 19-3

Fatalities-Income Benefits for Spouse and Children

	MAXIMUM WEEKLY PAYMENT		AMOUNT LIMIT		
State	Spouse plus Children	Spouse Only	Spouse plus Children	Spouse Only	Maximum Burial Allowance
Alaska	$650.00	$650.00	None	None	$1,000.00
California	154.00	154.00	$55,000	$50,000	1,500.00
D.C.	No Limit	No Limit	None	None	1,000.00
Georgia	110.00	110.00	44,000	32,500	1,000.00
Illinois	353.19	353.19	250,000	250,000	1,750.00
Kentucky	131.00	109.00	None	None	1,500.00
Maryland	241.00	241.00	None	None	1,200.00
Mississippi	98.00	98.00	44,100	44,100	1,000.00
Missouri	120.00	120.00	None	None	2,000.00
Ohio	258.00	258.00	None	None	1,200.00

Source: United States Chamber of Commerce, *Analysis of Workers' Compensation Laws*, 1980. Chart VII.

Copyright 1980. Analysis of Workers' Compensation Laws, Chamber of Commerce of the United States.

whether to insure in the fund or with a private insurance company, or qualify as self-insurers.

Employer's Risk

Industrial accidents create two risks for employers. First, employers are responsible to employees covered by the workers' compensation law for the benefits required by law. Second, they may become liable for injured employees who are *not* covered by the law.[2] These risks cannot be avoided without suspending operations—hardly a viable alternative. The first may be retained if the workers' compensation law of the state(s) in which the firm operates permits self-insurance, but the second is like other liability exposures in that retention is usually not feasible because of the magnitude of possible losses. Even where permitted, self-insurance is feasible only for large firms which have a sufficient number of exposure units (employees) to make accurate prediction of losses possible. Whatever alternative the risk manager chooses, loss prevention and control are imperative if costs are to be kept within reasonable bounds and assets and income protected.

WORKERS' COMPENSATION INSURANCE

Both risks just mentioned can be transferred to an insurer by purchasing a Workers' Compensation and Employers' Liability Policy.

Coverage

The Workers' Compensation and Employers' Liability Policy has two parts: Coverage A and Coverage B. Under Coverage A, entitled "Workers' Compensation," the insurer agrees:

> to pay promptly when due all compensation and other benefits required of the insured by the workers' compensation law.

The policy defines "workers' compensation law" as the law of any state designated in the declarations and specifically includes any occupational disease law of that state. The Workers' Compensation portion of the policy is directly for the benefit of employees covered by the law. The insurer assumes the obligations of the insured under the law and is bound by the terms of the law as well as the actions of the industrial commission or other state body having jurisdiction. Any changes in the workers' compensation law are covered automatically by the policy.

---

2. For example, many workers' compensation laws exclude casual workers. Injured employees who are classified as casual workers are not entitled to benefits under the law but may recover damages from the employer if they can prove that their injuries were caused by the employer's negligence. The employer's liability risk with regard to excluded employees is the same as it would be if there were no workers' compensation law.

Coverage B provides employers' liability protection. The insurer agrees to pay damages for which the employer becomes legally obligated because of:

bodily injury by accident or disease, including death at any time resulting therefrom . . . by any employee of the insured arising out of and in the course of his employment by the insured either in operations in a state designated in . . . the declarations or in operations necessary or incidental thereto.

The policy also provides the defense, settlement, and supplementary payments common to most liability policies. The combination of Coverages A and B provides complete protection for whatever responsibility the employer may have in connection with injury or disease suffered by employees through their employment.

Cost

Based on payroll. The premium for workers' compensation insurance is based on the payroll paid by the employer. A charge is made for each $100 of payroll for each classification of employee. This rate varies with the degree of hazard of the occupation.[3] For example, the highest rate in one state, which has about average rates, is $62.72 per $100 of payroll. This is for classification number 5701, wrecking buildings. On the other hand, clerical classifications in the same state are rated at 39 cents per $100 of payroll.

Factors affecting rate. The rate for workers' compensation insurance is influenced not only by the degree of hazard of the occupational classification but also by the nature of the law and its administration. If the benefits of the law are high, rates will tend to be high. If they are low, rates will tend to be low. Moreover, given any law—whether benefits stipulated by the law are high, low, or otherwise—its administration will affect premium rates. If those who administer the law are conservative in their evaluation of borderline cases, premium rates will be lower than is the case where administrators are less circumspect in parceling out employers' and insurance companies' money.[4] Most laws provide that either the claimant or the insurer may appeal a decision of the administrative board in court on questions of law, but if both the board and the courts are inclined toward generosity, the effect is to increase workers' compensation costs.

Workers' compensation may be a significant expense for the employer, depending upon a number of factors.

---

3. Rates are made for each state and depend upon the experience under the law in that state. Thus, the rate for the same occupational classification may differ from state to state.

4. This is not to imply that they should be one way or the other. The discussion is concerned with factors that influence cost to the employer.

Given any particular law and its administration, costs for the firm are influenced by the frequency and severity of injuries suffered by workers covered. The more injuries there are, the more workers will be receiving benefits. The more severe such injuries, the longer such benefits must be paid. It is not unusual to find firms in hazardous industries which have workers' compensation costs running from 10 to 30 percent of payroll. This can have a significant impact on labor costs. Moreover, there are many other costs for employees, such as Social Security and unemployment compensation taxes and voluntary employee benefits (group life and health insurance or group pensions). The combined effect of all these payroll-related costs is to increase total expenses markedly.

SELF-INSURANCE

Most state workers' compensation laws permit an employer to retain the workers' compensation risk if financial ability to pay claims can be proven. Some states permit the risk to be retained only by employers who furnish a bond guaranteeing payment of benefits.

The major question for the self-insurance of the workers' compensation risk is whether the firm has a large enough number of exposure units (employees) so that its losses are reasonably stable and can be predicted with some accuracy. Clearly, an employer with three employees cannot make an accurate prediction of workers' compensation benefit costs for next year. Such costs may be zero one year and several thousand dollars another year. On the other hand, as the size of the firm increases in terms of the number of its employees, workers' compensation losses become more stable and more predictable. Just how stable losses must be in order for self-insurance to be feasible depends upon the employer's ability and willingness to pay for losses which exceed expectations.

STATE FUNDS

A third method of assuring benefit payments to injured workers is the state fund. State funds are similar to private insurers except that (1) they are operated by an agency of the state government, and (2) they are concerned only with benefit payments under the workers' compensation law and do not assume the employers' liability risk. This must be insured privately. The employer pays a premium (or tax) to the state fund and the fund, in turn, provides the benefits to which injured employees are entitled. Some state funds decrease rates for employers or classes of employers if their experience warrants it.

SECOND-INJURY FUNDS

Nature and Purpose

If two employees each lose one eye in an industrial accident, the cost in workers' compensation benefits for each will be equal. If one of these employees had previously lost an eye, however, the cost of benefits for him or her would be much greater than for the other worker. Obviously, the loss of both eyes is a much greater handicap than the loss of one. If the employer has to pay the total cost of both the previous injury and the subsequent injury, he or she will be unwilling to hire workers who are handicapped. To avoid this situation, "second-injury" funds have been established under most workers' compensation laws. When a subsequent injury occurs, the employee is compensated for the disability resulting from the combined injuries. The insurer (or employer) who pays the benefit is then reimbursed by the second-injury fund for the amount by which the combined disability benefits exceed the benefit which would have been paid for only for the last injury.

Financing

Second-injury funds are financed in a variety of ways. Some receive appropriations from the state. Others receive moneys from a charge made against an employer or an insurer when a worker who has been killed on the job does not leave any dependents. Some states finance the fund by annual assessments on insurers and self-insurers.

UNEMPLOYMENT COMPENSATION

State Laws

State unemployment compensation programs were established as a result of federal legislation. Each state creates, finances, and administers its own law. Like workers' compensation, the law transfers to the employer at least part of the financial element of a risk faced by the employee. Unlike workers' compensation, however, the firm's risk manager has no choice with regard to how the risk is handled. The firm bears the burden. Management can, however, reduce the cost by stabilizing the firm's employment and preventing payment of unjustified benefits.

Federal tax offset. Prior to the adoption of the Social Security Act of 1935, there was considerable opposition to the idea of state laws to deal with the problem of unemployment compensation. This opposition stemmed at least partly from the fear that a state which adopted such a program would place business and industry within its borders at a competitive disadvantage unless all states had similar legislation. The unemployment provisions of the Social Security Act solved this problem by placing a 3.4 percent tax on payrolls and providing that employers who pay the tax are permitted to offset 2.7 percent by proving that an equivalent amount has been paid into a state system of unemployment compensation which meets the standards set forth by the federal law.[5]

---

5. Employers whose state tax is less than 3 percent as a result of experience rating are permitted to offset 90 percent of what they would have paid without experience rating. Without this provision, experience rating could not be used to reduce the employer's tax burden.

Firms subject to tax. The federal tax applies to firms that have one or more employees in each of twenty weeks during the year. Only the first $6,000 of annual wages of each employee is subject to the tax. Certain occupations and organizations are excluded: agriculture, domestic service, casual labor, certain public service and nonprofit charitable, educational, literary, religious, and scientific organizations.

Coverage

The federal law established minimum standards for coverage and benefits. Unless a state law meets the standards, no tax offset is permitted. Every state meets the standards and in many cases they are exceeded. Today, all states cover state and local government employees, several cover farm workers, and a few cover domestic workers. About 97 percent of the civilian labor force is covered.

Unemployment compensation is designed to relieve workers in certain industries and occupations of part of the economic burden of unemployment to which they are subjected through no fault of their own. Three aspects of benefit payments are important: (1) amount and duration, (2) qualifications for benefits, and (3) disqualifications.

Amount and duration. The amount of the weekly benefit payment a worker may receive while unemployed varies according to the benefit formula in the law of each state. Usually it is about one-half to two-thirds the worker's full-time weekly pay within specified limits. The maximum ranges from $82 to $192 a week for a worker without dependents. Minimum benefits range from $5 to $38 a week. Eleven states provide an additional allowance for certain dependents of the unemployed worker.

Most state laws have a waiting period—typically one week—between the time an unemployed worker files a claim for benefits and the time benefit payments begin. This is designed to place the burden of short-term temporary unemployment on the worker as well as to decrease the cost of the plan, thereby making possible greater coverage of more significant unemployment losses with the money available. The number of weeks for which benefits are paid is a function of the work history of the worker. Those whose earnings record is the highest and the longest are entitled to the largest benefits for the maximum length of time. The maximum number of weeks benefits can be paid ranges from 20 to 36, but 26 weeks is typical. The trend is to increase the period for which benefits are paid, and some state laws provide for the payment of additional benefits for a limited period to workers who have exhausted their regular unemployment benefits during a period of high unemployment.

Qualifications for benefits. In order to qualify for benefits, unemployed workers must fulfill certain conditions. They must register for work at a public employment office and file a claim for benefits. They must have been employed in a job covered by the state unemployment compensation law.[6] They must have earned a specified amount of pay or worked for a specified length of time, or both. They must be able to work, available for work, and willing to take a suitable job if it is offered to them. In most states, an unemployed worker who is sick and, therefore, unable to work is not entitled to unemployment compensation benefits. Some states, however, permit payments to disabled workers who are otherwise qualified.[7]

Disqualifications. Unemployed workers may be disqualified from benefits even if they meet the qualifications described above. Most state laws disqualify those who quit voluntarily without good cause or were discharged for just cause. Those who refuse to apply for or accept suitable work, or are unemployed because of a work stoppage caused by a labor dispute may be disqualified. Other causes for disqualification are: receiving pay from a former employer, receiving workers' compensation benefits, or receiving Social Security benefits.

The effect of disqualification varies from state to state. In some cases, it means that the unemployed worker receives no benefits until he or she has again qualified by being employed for a specified length of time in covered work. In other cases, disqualification results in an increase in the waiting period. Some state laws not only increase the waiting period but also decrease the benefits.

How Benefits are Financed

Noncontributory. Most unemployment compensation insurance is noncontributory; employers pay all the cost in most states. The Federal Unemployment Tax Act places a tax on employers at the rate of 3.4 percent of workers' pay in covered jobs, excluding anything over $6,000 paid to a worker in a year. Up to 2.7 percent can be offset by the employers who pay a state tax or from which they have been excused through experience rating. Thus, the maximum state tax which can be offset is 2.7 percent. Revenue from this tax belongs to the state for the payment of benefits under its plan. The remaining part of the federal tax goes into general federal revenues. Congress appropriates money for grants to the states for their administration of the program. If appropriations for this purpose are less than the federal share of the payroll tax, the remainder of such revenue is put into a reserve fund for aid to the states in payment of benefits when state reserves are low.

Experience rating. All states have experience rating; i.e., they reduce the contribution of employers whose workers have little unemployment.

---

6. An unemployed federal civilian or ex-serviceperson may be entitled to benefits under the conditions of a state law for determining benefit eligibility. The amount he or she may receive will be the same as if federal pay had been covered under the state law. Costs of the benefits are paid by the federal government.

7. Several states have compulsory temporary disability insurance laws to provide income (and, in one state, medical) benefits for disabled workers who are not receiving unemployment benefits. Some of these plans pay partial benefits to workers receiving workers' compensation benefits. Others exclude them.

The theory of this rating system is that it will encourage employers to reduce unemployment to the extent that they have control over it. This should help stabilize employment. One other effect is to make employers interested in disqualifying workers who apply for benefits, because it is benefits paid out of their account that reflect their experience under the plan.[8] This has led to considerable discussion of disqualification standards and administration.

Administration

The federal portion of the unemployment compensation insurance program is administered by the Bureau of Employment Security in the Department of Labor. Every state has its own employment security agency; some of them are independent; others are in the State Department of Labor or some other state agency. Typically, the agency is also responsible for the administration of state employment service offices. There are more than 2,500 such offices in the United States where claims for benefits may be filed. Claimants apply for benefits and register for employment at the same time. The function of the office is to find employment or provide them with benefits.

---

8. This does not mean that employers try to cheat employees out of the benefits to which they are entitled. There are many borderline cases in which there is room for argument about whether or not the unemployed worker is really *involuntarily* unemployed. Experience rating emphasizes the fact that employers pay the cost of benefits and motivates them to be interested in disqualifications. As in other human relations situations, one can find examples of bad behavior by either employers or employees.

Consumer Applications
Reducing Workers' Compensation Costs

As we noted earlier, workers' compensation costs can be a significant burden for your firm. Whatever their size, however, they understate the total cost of occupational injury and disease. If your firm insures this risk, the premium you pay is the direct cost. It's visible and you are very much aware of it. You may not be aware that indirect costs of industrial accidents, such as lost time, spoiled materials, and impairment of worker morale, can be just as significant. How can you reduce these costs? First, by loss prevention and control. Second, you *may* reduce costs by self-insuring the risk.

Loss Prevention and Control

Most industrial accidents are caused by a combination of physical hazard and faulty behavior. Once an accident begins to occur, the ultimate result is largely a matter of chance. Total loss costs are a function of accident frequency and severity. Frequency is a better indicator of safety performance than severity because chance plays a greater part in determining the seriousness of an injury than it does in determining frequency. To emphasize this, one risk manager said, "We look at every accident, regardless of how small it is, as a potential death. When a man falls and breaks his arm there is little that must be added to create a fatality."[9]

Accident prevention program

The first consideration is to reduce frequency by preventing accidents. Safety must be part of your thinking, planning, and supervising. Your safety program should be designed to do two things: (1) reduce hazard to a minimum, and (2) develop safe behavior in every employee. A safety engineer from your workers' compensation insurer can give you expert advice and help with your program. He or she can identify hazards so they can be corrected. This involves plant inspection, job safety analysis, and accident investigation.

The safety engineer can inspect your plant to observe housekeeping, machinery guarding, maintenance, and safety equipment. He or she can help you organize and implement a safety training program. He or she can analyze job safety to determine safe work methods and set job standards that promote safety. Your insurer will provide you with accident report forms and instruction on accident investigation. This is essential because every accident indicates either a hazardous condition or unsafe practices, or both. You must know the cause of accidents if you are going to prevent them. Inspection, job safety analysis, and acci-

9. H. Wayne Snider (ed.), *Risk Management* (Homewood, Illinois: Richard D. Irwin, 1964), p. 41.

dent investigation which lead consistently to corrective action are the foundation of accident prevention.

Loss Reduction.

Accident frequency cannot be reduced to zero, so not all losses can be prevented. After an employee has suffered an injury, however, you can take some action that will reduce the loss. First, if you provide immediate medical attention, you may save a life that would otherwise be lost. Moreover, recovery will be expedited. This is why many large plants have their own medical staff and hospital facilities. It is also why you should provide first-aid instruction for your employees. Second, arrange for an injured worker to take advantage of rehabilitation services. Rehabilitation is not always successful but experience has shown that remarkable progress is possible, especially if it is started soon enough after an injury. The effort is worthwhile from both the economic and humanitarian points of view. You, the employee, and society all benefit.

Insurance or Self-insurance?

Is your firm large enough to self-insure and, if so, can you save money by doing so? Unless you have a fairly large number of employees and your workers' compensation losses are reasonably stable, self-insurance is not feasible. Unless self-insurance will save money, it is not worthwhile. Where are the possibilities for saving money? Ask yourself the following questions about your present arrangement:

1. Does the insurer pay benefits too liberally?
2. Does it bear the risk of excessive losses?
3. Does it bear the risk of employers' liability?
4. Does it administer the program?
5. Does it make a profit on our business?

If you self-insure, will you reduce benefit payments? Unless the answer is yes, you would not save on that. Would you bear the risk of excessive losses and employers' liability? No, unless your firm is very large, you would have to insure those risks. Would you administer the program? Yes, and you might do it cheaper than the insurer. If the insurer makes a profit on your business, you could retain that by self-insuring. When you decide to self-insure, you are saying, "We can do it cheaper than they can," and maybe you can. But remember that someone will have to be responsible for loss prevention.

If your firm is large enough for self-insurance, your workers' compensation premium is *experience-rated.* What you pay this year is influenced by your loss experience during the past three years. The extent to which your rate goes up or down to reflect bad experience or good experience depends upon the size of your firm. The larger your firm, the more your experience influences the rate you pay during succeeding years.

If you want this year's experience to influence what you pay this year, you can insure on a *retrospective plan.* It involves payment of a minimum premium or a maximum premium, depending on your loss experience. Regardless of how favorable your experience is, you must pay at least the minimum premium. On the other hand, regardless of how bad your experience is, you pay no more than the maximum. Between the minimum and the maximum, your actual cost for the year depends on your experience that year.

Several plans are available, the difference being the minimum and maximum stipulated. If you are conservative, you will prefer a low minimum and a low maximum, but that is the most expensive. A low minimum and high maximum, on the other hand, is cheaper but it puts most of the burden of your experience on you. If you have an effective loss prevention and control program, you may choose the high maximum and save money on your workers' compensation insurance.

Discussion Questions

1. The purpose of second-injury funds is to encourage employers to hire the handicapped by eliminating the burden of additional workers' compensation payments involved. When you read the latest annual report from your state's second-injury fund, however, you find that virtually no disbursements have been made for several years. How would you interpret this?

2. Many workers' compensation laws exclude casual workers from coverage. Why?

3. A worker is entitled to workers' compensation benefits when disability "arises out of and in the course of" employment. A pregnant employee applies for medical and income benefits, alleging that her condition arose out of and in the course of the company's annual Christmas party. Is she entitled to benefits? Why or why not?

4. Is the rationale for no-fault auto insurance the same as that for workers' compensation? Please explain.

5. How do you account for the huge range in maximum weekly disability income benefits among the various states?

6. A worker who is unemployed because of import competition (e.g., auto manufacturing) can receive benefits of about 70 percent of his or her gross pay for up to a year under the Trade Adjustment Assistance program. How will such a program affect a worker's interest in finding a job? Does such a program contribute to inflation? If so, how?

7. Under Supplemental Unemployment Benefits, auto company funds pay the difference between all public unemployment compensation benefits and 90 percent of a worker's take-home pay for a period of one year. Do you think this is too much, too little, or about the right level of benefits? Please explain.

8. Ann and Dick both have excellent jobs in Boston. She is transferred to Los Angeles. Dick quits his job so he can go with her. Should he receive unemployment compensation benefits? Why or why not?

9. Do unemployment compensation benefits help stabilize our economy? Please explain.

10. Do you think experience rating of unemployment compensation contributions helps stabilize employment? Why or why not?

Cases

19-1 Ted Williams, a production foreman for Acme Machine Company, was discussing an unusual situation with Bill Johnson, a line supervisor.

"Bill, I've got a bit of a problem. That new applicant for the number 7 drill press job seems to be just the person we need. He has the skill and experience to handle the job. The fact that he has sight in only one eye doesn't affect his ability to perform adequately. Yet I am worried about two things. First, he said he lost his sight in the bad eye because of a steel shaving from a drill press ten years ago. That bothers me about this job, and a possible reoccurrence. Second, I know that management would be upset if he lost his only good eye because he would be totally blind and the workers' compensation settlement would be much higher for him than for a less experienced worker with two good eyes. Its a hard decision for me to make."

Bill replied, "I don't know much about the technical aspects of that problem, but I think I would hire the experienced fellow."

1. What obligation (if any) does the company have toward the new man if he is hired to make his workplace "extra" safe?

2. How much added workers' compensation risk will the company be assuming by hiring the one-eyed worker rather than a worker with normal vision?

19-2 Professor Applegate had just finished his lecture to the class on the theory of unemployment compensation. In the hall Jack Armbuster told his friend that his father's company, Armbuster Construction, paid rather extensive unemployment premiums due to the seasonal nature of their work. Jack said that Professor Applegate's comment that unemployment payments tended to keep skilled labor in a market through short periods of unemployment seemed to make sense to him. Jack said he could now see some possible benefit in that it may be better to pay higher unemployment premiums and have your crew ready to go back to work on a day's notice than have them all move a thousand miles away just as soon as they were laid-off due to weather. Jack's friend indicated he shared this view.

1. Does Professor Applegate's idea make sense to you? Why?

2. What argument can you make against it?

19-3 Jeanne quits her job because her boss continually makes advances to her. She applies for unemployment compensation benefits while she looks for another job, but her employer challenges her benefits on the grounds that her unemployment was voluntary because she quit her job with his firm.

1. What do you think her chances of collecting benefits really are?

2. Do you think that she *should* be able to collect?

3. Could an employer make a workplace so onerous as to force resignations in order to escape unemployment compensation costs?

19-4 As risk manager for Titanic Corp., you want to embark on a stringent work safety program which would cost the business at least $500,000 per year for the next three years, and $300,000 per year thereafter. Workers' compensation losses average about $600,000 per year, and you estimate that you can reduce them by one-third. Your plan is opposed by the financial vice-president as a "bleeding heart" program which is not even close to being cost efficient.

1. In light of your knowledge of workers' compensation costs, employers liability exposures, and trends in court decisions, what arguments can you make in favor of the safety program?

Chapter Twenty:
MANAGING EMPLOYEE BENEFITS

INTRODUCTION

When we discussed a program of life and health protection for the Moran family in Chapter 13, the vital role played by Social Security benefits and those provided by the employer was obvious. If the family did not have such benefits, the burden of paying for all its needs would be unbearable. In this chapter, we will examine the nature of employee benefits in some detail. Special attention will be given to the following:

1. Group life and health insurance

2. Group pensions

3. Group deferred profit-sharing plans.

GROUP LIFE AND HEALTH INSURANCE

Nature

The basic function of group life and health insurance is the same as that of individual insurance, namely, to provide protection against loss caused by death or disability. To the person who is covered, the two forms of insurance are fundamentally the same. Group insurance differs from individual insurance, however, both in administration and underwriting.[1]

---

1. Another difference is that group life insurance contracts typically contain no exclusions. The benefits are payable in the event of death from any cause; there is not even a suicide clause.

Administration.   The administration of group insurance differs from individual insurance in that the contract is made with the employer rather than each individual. Moreover, if the group is large, the employer may be responsible for the record keeping ordinarily done by the insurer.

In group insurance, the employer receives the policy which describes all the terms and conditions of the contract. The employer, in turn, provides each insured employee with a certificate showing his or her name, the amount of insurance, and the beneficiary. Employees also receive a booklet describing the plan. It is distributed to employees by the employer at the time the plan goes into effect or when they are employed, whichever is later.

Underwriting.   Individual life and health insurance involves individual underwriting. That is, the purchaser files an application and, in many cases, takes a medical examination. On the basis of this information and that obtained from other sources, the underwriter decides whether or not to issue insurance, and on what terms. The merits of each application are decided individually. Group insurance, on the other hand, does not involve an application to the insurer by each participant, or— except in some very small groups—a medical examination.[2] Instead of selecting individual insureds, the insurance company selects on the basis of the group, for which the employer makes application. If the group is satisfactory, no consideration is given to the health or habits of individuals within the group.

Benefits

Life insurance.   In order to prevent employees in the group who are uninsurable as individuals from acquiring disproportionate amounts of life insurance under the group plan, various methods are used to prevent individuals from having any choice in the matter. Some plans provide the same amount of insurance for every employee. Others determine the amount by *position*. A third system is to relate the amount of insurance to years of *service*. A fourth method is to relate the amount of insurance to *earnings*. Finally, a plan may use some combination of these methods of determining the amount of life insurance for each employee.[3]

Most group life insurance is written on the yearly renewable term plan. Because temporary protection is not as desirable as permanent protection, however, some group life insurance plans utilize permanent insurance. Group permanent may be written on a group paid-up or a level premium basis.

---

2. However, an employee who does not become a participant at the time the plan is installed or when he or she is first employed (whichever is later) may be required to provide evidence of insurability if he or she decides to become a participant at a later date.

3.   Although some states have legal limitations on the amount of insurance which may be written on any individual in a group, most do not. Insurers have their own underwriting limitations, which are usually related to the total volume of insurance on the group.

Group paid-up is a combination of accumulating units of single premium whole life insurance and decreasing units of group term life insurance. As monthly premiums are paid, the employee's contribution is used to buy a specified amount of paid-up insurance and the employer's portion of the premium is used to buy term insurance. As the amount of paid-up insurance increases, the amount of term insurance decreases. Employer contributions to a group paid-up plan are deductible as a business expense but are not considered taxable income to employees so long as the employer makes no contribution to the paid-up values.

Level premium group permanent is similar to group term except that whole life or endowment insurance is purchased instead of term insurance. It has been used primarily for the funding of pension benefits rather than the provision of life insurance protection, however, because when used for the latter purpose, employer contributions toward the cost of permanent insurance are considered taxable income for employees.

Health insurance. Health insurance benefits provided by an employer on a group basis are similar to, if not identical with, those discussed in Chapter 11. One difference is that some of the larger group plans arrange for medical benefits through a Health Maintenance Organization (HMO). HMO's provide a comprehensive range of health care services, including physicians' services, outpatient and inpatient hospital care, and emergency health services, with a heavy emphasis on preventive health services. Most of them employ physicians and other health care professionals on a salaried basis to provide services to a specific group of subscribers.

Under the Health Maintenance Organization Act of 1973 federal financial aid is available to qualified HMO's. It requires that employers with 25 or more employees who offer a health benefits plan must include the option of membership in a federally qualified HMO if one is available. Thus far, there are only about 200 HMO's in operation, but they provide service to several million people. Sponsors include insurance companies, government units, Blue Cross-Blue Shield, hospitals, medical schools, consumer groups, unions, and other organizations.

Cost

Premiums for group insurance plans are paid by the employer to the insurer. In some cases, the plan requires employees to pay part of the cost to the employer. Such plans are called *contributory*. The balance of the cost is paid by the employer. In other plans, the employer pays all the costs, in which case the plan is called *noncontributory*. Some group health insurance plans are noncontributory for the employee but require him or her to contribute if other members of the family are covered.

Group insurance costs less than individual insurance. The insurer deals with one insured instead of many. The employer takes care of much of the administration detail. Commission scales on group business are lower than they are on individual policies. Medical examinations are not needed because underwriting is done on a group basis. The employer pays part (or all) of the costs and is interested in weeding out false or padded claims for health care benefits.

Premiums paid by the firm are considered to be a deductible business expense for tax purposes but are not taxable income for the insured employee except on amounts of term life insurance in excess of $50,000 per person. On the other hand, contributions toward the premium made by the employee are not a deductible expense. Proceeds paid at death are not taxable income for the beneficiary but are included in the estate of the insured—if he or she is the owner—for federal estate tax purposes.

PENSIONS

Death and disability are two of the three great risks confronting the individual. Old age dependency is the third. Theoretically, the latter problem should be solved by the individual by saving a portion of his or her income every payday during his or her working years. As a practical matter, however, many people either cannot or will not do so. Moreover, for many people, keeping money is even more difficult than saving it. They are more adept at earning an income than they are at managing investments.

This problem has been partially solved by the Social Security program. For most people, however, Social Security retirement benefits do not provide enough income. So an important component of their compensation is not only life and health benefits during their working years but a pension provided by their employer when they retire.

An adequate retirement program has advantages for the employer as well as employees. First, it encourages older employees to retire and make room for new blood in the firm. This helps attract qualified employees who realize they will not have to wait until someone dies in order to receive a promotion. Second, it improves the morale of all concerned and thus contributes to efficiency. Finally, it makes a favorable public relations impact. In a unionized plant, of course, pensions are a proper subject for negotiation at the bargaining table.

Qualifying the Plan

Significance. A pension plan may be qualified or unqualified. The distinction between these two categories is important to both the employer and the employee because qualification affects the tax status of contributions made by the firm for the purpose of funding the plan. Unqualified plans are not approved by the Internal Revenue Service. Employer contributions to them are not a deductible business expense unless they are classified as compensation to the employee, in which case they would be taxable income for him or her.

Plans which meet the requirements of the tax laws for qualification, however, receive favorable tax treatment. With a qualified plan, employer contributions are deductible as a business expense but are not taxable income to the employee until they are received as benefits. Moreover, earnings on funds held by the trustee for the plan are not subject to income tax. Because funds required to provide benefits accumulate faster when tax sheltered, this reduces pension costs and makes higher benefits possible.

Requirements. In order to be qualified, a plan must fulfill requirements shown in Table 20-1. The purpose of these requirements is to prevent those in control of the firm from using the plan primarily for their own benefit rather than that of ordinary employees.

1. There must be a legally binding arrangement in writing and communicated to the employees.
2. The plan must be for the exclusive benefit of the employees or their beneficiaries.
3. It must be impossible for the principal or income of the plan to be diverted from these benefits to any other purpose.
4. The plan must benefit a broad class of employees and not discriminate in favor of officers, stockholders, supervisory personnel, or highly paid employees.
5. The plan must comply with the Employee Retirement Income Security Act (ERISA).

TABLE 20-1

Requirements for Plan Qualification

Designing the Plan

Eligibility. A pension plan must establish criteria for determining who is covered by the plan. Most plans do not cover all employees but exclude certain classes. For example, part-time or seasonal employees are usually not covered. A plan may apply to employees in one plant, one department, or to salaried employees only. Separate plans may be set up for those paid on an hourly basis. Individual employees are included in the plan only after they attain a specified age or after a specified number of years of service.[4] These eligibility requirements are designed to reduce turnover among those covered by the plan, reduce the cost of the plan, and simplify its administration.

Normal retirement age. Unless the age at which employees will retire is known, it is impossible to calculate the cost of benefits provided by the plan and estimate the rate at which funds must be accumulated. Therefore, every plan must establish a normal retirement age. Provision can then be made for early or deferred retirement—early retirement will reduce benefits and deferred retirement may increase them. The Social Security system stipulates age 65 as the normal retirement

---

4. This is partly to reduce costs and partly because most younger employees attach a rather low priority to benefits they may receive 40 years hence. Under ERISA, the maximum eligibility requirement permitted is the later of one year of service or age 25.

age, and most private pensions do the same.[5] This is because many private pensions provide benefits which are integrated with those of Social Security.[6]

Benefits.   A pension plan may provide for a defined contribution benefit or a defined benefit.

Defined Contribution.   A *defined contribution plan* is also called a *money purchase plan.* It establishes a rate of contribution, and the employee receives whatever benefit the contribution will provide at retirement. The benefit varies with the amount of the contribution, and the age, sex, and length of covered service of the employee prior to normal retirement age. This type of plan is not widely used but has been adopted in some cases as a result of union negotiation. In such cases, the employer's contribution is a specified number of cents per hour, or per ton of coal, and so on. Because of its simplicity, the money purchase plan is used by profit-sharing plans that allocate part of their funds to provide pension benefits.

Defined benefit.   A *defined benefit plan* may state that the employee is to receive a flat amount, such as $100 per month, or it may provide a formula by which the amount can be calculated. Thus, it may provide a specified percentage of current salary or the average of the past five (or other number of) years. Or, it may provide (say) $1 per month for each year of service, plus a specified percentage of current salary or average salary for a specified period. Another example would be a specified percentage (say 1 or 1.5) of final annual salary for each year of service.[7] The complexity of the formula which may be used is virtually unlimited. One problem which can occur, however, is that the formula may be so complicated that employees are unable to understand and appreciate the amount of benefit to which they will become entitled, thus losing for the firm part of the goodwill the plan was expected to create.

---

5.   Both men and women may now receive Social Security retirement benefits at age 62, but such benefits are less than those payable if retirement is postponed to age 65.

6.   An integrated plan makes Social Security retirement benefits an integral part of the total pension provided at retirement. The plan may provide, for example, a monthly pension of $500 including Social Security benefits. If the Social Security benefit is $200 per month, the employer provides $300 per month, but if the Social Security benefit is $300 per month, the employer provides only $200 per month. The offset cannot exceed 5/6 of Social Security benefits, however.

7.   Two types of service are involved: past service and future service. Past service refers to service prior to the installation of the plan. Future service refers to service subsequent to the installation of the plan. When credit is given for past service, the plan starts out with an initial past service liability at the date of its installation. In order to reduce the size of this liability, the percentage of credit for past service may be less than that for future service, or a limit may be put on the number of years of past service credit, or past credits may begin at (say) age 40 regardless of the age of the employee. Initial past service liability is a serious problem for the employer installing a pension plan.

Vesting. A pension plan may be contributory or noncontributory. An employee who contributes to a pension plan must be permitted to recover the contributions, with or without interest, if he or she leaves the firm. Vesting, or the employee's right to benefits for which the employer has made contributions, depends, however, upon the provisions of the plan. Prior to ERISA, a plan could provide for no vesting, in which case employees who left the firm prior to retirement would receive no benefit from the employer's contributions. Or, at the other extreme, a plan could provide for immediate vesting, which would give employees the full benefit of the employer's contributions regardless of when they withdrew.

Vesting provisions are important to you because they determine whether you will lose pension benefits if you change jobs. In order to prevent employees who spend a significant part of their working lives with one firm from losing pension benefits if they change employers, ERISA established minimum standards to assure full vesting within a reasonable period of time.

Financing the Plan

Under ERISA, virtually all private pension plans must be funded. A funded plan is one that accumulates funds during the period in which employees are actively working for the firm. Pension expense is charged against income earned by the firm, while pension obligations are accumulating instead of being deferred until employees have retired. There are two methods of funding: (1) self-administered, or (2) insured.

Self-administered Trusteed Plan. A self-administered trusteed plan does not involve the use of insurance, at least during the period when funds are being accumulated. The employer creates a trust to accumulate funds and disburse benefits to employees. The trustee responsible for the trust may be an individual, a bank, a trust company, or some combination of co-trustees. The duties of the trustee are to invest the funds contributed to the trust by the employer (and the employees, if contributory), accumulate the earnings, and pay benefits to eligible employees. Under such plans, a consulting actuary is employed to make estimates of the sums which should be put into the trust.

With a self-administered trusteed plan, the employer is a self-insurer. The trustee makes no guarantee with regard to earnings or investments. The consulting actuary does not guarantee that his or her estimates of the funds which should be accumulated will be accurate.[8] There is no guarantee as to the expense of operating the plan.

Insured Pension Plans. An employer who wants to fund the firm's pension plan through an insurance company has the options listed in Table 20-2.

---

8. There is no implication here that such estimates will *not* be accurate; the point is that they are not guaranteed for the employer as they would be with an insured plan.

TABLE 20-2

*Insured Pension
Plan Options*

1. Group deferred annuity contract
2. Deposit administration contract
3. Immediate participation guarantee contract
4. Separate accounts
5. Individual policy pension trust

Group deferred annuity contract.   The group annuity is similar to the retirement annuity policy discussed in Chapter 8 except that the contract is between the insurer and the employer. The latter receives a master contract, and certificates of participation are given to the individuals covered by the plan. Group plans usually require some minimum number of participants in order to make possible administrative economies. If the plan is contributory, at least 75 percent of those eligible must be covered. The plan provides for the purchase of specified amounts of deferred annuity each year. For example, $10 per month beginning at age 65 might be purchased each year for each employee. An employee who worked for 10 years would receive an annuity of $100 per month beginning at age 65, while an employee who worked for 35 years would receive an annuity of $350 per month at age 65.

Under this plan, the insurance company guarantees each unit of deferred annuity purchased. All actuarial work is done by the insurer, who provides administrative and investment services. Neither the employees nor the employer are subject to risk. The employer's only responsibility is to report essential information to the insurer and pay premiums.

Deposit administration contract.   This arrangement requires the employer to make regular payments to the insurance company on behalf of employees, but annuities are not purchased until the employee retires. Instead, contributions are accumulated at interest in a separate fund. The insurer has no responsibility to individual employees until they retire and annuities are purchased for them. The insurer does the actuarial work required to estimate the amount of annual deposits necessary to accumulate the funds to purchase annuities when employees retire. It also guarantees that funds deposited will be accumulated at a specified rate of interest and will be preserved. It does not, however, guarantee the adequacy of such funds. Prior to retirement, the employee's position is similar to that under an uninsured trusteed plan. After retirement, it is the same as it would be under a group deferred annuity contract.

Immediate participation guarantee contract. This plan is similar to a deposit administration plan in that the employer makes regular deposits to a fund managed by the insurance company. The insurance company receives deposits, makes investments, and pays benefits to retired employees. It also makes periodic evaluations of the plan to determine its actuarial soundness. The plan is like a self-administered trusteed plan in that costs are a function of its actual experience, which is reflected immediately in its operation. It is also similar to a trusteed plan in that the insurer makes no guarantee concerning the safety of investments or the return that is made. The fund is charged with administrative costs and investment losses and credited with investment gains and earnings.

The "guarantee" of the contract concerns employees who have retired; that is, the insurance company guarantees that they will receive the benefits to which they are entitled. This is done by providing that when an evaluation of the plan indicates that it is actuarially unsound, either the employer must deposit additional funds or the insurance company uses the funds in the account to purchase annuities for the retired employees. This converts the plan to a normal group annuity contract. Prior to retirement, there are no guarantees.

Separate accounts. Separate account plans are a modification of deposit administration contracts and are designed to give the insurer greater investment flexibility. They are not commingled with the insurer's other assets and, therefore, not subject to the investment limitations applicable to such assets. At least part of the employer's contributions are placed in separate accounts for investment in common stocks. Usually, the funds of many employers are pooled for investment purposes, although a large employer may arrange for a special separate account for his or her funds exclusively. Separate accounts may be used to fund either fixed-dollar or variable annuity benefits.

Individual policy pension trust. This plan provides pension and life insurance benefits by the creation of a trust into which the employer makes regular contributions. The trustee uses such funds to purchase individual policies on the life of each employee. Typically, a retirement income policy is purchased. When the policies bought, such as ordinary life, do not accumulate enough cash value to provide the retirement income benefits desired, split funding is used. That is, part of the funds are accumulated as life insurance policy cash values, and the balance is accumulated in a trust or through a deposit administration contract issued by an insurance company. If the employee is uninsurable for a death benefit, a retirement annuity may be purchased.

At the time individual policy plans were introduced, group requirements were more restrictive than today and many small firms had no alternative for funding their pension plans. They could not qualify for group plans and self-insurance was not feasible. Unfortunately, individual policy plans provide few—if any—of the advantages of group plans and are an expensive method of funding pension plan benefits. Cash values accumulate slowly during the early years of individual policies; when there is high employee turnover, a good deal of the money the employer puts into them is lost.

DEFERRED PROFIT-SHARING PLANS

A deferred profit-sharing plan is an arrangement whereby a firm puts part of its profits in trust for the benefit of employees. The share of profit allocated to each employee generally is related to his or her salary; that is, it might be 5 percent of annual salary, or 10 percent, and so on. Some employers also consider years of service in making allocations. Suppose, for example, that a plan provides for allocating an amount equal to 5 percent of annual basic salary for each employee who has been employed by the firm for 10 years or less, and 10 percent for employees who have been employed for over 10 years. Deposits would be made in the trust at the end of this year as follows:

Employee	Basic Salary	Years Service	Percent Deposit	Amount Deposit
Adams, J.	$16,000	8	5	$ 800
Brown, M.	20,000	11	10	2,000
Cramer, T.	30,000	7	5	1,500

When the plan meets the qualifications established by the Internal Revenue Code, contributions to the trust are deductible from income by the firm but are not taxable income to the employee until he or she receives them.

Qualifying the Plan

Deferred profit-sharing plans must meet requirements similar to those for a qualified pension plan in order to qualify for tax exemption under the Internal Revenue Code. Employees must be included on a nondiscriminatory basis. Benefits provided must not favor those in supervisory, managerial, or equity positions.[9] There may be differences based on salary and length of service, but the same standard must apply to all participants. Employee benefits must be nonforfeitable in the event of death, disability, or retirement. Vesting need not be immediate and full but must take place relatively rapidly in order for the plan to qualify.

---

9. Common stocks are referred to as "equities" because they represent ownership. A person who occupies an "equity position" in the firm is an owner or part owner. In a close corporation, stockholder-employees have "equity positions." Such people not only work for the firm, but also exercise ownership control and are in a position to favor themselves when establishing a profit-sharing plan.

Trust Funds

Trust funds accumulated by a profit-sharing plan may be used to buy life insurance or annuities for employees, or they may be used to provide disability benefits. They may also be invested in stocks, bonds, or any other type of investment permitted by the trust agreement. Investments may be managed in such a way as to provide a hedge against inflation. The fact that trust income is not taxable makes it possible for trust assets to accumulate at a faster rate than those held by a firm or an individual.

Consumer Applications
Getting the Most from Employee Benefits

If your salary is $750 a week, how big is your check? Do you look? Of course you do, and you're probably disappointed to see that it is about $500. Your salary, however, may be only three-fourths (or less) of your total compensation. The other fourth is employee benefits. Look at it this way: if your salary is $750 per week, your weekly check is probably $500, or two-thirds. Your employee benefits may be worth $250 per week and you don't have to pay income tax and take other deductions from them. If your employer did not provide these benefits, you would have to take *half* of your $500 paycheck to pay for them. On an after-tax basis, they probably account for a third of your total compensation. How can you use them to the best advantage? Two things: First, know your coverage. Know what the benefits are. Study your employee benefits booklet as carefully as you would inspect your new Corvette.[10] If there is anything you don't understand, ask your supervisor. If he or she doesn't know, keep asking until you find out. Second, *use* your knowledge. Don't buy any other insurance until you know what your employer provides. Now let's look at your employee benefits and make some specific suggestions.

---

10. Yes, I remember telling you not to buy a sports car because the auto insurance premium is high, but some of you will anyway.

Suggestions For You

Life Insurance
Don't count too much on your group life insurance on a permanent basis. It is probably term insurance and will be in force only as long as you are with your present employer. You can convert it to a permanent form if you quit your job and are no longer covered, but you will pay the premium and it will be substantial. Look at Gary Moran in Chapter 13. His employer provides him with $72,000 (twice his $36,000 annual salary) group life insurance. If he converted it to a permanent form, the annual premium would be almost $1,000 per year. Your group life insurance may be a major part of your protection program, but if you need permanent protection, don't depend on it. You can't take it with you in a term form if you leave your present job. Your next employer may offer you group life, but what if you leave to go into business for yourself? Or retire?

Who owns your group life insurance? Because the matter of ownership is usually not mentioned when you sign up for employee benefits, you are probably the owner. Is that the way you want it? If not, you will have to take the initiative to change ownership. If the clerk who handles employee benefits tells you it can't be done, keep pushing the matter. It doesn't cost your employer anything and it may be important to you. If you are the owner at the time of your death, the proceeds will become part of your estate for tax purposes.

Health Insurance
Sometimes when both spouses work and are covered by different group health insurance plans, they list each other as a dependent, thinking that two policies are better than one. Actually, your coverage is primary for you and excess for your spouse. Your insurance would provide benefits for him or her only after his or her own policy benefits have been exhausted. It is foolish to pay extra premium to have dependent coverage for your spouse on your policy unless it is far superior to his or hers.

What if you have children? Frequently, they are automatically covered by the husband's insurance and he pays extra premium for them. But is his insurance coverage better than hers? If hers is better and the premium for dependent coverage is reasonable, have her policy cover the children. *Caution:* If she quits or is laid off her job, be sure to add her and the children to the husband's coverage. On the other hand, if the husband quits or is laid off, be sure to add him to her coverage. This seems obvious but it is frequently overlooked.

Medical-surgical. Where does the surgical coverage in your health plan apply? In some cases, it is in-hospital only. If that is the case, remember that you will have to pay for surgery performed in the doctor's office. Let him or her know about this if you need minor surgery.

Does your health coverage have a deductible? Is the deductible waived for an accidental injury treated in the emergency room? Does treatment have to be within 48 hours of the accident? If so, from an economic point of view, if you're going to go to the emergency room, go now.

Beware of the pre-existing conditions provision. Some policies will not cover a preexisting condition for one year after you are first enrolled. Others exclude coverage until you are free of the condition for, say, six months. Whatever the provision is, you should be familiar with it. It may be prudent for you to see a doctor now about some problem for which you've previously had treatment. If postponing the visit for a short period of time will get you past the time when the pre-existing condition provision is effective, it may be prudent to wait. This is not to suggest that you should neglect health problems but to remind you that a great deal of health care is discretionary. If you know the coverage and use your knowledge, you can take care of your money *and* your health.

Disability Income. Beware of offsets against your long-term disability income benefit. Some plans offset Social Security disability income benefits or workers' compensation benefits. Some teachers' retirement system disability income benefits have so many offsets that they really don't provide much income to a disabled person. This is not to say that there should not be offsets, but to warn you that simply adding up all the disability income benefits you might receive may be misleading. Some of the benefits you add may, instead, be offset. Looked at from that point of view, your total disability income may be inadequate. Know your coverage!

Retirement Benefits

Offsets. Does your retirement benefit have a

Social Security offset? Most plans don't offset more than 50 percent of your Social Security benefit, but yours could. The larger the offset, the smaller the combination of the two. Instead of getting your retirement benefit *plus* Social Security, you get Social Security, plus your employer-provided benefit, minus some percentage of your Social Security benefit. This is not wrong in the sense that you are being cheated, but you should be aware of it for retirement planning purposes.

The freeze. Another thing you should be aware of is that the Social Security offset freezes when you retire. This means that it cannot increase as Social Security benefits increase. This has some significance for the timing of retirement. If your retirement has a Social Security benefit offset, it is better to retire just before an increase in Social Security benefits than just after. Suppose, for example, that you are now entitled to $600 per month Social Security retirement benefit and your firm's plan offsets half of it against your employer-provided benefit. That's $300 per month. Suppose Social Security retirement benefits are scheduled to increase 15 percent three months from now. If you retire after that increase instead of before, your offset will be $345 per month instead of $300 per month.

So what? As you read this, you are saying to yourself, "What's this got to do with me?" Nothing, directly. There may not be any Social Security by the time you retire. But as a person who has had one course in insurance, you may be something of an expert within the confines of your own family circle. You may be able to help your parents or grandparents or one of their friends. An expert doesn't know everything; he or she just knows something helpful that others either don't know or don't appreciate.

Suggestions for Your Employer

Why does your employer provide employee benefits? There are many reasons, of course, but a major one is to provide a form of compensation that will attract and keep better employees. How can this be accomplished? The better the benefits are, the more employees will appreciate them. But unless they understand what they are entitled to and actually get it, your employer will not get his or her money's worth. This involves communication and administration.

Communication
If you spend an amount equal to 25 percent of the payroll to provide benefits for your employees, why not spend a few more dollars to assure they understand what they're getting? Mere establishment of an employee benefit plan is not enough, regardless of how good it is. If the firm is to get its money's worth, active steps must be taken to inform employees about the plan when it is established and keep them informed as time goes by. Someone in the firm has to become a local expert on every aspect of the plan so there can be a constant flow of information. Having someone from an insurance company come in occasionally to explain benefits is helpful, but it isn't enough. Employees who have questions about coverage want answers now, not next month.

Administration
If the firm's objectives in establishing an employee benefit plan are to be attained, someone in the firm must be responsible for handling claims and insisting that employees get the benefits to which they are entitled. When the plan is created, the employer negotiates with the insurance company. He or she has both experience in negotiating and bargaining power. When benefit delivery time arrives, it is

the employer who understands (or should) what has been purchased and it is the employer who has the bargaining muscle. Example: what is a "reasonable and customary charge" for surgical procedure X? If the doctor says $200 but the insurer says $175, the employee can either pay the extra $25 now or spend months fighting with the insurer and then pay the $25. He or she doesn't have enough knowledge or enough bargaining power to negotiate with the insurer on an even footing. An employer who ignores this problem will not get his or her money's worth either in the form of benefits for employees or employee appreciation for the plan.

Cost Control

Many firms reduce employee benefits costs by hiring only healthy people. They try to weed out the unhealthy by requiring a physical examination prior to hiring. The result can be:

1. Reduction in sick leave
2. Reduction in health insurance cost
3. Reduction in workers' compensation cost
4. Reduction in group life insurance cost.

Group life and health insurance costs may also be controlled by monitoring your insurer's retention. The retention is the difference between total premiums paid to the insurer during the year and the sum of benefits to employees and dividends to the employer. It is a good measure of what it costs to have the insurer pay benefits, bear risk, and provide administrative service. You can compare it with that of other insurance companies. If it is relatively high and you express concern to your insurer, it may be reduced by an increase in dividends if experience has been favorable.[11] If you never question the retention, it is likely to be higher than would otherwise be the case.

Pension costs may also be reduced. Many employers who fund a pension plan with individual policies are concerned only with the size of the premium and the benefits their employees will receive at retirement. They disregard the rate at which cash values accumulate. They fail to appreciate the fact that when an employee withdraws, the nonvested portion of cash values is available to help pay premiums for those who remain, thereby reducing the deposits the employer must make. Your employer can reduce pension costs by comparing cash value growth rates before making a commitment for an insured pension plan. There is a wide variation among insurers on this score, so it pays to shop for the best.

Discussion Questions

1. It has been suggested that all private pension plans be required to provide full vesting at the end of one year of participation. If you were the owner of a firm employing 50 people and had a qualified pension plan, how would you react to this proposal? Please explain.

---

11. This statement is not pure theory; it is based on personal experience.

2. If you were an employee of a small firm, would you favor the proposal that full vesting be required for all private pension plans at the end of one year of participation? Why or why not?

3. As an employee, which would you prefer, a qualified or unqualified pension plan? Why?

4. Most employees prefer a noncontributory group life and health plan. What advantage might a contributory plan have for them?

5. As an employer, would you prefer a defined contribution pension plan or a defined benefit plan? Please explain.

6. Which is preferable from an employee's point of view: a defined contribution or a defined benefit pension plan? Please explain.

7. As an employee, would you prefer a deferred or an immediate (cash at the end of each year) profit-sharing plan? Please explain.

8. Some employers have deferred profit-sharing plans instead of pension plans. Why?

9. How do you account for the fact that most employers, especially small firms, do a poor job of communicating with employees about their employee benefit plans?

10. Social Security retirement benefits are adjusted annually to offset the effect of inflation but few private pension plans follow this practice. Why not?

Cases

20-1 Lloyd Olsen, the personnel manager of Sturdy Biscuit Company, is pondering a question of funding the company's pension plan. Sturdy Biscuit Co. employs 300 people and has a history of sound financial management. Knowing that he has to present a proposal to the board of directors next week, Lloyd is concerned about the funding method to be used by his company. He is considering presenting to the board the advantages and disadvantages of both a self-administered trusteed plan and an insured pension plan. He feels that once the board clearly understands the alternatives, they can make the best decision.

1. Help Lloyd construct a comparison of the two approaches.

2. Outline the advantages and disadvantages.

20-2 Mr. Henry Zantow, the corporation's comptroller, was discussing the supposed advantages of a "qualified" pension plan versus the "unqualified" plan with Darrell Hafner. Hafner agreed with Henry that a qualified plan certainly seemed the better of the two plans. Both Mr. Zantow and Mr. Hafner looked at each other and in the same breath said, "I wonder why anyone would choose an unqualified plan?"

1. Please respond to the question.

2. If the corporation decides to use a qualified plan, what must it do to be certain that its plan gains—and keeps—that status?

20-3 Jackson Appliances has 12 employees. The owner is considering some system to reward them for their loyalty and to provide some funds to help them with their living expenses after they retire.

1. What alternatives do you see for the owner to consider?

2. What are the advantages and disadvantages of each?

3. Which would you recommend?

20-4 Charles' company pension plan allowed him to begin participating at age 25. He worked for the company for 20 years, leaving at age 45. He was promised $20 per month in retirement benefits, to begin at age 65, for each year he was covered by the plan, but he finds when he leaves that he will not be allowed to take the money out of the plan. Instead, he must wait until he is 65 and take the benefits at that time.

1. Why would the law allow this arrangement?

2. Why not let Charles take the present value of his benefits with him to his new employer, and add this to his plan there?

3. Why not simply let him take the money out and use it as he sees fit today?

Chapter Twenty-One:
INSURANCE ISSUES AND CAREER OPPORTUNITIES

INTRODUCTION

By the time you get to this point in this book, you are aware of how complex insurance is and what a vital role it plays in our society. It is a costly but integral part of our daily lives. Does it work perfectly? No, it does not. And because insurance is so important, its imperfections become issues.

Some of the major current insurance issues are listed in Table 21-1. The first part of this chapter is devoted to them because of their significance to insurance consumers. The second part is concerned with the innumerable career opportunities available in insurance because a large work force is required to run the business and deal with these issues.

SOCIAL SECURITY ISSUES

The major Social Security issue is financing. Can (or will) our society support the system? Originally advance funded, it has for many years operated on an unfunded, pay-as-you-go basis. This generation of workers is paying for its current benefits, such as disability income and survivors' benefits, and benefits for those who are retired. Social Security taxes have increased much faster than the general level of prices and even faster than the cost of health care during the past two decades. At the same time, benefits have increased in both type and amount.

The number of retired workers has increased faster than the number working, so the burden is being borne by a shrinking sector of

TABLE 21-1

*Major Insurance
Issues*

Social Security		Life Insurance
Health Insurance		Auto Insurance
	Insurance Regulation	

society. With taxes at an all time high and talk of a taxpayers' revolt, retired workers are beginning to worry about the certainty of their benefits. At the same time, workers paying high taxes wonder what the future holds for them. Will the next generation pay for this generation's benefits? Is the Social Security system financially sound? If it were a private pension plan required to be advance funded, the answer would be negative. Combined Social Security trust funds are far less than the present value of future benefits. But on a pay-as-you-go basis, current funding will be adequate as long as the government can collect taxes.

Two suggestions have been made to reduce the burden of Social Security taxes. One is to reduce the amount of, or eliminate, the annual adjustment of benefits to offset inflation. While this would help to avoid increasing payroll taxes, it would place the burden of shrinking benefits (in real terms) on those least able to cope with it—the retired. Another suggestion is to raise the age level at which full retirement benefits are paid from age 65 to age 67, or even higher. The argument in favor of this change is that age 65 was chosen nearly a half century ago when life expectancy was considerably lower than it is now. Thus, a person who retires at age 65 today will receive far more benefits than a person who retired at age 65 several decades ago. Critics of this suggestion are quick to point out that those who retire now have paid considerably more in Social Security taxes than those who retired several decades ago. Moreover, the dollar isn't worth as much as it used to be, so they really aren't getting all that much in terms of real benefits.

LIFE INSURANCE ISSUES

The major current issue in life insurance is concerned with cost disclosure. What shall be disclosed and who shall be responsible for its disclosure? Considerable publicity has been given to the wide variation in the cost of life insurance policies. Publications such as *Consumer Reports, Money, Changing Times,* and others provide a great deal of information on the subject. In addition, more than 20 states now require that life insurance buyers be provided a Life Insurance Buyer's Guide prepared by the National Association of Insurance Commissioners. Industry critics, consumer advocates, and the Federal Trade Commission suggest, however, that more active steps should be taken by both regulatory agencies and life insurance companies to provide each purchaser with cost and other information. Based on this information, a rational choice can be made among the offerings of various insurance companies.

The NAIC Buyer's Guide lists the life insurance surrender cost index and the net payment cost index and tells you that "a policy with a small index number is generally a better buy than a comparable policy with a larger index number." It does not, unfortunately, provide cost comparisons to provide a bench mark against which you may decide whether a number is small or large. The Guide points out that the *equivalent level annual dividend* number "shows the part dividends play in determining the cost index of a participating policy" and says that adding this number to a policy's cost index allows you to compare total cost of similar policies before deducting dividends.

Critics suggest that the absence of data on the array of indexes among policies offered by various companies leaves the consumer in the dark. You have no way of knowing how a particular index for a particular policy compares with industry averages and extremes. Without a bench mark of some kind, they assert, it is difficult for you to follow the advice that you should "look for policies with lower cost index numbers."

Another concern is that the equivalent level annual dividend number may be used by an unscrupulous life insurance agent to make unrealistic comparisons between participating and guaranteed cost policies. This can be done by showing how dependent costs are on projected dividends and implying that such dividends may, in fact, be zero. While such a development is possible, the probability is so small that it may be disregarded. On the other hand, of course, attaching a probability of 1 to dividend projections may also be unwarranted.

Life insurance industry leaders are opposed to the use of *rate of return* as a measure of policy cost. The method used to calculate this return assumes that a portion of the premium is required to pay for the protection element of a cash value policy, and a portion is available to build up the cash value. The larger the amount assumed necessary for protection, the smaller the amount available for the cash value. The smaller the contribution to the savings component, the higher the rate of interest required to accumulate the cash value to the amounts specified for each year in the policy. Other things equal, the higher one assumes the cost for the protection element, the higher the rate of return, and *vice versa*.

A study published by the Federal Trade Commission in 1979 showed that the average rate of return for cash value policies ranged from awful to good. For a 35-year-old male, for example, who bought a participating whole life policy in 1977, the average of policies analyzed ranged from a negative 8+ percent over five years to not quite 5 percent over 30 years. The highest projected return over 30 years among such policies was almost 8 percent while the lowest was less than 2 percent. Publication of the study was announced in a press release which emphasized the low rates of return and asserted that millions of Americans were being bilked on their "investment" in cash value life insurance. To say that the life insurance industry had a collective fit over this widely circulated story is, indeed, an understatement. Immediate steps were taken first to prove that unrealistic assumptions made the results invalid, and second, get congress to prevail upon the FTC to lay off the life insurance industry.

HEALTH INSURANCE ISSUES

The major issues in health care and health insurance are:

1. How can health care be made universally available?

2. How should it be financed?

3. How can health care costs be controlled?

As Figure 21-1 shows, most people have some kind of health insurance, but many have either inadequate coverage or none. Many people do not have access to health care because they cannot pay the cost, either directly or through health insurance. As Figure 21-2 shows, the cost of health care more than tripled during the seventies and may rise even more rapidly during the eighties.

Various proposals for a national program to increase the availability of health care and finance it while at the same time controlling costs are referred to as national health insurance. The following plans have received considerable attention:

1. The Carter Plan

2. The Kennedy Plan

3. The Long Plan

The Carter Plan

This plan would cover everyone, under either private health insurance or a public plan for the elderly and poor. The plan would cover all hospital, medical, and surgical costs after a family or individual incurred $2,500 out-of-pocket expenses for medical expenses in one year. Employers would pay at least 75 percent and employees no more than 25 percent of premium costs. Benefits for the elderly and poor would be financed by state and federal taxes. The public program would be administered by a federal agency. The private program would be handled by individual insurance companies, health maintenance organizations, and employers with self-insured plans.

The Kennedy Plan

This plan would provide comprehensive health care services to everyone with no deductible. Employers would be required to provide health benefits and pay at least 65 percent of premium costs. The rest of the

Who Does, and Doesn't, Have Health Insurance

FIGURE 21-1

Private hospital insurance, including group plans, protects 179 million Americans.

And—

9 out of 10 of these people also have insurance covering surgery.

9 out of 10 of these people also had insurance on physicians' services other than surgery.

8 out of 10 of these people also have major-medical insurance.

BENEFITS PAID by these insurance policies in 1977 totaled $43 BILLION, almost 4 times as much as in 1967.

Yet—

18 MILLION AMERICANS still have no health-insurance coverage.

19 MILLION AMERICANS have insurance that does not cover ordinary hospital and physician services.

46 MILLION AMERICANS have inadequate insurance against large medical bills.

Source: *U.S. News & World Report,* June 25, 1979.

Reprinted from U.S. News & World Report, Copyright 1979 U.S. News & World Report, Inc.

cost would be financed through general tax revenues. A national health board would set insurance premium rates nationally and monitor the quality of care. The plan would be administered locally by state boards.

The Long Plan

Unlike the Carter and Kennedy plans, this plan would cover only employed or self-employed persons, their spouses, and dependents

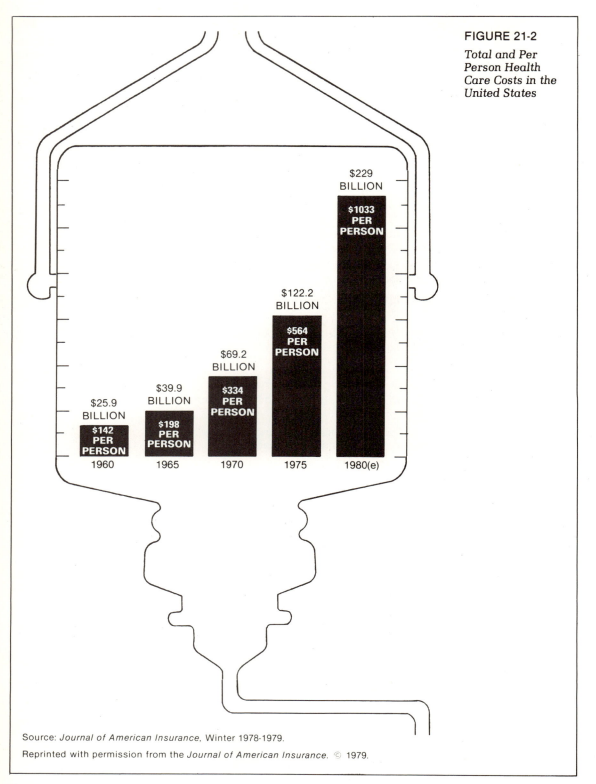

FIGURE 21-2

Total and Per Person Health Care Costs in the United States

$229 BILLION

$1033 PER PERSON

$122.2 BILLION

$564 PER PERSON

$69.2 BILLION

$334 PER PERSON

$39.9 BILLION

$198 PER PERSON

$25.9 BILLION

$142 PER PERSON

1960   1965   1970   1975   1980(e)

Source: *Journal of American Insurance*, Winter 1978-1979.

Reprinted with permission from the *Journal of American Insurance*. © 1979.

below age 26. Benefits would begin after an individual incurred $3,000 in out-of-pocket medical expenses ($5,000 for a family) in a single year. A separate medical assistance plan would provide catastrophic protection for individuals earning less than $3,000 a year. Medicare would be changed to provide catastrophic coverage for the elderly. Catastrophic insurance for the employed would be handled by private insurance carriers. The rest of the program would be administered by a federal agency.

Comparison

Annual cost estimates for the proposed plans are as follows:

Carter Plan	$24 billion
Kennedy Plan	$40 billion
Long Plan	$10 billion

The Carter and Long Plans have such large deductibles that many people would be faced with an unbearable burden for unplanned medical expenses. The Kennedy plan does not have this shortcoming but would cost almost four times as much as the Long plan and nearly twice that of the Carter plan. First-dollar coverage is expensive, but how can health care be provided for those who cannot bear a deductible?

Both the Carter and Kennedy plans include cost controls but the Long plan has none. The Carter plan would control hospital charges directly and establish guidelines for physicians fees by publishing a list of those who comply with federal fee schedules for their services. Experience with guidelines as a cost control device is not encouraging. The Kennedy plan, on the other hand, would put strict controls on both hospital and physicians fees. Opponents of cost controls point out that they sometimes reduce supply. Such a result would, of course, conflict with the objective of increasing the availability of health care services.

AUTO INSURANCE ISSUES

The major issues in auto insurance are:

1. How can adequate compensation for auto crash victims be assured?

2. Should the fault system be modified or abandoned?

3. How can availability of auto insurance be assured?

4. Are auto insurance premium rates fair?

Adequate Compensation

Every state has some kind of financial responsibility law to induce motorists to buy auto liability insurance so victims of their negligence will receive compensation. A typical law requires evidence of financial responsibility when a driver is involved in an accident. The simplest way to prove such responsibility is to have an auto liability insurance policy with specified limits, such as $10,000/$20,000. Most laws also require proof of financial responsibility from drivers who are convicted of specified violations, such as driving while intoxicated.

Several states also have unsatisfied judgment funds that respond to the problem of an injured motorist who obtains a judgment against the party at fault, but cannot collect because the party has neither insurance nor resources. The maximum amount the injured party may claim from the fund is usually the same as that established by the state's financial responsibility law. When the fund pays the judgment, the party at fault becomes indebted to the fund and his or her driving privilege is suspended until the fund is reimbursed.

Financial responsibility laws increased the percentage of drivers with auto liability insurance, but many remained uninsured. Therefore, about half the states require evidence of insurance prior to licensing the driver or the vehicle. Unfortunately, in many such states only about 80 or 90 percent of the drivers have insurance. Even a compulsory auto liability insurance law does not guarantee that you will not be injured by a financially irresponsible driver.

Should Fault be Abandoned?

In addition to financial responsibility laws, over half the states have mandatory first-party benefits laws which require that automobile insurance policies must provide specified benefits to specified persons in the event they are injured in, or die as a result of, an automobile crash. In most of these states, the insured must accept a policy that provides these benefits, but in a few the coverage may be rejected. Benefits are similar to those in the medical payments part of the Personal Auto Policy, except that they also cover wage loss of employed persons and replacement cost of services provided by other family members.

No-fault.   Mandatory first-party benefits are part of no-fault auto insurance; they are paid without regard to fault. A pure no-fault policy would provide *only* first-party benefits and the liability part of the policy would be eliminated. In order for such insurance to cover all the risks to assets and income related to automobile use and ownership, the concept of negligence liability with regard to automobiles would have to be scrapped. This would require legislation prohibiting tort action in such cases.

The impetus for such legislation is a Department of Transportation study which concluded that:

1. Many victims of auto accidents are uncompensated.

2. Many who suffer small losses are overcompensated.

3. Many who suffer large losses are undercompensated.

4. Long delays in payment are common.

5. The costs of attorneys, insurance companies, and courts are too large a proportion of total loss claims.

The DOT study recommended a no-fault system through two means:

(1) adoption of compulsory first-party insurance to cover economic losses caused by auto accidents, and (2) restriction of the right to sue for damages to cases involving large losses. As a result of this study and dissatisfaction with the existing system, about half the states that have mandatory first-party benefits provide some tort exemption. For example, suit for damages is prohibited unless injury results in death, serious disfigurement, disability beyond a specified number of days, or medical costs in excess of a specified amount, such as $500 or $1,000.

No-fault appraised. The appeal of no-fault is evidence that the tort system is slow, erratic in its results, and expensive from the point of view of the portion of the premium dollar used to compensate persons injured in automobile crashes. If the tort system could be by-passed, all the expenses of the process—including defense and plaintiff's counsel—could be eliminated. This would make more dollars available for compensation at no additional cost to insureds and, perhaps, even reduce the cost of insurance. Proponents of no-fault assert that enough money is spent on automobile insurance to compensate crash victims but that the tort system wastes funds on the question of fault. Therefore, the concept of fault should be abandoned and the funds used more effectively.

Opponents of no-fault include plaintiff's attorneys, who can hardly be classified as unbiased observers—as proponents have been quick to point out. Others who lack enthusiasm for no-fault point out that it is simply compulsory health insurance with restrictions on tort action. They observe that workers' compensation was designed to reduce litigation by abandoning employers' liability, but that in recent times litigation in that field has been increasing. They assert that many people who favor no-fault do so primarily because of the expectation that it will be cheaper than the present system when, in fact, it may cost more. They also point out that those who wish to cover the life and health risks associated with the automobile on a voluntary basis may do so without giving up their right to sue the party at fault; such insurance is readily available and has been for a long time.

Auto Insurance Availability

The assumption underlying laws requiring motorists to buy automobile liability insurance is that it is available. Unfortunately, some drivers cannot buy insurance through usual channels because, as a group, their losses are excessive. Presumably, this problem could be solved by charging higher premium rates for such drivers. But auto insurance rates are closely regulated in many states and insurers cannot adjust them easily. Where rates are permitted flexibility, there is a so-called "substandard" market in which some companies offer limited auto coverage to high-risk drivers at high premium rates.

The methods of creating a market for people who cannot buy auto insurance through the usual channels are listed in Table 21-2. Known as the *residual market*, they are created by law in the state in which they operate.

TABLE 21-2

*Auto Insurance
Residual Market*

| Auto Insurance Plans | Joint Underwriting Associations |
| Reinsurance Facilities | Maryland State Fund |

Auto Insurance Plans.   These plans were formerly called *assigned risk plans* because they operate on an assignment basis. Drivers who cannot buy auto liability insurance through the usual channels can apply to the plan. They are assigned to an insurer which must sell them coverage which meets the requirements of the financial responsibility law. Every company writing auto insurance in the state is a member of the plan and each must take its share of such business. If a company writes 10 percent of the auto insurance business in the state, it has to accept 10 percent of the qualified applicants. In most states, an insurer can reduce its quota by voluntarily insuring youthful drivers. Persons who have criminal records or frequent accidents or violations are excluded in some plans. Most motorists insured through the plan pay a surcharge in addition to the regular premium, although in some states those with good records pay the regular premium.

In spite of generally higher rates than the voluntary market, auto insurance plans have caused significant losses to the auto insurance industry. Many insureds dislike the plans because of high rates and the stigma connected with being assigned. Moreover, many insureds in such plans are not bad drivers on the basis of their driving records but have the misfortune to be in an undesirable classification (such as young, unmarried male), which prevents them from obtaining insurance through regular channels.

Reinsurance facilities.   Where there is a reinsurance facility—Massachusetts, North Carolina, New Hampshire, South Carolina—every auto insurer is required to issue auto insurance to any licensed driver who applies and can pay the premium. The insurer can transfer the burden of bad risks to the facility, a pool to which all auto insurers belong. As members of the pool, they share in both premiums and losses. The insured knows nothing about this arrangement; like all other insureds, he or she receives a policy issued by the company to which he or she applied.

Joint underwriting associations.   Where there is a joint underwriting association—Florida, Hawaii, and Missouri—all automobile insurers in the state are members and the association is, in effect, an insurance industry company. Several insurers are appointed servicing carriers to act as agents for the association. An applicant for insurance who cannot meet underwriting requirements in the regular market is issued a policy by the servicing carrier on behalf of the association; so far as he or she is concerned, that is his or her company. Premiums and losses are shared by members of the association (pooled).

Maryland state fund.   This government-operated residual market company charges high premiums to drivers who cannot obtain insurance through the regular market. In spite of high premiums, however, it has suffered heavy losses. Originally, it was to bear such losses itself, but the law now requires that the private insurance industry subsidize the fund.

Residual market evaluated.   Three groups are affected by attempts to make automobile insurance available to everybody—the insurance companies, bad risks, and other insureds. The insurance companies are responsible for establishing and managing the plans as well as bearing the losses they generate. Even though bad risks pay high prices for their insurance, others have to pay higher premium rates than they would if there was no involuntary market because most plans have suffered heavy losses. Thus, the good drivers as a group are paying part of the cost of providing auto liability insurance for bad drivers. An undue financial burden has been placed on insurance companies and, in turn, the insuring public.

Auto Insurance Premium Rates

Pricing insurance is different from pricing most goods and services for two reasons. First, costs depend on the future. Who knows how many losses there will be, how much they will cost, and when they will occur? Second, cost is influenced by the purchaser. The cost of a bottle of beer is the same whether you buy it or I buy it. On the other hand, if I drive 50,000 miles per year and you drive 10,000 miles per year, other things being equal, I am more likely to be involved in an auto crash than you are.

Laws regulating insurance require that insurance premium rates be adequate to assure the ability of the insurer to fulfill the promises it sells. They also require that rates be equitable. That is, they should be fair. This does not mean that everyone should pay the same price for a particular policy but that the price each person pays should reflect accurately the amount of risk he or she brings to the group of insureds.

Auto insurance is (1) virtually a necessity for most of us, (2) expensive for many people, and (3) sold at a wide range of prices which are greatly influenced by purchaser characteristics. As a result, there is considerable controversy about their fairness. It is claimed that the factors used to classify purchasers for pricing purposes are either entirely wrong or are given the wrong weight. Those objected to most frequently are: (1) age, (2) sex, (3) marital status, (4) driving record, and (5) place of residence.

Unmarried male drivers object to paying higher premiums than females, married males, and older drivers. People who live in urban areas feel that paying more for auto insurance than those who live in rural areas is unfair. A common complaint from young drivers is, "I have a perfect driving record, yet I pay more for auto insurance than some older people who have had an accident. My driving record proves that I'm a good risk, but I'm being ripped off." Fathers whose sons reach their teens and begin to drive the family car are equally vehement when their auto insurance premium leaps upward. How can all these apparent inequities be justified?

In 1980, the Florida Insurance Department dealt with the problem by prohibiting use of sex and marital status for auto insurance ratemaking, but the prohibition was temporarily stopped by court order. Testimony before the court established that there is actuarial justification for sex and marital status factors. The Louisiana Insurance Department issued a similar order but it was set aside by the court. In 1977, Los Angeles County sued the California Insurance Commissioner and two insurance companies, contending that geographical rating territories discriminated against urban residents. This led to a massive study of California's 14 million drivers.

The conclusion of the study was that no single factor, such as an individual's accident record, provides an adequate measure of insurance loss potential. The most accurate predictions are those based on a combination of factors, including driving record, age, sex, annual mileage, and place of residence. As Figure 21-3 illustrates, the study revealed that young male drivers have twice as many accidents as older males, and males of all ages have more accidents than females of the same age.

The California study also showed that varying rates by geographical territory is valid and justifies higher rates in urban than in rural areas. In addition, it was found that drivers who have had prior accidents are more apt to have accidents in a subsequent period but the vast majority of accidents in any given time period involve drivers who have had no previous accidents. Therefore, it appears that driving records should be used in estimating future loss potential of drivers who have had accidents, but they are not the only factor to be considered. A clean record does not necessarily imply a low risk. For insurance rating purposes, the study concludes, "factors other than the individual's past driving record must be assessed in order to properly predict the total cost of losses."

Premium rates for young single males are high because, as a class, their loss experience is high. Some critics of the present system, however, suggest that it is socially desirable to do away with age, sex, and marital status as classification factors. This has been done by law in several states. According to estimates of the National Association of Independent Insurers, however, this would result in premiums for young married couples rising 37 percent and those for unmarried females under 25 going up roughly 26 percent. Yet single males under age 25, the group expected to benefit from the change, would receive a rate decrease of only 14 percent.

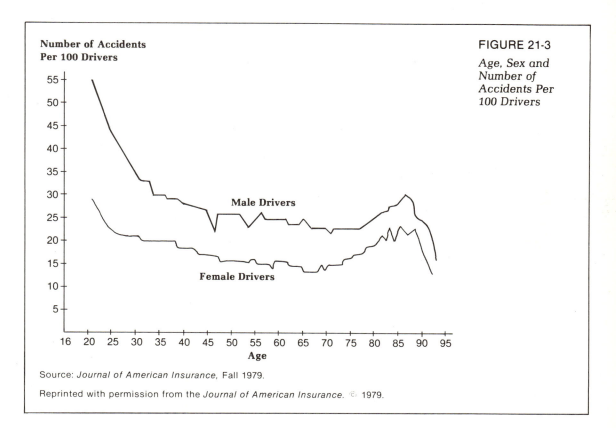

Number of Accidents
Per 100 Drivers

FIGURE 21-3

*Age, Sex and
Number of
Accidents Per
100 Drivers*

Source: *Journal of American Insurance,* Fall 1979.

Reprinted with permission from the *Journal of American Insurance.* © 1979.

INSURANCE REGULATION

The purpose of insurance is to reduce uncertainty. You buy insurance so that you don't have to worry about the various risks you face. But are you sure the policy you bought provides the protection you need? Did you get it for a fair price? Will the insurance company be able to fulfill its promises to you or will it be insolvent when that time comes? Theoretically, competition among hundreds of companies should result in the answer to all these questions being yes. Nearly two centuries of experience with the insurance industry in the United States has shown, however, that regulation is necessary in spite of the fact that there is considerable competition for your insurance dollars.

State Regulation

Most insurance regulation is done by the states although insurance company activities are also influenced by federal antitrust legislation concerning unfair trade practices. Following a U.S. Supreme Court decision in 1868 (*Paul v. Virginia*), the right of the states to regulate insurance was successfully defended until a decision in 1944 (*United States* v. *South-Eastern Underwriters Association et al*) ruled that insurance is subject to federal control. The insurance industry promptly persuaded congress to pass the McCarran-Ferguson Act, which says that regulation by the states is in the public interest. It also provides that federal antitrust laws apply to insurance only to the extent that such business is not regulated by the states.

State regulation is based on legislation which spells out requirements concerning licensing and operation of companies, agents, adjusters, and others. Capital and reserve requirements are stipulated by law. Insurance legislation is administered through a state insurance department headed by an insurance commissioner who has rather broad power to promulgate regulations. These regulations have the power of law. Standards for insurance policy forms are established and no policy can be sold in the state until approved by the state insurance department. Companies are required to submit annual reports to the department for audit and the commissioner has the power and duty to conduct regular examinations of companies to assure that they abide by the law and are in good financial condition. In most states, the commissioner has considerable authority if he or she wants to use it. For example, if a policy form appears unfair, the commissioner can refuse to permit its sale. In many states, premium rates for other than life insurance must be approved by the commissioner prior to being used.[1] This authority, along with the power to withhold a license, gives the commissioner a great deal of influence. An aggrieved party can always take the commissioner to court but it is cheaper and easier to go along with him or her most of the time.

Most insurance departments handle complaints from consumers and some of them do a good job. Some departments provide ready access for consumers by making WATS lines available and publicizing their interest in the consumer. A number of departments have published consumer guides to buying insurance, some of which are very well done and can be most helpful.

Is State Regulation Adequate?

This is another way of asking if state regulation is preferable to federal regulation. Proponents of state regulation claim that much insurance is local and the state can regulate it in accordance with local needs and conditions. They say that the states are doing a good job. Critics argue that state regulation is expensive because it involves duplication for multi-state insurers. At the same time, lack of uniformity among the states complicates compliance for these companies. They say federal regulation would be more uniform and more effective.

A 1979 report by the United States General Accounting Office asserts that "there are serious shortcomings in State laws and

---

1. This is known as "prior approval." Some states permit use of rates without prior approval but the commissioner has authority to disapprove them and prohibit their use.

regulatory activities with respect to protecting the interests of insurance consumers in the United States."[2] It says that most state insurance departments are not equipped to determine whether insurance consumers are being treated properly with regard to claims payments, premium rate-setting, and protection from unfair discrimination. The report suggests that state insurance department resources are generally inadequate and is generally critical of virtually all aspects of state regulation, including apparent lack of independence of state regulators. This report, along with Federal Trade Commission activities, should help keep the matter of state versus federal regulation of insurance a continuing issue.

CAREERS IN INSURANCE

When you read the title of this section, the first thing you thought of was selling, right? That is the reaction of most students, perhaps because the primary contact most people have with insurance is through the sales force. A common misconception is that the bulk of employment in the insurance business is in sales. Even worse, from the point of view of taking an unbiased look at a career in insurance, the typical view of an insurance agent is a person who spends his[3] day knocking on doors in a frantic attempt to sell another policy. While there are such people in the business, they are far from typical.

The purpose of this section is to give you enough information about careers in the insurance business so you can decide on the basis of facts rather than bias whether or not you should investigate further to see what the opportunities are for you.

Insurance Employment

The insurance business in the United States employs more than one and one-half million people. About one fourth are engaged in marketing and related services while the vast majority perform other functions. The insurance agents you are aware of are the "visible minority" in the insurance business. For every agent you see, there are three other people working in less visible but just as important jobs. In order to call attention to the variety of jobs in insurance, one company refers in a recruiting advertisement to "our 2,400 different job descriptions." We cannot list all of them but Table 21-3 provides some examples.

Insurance Jobs

Some of the jobs listed in Table 21-3 are common to all types of business organizations. Others, such as agent, branch manager, broker, have been discussed in earlier chapters. Some are specialists unique to the insurance business. Let's discuss them.

---

2. "Issues and Needed Improvements In State Regulation Of The Insurance Business," October 9, 1979. PAD-79-72A.

3. Although many insurance sales people are women, the common perception is that of a salesman.

		TABLE 21-3
		A Sample of Insurance Jobs

Accountant	Data Processing Analyst
Actuary	Employee Benefit Representative
Agent	General Agent
Advanced Underwriting Consultant	Legal Counsel
Bond Representative	Loss Control Engineer
Branch Manager	Personnel Manager
Broker	Premium Auditor
Broker Representative	Securities Analyst
Claim Adjuster	Underwriter

What is an *actuary*? An actuary is a highly specialized mathematician who deals with the financial and risk aspects of insurance, including determination of proper rates, reserves, and financial statements. Actuaries also participate in product development and management planning. One large company hires actuarial students and expects them to demonstrate technical expertise by passing the examinations required for admission into either the Society of Actuaries or the Casualty Actuarial Society. It encourages them by granting time off for study and paying for books and tuition. Many actuaries work for insurance companies, while others are employed by government or private consulting firms.[4]

What is an *advanced underwriting consultant*? This person is a problemsolver and source of information for a life insurance company's sales force in the technical aspects of business insurance and estate planning. This job involves study, research, and working with agents on a one-to-one basis.

An *employee benefit representative* (or a *brokerage representative*), on the other hand, helps agents and brokers sell the life insurance products required for employee benefit plans, installs the plans after they are sold, and provides service to policyholders. This person must have both technical knowledge in the employee benefits field and the ability to work with agents, employers, and employees.

A *bonding representative* works with agents and their clients on financial and technical matters concerned with qualifying for contract bonds. After an intensive company training program, they are experts

4. For further information about actuarial careers, write to: Society of Actuaries, 208 South LaSalle Street, Chicago 60604 or Casualty Actuarial Society, 200 East 42nd Street, New York City 10017.

in their field who deal frequently with contractors, engineers, attorneys, and top management in virtually all types of businesses. A bonding rep's recommendation plays an important part in the company's decision to write contract bonds involving hundreds of thousands or even millions of dollars.

A *loss control engineer* surveys the facilities of a company that applies for insurance and provides crucial information for the underwriting department. After the insurance has been provided, he or she makes regular safety inspections and makes recommendations designed to reduce losses. This service helps reduce premium levels for the insured and keeps the insurer informed about the risks it has assumed.

The *underwriter* to whom the loss control engineer provides information is the person who decides whether or not to insure risks and, if so, at what premium rate. Both underwriters and loss control engineers work closely with insurance agents in providing service for insureds.

Because the premium for many commercial insurance policies depends upon such factors as the payroll, the number of people employed, or the value of inventory, *premium auditors* visit insureds to examine their business records. A premium auditor has to learn a great deal about the operations of businesses the company insures in order to determine the premium they should pay.

Unlimited Opportunities

The jobs we have discussed are only a small sample of career opportunities in insurance. There are literally thousands of employers looking for young men and women to enter the business. Most of the opportunities they offer have two elements in common. First, employers prefer college graduates, although a specialized educational background is not usually required. What they are looking for is a literate person who has drive and the ability to learn. If you want to become an actuary, however, you must have a mathematics background. Or, if you want to become legal counsel for an insurance company, you must have a law degree.

Second, there is a strong emphasis on continuing education and training. Many students who enter the insurance business are shocked to learn that graduation from college does not mean the end of studying. On the contrary, they spend their first two or three months in the business going to school in the home office, followed by correspondence courses and seminars for the next two or three years. From then on, education and training take a decreasing part of the work week but never quite come to an end. Professionals in insurance sales devote some time to continuing education all through their careers.

Consumer Applications

Pursuing a Career in Insurance

Whatever your interests may be, there is an insurance job for you. Figure 21-4 shows where to get specific information. Some insurance jobs require specialized knowledge and skills but many are similar to other kinds of business. It may be a good idea to find out what an insurance career could do for you so you can compare it with other alternatives. How do you do this?

How do you find a summer or part-time job in insurance? First, contact your college placement office. Second, contact insurance company offices in your area. There may be some home offices or branch offices. Look in the Yellow Pages. Third, contact insurance agency offices in your area (Yellow Pages). They may not have a job for you, but many insurance sales people are eager to help young people

---

FIGURE 21-4

Insurance Career Information

Insurance Careers Magazine
  Box 4169, Memphis, TN 38104
Insurance company publications
Insurance company offices in your town
Local insurance agents
Your college placement office

If You Have Another Year or So of College

You have time to get some job experience and learn about the insurance business firsthand. The options available are shown in Table 21-4.

who express an interest in an insurance job. Fourth, your parents, or someone else you are related to, may have bought insurance from someone. Contact that "someone" and tell them you are looking for a job in insurance.

TABLE 21-4

How to Get Insurance Job Experience

Part-time job during school year
Full-time job during summer vacation
Internship

Fifth, contact the state or local insurance agents association. Association managers and staff know what's going on in the business and hear about jobs from time to time. Sixth, tell your insurance professor you are looking for a job.

What is an *internship* and how do you get one? An internship is a temporary employment arrangement between a student, an employer, and a college or university. The purpose is to give the student a sample of the business while doing work that provides a worthwhile learning experience. Generally, the student is paid wages by the employer and granted academic credit by his or her college or university. Figure 21-5 is an excerpt from an internship report for a University of South Carolina student who interned with an insurance company one semester. It shows some of the special assignments for which she was responsible. Your faculty advisor can help you get this experience.

If You are Graduating This Year

1. Send for a copy of *INSURANCE CAREERS* and read it carefully.
2. Register with your college placement service.
3. Interview every insurance recruiter who visits your campus.
4. Tell your faculty advisor you want an insurance job.
5. Tell your insurance agent you want an insurance job.
6. Study insurance company recruiting brochures.[5]

Project: Policy filings—State of Indiana. Our company filed all policy forms in Indiana upon approval for admission in 1979. Several policy forms were disapproved and had to be adjusted by endorsement or addition of further policyowner information on the policy face. Kathy coordinated refiles of these forms and circulated a memo inter-office to update all areas on the entire set of filings.

Project: Article for Quarterly Newsletter. Kathy prepared an article on selling life insurance to dual-income families for use in our quarterly field publication.

Project: Field Manual Revision. To provide our fieldmen with current home office operations information, Kathy is revising the company field manual. This project will take her into virtually every area of the home office.

FIGURE 21-5
Internship Projects

---

5. A 24-page brochure published by one large company says: "We've only skimmed the surface of techniques for discovering and pursuing a job. Your library is a good source for more information, as are the people in your college or university career counseling department. They can help you define your special interests and skills and give you advice about writing a resume and help to refine your interview style. The department will also have reference information about jobs, guides to finding them and an extensive collection of recruiting information produced by companies." Reprinted through the courtesy of AEtna Life and Casualty, Hartford, CT.

Discussion Questions

1. During the last 50 years, our society has created massive social security programs. Do you think people feel any more secure now than they did 50 years ago? Why or why not?

2. The cost of health care in the United States has risen faster than the cost of most other goods and services in the last decade. How do you account for this?

3. Which of the national health care plans do you think is most likely to be successful if adopted? Why?

4. It has been suggested that compulsory auto liability insurance and financial responsibility laws be repealed. Do you agree? Why or why not?

5. Do you think the price of auto insurance should be controlled by law? Why or why not?

6. Do you think "it is socially desirable to do away with age, sex, and marital status as classification factors" for auto insurance premium rates? Why or why not?

7. Do you think it would be socially desirable to do away with age and sex as classification factors for life insurance premium rates? Why or why not?

8. What has your State Insurance Department done to help you as an insurance consumer? What evidence do you have to back up your response to this question?

9. Some firms give a bonus to employees who recruit new personnel if the recruits stay a month or more. Employees of one large life insurance company receive $200 and a $750 videotape recorder for referring data processors and $1,000 for actuaries. What does this tell you about career opportunities in insurance?

10. What is your reaction to the internship projects listed in Figure 21-5?

Cases

21-1 Reno Tulip, a client of your insurance agency, recently commented to you that because he is only 20 years old his auto insurance should be lower, not higher, than a man of forty. Reno's logic was that his health and reflexes are better than those of an older person and he is better able to avoid accidents. He feels especially discriminated against because he has a clean driving record; no wrecks and no moving violations. He says auto insurance pricing is unfair and his insurance premium is too high.

1. Why is Reno's premium relatively high?

2. How does the insurance company determine auto premium rates?

3. Is this system equitable or inequitable? Support your position.

21-2 Assume that the Kennedy Plan to provide comprehensive health care services to every American becomes law early in 1981 and is to be administered by the Department of HEW. Benefits are to be provided beginning January 1, 1982. You are the administrator and responsible for the accomplishment of the plan's goals.

1. How can you control the cost of health care after the plan goes into operation?

2. How can you assure that the quality of health care service will not deteriorate?

3. What effect will the plan have on the people in the health insurance business? What advice do you now have for these people?

21-3 Teri Tunell will graduate from college next year. She has a major in English and a minor in mathematics. She has worked part-time as a salesperson in a local clothing store for the past two academic years. Last summer, she was a counselor in a summer camp for teenagers in Colorado. She told you recently that she is beginning to worry about a career after graduation but really doesn't know what she wants to do. She knows you are taking an insurance course, so she asks you about job opportunities in that field. She tells you, "I don't want to go around knocking on doors like some magazine subscription salesman."

1. Should you tell Teri about insurance job opportunities or should you tell her how to find out for herself?

2. If you decide on the latter approach, what would you tell her?

3. How can she find out what kind of job she may be qualified for?

21-4 Tom Randall is president and CEO of International Monumental All Lines Insurance Company. It has been in business for 47 years and is licensed in all states except New York. It has offices in 50 other countries, primarily in Europe and South America. One trade association it belongs to is publicly in favor of federal regulation of insurance to the virtual exclusion of the states. Another has taken a firm stand against federal regulation and is very much in favor of continued state regulation.

Tom is well-known and highly respected in the insurance business as well as in banking and related fields. He is recognized as a spokesman for big business but is a political moderate. Friends in the insurance business who favor federal control are urging him to come out in favor of it, while those who favor state regulation want him to make a public statement supporting their position.

1. Why may Mr. Randall be reluctant to take a public position on this issue?

2. What would you advise him to do? Why?

Appendixes

Appendix A

Whole Life Policy

THE COUNCIL LIFE INSURANCE COMPANY

The Council Life Insurance Company agrees to pay the benefits
provided in this policy, subject to its terms and conditions.
Executed at New York, New York on the Date of Issue.

David Olson

Secretary

Barbara Sloan

President

Life Policy — Participating

Amount payable at death of Insured $10,000.

Premiums payable to age 90.

Schedule of benefits and premiums page 2.

Right to Examine Policy—Please examine this policy carefully. The Owner may return
the policy for any reason within ten days after receiving it. If returned, the policy will be
considered void from the beginning and any premium paid will be refunded.

A GUIDE TO THE PROVISIONS OF THIS POLICY

Accidental Death Benefit	12
Beneficiaries	7
Cash Value, Extended Term and Paid-Up Insurance	5
Change of Policy	6
Contract	3
Dividends	4
Loans	6
Ownership	3
Premiums and Reinstatement	4
Specification	2
Waiver of Premium Right	11

Endorsements Made At Issue Appear After "General Provisions." Additional Benefits, If
Any, Are Provided By Rider.

Specifications

Plan and Additional Benefits	Amount	Premium	Years Payable
Whole Life (Premiums payable to age 90)	$10,000	$229.50	55
Waiver of Premium (To age 65)		4.30	30
Accidental Death (To age 70)	10,000	7.80	35

A premium is payable on the policy date and every 12 policy months thereafter. The first premium is $241.60.

TABLE OF GUARANTEED VALUES

END OF POLICY YEAR	CASH OR LOAN VALUE	PAID-UP INSURANCE	EXTENDED TERM INSURANCE YEARS	DAYS
1	$ 14	$ 30	0	152
2	174	450	4	182
3	338	860	8	65
4	506	1,250	10	344
5	676	1,640	12	360
6	879	2,070	14	335
7	1,084	2,500	16	147
8	1,293	2,910	17	207
9	1,504	3,300	18	177
10	1,719	3,690	19	78
11	1,908	4,000	19	209
12	2,099	4,300	19	306
13	2,294	4,590	20	8
14	2,490	4,870	20	47
15	2,690	5,140	20	65
16	2,891	5,410	20	66
17	3,095	5,660	20	52
18	3,301	5,910	20	27
19	3,508	6,150	19	358
20	3,718	6,390	19	317
AGE 60	4,620	7,200	18	111
AGE 65	5,504	7,860	16	147

Paid-up additions and dividend accumulations increase the cash values; indebtedness decreases them.
The percentage referred to in section 5.6 is 83.000%.

Direct Beneficiary   Helen M. Benson, wife of the insured

Owner   Thomas A. Benson, the insured

Insured	Thomas A. Benson	**Age and Sex**	35 Male
Policy Date	May 1, 1978	**Policy Number**	000/00
Date of Issue	May 1, 1978		

SECTION 1. THE CONTRACT

1.1 LIFE INSURANCE BENEFIT

The Council Life Insurance Company agrees, subject to the terms and conditions of this policy, to pay the Amount shown on page 2 to the beneficiary upon receipt at its Home Office of proof of the death of the Insured.

1.2 INCONTESTABILITY

This policy shall be incontestable after it has been in force during the lifetime of the Insured for two years from the Date of Issue.

1.3 SUICIDE

If within two years from the Date of Issue the Insured dies by suicide, the amount payable by the Company shall be limited to the premiums paid.

1.4 DATES

The contestable and suicide periods commence with the Date of Issue. Policy months, years and anniversaries are computed from the Policy Date. Both dates are shown on page 2 of this policy.

1.5 MISSTATEMENT OF AGE

If the age of the Insured has been misstated, the amount payable shall be the amount which the premiums paid would have purchased at the correct age.

1.6 GENERAL

This policy and the application, a copy of which is attached when the policy is issued, constitute the entire contract. All statements in the application are representations and not warranties. No statement shall void this policy or be used in defense of a claim under it unless contained in the application.

Only an officer of the Company is authorized to alter this policy or to waive any of the Company's rights or requirements.

All payments by the Company under this policy are payable at its Home Office.

SECTION 2. OWNERSHIP

2.1 THE OWNER

The Owner is as shown on page 2, or his successor or transferee. All policy rights and privileges may be exercised by the Owner without the consent of any beneficiary. Such rights and privileges may be exercised only during the lifetime of the Insured and thereafter to the extent permitted by Sections 8 and 9.

2.2 TRANSFER OF OWNERSHIP

The Owner may transfer the ownership of this policy by filing written evidence of transfer satisfactory to the Company at its Home Office and, unless waived by the Company, submitting the policy for endorsement to show the transfer.

2.3 COLLATERAL ASSIGNMENT

The Owner may assign this policy as collateral security. The Company assumes no responsibility for the validity or effect of any collateral assignment of this policy. The Company shall not be charged with notice of any assignment unless the assignment is in writing and filed at its Home Office before payment is made.

The interest of any beneficiary shall be subordinate to any collateral assignment made either before or after the beneficiary designation.

A collateral assignee is not an Owner and a collateral assignment is not a transfer of ownership.

SECTION 3. PREMIUMS AND REINSTATEMENT

3.1 PREMIUMS

(a) Payment. All premiums after the first are payable at the Home Office or to an authorized agent. A receipt signed by an officer of the Company will be provided upon request.

(b) Frequency Premiums may be paid annually, semiannually, or quarterly at the published rates for this policy. A change to any such frequency shall be effective upon acceptance by the Company of the premium for the changed frequency. Premiums may be paid on any other frequency approved by the Company.

(c) Default. If a premium is not paid on or before its due date, this policy shall terminate on the due date except as provided in Sections 3.1(d), 5.3 and 5.4.

(d) Grace Period. A grace period of 31 days shall be allowed for payment of a premium not paid on its due date. The policy shall continue in full force during this period. If the Insured dies during the grace period, the overdue premium shall be paid from the proceeds of the policy.

(e) Premium Refund at Death. The portion of any premium paid which applies to a period beyond the policy month in which the Insured died shall be refunded as part of the proceeds of this policy.

3.2 REINSTATEMENT

If the policy has not been surrendered for its cash value, it may be reinstated within five years after the due date of the unpaid premium provided the following conditions are satisfied:

(a) Within 31 days following expiration of the grace period, reinstatement may be made without evidence of insurability during the lifetime of the Insured by payment of the overdue premium.

(b) After 31 days following expiration of the grace period, reinstatement is subject to:

(i) receipt of evidence of insurability of the Insured satisfactory to the Company;
(ii) payment of all overdue premiums with interest from the due date of each at the rate of 6% compounded annually; or any lower rate established by the Company.

Any policy indebtedness existing on the due date of the unpaid premium, together with interest from that date, must be repaid or reinstated.

SECTION 4. DIVIDENDS

4.1 ANNUAL DIVIDENDS

This policy shall share in the divisible surplus, if any, of the Company. This policy's share shall be determined annually and credited as a dividend. Payment of the first dividend is contingent upon payment of the premium or premiums for the second policy year and shall be credited proportionately as each premium is paid. Thereafter, each dividend shall be payable on the policy anniversary.

4.2 USE OF DIVIDENDS

As directed by the Owner, dividends may be paid in cash or applied under one of the following:

(a) Paid-Up Additions. Dividends may be applied to purchase fully paid-up additional insurance. Paid-up additions will also share in the divisible surplus.

(b) Dividend Accumulations. Dividends may be left to accumulate at interest. Interest is credited at a rate of 3% compounded annually, or any higher rate established by the Company.

(c) Premium Payment. Dividends may be applied toward payment of any premium due within one year, if the balance of the premium is paid. If the balance is not paid, or if this policy is in force as paid-up insurance, the dividend will be applied to purchase paid-up additions.

If no direction is given by the Owner, dividends will be applied to purchase paid-up additions.

4.3 USE OF ADDITIONS AND ACCUMULATIONS

Paid-up additions and dividend accumulations increase the policy's cash value and loan value and are payable as part of the policy proceeds. Additions may be surrendered and accumulations withdrawn unless required under the Loan, Extended Term Insurance, or Paid-up Insurance provisions.

4.4 DIVIDEND AT DEATH

A dividend for the period from the beginning of the policy year to the end of the policy month in which the Insured dies shall be paid as part of the policy proceeds.

SECTION 5. CASH VALUE, EXTENDED TERM
AND PAID-UP INSURANCE

5.1 CASH VALUE

The cash value, when all premiums due have been paid, shall be the reserve on this policy less the deduction described in Section 5.5, plus the reserve for any paid-up additions and the amount of any dividend accumulations.

The cash value within three months after the due date of any unpaid premium shall be the cash value on the due date reduced by any subsequent surrender of paid-up additions or withdrawal of dividend accumulations. The cash value at any time after such three months shall be the reserve on the form of insurance then in force, plus the reserve for any paid-up additions and the amount of any dividend accumulations.

If this policy is surrendered within 31 days after a policy anniversary, the cash value shall be not less than the cash value on that anniversary.

5.2 CASH SURRENDER

The Owner may surrender this policy for its cash value less any indebtedness. The policy shall terminate upon receipt at the Home Office of this policy and a written surrender of all claims. Receipt of the policy may be waived by the Company.

The Company may defer paying the cash value for a period not exceeding six months from the date of surrender. If payment is deferred 30 days or more, interest shall be paid on the cash value less any indebtedness at the rate of 3% compounded annually from the date of surrender to the date of payment.

5.3 EXTENDED TERM INSURANCE

If any premium remains unpaid at the end of the grace period, this policy shall continue in force as nonparticipating extended term insurance. The amount of insurance shall be the amount of this policy, plus any paid-up additions and dividend accumulations, less any indebtedness. The term insurance shall begin as of the due date of the unpaid premium and its duration shall be determined by applying the cash value less any indebtedness as a net single premium at the attained age of the Insured. If the term insurance would extend to or beyond attained age 100, paid-up insurance under Section 5.4 below will be provided instead.

5.4 PAID-UP INSURANCE

In lieu of extended term insurance this policy may be continued in force as participating paid-up life insurance.

Paid-up insurance may be requested by written notice filed at the Home Office before, or within three months after, the due date of the unpaid premium. The insurance will be for the amount that the cash value will purchase as a net single premium at the attained age of the Insured. Any indebtedness shall remain outstanding.

5.5 TABLE OF GUARANTEED VALUES

The cash values, paid-up insurance, and extended term insurance shown on page 2 are for the end of the policy year indicated. These values are based on the assumption that premiums have been paid for the number of years stated and are exclusive of any paid-up additions, dividend accumulations, or indebtedness. During the policy year allowance shall be made for any portion of a year's premium paid and for the time elapsed in that year. Values for policy years not shown are calculated on the same basis as this table and will be furnished on request. All values are equal to or greater than those required by the State in which this policy is delivered.

In determining cash values a deduction is made from the reserve. During the first five policy years, the deduction for each $1,000 of Amount is $9 plus $.15 for each year of the Insured's issue age. After the fifth policy year, the deduction decreases yearly by one-fifth of the initial deduction until there is no deduction in the tenth and subsequent policy years. If the premium paying period is less than ten years, there is no deduction in the last two policy years of the premium paying period or thereafter.

5.6 RESERVES AND NET PREMIUMS

Reserves, net premiums and present values are determined in accordance with the Commissioners 1958 Standard Ordinary Mortality Table and 3% interest, except that for the first five years of any extended term insurance, the Commissioners 1958 Extended Term Insurance Table is used. All reserves are based on continuous payment of premiums and immediate payment of claims. Net annual premiums are the same in each policy year, except that if premiums are payable for more than 20 years, the net annual premium in the 21st and subsequent policy years is determined by applying the percentage shown on page 2 to the net annual premium for the 20th policy year. On the Policy Date, the present value of all future guaranteed benefits equals the present value of all future net annual premiums. The reserve at the end of any policy year is the excess of the present value of all future guaranteed benefits over the present value of all future net annual premiums. The reserve is exclusive of any additional benefits.

SECTION 6. LOANS

6.1 POLICY LOAN

The Owner may obtain a policy loan by assignment of this policy to the Company. The amount of the loan, plus any existing indebtedness, shall not exceed the loan value. No loan shall be granted if the policy is in force as extended term insurance. The Company may defer making a loan for six months unless the loan is to be used to pay premiums on policies issued by the Company.

6.2 PREMIUM LOAN

A premium loan shall be granted to pay an overdue premium if the premium loan option is in effect. If the loan value, less any indebtedness, is insufficient to pay the overdue premium, a premium will be paid for any other frequency permitted by this policy for which the loan value less any indebtedness is sufficient. The premium loan option may be elected or revoked by written notice filed at the Home Office.

6.3 LOAN VALUE

The loan value is the largest amount which, with accrued interest, does not exceed the cash value either on the next premium due date or at the end of one year from the date of the loan.

6.4 LOAN INTEREST

Interest is payable at the rate of 8% compounded annually, or at any lower rate established by the Company for any period during which the loan is outstanding.

The Company shall provide at least 30 days written notice to the Owner (or any other party designated by the Owner to receive notice under this policy) and any assignee recorded at the Home Office of any increase in interest rate on loans outstanding 40 or more days prior to the effective date of the increase.

Interest accrues on a daily basis from the date of the loan on policy loans and from the premium due date on premium loans, and is compounded annually. Interest unpaid on a loan anniversary is added to and becomes part of the loan principal and bears interest on the same terms.

6.5 INDEBTEDNESS

Indebtedness consists of unpaid policy and premium loans on the policy including accrued interest. Indebtedness may be repaid at any time. Any unpaid indebtedness will be deducted from the policy proceeds.

If indebtedness equals or exceeds the cash value, this policy shall terminate. Termination shall occur 31 days after a notice has been mailed to the address of record of the Owner and of any assignee recorded at the Home Office.

SECTION 7. CHANGE OF POLICY

7 CHANGE OF PLAN

The Owner may change this policy to any permanent life or endowment plan offered by the Company on the Date of Issue of this policy. The change may be made upon payment of any cost and subject to the conditions determined by the Company. For a change made after the first year to a plan having a higher reserve, the cost shall not exceed the difference in cash values or the difference in reserves, whichever is greater, plus 3½% of such difference.

SECTION 8. BENEFICIARIES

8.1 DESIGNATION AND CHANGE OF BENEFICIARIES

(a) By Owner. The Owner may designate and change direct and contingent beneficiaries and further payees of death proceeds:

(1) during the lifetime of the Insured.

(2) during the 60 days following the date of death of the Insured, if the Insured immediately before his death was not the Owner. Any such designation of direct beneficiary may not be changed. If the Owner is the direct beneficiary and elects a payment plan, any such designation of contingent beneficiaries and further payees may be changed.

(b) By Direct Beneficiary. The direct beneficiary may designate and change contingent beneficiaries and further payees if:

(1) the direct beneficiary is the Owner.

(2) at any time after the death of the Insured, no contingent beneficiary or further payee is living, and no designation is made by the Owner under Section 8.1 (a) (2).

(3) the direct beneficiary elects a payment plan after the death of the Insured, in which case the interest in the share of such direct beneficiary or any other payee designated by the Owner shall terminate.

(c) By Spouse (Marital Deduction Provision). Notwithstanding any provision of Section 8 or 9 of this policy to the contrary, if the Insured immediately before death was the Owner and if the direct beneficiary is the spouse of the Insured and survives the Insured, such direct beneficiary shall have the power to appoint all amounts payable under the policy either to the executors or administrators of the direct beneficiary's estate or to such other contingent beneficiaries and further payees as he may designate. The exercise of that power shall revoke any then existing designation of contingent beneficiaries and further payees and any election of a payment plan applying to them.

(d) Effective Date. Any designation or change of beneficiary shall be made by the filing and recording at the Home Office of a written request satisfactory to the Company. Unless waived by the Company, the request must be endorsed on the policy. Upon the recording, the request will take effect as of the date it was signed. The Company will not be held responsible for any payment or other action taken by it before the recording of the request.

8.2 SUCCESSION IN INTEREST OF BENEFICIARIES

(a) Direct Beneficiaries. The proceeds of this policy shall be payable in equal shares to the direct beneficiaries who survive to receive payment. The unpaid share of any direct beneficiary who dies while receiving payment shall be payable in equal shares to the direct beneficiaries who survive to receive payment.

(b) Contingent Beneficiaries. At the death of the last surviving direct beneficiary, payments due or to become due shall be payable in equal shares to the contingent beneficiaries who survive to receive payment. The unpaid share of any contingent beneficiary who dies while receiving payment shall be payable in equal shares to the contingent beneficiaries who survive to receive payment.

(c) Further Payees. At the death of the last to survive of the direct and contingent beneficiaries, the proceeds, or the withdrawal value of any payments due or to become due if a payment plan is in effect, shall be paid in one sum:

(1) in equal shares to the further payees who survive to receive payment; or
(2) if no further payees survive to receive payment, to the executors or administrators of the last to survive of the direct and contingent beneficiaries.

(d) Estate of Owner. If no direct or contingent beneficiaries or further payees survive the Insured, the proceeds shall be paid to the Owner or the executors or administrators of the Owner.

8.3 GENERAL

(a) Transfer of Ownership. A transfer of ownership will not change the interest of any beneficiary.

(b) Claims of Creditors. So far as permitted by law, no amount payable under this policy shall be subject to the claims of creditors of the payee.

(c) Succession under Payment Plans. A direct or contingent beneficiary succeeding to an interest in a payment plan shall continue under such plan subject to its terms, with the rights of transfer between plans and of withdrawal under plans as provided in this policy.

SECTION 9. PAYMENT OF POLICY BENEFITS

9.1 PAYMENT

Payment of policy benefits upon surrender or maturity will be made in cash or under one of the payment plans described in Section 9.2, if elected.

If policy benefits become payable by reason of the Insured's death, payment will be made under any payment plan then in effect. If no election of a payment plan is in effect, the proceeds will be held under the Interest Income Plan (Option A) with interest accumulating from the date of death until an election or cash withdrawal is made.

9.2 PAYMENT PLANS

(a) Interest Income Plan (Option A). The proceeds will earn interest which may be received in monthly payments or accumulated. The first interest payment is due one month after the plan becomes effective. Withdrawal of accumulated interest as well as full or partial proceeds may be made at any time.

(b) Installment Income Plans. Monthly installment income payments will be made as provided by the plan elected. The first payment is due on the date the plan becomes effective.

(1) Specified Period (Option B). Monthly installment income payments will be made providing for payment of the proceeds with interest over a specified period of one to 30 years. Withdrawal of the present value of any unpaid installments may be made at any time.

(2) Specified Amount (Option D). Monthly installment income payments will be made for a specified amount of not less than $5 per $1,000 of proceeds. Payments will continue until the entire proceeds with interest are paid, with the final payment not exceeding the unpaid balance. Withdrawal of the unpaid balance may be made at any time.

(c) Life Income Plans. Monthly life income payments will be made as provided by the plan elected. The first payment is due on the date the plan becomes effective. Proof of date of birth satisfactory to the Company must be furnished for any individual upon whose life income payments depend.

(1) Single Life Income (Option C). Monthly payments will be made for the selected certain period, if any, and thereafter during the remaining lifetime of the individual upon whose life income payments depend. The selections available are:

    (i) no certain period,
    (ii) a certain period of 10 or 20 years, or
    (iii) a refund certain period such that the sum of the income payments during the certain period will be equal to the proceeds applied under the plan, with the final payment not exceeding the unpaid balance.

(2) Joint and Survivor Life Income (Option E). Monthly payments will be made for a 10 year certain period and thereafter during the joint lifetime of the two individuals upon whose lives income payments depend and continuing during the remaining lifetime of the survivor.

(3) Withdrawal. Withdrawal of the present value of any unpaid income payments which were to be made during a certain period may be made at any time after the death of all individuals upon whose lives income payments depend.

(d) Payment Frequency. In lieu of monthly payments a quarterly, semiannual or annual frequency may be selected.

9.3 PAYMENT PLAN RATES

(a) Interest Income and Installment Income Plans. Proceeds under the Interest Income and Installment Income plans will earn interest at rates declared annually by the Company, but not less than a rate of 3% compounded annually. Interest in excess of 3% will increase payments, except that for the Installment Income Specified Amount Plan (Option D), excess interest will be applied to lengthen the period during which payments are made.

The present value for withdrawal purposes will be based on a rate of 3% compounded annually.

The Company may from time to time also make available higher guaranteed interest rates under the Interest Income and Installment Income plans, with certain conditions on withdrawal as then published by the Company for those plans.

(b) Life Income Plans. Life Income Plan payments will be based on rates declared by the Company. These rates will provide not less than 104% of the income provided by the Company's Immediate Annuities being offered on the date the plan becomes effective. The rates are based on the sex and age nearest birthday of any individual upon whose life income payments depend, and adjusted for any certain period and the immediate payment of the first income payment. In no event will payments under these rates be less than the minimums described in Section 9.3(c).

(c) Minimum Income Payments. Minimum monthly income payments for the Installment Income Plans (Options B and D) and the Life Income Plans (Options C and E) are shown in the Minimum Income Table. The minimum Life Income payments are determined as of the date the payment plan becomes effective and depend on the age nearest birthday adjusted for policy duration.

The adjusted age is equal to the age nearest birthday decreased by one year if more than 25 years have elapsed since the Policy Date, two years if more than 35 years have elapsed, three years if more than 40 years have elapsed, four years if more than 45 years have elapsed or five years if more than 50 years have elapsed.

9.4 ELECTION OF PAYMENT PLANS

(a) **Effective Date.** Election of payment plans for death proceeds made by the Owner and filed at the Home Office during the Insured's lifetime will be effective on the date of death of the Insured. All other elections of payment plans will be effective when filed at the Home Office, or later if specified.

(b) **Death Proceeds.** Payment plans for death proceeds may be elected:

(1) by the Owner during the lifetime of the Insured.

(2) by the Owner during the 60 days following the date of death of the Insured, if the Insured immediately before his death was not the Owner. Any such election may not be changed by the Owner.

(3) by a direct or contingent beneficiary to whom such proceeds become payable, if no election is then in effect and no election is made by the Owner under Section 9.4(b) (2).

(c) **Surrender or Maturity Proceeds.** Payment plans for surrender or maturity proceeds may be elected by the Owner for himself as direct beneficiary.

(d) **Transfers Between Payment Plans.** A direct or contingent beneficiary receiving payment under a payment plan with the right to withdraw may elect to transfer the withdrawal value to any other payment plan then available.

(e) **Life Income Plan Limitations.** An individual beneficiary may receive payments under a Life Income Plan only if the payments depend upon his life. A corporation may receive payments under a Life Income Plan only if the payments depend upon the life of the Insured, or a surviving spouse or dependent of the Insured.

(f) **Minimum Amounts.** Proceeds of less than $5,000 may not be applied without the Company's approval under any payment plan except the Interest Income Plan (Option A) with interest accumulated. The Company retains the right to change the payment frequency or pay the withdrawal value if payments under a payment plan are or become less than $25.

9.5 INCREASE OF MONTHLY INCOME

The direct beneficiary who is to receive the proceeds of this policy under a payment plan may increase the total monthly income by payment of an annuity premium to the Company. The premium, after deduction of charges not exceeding 2% and any applicable premium tax, shall be applied under the payment plan at the same rates as the policy proceeds. The net amount so applied may not exceed twice the proceeds payable under this policy.

MINIMUM INCOME TABLE

Minimum Monthly Income Payments Per $1,000 Proceeds

INSTALLMENT INCOME PLANS (Options B and D)

PERIOD (YEARS)	MONTHLY PAYMENT	PERIOD (YEARS)	MONTHLY PAYMENT	PERIOD (YEARS)	MONTHLY PAYMENT
1	$84.50	11	$8.86	21	$5.32
2	42.87	12	8.24	22	5.15
3	29.00	13	7.71	23	4.99
4	22.07	14	7.26	24	4.84
5	17.91	15	6.87	25	4.71
6	15.14	16	6.53	26	4.59
7	13.17	17	6.23	27	4.48
8	11.69	18	5.96	28	4.37
9	10.54	19	5.73	29	4.27
10	9.62	20	5.51	30	4.18

MINIMUM INCOME TABLE

Minimum Monthly Income Payments Per $1,000 Proceeds

LIFE INCOME PLANS

SINGLE LIFE MONTHLY PAYMENTS (Option C)					
ADJUSTED AGE		CERTAIN PERIOD			
MALE	FEMALE	NONE	10 YEARS	20 YEARS	REFUND
50	55	$ 4.62	$4.56	$4.34	$4.36
51	56	4.72	4.65	4.40	4.44
52	57	4.83	4.75	4.46	4.52
53	58	4.94	4.85	4.53	4.61
54	59	5.07	4.96	4.59	4.69
55	60	5.20	5.07	4.66	4.79
56	61	5.33	5.19	4.72	4.88
57	62	5.48	5.31	4.78	4.99
58	63	5.64	5.43	4.84	5.09
59	64	5.80	5.57	4.90	5.20
60	65	5.98	5.70	4.96	5.32
61	66	6.16	5.85	5.02	5.44
62	67	6.36	5.99	5.07	5.57
63	68	6.57	6.14	5.13	5.71
64	69	6.79	6.30	5.17	5.85
65	70	7.03	6.45	5.22	6.00
66	71	7.28	6.62	5.26	6.15
67	72	7.54	6.78	5.30	6.31
68	73	7.83	6.95	5.33	6.48
69	74	8.13	7.11	5.36	6.66
70	75	8.45	7.28	5.39	6.85
71	76	8.79	7.45	5.41	7.05
72	77	9.16	7.62	5.43	7.26
73	78	9.55	7.79	5.45	7.48
74	79	9.96	7.95	5.46	7.71
75	80	10.41	8.11	5.48	7.95

JOINT AND SURVIVOR MONTHLY PAYMENTS (Option E)

ADJUSTED AGE　　　　　　　　　　**JOINT PAYEE ADJUSTED AGE**

MALE		45	50	55	60	65	70	75
	FEMALE	50	55	60	65	70	75	80
45	50	$3.68	$3.80	$3.90	$3.97	$4.02	$4.06	$4.10
50	55	3.80	3.97	4.13	4.25	4.34	4.41	4.46
55	60	3.90	4.13	4.35	4.56	4.72	4.84	4.92
60	65	3.97	4.25	4.56	4.86	5.13	5.33	5.48
65	70	4.02	4.34	4.72	5.13	5.51	5.85	6.10
70	75	4.06	4.41	4.84	5.33	5.85	6.33	6.73
75	80	4.10	4.46	4.92	5.48	6.10	6.73	7.28

WAIVER OF PREMIUM BENEFIT

1. THE BENEFIT

If total disability of the Insured commences before the policy anniversary nearest his 60th birthday, the Company will waive the payment of premiums becoming due during total disability of the Insured.

If total disability of the Insured commences on or after the policy anniversary nearest his 60th birthday but before the policy anniversary nearest his 65th birthday, the Company will waive the payment of premiums becoming due during total disability of the Insured and before the policy anniversary nearest his 65th birthday.

The Company will refund that portion of any premium paid which applies to a period of total disability beyond the policy month in which the disability began.

The premium for this benefit is shown on page 2.

2. DEFINITION OF TOTAL DISABILITY

Total disability means disability which:

(a) resulted from bodily injury or disease;
(b) began after the Date of Issue of this policy and before the policy anniversary nearest the Insured's 65th birthday;
(c) has existed continuously for at least six months; and
(d) prevents the Insured from engaging in an occupation. During the first 24 months of disability, occupation means the occupation of the Insured at the time such disability began; thereafter it means any occupation for which he is reasonably fitted by education, training or experience, with due regard to his vocation and earnings prior to disability.

The total and irrecoverable loss of the sight of both eyes, or of speech or hearing, or of the use of both hands, or of both feet, or of one hand and one foot, shall be considered total disability, even if the Insured shall engage in an occupation.

3. PROOF OF DISABILITY

Before any premium is waived, proof of total disability must be received by the Company at its Home Office:

(a) during the lifetime of the Insured;
(b) during the continuance of total disability; and
(c) not later than one year after the policy anniversary nearest the Insured's 65th birthday.

Premiums will be waived although proof of total disability was not given within the time specified, if it is shown that it was given as soon as reasonably possible, but not later than one year after recovery.

4. PROOF OF CONTINUANCE OF DISABILITY

Proof of the continuance of total disability may be required once a year. If such proof is not furnished, no further premiums shall be waived. Further proof of continuance of disability will no longer be required if, on the policy anniversary nearest the Insured's 65th birthday, the Insured is then and has been totally and continuously disabled for five or more years.

5. PREMIUMS

Any premium becoming due during disability and before receipt of proof of total disability is payable and should be paid. Any such premiums paid shall be refunded by the Company upon acceptance of proof of total disability. If such premiums are not paid, this benefit shall be allowed if total disability is shown to have begun before the end of the grace period of the first unpaid premium.

If on any policy anniversary following the date of disablement the Insured continues to be disabled and this benefit has not terminated, an annual premium will be waived.

6. TERMINATION

This benefit shall be in effect while this policy is in force, but shall terminate on the policy anniversary nearest the Insured's 65th birthday unless the Insured is then totally disabled and such disability occurred prior to the policy anniversary nearest the Insured's 60th birthday. It may also be terminated within 31 days of a premium due date upon receipt at the Home Office of the Owner's written request.

ACCIDENTAL DEATH BENEFIT

1. THE BENEFIT

The Company agrees to pay an Accidental Death Benefit upon receipt at its Home Office of proof that the death of the Insured resulted, directly and independently of all other causes, from accidental bodily injury, provided that death occurred while this benefit was in effect.

2. PREMIUM AND AMOUNT OF BENEFIT

The premium for and the amount of this benefit are shown on page 2. This benefit shall be payable as part of the policy proceeds.

3. RISKS NOT ASSUMED

This benefit shall not be payable for death of the Insured resulting from suicide, for death resulting from or contributed to by bodily or mental infirmity or disease, or for any other death which did not result, directly and independently of all other causes, from accidental bodily injury.

Even though death resulted directly and independently of all other causes from accidental bodily injury, this benefit shall not be payable if the death of the Insured resulted from:

(a) Any act or incident of war. The word "war" includes any war, declared or undeclared, and armed aggression resisted by the armed forces of any country or combination of countries.

(b) Riding in any kind of aircraft, unless the Insured was riding solely as a passenger in an aircraft not operated by or for the Armed Forces, or descent from any kind of aircraft while in flight. An Insured who had any duties whatsoever at any time on the flight or any leg of the flight with respect to any purpose of the flight or to the aircraft or who was participating in training shall not be considered a passenger.

4. TERMINATION

This benefit shall be in effect while this policy is in force other than under the Extended Term Insurance or Paid-up Insurance provisions, but shall terminate on the policy anniversary nearest the Insured's 70th birthday. It may also be terminated within 31 days of a premium due date upon receipt at the Home Office of the Owner's written request.

David Olson

Secretary

THE COUNCIL LIFE INSURANCE COMPANY

RECEIPT FOR PAYMENT AND CONDITIONAL LIFE INSURANCE AGREEMENT

When premium is paid at the time of application, complete this Agreement and give to the Applicant. No other Agreement will be recognized by the Company. If premium is not paid—do not detach.

Name of Proposed Insured: THOMAS A. BENSON   Face Amount: $10,000   Plan: LIFE POLICY – PARTICIPATING

Received of Thomas A. Benson

the sum of $ 241.60 for the policy applied for in the application to THE COUNCIL INSURANCE COMPANY (CL) with the same date and number as this receipt. Checks, drafts, and money orders are accepted subject to collection.

NEW YORK, NEW YORK MAY 1, 19 78   J. R. Washington Agent.

Place and Date

CONDITIONAL LIFE INSURANCE AGREEMENT

I. **No Insurance Ever in Force.** No insurance shall be in force at any time if the proposed insured is not an acceptable risk on the Underwriting Date for the policy applied for according to CL's rules and standards. No insurance shall be in force under an Additional Benefit for which the proposed insured is not an acceptable risk.

II. **Conditional Life Insurance.** If the proposed insured is an acceptable risk on the Underwriting Date, the insurance shall be in force subject to the following maximum amounts if the proposed insured dies before the policy is issued:

Life Insurance			Accidental Death Benefit		
Age at Issue	Policies Issued at Standard Premiums	Policies Issued at Higher Premiums	Age at Issue	Maximum Amount	
0-24	$ 500,000	$250,000	0-14	$ 25,000	
25-45	1,000,000	500,000	15-19	50,000	
46-55	800,000	400,000	20-24	75,000	
56-65	400,000	200,000	25-60	150,000	
66-70	200,000	100,000	Over 60	-0-	
Over 70	-0-	-0-			

III. **Reduction in Maximum Amounts.** The maximum amounts set forth in the preceding table shall be reduced by any existing CL insurance on the life of the proposed insured with an Issue Date within 90 days of the date of this Agreement or by any pending prepaid applications for CL insurance on the life of the proposed insured with an Underwriting Date within 90 days of the date of this Agreement.

Termination of Conditional Life Insurance. If the proposed insured is an acceptable risk for the policy applied for according to CL's rules and standards only at a premium higher than the premium paid, any insurance under this Agreement shall terminate on the date stated in a notice mailed by CL to the applicant unless by such date the applicant accepts delivery of the policy and pays the additional premium required.

Underwriting Date. The Underwriting Date is the date of page 2 (90-2) of the application or the date of the medical examination [if required, otherwise the date of the nonmedical, page 4 (90-4)], whichever is the later.

III. **Premium Adjustment.** If the proposed insured is an acceptable risk for the policy applied for only at a premium higher than the premium paid and dies before paying the additional premium required, that additional premium shall be subtracted from the insurance benefit payable to the beneficiary.

IV. **Premium Refund.** Any premium paid for any insurance or Additional Benefit not issued or issued at a higher premium but not accepted by the applicant shall be returned to the applicant.

NOT A "BINDER"—NO INSURANCE WHERE SECTION I APPLIES—NO AGENT MAY MODIFY

PART I

Life Insurance Application To *The COUNCIL Life Insurance Company*

IMPORTANT NOTICE—This application is subject to approval by the Company's Home Office. Be sure all questions in all parts of the application are answered completely and accurately, since the application is the basis of the insurance contract and will become part of any policy issued.

1. Insured's Full Name (Please Print-Give title as Mr., Dr., Rev., etc.)

	Mo., Day, Yr. of Birth	Ins. Age	Sex	Place of Birth	Social Security No.
MR. THOMAS A. BENSON	APRIL 6, 1943	35	M	BOSTON, MASS.	000-00-0000

Single ☐ Married ☑ Widowed ☐ Divorced ☐ Separated ☐

2. Addresses last 5 yrs.

	Number	Street	City	State	Zip Code	County		Yrs.
Mail to Present □ Home: Former	217	E. 62 STREET	NEW YORK, N.Y.		10017	NEW YORK		6
☑ Business: Present	PEPPER, GRINSTEAD, & CROUCH	55 E. 49ᵗʰ ST			10017	NEW YORK		7
Former								

3. Occupation

	Title	Describe Exact Duties		Yrs.
Present	ATTORNEY	REPRESENTS CLIENTS IN LEGAL MATTERS		7
Former				

12. Face Amount $ **10,000** Plan **WL**
Accidental Death [ ] Waiver of Premium [ ]
Purchase Option—Regular [ ] Preferred [ ] PEP [ ] GOR [ ]
_____ units of Wife's Term—name:
$_____ initial amount Decreasing Term, _____ Years
(Joint [ ]) (Mot. Pro. [ ]) (Straight Line [ ])
Children's Term _____ Other: _____

13. Auto. Prem. Loan provision operative if available? Yes [ ] No [✓]

14. Dividend Option — Additions (for other than Term policies) [ ] Deposits [ ]
Reduce premium, if applicable, otherwise cash [✓]
Supplemental Protection (Keyman only) [ ]
1 Year Term—any balance to
Deposits [ ] Additions [ ] Reduce prem. (cash if mo.) [ ]

15. Beneficiary—for children's, wife's or joint insurance as provided in contract; for other insurance as follows, subject to policy's beneficiary provisions:

(Name)	(Relationship to Insured)	If living,	If not
1st HELEN M. BENSON	WIFE	[ ]	[ ]
2nd DAVID A. BENSON	SON	[ ]	[ ]
3rd		[ ]	[ ]

the executors or administrators of: Insured [✓] Other [ ] (use Remarks)
(Joint beneficiaries will receive equally or survivor, unless otherwise specified.)

16. Flexible Plan settlement (personal beneficiary only) [ ]

17. Rights—During Insured's lifetime all rights belong to
Insured [✓] Other: _____
Trustee [ ] (attach Trust)
(After Insured's death as provided in contract on wife's insurance.)

18. Premium—Frequency **ANNUAL** Amt. Paid $ **241.60** None [ ]
Have you received a Conditional Receipt? Yes [✓] No [ ]

---

4. a) Employer
b) Any change contemplated? Yes [ ] No [✓] (Explain in Remarks)

5. Have you ever — Yes / No
a) been rejected, deferred or discharged by the Armed Forces for medical reasons or applied for a government disability rating? [ ] [✓]
b) applied for insurance or for reinstatement which was declined, postponed, modified or rated? [ ] [✓]
c) used LSD, heroin, cocaine or methadone? [ ] [✓]

6. a) In the past 3 years have you
(i) had your driver's license suspended or revoked or been convicted of more than one speeding violation? [ ] [✓]
(ii) operated, been a crew member of, or had any duties aboard any kind of aircraft? [ ] [✓]
(iii) engaged in underwater diving below 40 feet, parachuting, or motor vehicle racing? [ ] [✓]
b) In the future, do you intend to engage in any activities mentioned in (ii) and (iii) of a) above? [ ] [✓]
(If "Yes" to 5a or any of 6, complete Supplemental Form 3375)

7. Have you smoked one or more cigarettes within the past 12 months? [✓] [ ]

8. Are other insurance applications pending or contemplated? [ ] [✓]

9. Do you intend to go to any foreign country? [✓] [ ]

10. Will coverage applied for replace or change any life insurance or annuities? (If "Yes", submit Replacement Form) [ ] [✓]

11. Total Life Insurance in force $ **35,000** None [ ]

REMARKS [Include details (company, date, amt., etc.) for all "Yes" answers to questions 4b, 5b, 5c, 8, 9 and 10]

Q9: PLANS VACATION IN SWITZERLAND

I agree that: (1) No one but the Company's President, a Vice-President or Secretary has authority to accept information not contained in the application, to modify or enlarge any contract, or to waive any requirement. (2) Except as otherwise provided in any conditional receipt issued, any policy issued shall take effect upon its delivery and payment of the first premium during the lifetime of each person to be insured. Due dates of later premiums shall be as specified in the policy.

Dated at *NEW YORK, N.Y.* on *MAY 1* 19 *78* Signature of Insured *Thomas A. Jensen*

Signature of Applicant (if other than Insured) who agrees to be bound by the representations and agreements in this and any other part of this

application _____   _____   _____
                          (Relationship)   (Complete address of Applicant)

Countersigned by *Ed Hattey*   _____
                   (Name)   Field Underwriter (Licensed Resident Agent)

PART 1A Statements Forming Part Of Application To *The COUNCIL Life Insurance Company*

[Complete this Part if any Non-Medical or Family Insurance is Applied For]

1. Name of Insured THOMAS A. BENSON Ins. Age 35 Height 6 ft. 1 in. Weight 185 lbs.

2. If Family, Children's, Wife's or Joint Insurance desired, other family members proposed for insurance:

Wife (include maiden name)	Sex	Ins. Age	Mo., Day, Yr. of Birth	Mo., Day, Yr. of Birth	Height ft. in.	Weight lbs.	Life in Force $	Place of Birth

Children	Sex	Ins. Age	Mo., Day, Yr. of Birth

3. Has any eligible dependent (a) been omitted from 2? Yes ☐ No ☐ (b) applied for insurance or for reinstatement which was declined, postponed, modified or rated or had a policy cancelled or renewal refused? Yes ☐ No ☐ (Give name, date, company in 8)

4. Have you or anyone else proposed for insurance, so far as you know, ever been treated for or had indication of (underline applicable item)

	Yes	No
a) high blood pressure? (If "Yes", list drugs prescribed and dates taken.)	☐	☑
b) chest pain, heart attack, rheumatic fever, heart murmur, irregular pulse or other disorder of the heart or blood vessels?	☐	☑
c) cancer, tumor, cyst, or any disorder of the thyroid, skin, or lymph glands?	☐	☑
d) diabetes or anemia or other blood disorder?	☐	☑
e) sugar, albumin, blood or pus in the urine, or venereal disease?	☐	☑
f) any disorder of the kidney, bladder, prostate, breast or reproductive organs?	☐	☑
g) ulcer, intestinal bleeding, hepatitis, colitis, or other disorder of the stomach, intestine, spleen, pancreas, liver or gall bladder?	☐	☑
h) asthma, tuberculosis, bronchitis, emphysema or other disorder of the lungs?	☐	☑
i) fainting, convulsions, migraine headache, paralysis, epilepsy or any mental or nervous disorder?	☐	☑
j) arthritis, gout, amputation, sciatica, back pain or other disorder of the muscles, bones or joints?	☐	☑
k) disorder of the eyes, ears, nose, throat or sinuses?	☐	☑
l) varicose veins, hemorrhoids, hernia or rectal disorder?	☐	☑
m) alcoholism or drug habit?	☐	☑

5. Have you or anyone else proposed for insurance, so far as you know, (underline applicable item)

	Yes	No
a) consulted or been examined or treated by any physician or practitioner in the past 5 years?	☑	☐
b) had, or been advised to have, an x-ray, cardiogram, blood or other diagnostic test in the past 5 years?	☑	☐
c) been a patient in a hospital, clinic, or other medical facility in the past 5 years?	☐	☑
d) ever had a surgical operation performed or advised?	☐	☑
e) ever made claim for disability or applied for compensation or retirement based on accident or sickness?	☐	☑

6. Are you or any other person proposed for insurance, so far as you know, in impaired physical or mental health, or under any kind of medication? ☐ Yes ☑ No

7. Weight change in last 6 months of adults proposed for insurance: N.A.

Name	Gain	Loss	Cause

8. Details of all "Yes" answers. For any checkup or routine examination, indicate what symptoms, if any, prompted it and include results of the examination and any special tests. Include clinic number if applicable.

Question No.	Name of Person	Illness & Treatment	No. of Attacks	Dates: Onset-Recovery	Doctor, Clinic or Hospital and Complete Address
5a	THOMAS A. BENSON	ANNUAL CHECKUP	—	—	LIFE EXTENSION INSTITUTE
5b	THOMAS A. BENSON	ROUTINE OF ANNUAL CHECKUP	—	—	"
5d	THOMAS A. BENSON	TONSILLECTOMY-AGE 5	1	JUNE 1949	BOSTON HOSPITAL, 2 PITTS STREET, BOSTON, MASS.

So far as may be lawful, I waive for myself and all persons claiming an interest in any insurance issued on this application, all provisions of law forbidding any physician or other person who has attended or examined, or who may attend or examine, me or any other person covered by such insurance, from disclosing any knowledge or information which he thereby acquired.

I represent the statements and answers in this and in any other part of this application to be true and complete to the best of my knowledge and belief, and offer them to the Company for the purpose of inducing it to issue the policy or policies and to accept the payment of premiums thereunder. I also agree that payment of the first premium (if after this date) shall be a representation by me that such statements and answers would be the same if made at the time of such payment.

Dated at NEW YORK, N.Y. on MAY 1, 19 78   Signature of Insured *Thomas A. Benson*

Witnessed by *Ed Hatty*   Signature of Wife (if insured) _____

Field Underwriter (Licensed Resident Agent)

AUTHORIZATION

For purposes of determining my eligibility for insurance, I hereby authorize any physician, practitioner, hospital, clinic, institution, insurance company, Medical Information Bureau, or other organization or person that has records or knowledge of me or my health to give any such information to the Council Life Insurance Company.

If application is made to The Council Life Insurance Company for insurance on any member of my family, this authorization also applies to such member. A photostatic copy of this authorization shall be as valid as the original.

Signed on MAY 1, 19 78   *Thomas A. Benson*

Signature of Insured

Appendix B

Personal Auto Policy

NAME OF COMPANY

PERSONAL AUTO POLICY

DECLARATIONS

Renewal of Number

No. PA

Named Insured and Mailing Address (No., Street, Apt., Town or City, County, State, Zip Code)

Policy Period:

From: To: 12:01 A.M. Standard Time

Description of Auto(s) or Trailer(s)

AUTO	Year	Trade Name — Model	VIN	Symbol	Age
1					
2					
3					
4					

The Auto(s) or Trailer(s) described in this policy is principally garaged at the above address unless otherwise stated:
(No., Street, Apt., Town or City, County, State, Zip Code)

Coverage is provided where a premium and a limit of liability are shown for the coverage.

Coverages	Limit of Liability		Premium			
			Auto 1	Auto 2	Auto 3	Auto 4
A. Liability		each accident	$	$	$	$
A. Liability						
Bodily Injury	$	each person				
	$	each accident	$	$	$	$
Property Damage	$	each accident	$	$	$	$
B. Medical Payments	$	each person	$	$	$	$
C. Uninsured Motorists	$	each accident				
C. Uninsured Motorists	$	each person	$	$	$	$
	$	each accident				
D. Damage to your Auto		Actual Cash Value minus				
1. Collision Loss	$	Deductible	$	$	$	$
2. Other than Collision Loss	$	Deductible	$	$	$	$
Towing and Labor Costs	$	each disablement	$	$	$	$

Endorsements made part of this Policy at time of issue:

		Auto 1	Auto 2	Auto 3	Auto 4
	Total Premium Per Auto	$	$	$	$

Endorsement Premium $

Total Premium $

Loss Payee
(Name and
address)

Countersigned:

By _____
Authorized Representative

THIS DECLARATIONS PAGE WITH PERSONAL AUTO POLICY PROVISIONS OR POLICY JACKET AND PERSONAL AUTO POLICY FORM, TOGETHER WITH ENDORSEMENTS, IF ANY, ISSUED TO FORM A PART THEREOF, COMPLETES THE ABOVE NUMBERED POLICY.

AGREEMENT

In return for payment of the premium and subject to all the terms of this policy, we agree with you as follows:

DEFINITIONS

Throughout this policy, "you" and "your" refer to the "named insured" shown in the Declarations and the spouse if a resident of the same household. "We", "us" and "our" refer to the Company providing this insurance. For purposes of this policy any private passenger type auto leased under a written agreement to any person for a continuous period of at least six months shall be deemed to be owned by that person.

Other words and phrases are defined. They are boldfaced when used.

"Your covered auto" means:

(a) Any vehicle shown in the Declarations.

(b) Any of the following types of vehicles of which you acquire ownership during the policy period, provided that you ask us to insure it within thirty days after you become the owner:

(1) a private passenger auto.

(2) if not used in any business or occupation, a pick-up, sedan delivery or panel truck.

If the vehicle replaces one shown in the Declarations, you have to ask us to insure it within thirty days only if you wish Damage to Your Auto Coverage to apply to the replacing vehicle.

(c) Any **trailer** you own.

(d) Any auto or **trailer** you do not own while used as a temporary substitute for any other vehicle described in this definition which is out of normal use because of its breakdown, repair, servicing, loss or destruction.

"Family member" means a person related to you by blood, marriage or adoption who is a resident of your household, including a ward or foster child.

"Occupying" means in, upon, getting in, on, out or off.

"Trailer" means a vehicle designed to be pulled by a private passenger type auto. It also means a farm wagon or farm implement while towed by a private passenger type auto or a pick-up, sedan delivery or panel truck.

PART A

LIABILITY COVERAGE

We will pay damages for bodily injury or property damage for which any **covered person** becomes legally responsible because of an auto accident. We will settle or defend, as we consider appropriate, any claim or suit asking for these damages. Our duty to settle or defend ends when our limit of liability for this coverage has been exhausted.

"Covered person" as used in this Part means:

1. You or any **family member** for the ownership, maintenance or use of any auto or **trailer.**

2. Any person using **your covered auto.**

3. For **your covered auto,** any person or organization but only with respect to legal responsibility for acts or omissions of a person for whom coverage is afforded under this Part.

4. For any auto or **trailer,** other than **your covered auto,** any person or organization but only with respect to legal responsibility for acts or omissions of you or any **family member** for whom coverage is afforded under this Part. This provision applies only if the person or organization does not own or hire the auto or **trailer.**

SUPPLEMENTARY PAYMENTS

In addition to our limit of liability, we will pay on behalf of a **covered person:**

1. Up to $250 for the cost of bail bonds required because of an accident, including related traffic law violations, resulting in bodily injury or property damage covered under this policy.

2. Premiums on appeal bonds and bonds to release attachments in any suit we defend.

3. Interest accruing after a judgment is entered in any suit we defend. Our duty to pay interest ends when we offer to pay that part of the judgment which does not exceed our limit of liability for this coverage.

4. Up to $50 a day for loss of earnings, but not other income, because of attendance at hearings or trials at our request.

5. Other reasonable expenses incurred at our request.

EXCLUSIONS

We do not provide Liability Coverage:

1. For any person who intentionally causes bodily injury or property damage.

2. For any person for damage to property owned or being transported by that person.

3. For any person for damage to property rented to, used by, or in the care of that person. This exclusion does not apply to damage to a residence or private garage. It also does not apply to damage to any of the following type vehicles not owned by or furnished or available for the regular use of you or any **family member:**

   a. private passenger autos;
   b. **trailers;** or
   c. pick-up, sedan delivery or panel trucks.

4. For any person for bodily injury to an employee of that person during the course of employment. This exclusion does not apply to bodily injury to a domestic employee unless workers' or workmen's compensation benefits are required or available for that domestic employee.

5. For any person's liability arising out of the ownership or operation of a vehicle while it is being used to carry persons or property for a fee. This exclusion does not apply to a share-the-expense car pool.

6. For any person while employed or otherwise engaged in the business or occupation of selling, repairing, servicing, storing or parking of vehicles designed for use mainly on public highways, including road testing and delivery. This exclusion does not apply to the ownership, maintenance or use of **your covered auto** by you, any **family member,** or any partner, agent or employee of you or any **family member.**

7. For any person maintaining or using any vehicle while that person is employed or otherwise engaged in any business or occupation not described in Exclusion 6. This exclusion does not apply to the maintenance or use of a private passenger type auto. It also does not apply to the maintenance or use of a pick-up, sedan delivery or panel truck that you own.

8. For the ownership, maintenance, or use of a motorcycle or any other self-propelled vehicle having less than four wheels.

9. For the ownership, maintenance or use of any vehicle, other than **your covered auto,** which is owned by you or furnished or available for your regular use.

10. For the ownership, maintenance or use of any vehicle, other than **your covered auto,** which is owned by or furnished or available for the regular use of any **family member.** However, this exclusion does not apply to you.

11. For any person using a vehicle without a reasonable belief that the person is entitled to do so.

12. For any person for bodily injury or property damage for which that person is an insured under a nuclear energy liability policy or would be an insured but for its termination upon exhaustion of its limit of liability. A nuclear energy liability policy is a policy issued by Nuclear Energy Liability Insurance Association, Mutual Atomic Energy Liability Underwriters, Nuclear Insurance Association of Canada, or any of their successors.

LIMIT OF LIABILITY

The limit of liability shown in the Declarations for this coverage is our maximum limit of liability for all damages resulting from any one auto accident. This is the most we will pay regardless of the number of **covered persons,** claims made, vehicles or premiums shown in the Declarations, or vehicles involved in the auto accident.

We will apply the limit of liability to provide any separate limits required by law for bodily injury and property damage liability. However, this provision will not change our total limit of liability.

OUT OF STATE COVERAGE

If an auto accident to which this policy applies occurs in any state or province other than the one in which **your covered auto** is principally garaged, we will interpret your policy for that accident as follows:

1. If the state or province has a financial responsibility or similar law specifying limits of liability for bodily injury or property damage higher than the limit shown in the Declarations, your policy will provide the higher specified limit;

2. If the state or province has a compulsory insurance or similar law requiring a nonresident to maintain insurance whenever the nonresident uses a vehicle in that state or province, your policy will provide the required minimum amounts and types of coverage.

No one will be entitled to duplicate payments for the same elements of loss as a result of the application of this provision.

FINANCIAL RESPONSIBILITY REQUIRED

If we certify this policy as proof of financial responsibility for the future under any financial responsibility law, this policy shall comply with the provisions of the law to the extent of the coverage required.

OTHER INSURANCE

If there is other applicable liability insurance we will pay only our share. Our share is the proportion that our limit of liability bears to the total of all applicable limits. However, any insurance we provide for a vehicle you do not own shall be excess over any other collectible insurance.

PART B

MEDICAL PAYMENTS COVERAGE

We will pay reasonable expenses incurred for necessary medical and funeral services because of bodily injury caused by accident and sustained by a **covered person.** We will pay only those expenses incurred within three years from the date of the accident.

"Covered person" as used in this Part means:

1. You or any **family member** while **occupying,** or as a pedestrian when struck by, a motor vehicle designed for use mainly on public roads or by a trailer of any type.

2. Any other person while **occupying your covered auto.**

EXCLUSIONS

We do not provide Medical Payments Coverage for any person:

1. For bodily injury sustained while **occupying** a motorcycle.

2. For bodily injury sustained while **occupying your covered auto** when it is being used to carry persons or property for a fee. This exclusion does not apply to a share-the-expense car pool.

3. For bodily injury sustained while **occupying** any vehicle located for use as a residence or premises.

4. For bodily injury occurring during the course of employment if workers' or workmen's compensation benefits are required or available for the bodily injury.

5. For bodily injury sustained while **occupying** or, when struck by, any vehicle (other than **your covered auto**) which is owned by you or furnished or available for your regular use.

6. For bodily injury sustained while **occupying** or, when struck by, any vehicle (other than **your covered auto**) which is owned by or furnished or available for the regular use of any **family member.** However, this exclusion does not apply to you.

7. For bodily injury sustained while **occupying** a vehicle without a reasonable belief that the person is entitled to do so.

8. For bodily injury sustained while **occupying** a vehicle when it is being used in the business or occupation of a **covered person.** This exclusion does not apply to bodily injury sustained while **occupying** a private passenger type auto. It also does not apply to bodily injury sustained while **occupying** a pick-up, sedan delivery or panel truck that you own.

9. For bodily injury caused by discharge of a nuclear weapon (even if accidental), war (declared or undeclared), civil war, insurrection, rebellion or revolution or any consequence of any of these.

10. For bodily injury from any nuclear reaction, radiation or radioactive contamination, all whether controlled or uncontrolled or however caused, or any consequence of any of these.

LIMIT OF LIABILITY

The limit of liability shown in the Declarations for this coverage is our maximum limit of liability for each person injured in any one accident. This is the most we will pay regardless of the number of **covered persons,** claims made, vehicles or premiums shown in the Declarations, or vehicles involved in the accident.

Any amounts otherwise payable for expenses under this coverage shall be reduced by any amounts paid or payable for the same expenses under any Auto Liability or Uninsured Motorists Coverage provided by this policy.

No payment will be made under this coverage unless the injured person or his legal representative agrees in writing that any payment shall be applied toward any settlement or judgment that person receives under any Auto Liability or Uninsured Motorists Coverage provided by this policy.

OTHER INSURANCE

If there is other applicable auto medical payments insurance we will pay only our share. Our share is the proportion that our limit of liability bears to the total of all applicable limits. However, any insurance we provide with respect to a vehicle you do not own shall be excess over any other collectible auto insurance providing payments for medical or funeral expenses.

PART C

UNINSURED MOTORISTS COVERAGE

We will pay damages which a **covered person** is legally entitled to recover from the owner or operator of an **uninsured motor vehicle** because of bodily injury sustained by a **covered person** and caused by an accident. The owner's or operator's liability for these damages must arise out of the ownership, maintenance or use of the **uninsured motor vehicle.**

Any judgment for damages arising out of a suit brought without our written consent is not binding on us.

"Covered person" as used in this Part means:
1. You or any **family member.**
2. Any other person **occupying your covered auto.**
3. Any person for damages that person is entitled to recover because of bodily injury to which this coverage applies sustained by a person described in 1. or 2. above.

"Uninsured motor vehicle" means a land motor vehicle or trailer of any type:

1. To which no bodily injury liability bond or policy applies at the time of the accident.

2. To which a bodily injury liability bond or policy applies at the time of the accident but its limit for bodily injury liability is less than the minimum limit for bodily injury liability specified by the financial responsibility law of the state in which **your covered auto** is principally garaged.

3. Which is a hit and run vehicle whose operator or owner cannot be identified and which hits:
    a. you or any **family member;**
    b. a vehicle which you or any **family member** are **occupying;** or
    c. **your covered auto.**

4. To which a bodily injury liability bond or policy applies at the time of the accident, but the bonding or insuring company denies coverage or is or becomes insolvent.

However, **"uninsured motor vehicle"** does not include any vehicle:

1. Owned by or furnished or available for the regular use of you or any **family member.**

2. Owned or operated by a self-insurer under any applicable motor vehicle law.

3. Owned by any governmental unit or agency.

4. Operated on rails or crawler treads.

5. Which is a farm type tractor or equipment designed mainly for use off public roads while not on public roads.

6. While located for use as a residence or premises.

EXCLUSIONS

A. We do not provide Uninsured Motorists Coverage for bodily injury sustained by any person:

1. While **occupying,** or when struck by, any motor vehicle or trailer of any type owned by you or any **family member** which is not insured for this coverage under this policy.

2. If that person or the legal representative settles the bodily injury claim without our consent.

3. While **occupying your covered auto** when it is being used to carry persons or property for a fee. This exclusion does not apply to a share-the-expense car pool.

4. Using a vehicle without a reasonable belief that the person is entitled to do so.

B. This coverage shall not apply directly or indirectly to benefit any insurer or self-insurer under any workers' or workmen's compensation, disability benefits or similar law.

LIMIT OF LIABILITY

The limit of liability shown in the Declarations for this coverage is our maximum limit of liability for all damages resulting from any one accident. This is the most we will pay regardless of the number of **covered persons,** claims made, vehicles or premiums shown in the Declarations, or vehicles involved in the accident.

Any amounts otherwise payable for damages under this coverage shall be reduced by:

1. all sums paid because of the bodily injury by or on behalf of persons or organizations who may be legally responsible. This includes all sums paid under the Liability Coverage of this policy, and

2. all sums paid or payable because of the bodily injury under any workers' or workmen's compensation, disability benefits law or any similar law.

Any payment under this coverage to or for a **covered person** will reduce any amount that person is entitled to recover under the Liability Coverage of this policy.

OTHER INSURANCE	If there is other applicable similar insurance we will pay only our share. Our share is the proportion that our limit of liability bears to the total of all applicable limits. However, any insurance we provide with respect to a vehicle you do not own shall be excess over any other collectible insurance.
ARBITRATION	If we and a **covered person** disagree whether that person is legally entitled to recover damages from the owner or operator of an **uninsured motor vehicle** or do not agree as to the amount of damages, either party may make a written demand for arbitration. In this event, each party will select an arbitrator. The two arbitrators will select a third. If they cannot agree within 30 days, either may request that selection be made by a judge of a court having jurisdiction. Each party will pay the expenses it incurs, and bear the expenses of the third arbitrator equally.
	Unless both parties agree otherwise, arbitration will take place in the county and state in which the **covered person** lives. Local rules of law as to procedure and evidence will apply. A decision agreed to by two of the arbitrators will be binding.

PART D

COVERAGE FOR DAMAGE TO YOUR AUTO	We will pay for direct and accidental loss to **your covered auto**, including its equipment, minus any applicable deductible shown in the Declarations. However, we will pay for loss caused by **collision** only if the Declarations indicate that Collision Coverage is afforded.
	"Collision" means the upset, or collision with another object of **your covered auto**. However, the following are not considered "collision":
	Loss caused by missiles, falling objects, fire, theft or larceny, explosion, earthquake, windstorm, hail, water, flood, malicious mischief or vandalism, riot or civil commotion, contact with bird or animal or breakage of glass. If breakage of glass is caused by a **collision**, you may elect to have it considered a loss caused by **collision**.
TRANSPORTATION EXPENSES	In addition, we will pay up to $10 per day, to a maximum of $300, for transportation expenses incurred by you because of the total theft of **your covered auto**. We will pay only transportation expenses incurred during the period beginning 48 hours after the theft and ending when **your covered auto** is returned to use or we pay for its loss.
EXCLUSIONS	We will not pay for:

1. Loss to **your covered auto** which occurs while it is used to carry persons or property for a fee. This exclusion does not apply to a share-the-expense car pool.

2. Damage due and confined to wear and tear, freezing, mechanical or electrical breakdown or failure or road damage to tires. This exclusion does not apply if the damage results from the total theft of **your covered auto.**

3. Loss due to radioactive contamination.

4. Loss due to discharge of any nuclear weapon (even if accidental), war (declared or undeclared), civil war, insurrection, rebellion or revolution, or any consequence of any of these.

5. Loss to equipment designed for the reproduction of sound, unless the equipment is permanently installed in **your covered auto.**

6. Loss to tapes, records or other devices for use with equipment designed for the reproduction of sound.

7. Loss to a camper body or **trailer** not shown in the Declarations. This exclusion does not apply to a camper body or **trailer** of which you acquire ownership during the policy period if you ask us to insure it within thirty days after you become the owner.

8. Loss to any vehicle while used as a temporary substitute for a vehicle you own which is out of normal use because of its breakdown, repair, servicing, loss or destruction.

9. Loss to TV antennas, awnings, cabanas or equipment designed to create additional living facilities.

10. Loss to any sound receiving or sound receiving and transmitting equipment designed for use as a citizens band radio, two-way mobile radio, telephone, or scanning monitor receiver, or their accessories or antennas.

LIMIT OF LIABILITY	Our limit of liability for loss will be the lesser of: 1. The actual cash value of the stolen or damaged property, or 2. The amount necessary to repair or replace the property.
PAYMENT OF LOSS	We may pay for loss in money or repair or replace the damaged or stolen property. We may, at our expense, return any stolen property to you or to the address shown in this policy. If we return stolen property we will pay for any damage resulting from the theft. We may keep all or part of the property at an agreed or appraised value.
NO BENEFIT TO BAILEE	This insurance shall not directly or indirectly benefit any carrier or other bailee.
OTHER INSURANCE	If other insurance also covers the loss we will pay only our share. Our share is the proportion that our limit of liability bears to the total of all applicable limits.

PART E

DUTIES AFTER AN ACCIDENT OR LOSS

We must be notified promptly of how, when and where the accident or loss happened. Notice should also include the names and addresses of any injured persons and of any witnesses.

A person seeking any coverage must:

1. Cooperate with us in the investigation, settlement or defense of any claim or suit.

2. Promptly send us copies of any notices or legal papers received in connection with the accident or loss.

3. Submit, at our expense and as often as we reasonably require, to physical examinations by physicians we select.

4. Authorize us to obtain medical reports and other pertinent records.

5. Submit a proof of loss when required by us.

A person seeking Uninsured Motorist Coverage must also:
1. Promptly notify the police if a hit-and-run driver is involved.
2. Promptly send us copies of the legal papers if a suit is brought.

A person seeking Coverage for Damage to Your Auto must also:

1. Take reasonable steps after loss, at our expense, to protect **your covered auto** and its equipment from further loss.

2. Promptly notify the police if **your covered auto** is stolen.

3. Permit us to inspect and appraise the damaged property before its repair or disposal.

PART F

**GENERAL
PROVISIONS**

1. **POLICY PERIOD AND TERRITORY**

This policy applies only to accidents and losses which occur during the policy period as shown in the Declarations, and within the policy territory.

The policy territory is the United States of America, its territories or possessions, or Canada. This policy also applies to loss to, or accidents involving, **your covered auto** while being transported between their ports.

2. **CHANGES**

This policy contains all the agreements between you and us. Its terms may not be changed or waived except by endorsement issued by us. If a change requires a premium adjustment, we will adjust the premium as of the effective date of change. If we revise this policy form to provide more coverage without additional premium charge, your policy will automatically provide the additional coverage as of the day the revision is effective in your state.

3. **LEGAL ACTION AGAINST US**

No legal action may be brought against us until there has been full compliance with all the terms of this policy. In addition, under the Liability Coverage, no legal action may be brought against us until we agree in writing that the **covered person** has an obligation to pay or until the amount of that obligation has been finally determined by judgment after trial. No person or organization has any right under this policy to bring us into any action to determine the liability of a **covered person.**

4. **TRANSFER OF YOUR INTEREST IN THIS POLICY**

Your rights and duties under this policy may not be assigned without our written consent. However, if a named insured shown in the Declarations dies, coverage will be provided until the end of the policy period for:

(a) The surviving spouse if resident in the same household at the time of death, as if a named insured shown in the Declarations;

(b) The legal representative of the deceased person as if a named insured shown in the Declarations. This applies only with respect to the representative's legal responsibility for the maintenance or use of **your covered auto.**

5. **OUR RIGHT TO RECOVER PAYMENT**

A. If we make a payment under this policy and the person to or for whom payment was made has a right to recover damages from another we shall be subrogated to that right. That person shall do whatever is necessary to enable us to exercise our rights and shall do nothing after loss to prejudice them.

B. If we make a payment under this policy and the person to or for whom payment is made recovers damages from another, that person shall hold in trust for us the proceeds of the recovery and shall reimburse us to the extent of our payment.

6. **TERMINATION**

A. Cancellation. This policy may be cancelled during the policy period as follows:

1. The named insured shown in the Declarations may cancel by returning this policy to us or by giving us advance written notice of the date cancellation is to take effect.

2. We may cancel by mailing to the named insured shown in the Declarations at the address shown in this policy,

(a) at least 10 days notice

(1) if cancellation is for nonpayment of premium; or

(2) if notice is mailed during the first 60 days this policy is in effect and this is not a renewal or continuation policy;

(b) at least 20 days notice in all other cases.

3. After this policy is in effect for 60 days and this is not a renewal or continuation policy, we will cancel only:

(a) for nonpayment of premium; or

(b) if your driver's license or that of any other driver who lives with you or customarily uses **your covered auto** has been suspended or revoked during the policy period; or if the policy period is other than one year, since the last anniversary of the original effective date.

B. Nonrenewal. If we decide not to renew or continue this policy we will mail notice to the named insured shown in the Declarations at the address shown in this policy at least 20 days before the end of the policy period. However, if the policy period is other than one year, we will have the right not to renew or continue it only at each anniversary of its original effective date.

C. Automatic Termination. If we offer to renew or continue and you or your representative do not accept, this policy will automatically terminate at the end of the current policy period. Failure to pay the required renewal or continuation premium when due shall mean that you have not accepted our offer.

If you obtain other insurance on **your covered auto,** any similar insurance provided by this policy will terminate as to that auto on the effective date of the other insurance.

D. Other Termination Provisions.

1. If the law in effect in your state at the time this policy is issued, renewed or continued, requires any longer notice period or any special form of or procedure for giving notice, or modifies any of the stated termination reasons, we will comply with those requirements.

2. We may deliver any notice instead of mailing it. Proof of mailing of any notice shall be sufficient proof of notice.

3. If this policy is cancelled, you may be entitled to a premium refund. If so, we will send you the refund. However, making or offering to make the refund is not a condition of cancellation.

4. The effective date of cancellation stated in the notice shall become the end of the policy period.

7. **TWO OR MORE AUTO POLICIES**

If this policy and any other auto insurance policy issued to you by us apply to the same accident, the maximum limit of our liability under all the policies shall not exceed the highest applicable limit of liability under any one policy.

8. **BANKRUPTCY**

Bankruptcy or insolvency of the **covered person** shall not relieve us of any obligations under this policy.

Homeowners Policy

RENEWAL OF NUMBER

NAME OF COMPANY

**HOMEOWNERS POLICY
DECLARATIONS**

No. H

Named Insured and Mailing Address (No., Street, Apt., Town or City, County, State, Zip Code)

Policy Period: Years   From: To: 12:01 A.M. Standard Time at the **residence premises**.

The **residence premises** covered by this policy is located at the above address unless otherwise stated: (No., Street, Apt., Town or City, County, State, Zip Code)

Coverage is provided where a premium or limit of liability is shown for the coverage.

Coverages and Limit of Liability	Section I Coverages				Section II Coverages	
	A. Dwelling	B. Other Structures	C. Personal Property	D. Loss of Use	E. Personal Liability Each occurrence	F. Medical Payments to Others Each person
	$	$	$	$	$	$
Premium	Basic Policy Premium	Additional Premiums			Total Prepaid Premium	Payable: At each subsequent At Inception (and) anniversary
						Premium if paid in installments
	$	$	$	$	$	$
						$
				Premium for Scheduled Personal Property $		$
				Combined Premium $		$

Form and Endorsements made part of this Policy at time of issue: (Insert Number(s) and Edition Date(s))

Form HO-   Endorsement(s) HO-

DEDUCT-IBLE	SECTION I	OTHER	In case of a loss under Section I,
	$	$	we cover only that part of the loss over the deductible stated.

Section II

Other **insured locations**: (No., Street, Apt., Town or City, County, State, Zip Code)

Special State Provisions	South Carolina: Valuation Clause (Cov. A)	Minnesota: Insurable Value (Cov. A)	New York: Coinsurance Clause Applies
	$	$	☐ Yes ☐ No

Mortgagee (Name and address)

Countersigned:

By _____

Authorized Representative

RATING INFORMATION

NUMBER OF FAMILIES	Not Town/rowhouse— Number of Families 1 2 3 4 9 over	Town/rowhouse— Family units in Fire Div. 3-4 5-8 9 over	If YES Number of Families— HO-4 and HO-6 Rented to others Not rented to others 1-4 5-10 11-40 over 40	If NO Number of Families	Year of Constr.

Code (1) (3) (6) (8) (4) (9) | Code No Yes (9) | Code No Yes (1) (2) (3) (4) (5) (6) (7) (8) | Year Code

CONSTRUCTION Frame (1) Brick, Stone or Masonry Veneer (2) Brick, Stone or Masonry (3) | Approved Roof | Frame with Aluminum or (5) Plastic Siding | Fire (4) Resistive | Mobile Homes enclosed Foundation | Mobile Homes Not enclosed Foundation (6) | Mobile Homes (7) | Modular Homes rated as Frame (8) | Specifically Rated—Not Fire Resistive (9) | Unapproved Roof

PROTECTION Code | Not more than _____ feet from hydrant | Not more than _____ miles from Fire Dept. | Southern: Inside City limits | Inside City Protected Suburb | Inside Fire District | Fire District or Town ( )

ZONE Code

PREMIUM GR. NO.

DEDUCTIBLE: Type Code | Size Code | Section I $ | Other $

STATISTICAL REPORTING INFORMATION Codes No. Type Classif. Cov. E Cov. F | Premium: Prepaid; If paid in Installments; Payable at: Inception | Each Anniversary

		Premium: Prepaid	Payable at: Inception	Each Anniversary
Snowmobiles	( ) (—)	$	$	$
Watercraft	( ) (2)	$	$	$
Outboard Motor	( ) ( )	$	$	$

ALL OTHER PREMIUMS (except Scheduled Personal Property) | $ | $ | $

(a) The **residence premises** is not seasonal; (b) no **business** pursuits are conducted on the **residence premises;** (c) the **residence premises** is the only premises where the Named Insured or spouse maintains a residence other than business or farm properties; (d) the **Insured** has no full time **residence employee(s)**; (e) the **Insured** has no outboard motor(s) or watercraft otherwise excluded under this policy for which coverage is desired. Exception, if any, to (a), (b), (c), (d) or (e)*.

*Absence of an entry means "no exceptions".

THIS DECLARATIONS PAGE, WITH POLICY JACKET, HOMEOWNERS POLICY FORM, AND ENDORSEMENTS IF ANY, ISSUED TO FORM A PART THEREOF, COMPLETES THE ABOVE NUMBERED HOMEOWNERS POLICY.

**Homeowners 3
Special Form
Ed. 7-77**

AGREEMENT

We will provide the insurance described in this policy in return for the premium and compliance with all applicable provisions of this policy.

DEFINITIONS

Throughout this policy, "you" and "your" refer to the "named insured" shown in the Declarations and the spouse if a resident of the same household, and "we", "us" and "our" refer to the Company providing this insurance. In addition, certain words and phrases are defined as follows:

1. "bodily injury" means bodily harm, sickness or disease, including required care, loss of services and death resulting therefrom.

2. "business" includes trade, profession or occupation.

3. "insured" means you and the following residents of your household:

a. your relatives;

b. any other person under the age of 21 who is in the care of any person named above.

Under Section II, **"insured"** also means:

c. with respect to animals or watercraft to which this policy applies, any person or organization legally responsible for these animals or watercraft which are owned by you or any person included in 3a or 3b. A person or organization using or having custody of these animals or watercraft in the course of any **business,** or without permission of the owner is not an **insured;**

d. with respect to any vehicle to which this policy applies, any person while engaged in your employment or the employment of any person included in 3a or 3b.

4. "insured location" means:

a. the **residence premises;**

b. the part of any other premises, other structures, and grounds, used by you as a residence and which is shown in the Declarations or which is acquired by you during the policy period for your use as a residence;

c. any premises used by you in connection with the premises included in 4a or 4b;

d. any part of a premises not owned by any **insured** but where any **insured** is temporarily residing;

e. vacant land owned by or rented to any **insured** other than farm land;

f. land owned by or rented to any **insured** on which a one or two family dwelling is being constructed as a residence for any **insured;**

g. individual or family cemetery plots or burial vaults of any **insured;**

h. any part of a premises occasionally rented to any **insured** for other than **business** purposes.

5. "motor vehicle" means:

a. a motorized land vehicle designed for travel on public roads or subject to motor vehicle registration. A motorized land vehicle in dead storage on an **insured location** is not a **motor vehicle.**

b. a trailer or semi-trailer designed for travel on public roads and subject to motor vehicle registration. A boat, camp, home or utility trailer not being towed by or carried on a vehicle included in 5a is not a **motor vehicle;**

c. a motorized golf cart, snowmobile, or other motorized land vehicle owned by any **insured** and designed for recreational use off public roads, while off an **insured location.** A motorized golf cart while used for golfing purposes is not a **motor vehicle;**

d. any vehicle while being towed by or carried on a vehicle included in 5a, 5b or 5c.

6. "property damage" means physical injury to or destruction of tangible property, including loss of use of this property.

HO-3 Ed. 7-77   Copyright, Insurance Services Office, 1975, 1977

7. **"residence employee"** means an employee of any **insured** who performs duties in connection with the maintenance or use of the **residence premises,** including household or domestic services, or who performs duties elsewhere of a similar nature not in connection with the **business** of any **insured.**

8. **"residence premises"** means the one or two family dwelling, other structures, and grounds or that part of any other building where you reside and which is shown as the "residence premises" in the Declarations.

SECTION I—COVERAGES

**COVERAGE A
DWELLING**

We cover:

a. the dwelling on the **residence premises** shown in the Declarations used principally as a private residence, including structures attached to the dwelling; and

b. materials and supplies located on or adjacent to the **residence premises** for use in the construction, alteration or repair of the dwelling or other structures on the **residence premises.**

**COVERAGE B
OTHER
STRUCTURES**

We cover other structures on the **residence premises,** separated from the dwelling by clear space. Structures connected to the dwelling by only a fence, utility line, or similar connection are considered to be other structures.

We do not cover other structures:

a. used in whole or in part for **business** purposes; or

b. rented or held for rental to any person not a tenant of the dwelling, unless used solely as a private garage.

**COVERAGE C
PERSONAL
PROPERTY**

We cover personal property owned or used by any **insured** while it is anywhere in the world. At your request, we will cover personal property owned by others while the property is on the part of the **residence premises** occupied by any **insured.** In addition, we will cover at your request, personal property owned by a guest or a **residence employee,** while the property is in any residence occupied by any **insured.**

Our limit of liability for personal property usually situated at any **insured's** residence, other than the **residence premises,** is 10% of the limit of liability for Coverage C, or $1000, whichever is greater. Personal property in a newly acquired principal residence is not subject to this limitation for the 30 days immediately after you begin to move the property there.

Special Limits of Liability. These limits do not increase the Coverage C limit of liability. The special limit for each following numbered category is the total limit for each occurrence for all property in that numbered category.

1. $100 on money, bank notes, bullion, gold other than goldware, silver other than silverware, platinum, coins and medals.

2. $500 on securities, accounts, deeds, evidences of debt, letters of credit, notes other than bank notes, manuscripts, passports, tickets and stamps.

3. $500 on watercraft, including their trailers, furnishings, equipment and outboard motors.

4. $500 on trailers not used with watercraft.

5. $500 on grave markers.

6. $500 for loss by theft of jewelry, watches, furs, precious and semi-precious stones.

7. $1000 for loss by theft of silverware, silver-plated ware, goldware, gold-plated ware and pewterware.

8. $1000 for loss by theft of guns.

Property Not Covered. We do not cover:

1. articles separately described and specifically insured in this or any other insurance;

2. animals, birds or fish;

3. motorized land vehicles except those used to service an **insured's** residence which are not licensed for road use;

4. any device or instrument, including any accessories or antennas, for the transmitting, recording, receiving or reproduction of sound which is operated by power from the electrical system of a **motor vehicle,** or any tape, wire, record, disc or other medium for use with any such device or instrument while any of this property is in or upon a **motor vehicle;**

HO-3 Ed. 7-77

5. aircraft and parts;

6. property of roomers, boarders and other tenants, except property of roomers and boarders related to any **insured;**

7. property contained in an apartment regularly rented or held for rental to others by any **insured;**

8. property rented or held for rental to others away from the **residence premises;**

9. **business** property in storage or held as a sample or for sale or delivery after sale;

10. **business** property pertaining to a **business** actually conducted on the **residence premises;**

11. **business** property away from the **residence premises.**

**COVERAGE D
LOSS OF USE**

The limit of liability for Coverage D is the total limit for all the following coverages.

1. Additional Living Expense. If a loss covered under this Section makes the **residence premises** uninhabitable, we cover any necessary increase in living expenses incurred by you so that your household can maintain its normal standard of living. Payment shall be for the shortest time required to repair or replace the premises or, if you permanently relocate, the shortest time required for your household to settle elsewhere. This period of time is not limited by expiration of this policy.

2. Fair Rental Value. If a loss covered under this Section makes that part of the **residence premises** rented to others or held for rental by you uninhabitable, we cover its fair rental value. Payment shall be for the shortest time required to repair or replace the part of the premises rented or held for rental. This period of time is not limited by expiration of this policy. Fair rental value shall not include any expense that does not continue while that part of the **residence premises** rented or held for rental is uninhabitable.

3. Prohibited Use. If a civil authority prohibits you from use of the **residence premises** as a result of direct damage to neighboring premises by a Peril Insured Against in this policy, we cover any resulting Additional Living Expense and Fair Rental Value loss for a period not exceeding two weeks during which use is prohibited.

We do not cover loss or expense due to cancellation of a lease or agreement.

**ADDITIONAL
COVERAGES**

1. Debris Removal. We will pay the reasonable expense incurred by you in the removal of debris of covered property provided coverage is afforded for the peril causing the loss. Debris removal expense is included in the limit of liability applying to the damaged property. When the amount payable for the actual damage to the property plus the expense for debris removal exceeds the limit of liability for the damaged property, an additional 5% of that limit of liability will be available to cover debris removal expense.

2. Reasonable Repairs. We will pay the reasonable cost incurred by you for necessary repairs made solely to protect covered property from further damage provided coverage is afforded for the peril causing the loss. This coverage does not increase the limit of liability applying to the property being repaired.

3. Trees, Shrubs and Other Plants. We cover trees, shrubs, plants or lawns, on the **residence premises,** for loss caused by the following Perils Insured Against: Fire or lightning, Explosion, Riot or civil commotion, Aircraft, Vehicles not owned or operated by a resident of the **residence premises,** Vandalism or malicious mischief or Theft. The limit of liability for this coverage shall not exceed 5% of the limit of liability that applies to the dwelling for all trees, shrubs, plants and lawns nor more than $500 for any one tree, shrub or plant. We do not cover property grown for **business** purposes.

4. Fire Department Service Charge. We will pay up to $250 for your liability assumed by contract or agreement for fire department charges incurred when the fire department is called to save or protect covered property from a Peril Insured Against. No deductible applies to this coverage.

5. Property Removed. Covered property while being removed from a premises endangered by a Peril Insured Against and for not more than 30 days while removed is covered for direct loss from any cause. This coverage does not change the limit of liability applying to the property being removed.

6. Credit Card, Forgery and Counterfeit Money. We will pay up to $500 for:

a. the legal obligation of any **insured** to pay because of the theft or unauthorized use of credit cards issued to or registered in any **insured's** name.

We do not cover use by a resident of your household. a person who has been entrusted with the credit card. or any person if any **insured** has not complied with all terms and conditions under which the credit card is issued.

b. loss to any **insured** caused by forgery or alteration of any check or negotiable instrument; and

c. loss to any **insured** through acceptance in good faith of counterfeit United States or Canadian paper currency.

We do not cover loss arising out of **business** pursuits or dishonesty of any **insured**. No deductible applies to this coverage.

Defense:

a. We may make any investigation and settle any claim or suit that we decide is appropriate. Our obligation to defend any claim or suit ends when the amount we pay for the loss equals our limit of liability.

b. If a claim is made or a suit is brought against any **insured** for liability under the Credit Card coverage. we will provide a defense at our expense by counsel of our choice.

c. We have the option to defend at our expense any **insured** or any **insured's** bank against any suit for the enforcement of payment under the Forgery coverage.

SECTION I—PERILS INSURED AGAINST

**Coverage A
Dwelling
and
Coverage B
Other
Structures**

We insure for all risks of physical loss to the property described in Coverages A and B except:

1. losses excluded under Section I—Exclusions;

2. freezing of a plumbing. heating or air conditioning system or of a household appliance. or by discharge. leakage or overflow from within the system or appliance caused by freezing. while the dwelling is vacant. unoccupied or being constructed unless you have used reasonable care to:

a. maintain heat in the building; or

b. shut off the water supply and drain the system and appliances of water;

3. freezing. thawing. pressure or weight of water or ice. whether driven by wind or not. to a fence. pavement. patio. swimming pool. foundation. retaining wall. bulkhead. pier. wharf or dock;

4. theft in or to a dwelling under construction. or of materials and supplies for use in the construction until the dwelling is completed and occupied;

5. vandalism and malicious mischief or breakage of glass and safety glazing materials if the dwelling has been vacant for more than 30 consecutive days immediately before the loss. A dwelling being constructed is not considered vacant;

6. continuous or repeated seepage or leakage of water or steam over a period of time from within a plumbing. heating or air conditioning system or from within a household appliance;

7. wear and tear; marring; deterioration; inherent vice; latent defect; mechanical breakdown; rust; mold; wet or dry rot; contamination; smog; smoke from agricultural smudging or industrial operations; settling. cracking. shrinking. bulging. or expansion of pavements. patios. foundations. walls. floors. roofs or ceilings; birds. vermin. rodents. insects or domestic animals. If any of these cause water to escape from a plumbing. heating or air conditioning system or household appliance. we cover loss caused by the water. We also cover the cost of tearing out and replacing any part of a building necessary to repair the system or appliance. We do not cover loss to the system or appliance from which this water escaped.

Under items 2 thru 7, any ensuing loss not excluded is covered.

**Coverage C
Personal
Property**

We insure for direct loss to property described in Coverage C caused by:

1. **Fire or lightning.**

2. **Windstorm or hail.**

This peril does not include loss to the property contained in a building caused by rain. snow. sleet. sand or dust unless the direct force of wind or hail damages the building causing an opening in a roof or wall and the rain. snow. sleet. sand or dust enters through this opening.

HO-3 Ed. 7-77

This peril includes loss to watercraft and their trailers, furnishings, equipment, and outboard motors, only while inside a fully enclosed building.

3. Explosion.

4. Riot or civil commotion.

5. Aircraft, including self-propelled missiles and spacecraft.

6. Vehicles.

7. Smoke, meaning sudden and accidental damage from smoke.
This peril does not include loss caused by smoke from agricultural smudging or industrial operations.

8. Vandalism or malicious mischief.

9. Theft, including attempted theft and loss of property from a known location when it is likely that the property has been stolen.
This peril does not include loss caused by theft:

    a. committed by any **insured;**

    b. in or to a dwelling under construction, or of materials and supplies for use in the construction until the dwelling is completed and occupied; or

    c. from any part of a **residence premises** rented by an **insured** to other than an **insured.**

This peril does not include loss caused by theft that occurs away from the **residence premises** of:

    a. property while at any other residence owned, rented to, or occupied by any **insured,** except while any **insured** is temporarily residing there. Property of a student who is an **insured** is covered while at a residence away from home if the student has been there at any time during the 45 days immediately before the loss;

    b. unattended property in or on any **motor vehicle** or trailer, other than a public conveyance, unless there is forcible entry into the vehicle while all its doors, windows and other openings are closed and locked and there are visible marks of the forcible entry; or the vehicle is stolen and not recovered within 30 days.
Property is not unattended when any **insured** has entrusted the keys of the vehicle to a custodian.

    c. watercraft, including its furnishings, equipment and outboard motors. Other property in or on any private watercraft is covered if the loss results from forcible entry into a securely locked compartment and there are visible marks of the forcible entry; or

    d. trailers and campers.

10. Falling objects.
This peril does not include loss to property contained in a building unless the roof or an exterior wall of the building is first damaged by a falling object. Damage to the falling object itself is not included.

11. Weight of ice, snow or sleet which causes damage to property contained in a building.

12. Collapse of a building or any part of a building.
This peril does not include settling, cracking, shrinking, bulging or expansion.

13. Accidental discharge or overflow of water or steam from within a plumbing, heating or air conditioning system or from within a household appliance.
This peril does not include loss:

    a. to the appliance from which the water or steam escaped;

    b. caused by or resulting from freezing;

    c. on the **residence premises** caused by accidental discharge or overflow which occurs off the **residence premises.**

14. Sudden and accidental tearing asunder, cracking, burning or bulging of a steam or hot water heating system, an air conditioning system, or an appliance for heating water.
We do not cover loss caused by or resulting from freezing under this peril.

15. Freezing of a plumbing, heating or air conditioning system or of a household appliance.
This peril does not include loss on the **residence premises** while the dwelling is unoccupied, unless you have used reasonable care to:

    a. maintain heat in the building; or

    b. shut off the water supply and drain the system and appliances of water.

16. Sudden and accidental damage from artificially generated electrical current.
This peril does not include loss to a tube, transistor or similar electronic component.

SECTION I—EXCLUSIONS

We do not cover loss resulting directly or indirectly from:

1. Ordinance or Law, meaning enforcement of any ordinance or law regulating the construction, repair, or demolition of a building or other structure, unless specifically provided under this policy.

2. Earth Movement. Direct loss by fire, explosion, theft, or breakage of glass or safety glazing materials resulting from earth movement is covered.

3. Water Damage, meaning:

a. flood, surface water, waves, tidal water, overflow of a body of water, or spray from any of these, whether or not driven by wind;

b. water which backs up through sewers or drains; or

c. water below the surface of the ground, including water which exerts pressure on, or seeps or leaks through a building, sidewalk, driveway, foundation, swimming pool or other structure.

Direct loss by fire, explosion or theft resulting from water damage is covered.

4. Power Interruption, meaning the interruption of power or other utility service if the interruption takes place away from the **residence premises.** If a Peril Insured Against ensues on the **residence premises,** we will pay only for loss caused by the ensuing peril.

5. Neglect, meaning neglect of the **insured** to use all reasonable means to save and preserve property at and after the time of a loss, or when property is endangered by a Peril Insured Against.

6. War, including undeclared war, civil war, insurrection, rebellion, revolution, warlike act by a military force or military personnel, destruction or seizure or use for a military purpose, and including any consequence of any of these. Discharge of a nuclear weapon shall be deemed a warlike act even if accidental.

7. Nuclear Hazard, to the extent set forth in the Nuclear Hazard Clause of Section I—Conditions.

SECTION I—CONDITIONS

1. Insurable Interest and Limit of Liability. Even if more than one person has an insurable interest in the property covered, we shall not be liable:

a. to the **insured** for an amount greater than the **insured's** interest; nor

b. for more than the applicable limit of liability.

2. Your Duties After Loss. In case of a loss to which this insurance may apply, you shall see that the following duties are performed:

a. give immediate notice to us or our agent, and in case of theft also to the police. In case of loss under the Credit Card coverage also notify the credit card company;

b. protect the property from further damage, make reasonable and necessary repairs required to protect the property, and keep an accurate record of repair expenditures;

c. prepare an inventory of damaged personal property showing in detail, the quantity, description, actual cash value and amount of loss. Attach to the inventory all bills, receipts and related documents that substantiate the figures in the inventory;

d. exhibit the damaged property as often as we reasonably require and submit to examination under oath;

e. submit to us, within 60 days after we request, your signed, sworn statement of loss which sets forth, to the best of your knowledge and belief:

(1) the time and cause of loss;

(2) interest of the **insured** and all others in the property involved and all encumbrances on the property;

(3) other insurance which may cover the loss;

(4) changes in title or occupancy of the property during the term of the policy;

HO-3 Ed. 7-77

(5) specifications of any damaged building and detailed estimates for repair of the damage;

(6) an inventory of damaged personal property described in 2c;

(7) receipts for additional living expenses incurred and records supporting the fair rental value loss;

(8) evidence or affidavit supporting a claim under the Credit Card, Forgery and Counterfeit Money coverage, stating the amount and cause of loss.

3. Loss Settlement. Covered property losses are settled as follows:

a. Personal property and structures that are not buildings at actual cash value at the time of loss but not exceeding the amount necessary to repair or replace;

b. Carpeting, domestic appliances, awnings, outdoor antennas and outdoor equipment, whether or not attached to buildings, at actual cash value at the time of loss but not exceeding the amount necessary to repair or replace;

c. Buildings under Coverage A or B at replacement cost without deduction for depreciation, subject to the following:

(1) If at the time of loss the amount of insurance in this policy on the damaged building is 80% or more of the full replacement cost of the building immediately prior to the loss, we will pay the cost of repair or replacement, without deduction for depreciation, but not exceeding the smallest of the following amounts:

(a) the limit of liability under this policy applying to the building;

(b) the replacement cost of that part of the building damaged for equivalent construction and use on the same premises; or

(c) the amount actually and necessarily spent to repair or replace the damaged building.

(2) If at the time of loss the amount of insurance in this policy on the damaged building is less than 80% of the full replacement cost of the building immediately prior to the loss, we will pay the larger of the following amounts, but not exceeding the limit of liability under this policy applying to the building:

(a) the actual cash value of that part of the building damaged; or

(b) that proportion of the cost to repair or replace, without deduction for depreciation, of that part of the building damaged, which the total amount of insurance in this policy on the damaged building bears to 80% of the replacement cost of the building.

(3) In determining the amount of insurance required to equal 80% of the full replacement cost of the building immediately prior to the loss, you shall disregard the value of excavations, foundations, piers and other supports which are below the undersurface of the lowest basement floor or, where there is no basement, which are below the surface of the ground inside the foundation walls, and underground flues, pipes, wiring and drains.

(4) When the cost to repair or replace the damage is more than $1000 or more than 5% of the amount of insurance in this policy on the building, whichever is less, we will pay no more than the actual cash value of the damage until actual repair or replacement is completed.

(5) You may disregard the replacement cost loss settlement provisions and make claim under this policy for loss or damage to buildings on an actual cash value basis and then make claim within 180 days after loss for any additional liability on a replacement cost basis.

4. Loss to a Pair or Set. In case of loss to a pair or set we may elect to:

a. repair or replace any part to restore the pair or set to its value before the loss; or

b. pay the difference between actual cash value of the property before and after the loss.

5. Glass Replacement. Loss for damage to glass caused by a Peril Insured Against shall be settled on the basis of replacement with safety glazing materials when required by ordinance or law.

6. Appraisal. If you and we fail to agree on the amount of loss, either one can demand that the amount of the loss be set by appraisal. If either makes a written demand for appraisal, each shall select a competent, independent appraiser and notify the other of the appraiser's identity within 20 days of receipt of the written demand. The two appraisers shall then select a competent, impartial umpire. If the two appraisers are unable to agree upon an umpire within 15 days, you or we can ask a judge of a court of record in the state where the **residence premises** is located to select an umpire. The appraisers shall then set the amount of the loss. If the appraisers submit a written report of an agreement to us, the amount agreed upon shall be the amount of the loss. If the appraisers fail to agree within a reasonable time, they shall submit their differences to the umpire. Written agreement signed by any two of these three shall set the amount of the loss. Each appraiser shall be paid by the party selecting that appraiser. Other expenses of the appraisal and the compensation of the umpire shall be paid equally by you and us.

7. Other Insurance. If a loss covered by this policy is also covered by other insurance, we will pay only the proportion of the loss that the limit of liability that applies under this policy bears to the total amount of insurance covering the loss.

8. Suit Against Us. No action shall be brought unless there has been compliance with the policy provisions and the action is started within one year after the occurrence causing loss or damage.

9. Our Option. If we give you written notice within 30 days after we receive your signed, sworn statement of loss, we may repair or replace any part of the property damaged with equivalent property.

10. Loss Payment. We will adjust all losses with you. We will pay you unless some other person is named in the policy to receive payment. Payment for loss will be made within 30 days after we reach agreement with you, entry of a final judgment, or the filing of an appraisal award with us.

11. Abandonment of Property. We need not accept any property abandoned by any **insured.**

12. Mortgage Clause.

The word "mortgagee" includes trustee.

If a mortgagee is named in this policy, any loss payable under Coverage A or B shall be paid to the mortgagee and you, as interests appear. If more than one mortgagee is named, the order of payment shall be the same as the order or precedence of the mortgages.

If we deny your claim, that denial shall not apply to a valid claim of the mortgagee, if the mortgagee:

    a. notifies us of any change in ownership, occupancy or substantial change in risk of which the mortgagee is aware;

    b. pays any premium due under this policy on demand if you have neglected to pay the premium;

    c. submits a signed, sworn statement of loss within 60 days after receiving notice from us of your failure to do so. Policy conditions relating to Appraisal, Suit Against Us and Loss Payment apply to the mortgagee.

If the policy is cancelled by us, the mortgagee shall be notified at least 10 days before the date cancellation takes effect.

If we pay the mortgagee for any loss and deny payment to you:

    a. we are subrogated to all the rights of the mortgagee granted under the mortgage on the property; or

    b. at our option, we may pay to the mortgagee the whole principal on the mortgage plus any accrued interest. In this event, we shall receive a full assignment and transfer of the mortgage and all securities held as collateral to the mortgage debt.

Subrogation shall not impair the right of the mortgagee to recover the full amount of the mortgagee's claim.

13. No Benefit to Bailee. We will not recognize any assignment or grant any coverage for the benefit of any person or organization holding, storing or transporting property for a fee regardless of any other provision of this policy.

14. Nuclear Hazard Clause.

    a. "Nuclear Hazard" means any nuclear reaction, radiation, or radioactive contamination, all whether controlled or uncontrolled or however caused, or any consequence of any of these.

    b. Loss caused by the nuclear hazard shall not be considered loss caused by fire, explosion, or smoke, whether these perils are specifically named in or otherwise included within the Perils Insured Against in Section I.

    c. This policy does not apply under Section I to loss caused directly or indirectly by nuclear hazard, except that direct loss by fire resulting from the nuclear hazard is covered.

SECTION II—LIABILITY COVERAGES

COVERAGE E PERSONAL LIABILITY

If a claim is made or a suit is brought against any **insured** for damages because of **bodily injury** or **property damage** to which this coverage applies, we will:

a. pay up to our limit of liability for the damages for which the **insured** is legally liable; and

b. provide a defense at our expense by counsel of our choice. We may make any investigation and settle any claim or suit that we decide is appropriate. Our obligation to defend any claim or suit ends when the amount we pay for damages resulting from the occurrence equals our limit of liability.

COVERAGE F MEDICAL PAYMENTS TO OTHERS

We will pay the necessary medical expenses incurred or medically ascertained within three years from the date of an accident causing **bodily injury.** Medical expenses means reasonable charges for medical, surgical, x-ray, dental, ambulance, hospital, professional nursing, prosthetic devices and funeral services. This coverage does not apply to you or regular residents of your household other than **residence employees.** As to others, this coverage applies only:

a. to a person on the **insured location** with the permission of any **insured;** or

b. to a person off the **insured location,** if the **bodily injury:**

(1) arises out of a condition in the **insured location** or the ways immediately adjoining;

(2) is caused by the activities of any **insured;**

(3) is caused by a **residence employee** in the course of the **residence employee's** employment by any **insured;** or

(4) is caused by an animal owned by or in the care of any **insured.**

SECTION II—EXCLUSIONS

1. Coverage E—Personal Liability and Coverage F—Medical Payments to Others do not apply to **bodily injury** or **property damage:**

a. which is expected or intended by the **insured;**

b. arising out of **business** pursuits of any **insured** or the rental or holding for rental of any part of any premises by any **insured.**

This exclusion does not apply to:

(1) activities which are ordinarily incident to non-**business** pursuits; or

(2) the rental or holding for rental of a residence of yours:

(a) on an occasional basis for the exclusive use as a residence;

(b) in part, unless intended for use as a residence by more than two roomers or boarders; or

(c) in part, as an office, school, studio or private garage;

c. arising out of the rendering or failing to render professional services;

d. arising out of any premises owned or rented to any **insured** which is not an **insured location;**

e. arising out of the ownership, maintenance, use, loading or unloading of:

(1) an aircraft;

(2) a **motor vehicle** owned or operated by, or rented or loaned to any **insured;** or

(3) a watercraft:

(a) owned by or rented to any **insured** if the watercraft has inboard or inboard-outdrive motor power of more than 50 horsepower or is a sailing vessel, with or without auxiliary power, 26 feet or more in overall length; or

(b) powered by one or more outboard motors with more than 25 total horsepower, owned by any **insured** at the inception of this policy. If you report in writing to us within 45 days after acquisition, an intention to insure any outboard motors acquired prior to the policy period, coverage will apply.

f. caused directly or indirectly by war, including undeclared war, civil war, insurrection, rebellion, revolution, warlike act by a military force or military personnel, destruction or seizure or use for a military purpose, and including any consequence of any of these. Discharge of a nuclear weapon shall be deemed a warlike act even if accidental.

Exclusion e(3) does not apply while the watercraft is stored and exclusions d and e do not apply to **bodily injury** to any **residence employee** arising out of and in the course of the **residence employee's** employment by any **insured.**

2. **Coverage E—Personal Liability,** does not apply to:

a. liability assumed under any unwritten contract or agreement, or by contract or agreement in connection with any **business** of the **insured;**

b. **property damage** to property owned by the **insured;**

c. **property damage** to property rented to, occupied or used by or in the care of the **insured.** This exclusion does not apply to **property damage** caused by fire, smoke or explosion;

d. **bodily injury** to any person eligible to receive any benefits required to be provided or voluntarily provided by the **insured** under any worker's or workmen's compensation, non-occupational disability, or occupational disease law; or

e. **bodily injury** or **property damage** for which any **insured** under this policy is also an insured under a nuclear energy liability policy or would be an insured but for its termination upon exhaustion of its limit of liability. A nuclear energy liability policy is a policy issued by Nuclear Energy Liability Insurance Association, Mutual Atomic Energy Liability Underwriters, Nuclear Insurance Association of Canada, or any of their successors.

3. **Coverage F—Medical Payments to Others,** does not apply to **bodily injury:**

a. to a **residence employee** if it occurs off the **insured location** and does not arise out of or in the course of the **residence employee's** employment by any **insured;**

b. to any person, eligible to receive any benefits required to be provided or voluntarily provided under any worker's or workmen's compensation, non-occupational disability or occupational disease law;

c. from any nuclear reaction, radiation or radioactive contamination, all whether controlled or uncontrolled or however caused, or any consequence of any of these.

SECTION II—ADDITIONAL COVERAGES

We cover the following in addition to the limits of liability:

1. **Claim Expenses.** We pay:

a. expenses incurred by us and costs taxed against any **insured** in any suit we defend;

b. premiums on bonds required in a suit defended by us, but not for bond amounts greater than the limit of liability for Coverage E. We are not obligated to apply for or furnish any bond;

c. reasonable expenses incurred by any **insured** at our request, including actual loss of earnings (but not loss of other income) up to $50 per day for assisting us in the investigation or defense of any claim or suit;

d. interest on the entire judgment which accrues after entry of the judgment and before we pay or tender, or deposit in court that part of the judgment which does not exceed the limit of liability that applies.

2. **First Aid Expenses.** We will pay expenses for first aid to others incurred by any **insured** for **bodily injury** covered under this policy. We will not pay for first aid to you or any other **insured.**

3. **Damage to Property of Others.** We will pay up to $250 per occurrence for **property damage** to property of others caused by any **insured.**

We will not pay for **property damage:**

a. to property covered under Section I of this policy;

b. caused intentionally by any **insured** who is 13 years of age or older;

c. to property owned by or rented to any **insured,** a tenant of any **insured,** or a resident in your household; or

d. arising out of:

(1) **business** pursuits;
(2) any act or omission in connection with a premises owned, rented or controlled by any **insured,** other than the **insured location;** or
(3) the ownership, maintenance, or use of a **motor vehicle,** aircraft or watercraft.

SECTION II—CONDITIONS

1. Limit of Liability. Regardless of the number of **insureds,** claims made or persons injured, our total liability under Coverage E stated in this policy for all damages resulting from any one occurrence shall not exceed the limit of liability for Coverage E stated in the Declarations. All **bodily injury** and **property damage** resulting from any one accident or from continuous or repeated exposure to substantially the same general conditions shall be considered to be the result of one occurrence.

Our total liability under Coverage F for all medical expense payable for **bodily injury** to one person as the result of one accident shall not exceed the limit of liability for Coverage F stated in the Declarations.

2. Severability of Insurance. This insurance applies separately to each **insured.** This condition shall not increase our limit of liability for any one occurrence.

3. Duties After Loss. In case of an accident or occurrence, the **insured** shall perform the following duties that apply. You shall cooperate with us in seeing that these duties are performed:

a. give written notice to us or our agent as soon as practicable, which sets forth:
(1) the identity of the policy and **insured;**
(2) reasonably available information on the time, place and circumstances of the accident or occurrence; and
(3) names and addresses of any claimants and available witnesses;

b. forward to us every notice, demand, summons or other process relating to the accident or occurrence;

c. at our request, assist in:
(1) making settlement;
(2) the enforcement of any right of contribution or indemnity against any person or organization who may be liable to any **insured;**
(3) the conduct of suits and attend hearings and trials;
(4) securing and giving evidence and obtaining the attendance of witnesses;

d. under the coverage—Damage to the Property of Others—submit to us within 60 days after the loss, a sworn statement of loss and exhibit the damaged property, if within the **insured's** control;

e. the **insured** shall not, except at the **insured's** own cost, voluntarily make any payment, assume any obligation or incur any expense other than for first aid to others at the time of the **bodily injury.**

4. Duties of an Injured Person—Coverage F—Medical Payments to Others. The injured person or someone acting on behalf of the injured person shall:

a. give us written proof of claim, under oath if required, as soon as practicable;

b. execute authorization to allow us to obtain copies of medical reports and records; and

c. the injured person shall submit to physical examination by a physician selected by us when and as often as we reasonably require.

5. Payment of Claim—Coverage F—Medical Payments to Others. Payment under this coverage is not an admission of liability by any **insured** or us.

6. Suit Against Us. No action shall be brought against us unless there has been compliance with the policy provisions.

No one shall have any right to join us as a party to any action against any **insured.** Further, no action with respect to Coverage E shall be brought against us until the obligation of the **insured** has been determined by final judgment or agreement signed by us.

7. Bankruptcy of any Insured. Bankruptcy or insolvency of any **insured** shall not relieve us of any of our obligations under this policy.

8. Other Insurance—Coverage E—Personal Liability. This insurance is excess over any other valid and collectible insurance except insurance written specifically to cover as excess over the limits of liability that apply in this policy.

SECTION I AND SECTION II—CONDITIONS

1. Policy Period. This policy applies only to loss under Section I or **bodily injury** or **property damage** under Section II, which occurs during the policy period.

2. Concealment or Fraud. We do not provide coverage for any **insured** who has intentionally concealed or misrepresented any material fact or circumstance relating to this insurance.

3. Liberalization Clause. If we adopt any revision which would broaden the coverage under this policy without additional premium within 60 days prior to or during the policy period, the broadened coverage will immediately apply to this policy.

4. Waiver or Change of Policy Provisions. A waiver or change of any provision of this policy must be in writing by us to be valid. Our request for an appraisal or examination shall not waive any of our rights.

5. Cancellation.

a. You may cancel this policy at any time by returning it to us or by notifying us in writing of the date cancellation is to take effect.

b. We may cancel this policy only for the reasons stated in this condition by notifying you in writing of the date cancellation takes effect. This cancellation notice may be delivered to you, or mailed to you at your mailing address shown in the Declarations. Proof of mailing shall be sufficient proof of notice:

(1) When you have not paid the premium, whether payable to us or to our agent or under any finance or credit plan, we may cancel at any time by notifying you at least 10 days before the date cancellation takes effect.

(2) When this policy has been in effect for less than 60 days and is not a renewal with us, we may cancel for any reason by notifying you at least 10 days before the date cancellation takes effect.

(3) When this policy has been in effect for 60 days or more, or at any time if it is a renewal with us, we may cancel if there has been a material misrepresentation of fact which if known to us would have caused us not to issue the policy or if the risk has changed substantially since the policy was issued. This can be done by notifying you at least 30 days before the date cancellation takes effect.

(4) When this policy is written for a period longer than one year, we may cancel for any reason at anniversary by notifying you at least 30 days before the date cancellation takes effect.

c. When this policy is cancelled, the premium for the period from the date of cancellation to the expiration date will be refunded. When you request cancellation, the return premium will be based on our short rate table. When we cancel, the return premium will be pro rata.

d. If the return premium is not refunded with the notice of cancellation or when this policy is returned to us, we will refund it within a reasonable time after the date cancellation takes effect.

6. Non-Renewal. We may elect not to renew this policy. We may do so by delivery to you, or mailing to you at your mailing address shown in the Declarations, written notice at least 30 days before the expiration date of this policy. Proof of mailing shall be sufficient proof of notice.

7. Assignment. Assignment of this policy shall not be valid unless we give our written consent.

8. Subrogation. Any **insured** may waive in writing before a loss all rights of recovery against any person. If not waived, we may require an assignment of rights of recovery for a loss to the extent that payment is made by us.

If an assignment is sought, any **insured** shall sign and deliver all related papers and cooperate with us in any reasonable manner.

Subrogation does not apply under Section II to Medical Payments to Others or Damage to Property of Others.

9. Death. If any person named in the Declarations or the spouse, if a resident of the same household, dies:

a. we insure the legal representative of the deceased but only with respect to the premises and property of the deceased covered under the policy at the time of death;

b. **insured** includes:

(1) any member of your household who is an **insured** at the time of your death, but only while a resident of the **residence premises;** and

(2) with respect to your property, the person having proper temporary custody of the property until appointment and qualification of a legal representative.

Appendix D

Businessowners Policy

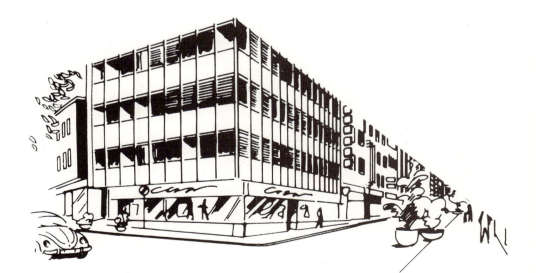

NAME OF COMPANY

DECLARATIONS

Renewal of Number

☐ STANDARD BUSINESSOWNERS POLICY
☐ SPECIAL BUSINESSOWNERS POLICY

No. SBP

Item 1. Named Insured and Mailing Address (No., Street, City or Town, County, State, Zip Code)

Item 2. Policy Period:

From   To

Beginning and ending at 12 noon Standard Time (12:01 A.M. in California and Oregon) at the location of the described premises.

Item 3. The Named Insured is:

☐ Individual   ☐ Partnership   ☐ Corporation   ☐ Joint Venture   ☐ Other: _____
                                                                    (SPECIFY)

Item 4. Mortgagee: _____
                       (NAME AND ADDRESS)

Item 5. Business of the Named Insured:

Item 6. In Consideration of the premium, insurance is provided the named insured with respect to those premises described in the Schedule below and with respect to those coverages and kinds of property for which a specific limit of liability is shown, subject to all of the terms of this policy including forms and endorsements made a part hereof:

SCHEDULE

Described premises: (Enter "same" if same location as in Item 1)

No. 1
No. 2
No. 3

SECTION I—BUILDING(S), BUSINESS PERSONAL PROPERTY, LOSS OF INCOME AND MONEY AND SECURITIES

LIMITS OF LIABILITY

Loc. No.	Bldg. No.	Loc. No.	Bldg. No.	Loc. No.	Bldg. No.	Loc. No.	Bldg. No.	COVERAGE	Deductible—Coverages A & B: $100 as specified in this policy.
* $		* $		* $		* $		A. Building(s)	
$		$		$		$		B. Business Personal Property	
								C. Loss of Income *(Not Applicable To Standard Businessowners Policy)*	

Actual Business Loss Sustained, Not exceeding 12 Consecutive Months.
$10,000 On Premises $2,000 Off Premises   D Money and Securities *(Not Applicable To Standard Businessowners Policy)*

*Automatic Increase in Insurance: Coverage A — Building(s) shall be automatically increased by 2% or __% whichever is greater, at the end of each period of three months after the inception date of the policy.

SECTION II—COMPREHENSIVE BUSINESS LIABILITY COVERAGE

LIMITS OF LIABILITY

		COVERAGE
$	each occurrence { The limit of liability with respect to the completed operations and products hazards combined is an aggregate limit for all occurrences during the policy period. }	E — Business Liability
$50,000 each occurrence		Fire Legal Liability
$ 1,000 each person $10,000 each accident		F — Medical Payments

Item 7. Optional Coverages. The following optional coverages are afforded under this policy only when designated by an "X" in the box(es) shown below. (These Coverages are subject to deductibles specified in this policy.)

LIMITS OF LIABILITY

	COVERAGES
$5,000 each occurrence	☐ Employee Dishonesty
$	☐ Exterior Signs
	☐ Exterior Grade Floor Glass
Included under Coverage A or Coverage B	☐ Burglary and Robbery *(Not Applicable To Special Businessowners Policy)*
Refer to Pages 6 & 7 of Form MLB-700	☐ Boiler, Pressure Vessels and Air Conditioning Equipment
Included under Coverage A or Coverage B	☐ Other (Describe)
$	

Item 8. Policy forms and endorsements attached at inception, if any

Item 9. Annual Premium for the Policy (and Optional Coverages, if any) $
Countersigned:

By _____
Authorized Representative

THIS DECLARATIONS PAGE WITH POLICY JACKET, BUSINESSOWNERS POLICY "MLB-700" OR "MLB-701" AND ENDORSEMENTS, IF ANY, ISSUED TO FORM A PART THEREOF, COMPLETES THE ABOVE NUMBERED POLICY.

SECTION I—PROPERTY COVERAGES

**COVERAGE A
BUILDINGS**

This policy covers the replacement cost of the building(s) at the premises described in the Declarations for which a limit of liability is shown, including, all while on the premises, the following:

1. all garages, storage buildings and appurtenant structures usual to the occupancy of the insured;

2. fixtures, machinery and equipment constituting a permanent part of and pertaining to the service of the building;

3. personal property of the insured used for the maintenance and service of the building, including fire extinguishing apparatus, floor coverings, and appliances for refrigerating, ventilating, cooking, dishwashing and laundering;

4. outdoor furniture and yard fixtures;

5. personal property owned by the insured in apartments or rooms furnished by the insured as landlord;

6. trees, shrubs and plants at the described premises for not more than $250 on any one tree, shrub or plant, including expense incurred for removing all debris thereof, however, the total liability of the Company shall not exceed $1,000 in the aggregate for any one loss.

DEBRIS REMOVAL: This policy covers, as an additional amount of insurance, expenses incurred in the removal of the debris of the property covered occasioned by loss as insured against in this policy.

AUTOMATIC INCREASE IN INSURANCE: The limit of liability shown in the Declarations with respect to Coverage A—Buildings shall automatically be increased at the end of each period of three months after inception date of this policy by the percentage shown in the Declarations.

**COVERAGE B
BUSINESS
PERSONAL
PROPERTY**

This policy covers replacement cost of the Business Personal Property owned by the insured, usual to the occupancy of the insured, at the premises described in the Declarations for which a limit of liability is shown, including:

1. similar property held by the insured and belonging in whole or in part to others but not exceeding the amount for which the insured is legally liable, including the value of labor, materials, and charges furnished, performed or incurred by the insured; and

2. tenant's improvements and betterments, meaning the insured's use interest in fixtures, alterations, installations or additions comprising a part of the building occupied but not owned by the insured and made or acquired at the expense of the insured, exclusive of rent paid by the insured, but which are not legally subject to removal by the insured;

while (1) in or on the building(s), or (2) in the open (including within vehicles) on or within 100 feet of the described premises.

DEBRIS REMOVAL: This policy covers, as an additional amount of insurance, expenses incurred in the removal of the debris of the property covered occasioned by loss as insured against in this policy.

SEASONAL AUTOMATIC INCREASE: When a limit of liability is shown in the Declarations for Coverage B—Business Personal Property, the limit of liability for Coverage B is automatically increased by 25% to provide for seasonal variations. However, this increase shall not apply unless the limit of liability shown in the Declarations is 100% or more of the insured's average monthly values for the 12 months immediately preceding the date of loss, or in the event the insured has been in business for less than 12 months, such shorter period of time.

PERSONAL PROPERTY OFF PREMISES: When a limit of liability is shown in the Declarations for Coverage B—Business Personal Property, this policy also covers the business personal property of the insured (excluding money and securities) and similar property held by the insured and belonging in whole or in part to others for not more than $1,000 for all losses arising out of any one occurrence while such property is in due course of transit, or otherwise temporarily away from the described premises.

PERSONAL PROPERTY AT NEWLY ACQUIRED LOCATIONS: When a limit of liability is shown in the Declarations for Coverage B—Business Personal Property, this policy also covers the business personal property of the insured for not exceeding $10,000 while at premises owned, leased or operated by the insured, other than those described in the Declarations, but this coverage shall cease thirty (30) days from the date of acquisition of such premises or on the date values at such locations are reported to the Company or on the expiration date of the policy, whichever occurs first.

COVERAGE C LOSS OF INCOME

This policy covers the actual business loss sustained by the insured and the expenses necessarily incurred to resume normal business operations resulting from the interruption of business or the untenantability of the premises when the building or the personal property is damaged as a direct result of an insured peril. The actual business loss sustained by the insured shall not exceed:

1. the reduction in gross earnings, less charges and expenses which do not necessarily continue during the interruption of business; and
2. the reduction in rents, less charges and expenses which do not necessarily continue during the period of untenantability.

The actual business loss sustained shall not include charges and expenses which do not necessarily continue during the interruption of business or during the untenantability of the premises.

Loss of income shall be payable for only such length of time as would be required to resume normal business operations but not exceeding such length of time as would be required to rebuild, repair or replace such part of the building or personal property as has been damaged or destroyed as a direct result of an insured peril. Such loss shall not exceed twelve consecutive months from the date of loss and shall not be limited by the expiration date of this policy. The insured is required to resume normal business operations as promptly as possible and shall use all available means to eliminate any unnecessary delay.

The term "normal business operations" of the insured means the condition that would have existed had no loss occurred.

RESUMPTION OF OPERATIONS: It is a condition of this insurance that if the insured could reduce the loss resulting from the interruption of business:

1. by complete or partial resumption of operation of the property herein described, whether damaged or not; or
2. by making use of merchandise or other property at the locations described herein or elsewhere; or
3. by making use of stock at the locations described herein or elsewhere;

such reduction shall be taken into account in arriving at the amount of loss hereunder.

LIMITATIONS: The Company shall not be liable for any increase of loss which may be occasioned by:

1. interference at the described premises by strikers or other persons with rebuilding, repairing or replacing the property or with the resumption or continuation of business; or
2. the suspension, lapse or cancellation of any lease, license, contract or order unless such suspension, lapse or cancellation results directly from the interruption of business, and then the Company shall be liable for only such loss as affects the insured's earnings during, and limited to, the period of indemnity covered under this policy.

PROPERTY NOT COVERED

This policy does not cover:

1. exterior signs unless insured under Optional Coverages;
2. growing crops and lawns;
3. aircraft, automobiles, motortrucks and other vehicles subject to motor vehicle registration, or watercraft (including motors, equipment and accessories) while afloat;
4. bullion, money and securities.

PROPERTY SUBJECT TO LIMITATIONS

The following property is subject to the limitations described below:

1. valuable papers and records meaning books of account, manuscripts, abstracts, drawings, card index systems and other records (except film, tape, disc, drum, cell and other magnetic recording or storage media for electronic data processing) are covered for not exceeding the cost of blank books, cards or other blank material plus the cost of labor incurred by the insured for transcribing or copying such records; and
2. film, tape, disc, drum, cell and other magnetic recording or storage media for electronic data processing are covered for not exceeding the cost of such media in unexposed or blank form.

Ed. 8-76

SECTION I—PERILS AND EXCLUSIONS

**PERILS
INSURED**

This policy insures against all direct loss, subject to all the provisions contained herein, for loss caused by:

1. Fire.

2. Lightning.

3. Windstorm or Hail, excluding loss caused directly or indirectly:

    (a) by frost or cold weather, or by ice (other than hail), snow or sleet, whether driven by wind or not;

    (b) by rain, snow, sand or dust, whether. driven by wind or not. unless the building containing the property covered shall first sustain an actual damage to roof or walls by direct action of wind or hail. In such event, the Company shall be liable for loss to the interior of the building or the property covered therein as may be caused by rain, snow, sand or dust entering the building through openings in the roof or walls made by direct action of wind or hail;

    (c) to the following property when outside of buildings:

        (1) awnings of fabric or slat construction, including their supports;

        (2) radio or television antennas, including their lead-in wiring, masts, or towers.

4. Explosion. including direct loss resulting from the explosion of accumulated gases or unconsumed fuel within the firebox (or combustion chamber) of any fired vessel or within the flues or passages which conduct the gases of combustion therefrom.

    (a) This Company shall not be liable for loss by explosion of steam boilers, steam pipes, steam turbines or steam engines. if owned by. leased by, or operated under the control of the insured.

    (b) The following are not explosions within the intent or meaning of these provisions:

        (1) shock waves caused by aircraft, generally known as "sonic boom";

        (2) electric arcing;

        (3) rupture or bursting of rotating or moving parts of machinery caused by centrifugal force or mechanical breakdown;

        (4) water hammer;

        (5) rupture or bursting of water pipes;

        (6) rupture or bursting due to expansion or swelling of the contents of any building or structure, caused by or resulting from water;

        (7) rupture, bursting or operation of pressure relief devices.

5. Smoke, meaning sudden and accidental damage from smoke, other than smoke from agricultural smudging or industrial operations.

6. Aircraft or Vehicles, meaning only direct loss resulting from actual physical contact of an aircraft or a vehicle with the property covered or with the building(s) containing the property covered. except that loss by aircraft includes direct loss by objects falling therefrom.

    The Company shall not be liable for loss:

    (a) by any vehicle owned or operated by an insured or by any tenant of the described premises;

    (b) by any vehicle to fences, driveways, walks, or when outside of buildings, to trees, shrubs or plants;

    (c) to any aircraft or vehicle including its contents other than stocks of aircraft or vehicles in process of manufacture or for sale;

    The word "vehicles" means vehicles running on land or tracks but not aircraft. The word "aircraft" shall include self-propelled missiles and spacecraft.

7. Riot, Riot Attending a Strike or Civil Commotion. including direct loss by acts of striking employees of the owner or tenant(s) of the building(s) while occupied by said striking employees and shall also include direct loss from pillage and looting occurring during and at the immediate place of a riot,

riot attending a strike or civil commotion. The Company shall not be liable for loss resulting from damage to or destruction of the property due to change in temperature or humidity or interruption of operations whether or not such loss is covered by this policy as to other perils.

8. Vandalism or Malicious Mischief, meaning only the willful and malicious damage to or destruction of the property covered.

The Company shall not be liable for loss:

(a) to glass (other than glass building blocks) constituting part of a building, structure or an outside sign;

(b) by pilferage, theft, burglary or larceny except that this Company shall be liable for willful damage to the building(s) covered caused by burglars;

(c) by explosion of steam boilers, steam pipes, steam turbines or steam engines, if owned by, leased by,' or operated under the control of the named insured; or by rupture or bursting of rotating or moving parts of machinery caused by centrifugal force or mechanical breakdown; but this exclusion shall apply only to loss or damage to the object itself;

(d) from depreciation, delay, deterioration or loss of market; nor for any loss resulting from change in temperature or humidity;

(e) if the described building(s) had been vacant or unoccupied beyond a period of thirty (30) consecutive days immediately preceding the loss, whether or not such period commenced prior to the inception date of this policy.

9. Sprinkler Leakage, meaning leakage or discharge of water or other substance from within an automatic sprinkler, or direct loss caused by collapse or fall of a tank forming a part of such system.

This policy shall also cover, when the insured is the building owner, the cost of repairs or replacement of the automatic sprinkler system when damage sustained is caused directly by:

(1) breakage of any of its parts resulting in sprinkler leakage, or

(2) freezing.

The term "Automatic Sprinkler System" means any automatic fire protective system, including sprinklers, discharge nozzles and ducts, pipes, valves, fittings, tanks (including component parts and supports thereof), pumps and fire protection mains, all connected with and constituting a part of an automatic fire protective system; and nonautomatic fire protective systems, hydrants, standpipes or outlets supplied from an automatic fire protective system.

This Company shall not be liable for sprinkler leakage loss:

(a) occurring during and resulting from the making of repairs, alterations or extensions involving a wall or supports of a floor or roof, the installation of or change in any automatic sprinkler system at the premises described in the Declarations made a part of this policy after a period of fifteen (15) consecutive days from the beginning of such operations;

(b) while the building is vacant or unoccupied;

(c) caused directly or indirectly by fire, lightning, windstorm, earthquake, blasting, explosion, rupture or bursting of steam boilers or flywheels, riot, civil commotion, and water, except from within an automatic sprinkler system.

10. With respect to property in due course of transit, the following additional perils shall apply:

(a) collision, derailment or overturn of a transporting conveyance;

(b) stranding or sinking of vessels; and

(c) collapse of bridges, culverts, docks or wharves.

EXCLUSIONS The Company shall not be liable for loss:

1. occasioned directly or indirectly by enforcement of any ordinance or law regulating the construction, repair or demolition of buildings or structures;

2. caused by or resulting from power, heating or cooling failure, unless such failure results from physical damage to power, heating or cooling equipment

situated on premises where the property covered is located, caused by perils not otherwise excluded. Also, the Company shall not be liable under this exclusion for any loss resulting from riot, riot attending a strike, civil commotion, or vandalism or malicious mischief;

3. caused by any electrical injury or disturbance of electrical appliances, devices, fixtures, or wiring caused by electrical currents artifically generated unless fire as insured against ensues and then this Company shall be liable for only loss caused by the ensuing fire;

4. caused by, resulting from, contributed to, or aggravated by any of the following:

   (a) earth movement, including but not limited to earthquake, landslide, mudflow, earth sinking, earth rising or shifting;

   (b) flood, surface water, waves, tidal water or tidal waves, overflow of streams or other bodies of water, or spray from any of the foregoing, all whether driven by wind or not;

   (c) water which backs up through sewers or drains;

   (d) water below the surface of the ground including that which exerts pressure on or flows, seeps or leaks through sidewalks, driveways, foundations, walls, basement or other floors, or through doors, windows or any other openings in such sidewalks, driveways, foundations, walls or floors;

   unless fire or explosion as insured against ensues, and then this Company shall be liable for only loss caused by the ensuing fire or explosion;

5. due to delay or loss of market.

SECTION I—OPTIONAL COVERAGES

The following Optional Coverages are subject to all the terms and conditions applicable to Section I of this policy, except as otherwise provided for herein.

EMPLOYEE DISHONESTY

When coverage is designated in the Declarations for Employee Dishonesty, this policy provides coverage for loss of money and other business personal property by dishonest or fraudulent acts of the named insured's employees for an amount not exceeding the limit of liability shown in the Declarations and subject to the following conditions:

1. the limit of the Company's liability for loss shall not exceed the replacement cost thereof at the time of loss, provided, however, at the option of the insured, payment of the cost of replacing securities may be determined by the market value at the time of such settlement;

2. this policy shall not apply to loss due to any dishonest or fraudulent act by the insured or by any partner, joint venture, officer, director or trustee, whether acting alone or in collusion with others;

3. insurance hereunder shall be deemed cancelled as to any employee immediately upon discovery by the insured, or any partner or officer, of any fraudulent or dishonest act of such employee;

4. dishonest or fraudulent acts or a series of similar or related acts of any employee acting alone or in collusion with others during the policy period shall be deemed to be one occurrence for the purpose of applying the deductible and the limit of liability;

5. loss is covered only if discovered not later than one year from the end of the policy period, and then this insurance shall apply only to loss sustained during the policy period;

6. if more than one insured is covered under this policy, the liability of the Company shall not exceed the amount for which the Company would be liable if there was only one insured;

7. regardless of the number of years this policy shall continue in force, the limit of liability shown in the Declarations shall not be cumulative from year to year.

Loss Under Prior Bond or Policy: The Company agrees that this optional coverage applies to loss which would have been recoverable by the insured or by any predecessor in the interest of the insured under a prior bond or policy, except for the fact that the time within which to discover loss thereunder had expired; provided:

1. coverage under this optional coverage is substituted for the prior bond or insurance policy at the time the prior bond or insurance policy is terminated, cancelled or allowed to expire;
2. the insurance under this condition shall not increase the limit of liability under Employee Dishonesty coverage;
3. such loss would have been covered under this optional coverage had this coverage subject to all its conditions and limitations at the time of such substitution, been in force when the acts or events causing such loss occurred; and
4. recovery under this optional coverage shall not exceed the smaller of the following:
    (a) the amount which would have been recoverable under such prior bond or insurance policy had such prior bond or policy continued in force until the discovery of such loss; or
    (b) the amount which would have been recoverable under this optional coverage had this coverage been in force when such acts or events were committed.

EXTERIOR SIGNS

When coverage is designated in the Declarations for Exterior Signs, coverage is provided for an amount not exceeding the limits of liability shown in the Declarations for loss to all exterior signs which are the property of the insured or the property of others in the care, custody or control of the insured, on the premises described in the Declarations for direct physical loss excluding wear and tear, latent defect, corrosion or rust, or mechanical breakdown.

The PERILS AND EXCLUSIONS provisions contained in this policy, except the Section I—War Risk, Governmental Action and Nuclear Exclusions, do not apply to this optional coverage.

EXTERIOR GRADE FLOOR GLASS

When coverage is designated in the Declarations for Exterior Grade Floor Glass, this policy shall apply to all exterior grade floor and basement glass, including encasing frames and all lettering or ornamentation thereon, which are the property of the insured or the property of others in the care, custody or control of the insured in the building described in the Declarations, for direct physical loss excluding wear and tear, latent defect, corrosion or rust. Such insurance shall also include the expense of boarding up damaged openings, installing temporary plates and removing or replacing obstructions when necessary.

The PERILS AND EXCLUSIONS provisions contained in this policy, except the Section I—War Risk, Governmental Action and Nuclear Exclusions, do not apply to this optional coverage.

BURGLARY AND ROBBERY

When coverage is designated in the Declarations for Burglary and Robbery, this policy covers loss by burglary and robbery to:

1. business personal property, (excluding money and securities) on the described premises for an amount not to exceed 25% of the limit of liability of Coverage B—Business Personal Property; and
2. money and securities while in or on the described premises or within a bank or savings institution for an amount not to exceed $5,000;
3. money and securities while enroute to or from the described premises, bank or savings institution, or within the living quarters of the custodian of such funds for an amount not to exceed $2,000.

Burglary means the abstraction of insured property from within the premises by a person making felonious entry or exit therein or therefrom by actual force and violence, evidenced by visible marks made by tools, explosives, electricity, chemicals, or physical damage to the exterior or interior of the premises at the place of such entry or exit.

Robbery means the taking of insured property:

1. by violence inflicted upon a messenger or custodian;
2. by putting him in fear of violence;
3. by any other overt felonious act committed in his presence and of which he was actually cognizant, provided such other act is not committed by an officer, partner, or employee of the insured; and
4. from the person of a messenger or custodian who has been killed or rendered unconscious when such property is in his direct care and custody.

Ed. 8-76

EXCLUSIONS

The Company shall not be liable, as respects these perils, for any loss:

1. to household and personal effects contained in living quarters occupied by the insured, any officer, director, stockholder or partner of the insured or relatives of any of the foregoing;

2. to accounts, deeds, evidences of debt and manuscripts;

3. caused by unexplained or mysterious disappearance of property, or shortage of property disclosed on taking inventory;

4. caused by any fraudulent, dishonest or criminal act done by or at the instigation of any insured, partner or joint venture in or of any insured, or officer, director, or trustee of any insured; pilferage, appropriation or concealment of any property covered due to any fraudulent, dishonest, or criminal act of any employee while working or otherwise, or agent of any insured, or any person to whom the property covered may be entrusted;

5. caused by voluntary parting with title or possession of any property by the insured or others to whom the property may be entrusted if induced to do so by any fraudulent scheme, trick, device, or false pretense;

6. caused by delay or consequential loss of any nature;

7. occurring during a fire.

PROPERTY SUBJECT TO LIMITATIONS

The following property is subject to these additional limitations:

1. fur and fur garments are covered for not exceeding loss in the aggregate of $1,000 in any one occurrence;

2. jewelry and watches, watch movements, jewels, pearls, precious and semi-precious stones, gold, silver, platinum and other precious alloys or metals are covered for not exceeding loss in the aggregate of $1,000 in any one occurrence. This limitation shall not apply to jewelry and watches valued at $25 or less per item.

BOILER, PRESSURE VESSELS & AIR CONDITIONING EQUIPMENT

When coverage is designated in the Declarations for Boiler, Pressure Vessels and Air Conditioning Equipment, this policy provides coverage for loss from an Accident to an Object, as defined herein which is owned by, leased by, or operated under the control of the insured.

Boiler and Pressure Vessels—Object shall mean:

1. any steam heating or hot water heating boiler;

2. any condensate return tank used in connection with a steam heating boiler;

3. any expansion tank used in connection with a hot water heating boiler;

4. any hot water heater;

5. any other fired or unfired vessel used for maintenance or service of the premises where they are located and not used in processing or manufacturing;

6. any piping used in connection with a steam heating boiler which contains steam or condensate thereof, with valves, fittings, traps and separators thereon; and

7. any feedwater piping between any steam heating boiler and its feed pump or injector.

Air Conditioning Equipment—Object shall mean:

1. any "air conditioning unit" which has a capacity of more than 60,000 Btu/hr or less than 600,000 Btu/hr, including;

2. all interconnected vessels, coils and piping which contain refrigerant, or within which refrigerant is circulated, together with valves and fittings on such vessels, coils and piping;

3. any vessel, heated directly or indirectly, which functions as a generator, regenerator or concentrator and which forms a part of an absorption type unit;

4. all compressors, pumps, fans and blowers used solely with such unit, together with their driving electric motors;

5. all control equipment used solely with the unit, excluding any wiring or piping leading to or from the unit; and

6.   all vessels, radiators, inductors, convectors and coils, together with valves and fittings thereon, which are connected to or used with the unit and within which steam, water, brine or other solution is circulated for cooling, humidifying or space heating; and all piping containing water, brine or other solution interconnecting such vessels, radiators, inductors, convectors and coils, together with valves and fittings on such piping, but excluding any vessel, cooling tower, reservoir or other source of supply of cooling water for any condenser or compressor, together with any water piping leading to or from such source of supply.

Accident shall mean a sudden and accidental breakdown of the Object covered, which manifests itself at the time of the breakdown by physical damage to the Object covered which necessitates repair or replacement of such Object.

Accident shall not mean:

1.   depletion, deterioration, corrosion or erosion of material; wear and tear, leakage at any valve, fitting, shaft seal, gland packing, joint or connection;

2.   the breakdown of any vacuum tube, gas tube, brush, electronic computer, electronic data processing equipment, structure or foundation supporting the property covered or any part thereof;

3.   the functioning of any safety device or protective device; nor

4.   the explosion of gas or unconsumed fuel within the furnace of any Object or within the passages from the furnace of said Object to the atmosphere.

The Company shall not be liable for loss to:

1.   any boiler, fired vessel or air conditioning equipment while said equipment is undergoing hydrostatic, pneumatic or gas pressure test, or while said equipment is undergoing an insulation breakdown test or is being dried out;

2.   any boiler setting, any insulating or refractory material, any part of a boiler or vessel which is not under vacuum or internal pressure other than static pressure of contents (other than a condensate return tank), any reciprocating, rotating or electrical apparatus within or forming a part of a boiler or vessel, any piping not on the premises of the insured.

INSPECTION AND SUSPENSION

The Company shall be permitted but not obligated to inspect, at all reasonable times, any insured Object. Neither the Company's right to make inspections nor the making thereof nor any report thereon shall constitute an undertaking, on behalf of or for the benefit of the named insured or others, to determine or warrant that such Object is safe or healthful.

Upon discovery of a dangerous condition with respect to any Object, any representative of the Company may immediately suspend the insurance with respect to an Accident to said Object by written notice mailed or delivered to the insured at the mailing address shown in the Declarations, or at the location of the Object. The insured shall be credited the unearned portion of the premium paid for such suspended insurance, pro rata, for the period of suspension.

SECTION I—DEDUCTIBLE

DEDUCTIBLE

This deductible clause does not apply to coverage as provided for Loss of Income.

1.   The sum of $100 shall be deducted from the amount of loss to property in any one occurrence. This deductible shall apply:

   (a)   separately to each building, including personal property therein;

   (b)   separately to personal property in each building if no coverage is provided on the containing building;

   (c)   separately to personal property in the open (including within vehicles).

The aggregate amount of this deductible in any one occurrence shall not exceed $1,000.

2.   When coverage is designated in the Declarations for Employee Dishonesty or Burglary and Robbery, each loss under such coverage shall be adjusted separately and from the amount of each such adjusted loss the sum of $250 shall be deducted.

SECTION II—COMPREHENSIVE BUSINESS LIABILITY

COVERAGE E BUSINESS LIABILITY

The Company will pay on behalf of the **insured** all sums which the **insured** shall become legally obligated to pay as damages because of **bodily injury, property damage** or **personal injury** caused by an **occurrence** to which this insurance applies.

The total liability of the Company for all damages, including **completed operations hazard, products hazard,** and damages for care and loss of services, as a result of any one **occurrence** shall not exceed the limit of liability stated in the Declarations as applicable to each **occurrence.**

As stated in the Declarations however, the limit of liability shown under Coverage E—Business Liability is an aggregate limit for all **occurrences** during the policy period with respect to the **completed operations hazard** and **products hazard** combined.

FIRE LEGAL LIABILITY: The Company will also pay on behalf of the **insured** all sums which the **insured** shall become legally obligated to pay for **property damage** to structures rented to or occupied by the **named insured,** including fixtures permanently attached thereto, if such **property damage** arises out of fire or explosion. The total liability of the Company for all damages as a result of any one fire or explosion, or a series or combination of such fires and explosions, shall not exceed $50,000 for each **occurrence.**

The above limits shall apply regardless of the following:

1. the number of persons or organizations insured under this policy;
2. the number of persons or organizations who have sustained injury or damage;
3. the number of claims made or causes of action or suits brought because of injury or damage.

For the purpose of determining the limit of the Company's liability, all **bodily injury** and **property damage** arising out of a continuous or repeated exposure to substantially the same general conditions shall be considered as arising out of one **occurrence.**

RIGHT AND DUTY TO DEFEND

The Company shall have the right and duty to defend any claim or suit against the **insured** seeking damages payable under this policy, even though the allegations of the suit may be groundless, false or fraudulent. The Company may make such investigations and settlements of any claim or suit as it deems expedient. The Company is not obligated to pay any claim or judgment or to defend any suit after the applicable limit of the Company's liability has been exhausted by payment of judgments or settlements.

SUPPLEMENTARY PAYMENTS

The Company will pay, in addition to the applicable limit of liability:

1. all expenses incurred by the Company;
2. all cost taxed against the **insured** in any suit defended by the Company and all interest on the entire amount of any judgment which accrues after entry of the judgment and before the Company has paid or tendered or deposited in court that part of the judgment which does not exceed the limit of the Company's liability;
3. premium on appeal bonds in any such suit;
4. premiums on bonds to release attachments in any such suit for an amount not in excess of the applicable limit of liability of this policy;
5. expenses incurred by the **insured** for first aid to others at the time of an accident for **bodily injury** to which this policy applies; and
6. reasonable expenses incurred by the **insured** at the Company's request in assisting the Company in the investigation or defense of any claim or suit, including actual loss of earnings not to exceed $50 per day.

BUSINESS LIABILITY EXCLUSIONS

Under Coverage E, this policy does not apply:

1. to **bodily injury** or **property damage** arising out of the ownership, maintenance, operation, use, loading or unloading of:
   (a) any **automobile** or aircraft owned or operated by or rented or loaned to any **insured;** or
   (b) any other **automobile** or aircraft operated by any person in the course of his employment by any **insured.**

This exclusion does not apply to the parking of an **automobile** on premises owned by, rented to or controlled by the **named insured** or the ways immediately adjoining, if such **automobile** is not owned by or rented or loaned to any **insured.**

This exclusion does not apply to the use in the business of the **named insured** of a non-owned **private passenger automobile** by any person, other than the **named insured,** or the occasional and infrequent use of a non-owned **commercial automobile** by an employee of the **named insured** in such business;

2.   to **bodily injury** or **property damage** arising out of:

(a)   the ownership, maintenance, operation, use, loading or unloading of any land motor vehicle (1) not subject to motor vehicle registration, or (2) not designed for use principally off public roads while being used in any prearranged or organized racing, speed or demolition contest or in any stunting activity or in practice or preparation for any such contest or activity; or

(b)   the operation or use of any snowmobile or trailer designed for use therewith.

Exclusion 2(a) does not apply to any land motor vehicle not subject to motor vehicle registration provided such vehicle is maintained for use exclusively on premises owned by or rented to the **named insured** including the ways immediately adjoining;

3.   to **bodily injury** or **property damage** arising out of the ownership, maintenance, operation, use, loading or unloading of:

(a)   any watercraft owned or operated by or rented or loaned to any **insured;** or

(b)   any other watercraft operated by any person in the course of his employment by any **insured;**

but this exclusion does not apply to watercraft while ashore on premises owned by, rented to or controlled by the **named insured;**

4.   to liability assumed by the **insured** under any **contract** or agreement except a **contract** as defined in this policy;

5.   to **bodily injury** or **property damage** arising out of the discharge, dispersal, release or escape of smoke, vapors, soot, fumes, acids, alkalis, toxic chemicals, liquids or gases, waste materials or other irritants, contaminants or pollutants into or upon land, the atmosphere or any watercourse or body of water; but this exclusion does not apply if such discharge, dispersal, release or escape is sudden and accidental;

6.   to any obligation of which the **insured** or any carrier as his insurer may be held liable under any workers' or workmen's compensation, unemployment compensation or disability benefits law, or under any similar law;

7.   to **bodily injury** or **property damage** for which the **insured** or his indemnitee may be held liable:

(a)   as a person or organization engaged in the business of manufacturing, distributing, selling or serving alcoholic beverages; or

(b)   if not so engaged, as an owner or lessor of premises used for such purposes,

if such liability is imposed

(1)   by, or because of the violation of any statute, ordinance or regulation pertaining to the sale, gift, distribution or use of any alcoholic beverage, or

(2)   by reason of the selling, serving or giving of any alcoholic beverage to a minor or to a person under the influence of alcohol or which causes or contributes to the intoxication of any person;

but part (2) of this exclusion does not apply with respect to liability of the **insured** or his indemnitee as an owner or lessor described in (b) above.

This entire exclusion does not apply to liability imposed on the **insured** as the result of the giving or serving of alcoholic beverages at functions incidental to the **named insured's** business, provided the **named insured** is not engaged in the business of manufacturing, distributing, selling or serving of alcoholic beverages and provided further that there has been no intentional violation of any statute, regulation, or ordinance committed by or at the direction of the **insured;**

Ed. 8-76

8. to **bodily injury** or **property damage** due to rendering of or failure to render any professional service, including but not limited to:

    (a) legal, accounting, advertising, engineering, drafting, architectural, and

    (b) medical, dental, pharmacological, cosmetic, hearing aid, optical, or ear piercing services;

but with respect to pharmacological services, this exclusion does not apply to any **insured** doing business as a retail drug store;

9. to **bodily injury** to any employee of the **insured** arising out of and in the course of his employment by the **insured** or to any obligation of the **insured** to indemnify another because of damages arising out of such injury; but this exclusion does not apply to liability assumed by the **insured** under a **contract;**

10. with respect to insurance afforded to any employee of the **named insured** other than an executive officer:

    (a) to **bodily injury** to:

        (1) another employee of the **named insured** arising out of and in the course of his employment;

        (2) the **named insured,** or if the **named insured** is a partnership or joint venture, any partner or member thereof;

    (b) to **property damage** to property owned, occupied or used by, rented to, in the care, custody or control of, or over which physical control is being exercised for any purpose by:

        (1) another employee of the **named insured;**

        (2) the **named insured,** or if the **named insured** is a partnership or joint venture, any partner or member thereof;

11. to damage to property:

    (a) owned or occupied by or rented to the **insured,** or, except with respect to the use of elevators, to property held by the **insured** for sale or entrusted to the **insured** for storage or safekeeping; but this exclusion does not apply to **property damage** to structures rented to or occupied by the **named insured,** including fixtures permanently attached thereto, if such **property damage** arises out of fire or explosion for which coverage is specifically granted for Fire Legal Liability—Coverage E;

    (b) except with respect to liability under a written sidetrack agreement or the use of elevators to:

        (1) property while on premises owned by or rented to the **insured** for the purpose of having operations performed on such property by or on behalf of the **insured;**

        (2) tools or equipment while being used by the **insured** in performing his operations;

        (3) property in the custody of the **insured** which is to be installed, erected or used in construction by the **insured;**

        (4) that particular part of any property, not on premises owned by or rented to the **insured:**

            (i) upon which operations are being performed by or on behalf of the **insured** at the time of the **property damage** arising out of such operations;

            (ii) out of which any **property damage** arises; or

            (iii) the restoration, repair or replacement of which has been made or is necessary by reason of faulty workmanship thereon by or on behalf of the **insured;**

    (c) with respect to the **completed operations hazard,** to work performed by the **named insured** arising out of the work or any portion thereof, or out of materials, parts or equipment furnished in connection therewith;

12. to **property damage** to premises alienated by the **named insured** arising out of such premises or any part thereof;

13. to **property damage** to the **named insured's products** arising out of such **products** or any part of such **products;**

14. to loss of use of tangible property which has not been physically injured or destroyed resulting from:

    (a) a delay in or lack of performance by or on behalf of the **named insured** of any **contract** or agreement: or

    (b) the failure of the **named insured's products** or work performed by or on behalf of the **named insured** to meet the level of performance, quality, fitness or durability warranted or represented by the **named insured;**

    but this exclusion does not apply to loss of use of other tangible property resulting from the sudden and accidental physical injury to or destruction of the **named insured's products** or work performed by or on behalf of the **named insured** after such **products** or work have been put to use by any person or organization other than an **insured;**

15. to damages claimed for the withdrawal, inspection, repair, replacement, or loss of use of the **named insured's products** or work completed by or for the **named insured** or for any property of which such **products** or work form a part, if such **products,** work or property are withdrawn from the market or from use because of any known or suspected defect or deficiency therein;

16. to **personal injury** arising out of the willful violation of a penal statute or ordinance committed by or with knowledge or consent of any **insured;**

17. to **personal injury** arising out of any publication or utterance described in Item (b) of the Definitions of **personal injury:**

    (a) if the first injurious publication or utterance of the same or similar material by or on behalf of the **named insured** was made prior to the effective date of this insurance; or

    (b) concerning any organization or business enterprise or its **products** or services made by or at the direction of any **insured** with knowledge of the falsity thereof.

SECTION II—MEDICAL PAYMENTS

COVERAGE F MEDICAL PAYMENTS

The Company will pay up to $1,000 for reasonable **medical expenses** incurred by any person who requires medical services because of an accident arising out of business operations with respect to which the **named insured** is afforded coverage for **bodily injury** liability, except for liability arising out of use of a **non-owned automobile.**

The **medical expenses** must be incurred within one year after the accident and must result directly from the accident.

The Company will not pay more than $10,000 for all **medical expenses** incurred by all persons requiring medical services in any one accident.

As soon as practicable the injured person or someone on his behalf shall give to the Company written proof of claim for **medical expenses,** under oath if required, and shall after each request from the Company, execute authorization to enable the Company to obtain medical reports and copies of records. The injured person shall submit to physical examinations by physicians selected by the Company when and as often as the Company may reasonably require.

The Company may pay the injured person or any person or organization rendering the services and the payment shall reduce the amount payable hereunder for such injury. Payment hereunder shall not constitute an admission of liability of any person or, except hereunder, of the Company.

MEDICAL PAYMENTS EXCLUSIONS

Under Coverage F. this policy does not apply:

1. to **bodily injury** excluded under Coverage E—Business Liability;

2. to **bodily injury** to any person while engaged in maintenance and repair of the insured premises or alteration. demolition or new construction at such premises;

3. to **bodily injury** arising out of operations performed for the **named insured** by independent contractors ,other than (a) maintenance and repair of the insured premises, or (b) structural alterations at such premises which do not involve changing the size of or moving buildings or other structures;

4. to **bodily injury** to the **named insured,** any partner therein. any tenant or other person regularly residing on the insured premises or any employee of any of the foregoing if the **bodily injury** arises out of and in the course of his employment;

5. to **bodily injury** to any other tenant if the **bodily injury** occurs on that part of the insured premises rented from the **named insured** or to any employee of such tenant if the **bodily injury** occurs on the tenant's part of the insured premises and arises out of and in the course of his employment for the tenant;

6. to **bodily injury** to any person if any benefits for such **bodily injury** are payable or required to be provided under any workers' or workmen's compensation. unemployment compensation or disability benefits law. or under any similar law;

7. to any **medical expense** for services by the **named insured,** any employee thereof or any person or organization under **contract** to the **named insured** to provide such services;

8. to **bodily injury** to any person practicing, instructing or participating in any physical training, sport, athletic activity or contest;

9. to **bodily injury** included within the **completed operations hazard** or the **products hazard.**

SECTION I AND SECTION II—WAR RISK, GOVERNMENTAL ACTION AND NUCLEAR EXCLUSIONS

This policy under Section I and Section II shall not apply to loss, **bodily injury** or **property damage** caused, directly or indirectly, by or due to any act or condition incident to the following:

1. hostile or warlike action in time of peace or war. including action in hindering, combating or defending against an actual. impending or expected attack (a) by any government or sovereign power (de jure or de facto), or by any authority maintaining or using military, naval or air forces; or (b) by military, naval or air forces; or (c) by an agent of any such government. power, authority or forces, it being understood that any discharge, explosion or use of any weapon of war employing nuclear fission or fusion shall be conclusively presumed to be such a hostile or warlike action by such a government, power. authority or forces;

2. insurrection. rebellion. revolution. civil war. usurped power, or action taken by governmental authority in hindering. combating or defending against such an occurrence; seizure or destruction under quarantine or custom's regulations. confiscation by order of any government or public authority, or risks of contraband or illegal transportation or trade.

SECTION I ONLY

1. Nuclear Clause: The word "fire" in this policy is not intended to and does not embrace nuclear reaction or nuclear radiation or radioactive contamination. all whether controlled or uncontrolled. and loss by nuclear reaction or nuclear radiation or radioactive contamination is not intended to be and is not insured against by this policy. whether such loss be direct or indirect, proximate or remote. or be in whole or in part caused by. contributed to. or aggravated by "fire" or any other perils insured against by this policy. How-

ever, subject to the foregoing and all provisions of this policy, direct loss by "fire" resulting from nuclear reaction or nuclear radiation or radioactive contamination is insured against by this policy.

2. Nuclear Clause (Applicable only in New York): This policy does not cover loss or damage caused by nuclear reaction or nuclear radiation or radioactive contamination, all whether directly or indirectly resulting from an insured peril under this policy.

3. Nuclear Exclusion: Loss by nuclear reaction or nuclear radiation or radioactive contamination, all whether controlled or uncontrolled, or due to any act or condition incident to any of the foregoing is not insured against by this policy, whether such loss be direct or indirect, proximate or remote, or be in whole or in part caused by, contributed to, or aggravated by any of the perils insured against by this policy; and nuclear reaction or nuclear radiation or radioactive contamination, all whether controlled or uncontrolled, is not "explosion" or "smoke". This clause applies to all perils insured against hereunder except the peril of fire, which is otherwise provided for in the nuclear clause above.

| **SECTION II ONLY** | It is agreed that: |

1. The policy does not apply:

(a) Under any Liability Coverage, to **bodily injury** or **property damage**

(1) with respect to which an **insured** under the policy is also an **insured** under a nuclear energy liability policy issued by Nuclear Energy Liability Insurance Association, Mutual Atomic Energy Liability Insurance Association, Mutual Atomic Energy Liability Underwriters or Nuclear Insurance Association of Canada, or would be an **insured** under any such policy but for its termination upon exhaustion of its limit of liability; or

(2) resulting from the **hazardous properties** of **nuclear material** and with respect to which (a) any person or organization is required to maintain financial protection pursuant to the Atomic Energy Act of 1954, or any law amendatory thereof, or (b) the **insured** is, or had this policy not been issued would be, entitled to indemnity from the United States of America, or any agency thereof, under any agreement entered into by the United States of America, or any agency thereof, with any person or organization;

(b) Under any Medical Payments Coverage, or under any Supplementary Payments provision relating to first aid, to expenses incurred with respect to **bodily injury** resulting from the **hazardous properties** of **nuclear material** and arising out of the operation of a **nuclear facility** by any person or organization;

(c) Under any Liability Coverage, to **bodily injury** or **property damage** resulting from the **hazardous properties** of **nuclear material,** if

(1) the **nuclear material** (a) is at any **nuclear facility** owned by, or operated by or on behalf of, an **insured** or (b) has been discharged or dispersed therefrom;

(2) the **nuclear material** is contained in **spent fuel** or **waste** at any time possessed, handled, used, processed, stored, transported or disposed of by or on behalf of an **insured;** or

(3) the **bodily injury** or **property damage** arises out of the furnishing by an **insured** of services, materials, parts or equipment in connection with the planning, construction, maintenance, operation or use of any **nuclear facility,** but if such facility is located within the United States of America, its territories or possessions or Canada, this exclusion (c) applies only to **property damage** to such **nuclear facility** and any property thereat.

2. As used in this exclusion:

"**hazardous properties**" include radioactive, toxic or explosive properties;

"**nuclear material**" means **source material, special nuclear material** or **byproduct material;**

"source material", "special nuclear material", and "byproduct material" have the meanings given them in the Atomic Energy Act of 1954 or in any law amendatory thereof;

"spent fuel" means any fuel element or fuel component, solid or liquid, which has been used or exposed to radiation in a nuclear reactor;

"waste" means any waste material (1) containing byproduct material and (2) resulting from the operation by any person or organization of any nuclear facility included within the definition of nuclear facility under paragraph (1) or (2) thereof;

"nuclear facility" means

(a) any nuclear reactor,

(b) any equipment or device designed or used for (1) separating the iso-topes of uranium or plutonium, (2) processing or utilizing spent fuel, or (3) handling, processing or packaging waste,

(c) any equipment or device used for the processing, fabricating or alloy-ing of special nuclear material if at any time the total amount of such material in the custody of the insured at the premises where such equipment or device is located consists of or contains more than 25 grams of plutonium or uranium 233 or any combination thereof, or more than 250 grams of uranium 235,

(d) any structure, basin, excavation, premises or place prepared or used for the storage or disposal of waste,

and includes the site on which any of the foregoing is located, all operations conducted on such site and all premises used for such operations;

"nuclear reactor" means any apparatus designed or used to sustain nu-clear fission in a self-supporting chain reaction or to contain a critical mass of fissionable material;

"property damage" includes all forms of radioactive contamination of property.

GENERAL CONDITIONS

The following Conditions apply to Section I and Section II except as otherwise in-dicated. Additional Conditions or modifications of the following Conditions may appear in the specific coverage sections.

1. **PREMIUM**

All premiums for this insurance shall be computed in accordance with the Company's rules, rates, rating plans, premiums and minimum premiums applicable to the insurance afforded herein.

The Company may because of undeclared exposures or change in the in-sured's business operation, acquisition or use of locations not shown in the Declarations require an additional premium in accordance with the rates, rules and forms of the Company in effect at the time of the change.

Subject to the consent of this Company and subject to the premiums, rules and forms then in effect for this Company, this policy may be continued in force by payment of the required continuation premium for each successive one year period. Such continuation premium must be paid to the Company prior to each anniversary date of this policy. If not so paid, the policy shall expire on the first anniversary date that the said premium has not been re-ceived by the Company.

2. **CANCELLATION**

The **named insured** may cancel this policy by mailing to the Company written notice stating when thereafter such cancellation shall be effective. This policy may be cancelled by the Company for reasons of other than nonpayment of premium by mailing to the **named insured** and mortgagee at the mailing address shown in the Declarations, written notice stating when, not less than thirty (30) days thereafter, such cancellation shall be effective. The mailing or delivery of notice as aforesaid shall be sufficient proof of notice.

In the event of such cancellation the returned premium shall be computed as follows:

(a) if the Company cancels, for reasons other than nonpayment, the return premium shall be computed pro rata; and

(b) if the **named insured** cancels, the return premium shall be ninety percent (90%) of the unearned premium computed on a pro rata basis.

Premium adjustment may be made at the time cancellation is effected and, if not then made, shall be made as soon as practicable after cancellation becomes effective. The Company's check or the check of its representative mailed or delivered as aforesaid shall be a sufficient tender of any refund of premium due to the **insured** but payment or tender of unearned premium is not a condition of cancellation.

If the **insured** fails to make payment of the premium for this policy or any installment payment, whether payable directly to the Company or its agent or indirectly under any premium finance plan or extension of credit, this policy may be cancelled by mailing to the **insured** written notice stating that not less than ten (10) days thereafter, such cancellation shall be effective.

In the event of such cancellation the earned premium shall be computed pro rata.

3. **POLICY PERIOD, TERRITORY**
   (a) Section I of this policy applies only to loss to property during the policy period while such property is within or between the fifty states of the United States of America, District of Columbia and Puerto Rico unless otherwise limited.
   (b) Section II of this policy applies only to:
       (1) **bodily injury** or **property damage** which occurs within the policy territory; or
       (2) **personal injury** committed during the policy period within the policy territory.
   (c) As respects Section II of this policy, the term policy territory means:
       (1) the United States of America, its territories or possessions, or Canada; or
       (2) international waters or air space, provided the **bodily injury** or **property damage** does not occur in the course of travel or transportation to or from any other country, state or nation; or
       (3) anywhere in the world with respect to damages because of **bodily injury** or **property damage** arising out of a **product** which was sold for use or consumption within the territory described in paragraph (1) above, provided the original suit for such damages is brought within such territory.

4. **TIME OF INCEPTION**
   To the extent that coverage in this policy replaces coverage in other policies terminating 12:01 A.M. (Standard Time) on the inception date of this policy, this policy shall be effective at 12:01 A.M. (Standard Time) instead of at Noon Standard Time.

5. **CONCEALMENT OR FRAUD**
   This policy is void if any **insured** has intentionally concealed or misrepresented any material fact or circumstance relating to this insurance.

6. **ASSIGNMENT**
   Assignment of interest under this policy shall not bind the Company until its consent is endorsed hereon. However, if the **named insured** shall die, this insurance shall apply:
   (a) to the **named insured's** legal representative, as the **named insured,** but only while acting within the scope of his duties as such; or
   (b) to the person having temporary custody of the property of the **named insured** but only until the appointment and qualification of the legal representative.

7. **SUBROGATION**
   (a) In the event of any payment under this policy, the Company shall be subrogated to all the **insured's** rights of recovery against any person or organization and the **insured** shall execute and deliver instruments and papers and do whatever else is necessary to secure such rights. The **insured** shall do nothing after loss to prejudice such rights.
   (b) The Company shall not be bound to pay any loss if the **insured** has impaired any right of recovery for loss; however, it is agreed that the **insured** may:

(1) as respects property while on the premises of the **insured,** release others in writing from liability for loss prior to loss, and such release shall not affect the right of the **insured** to recover hereunder; and

(2) as respects property in transit, accept such bills of lading, receipts or contracts of transportation as are ordinarily issued by carriers containing a limitation as to the value of such goods or merchandise.

8. **INSPECTION AND AUDIT**

The Company shall be permitted but not obligated to inspect the **named insured's** property and operations at any time. Neither the Company's right to make inspections nor the making thereof nor any report thereon shall constitute an undertaking, on behalf of or for the benefit of the **named insured** or others, to determine or warrant that such property or operations are safe or healthful, or are in compliance with any law, rule or regulation.

The Company may examine and audit the **named insured's** books and records at any time during the policy period and extensions thereof and within three years after the final termination of this policy, as far as they relate to the subject matter of this insurance.

9. **LIBERALIZATION CLAUSE**

In the event any filing is submitted to the insurance supervisory authorities on behalf of the Company, and:

(a) the filing is approved or accepted by the insurance authorities to be effective while this policy is in force or within 45 days prior to its inception; and

(b) the filing includes insurance forms or other provisions that would extend or broaden this insurance by endorsement or substitution of form, without additional premium;

the benefit of such extended or broadened insurance shall inure to the benefit of the **insured** as though the endorsement or substitution of form had been made a part hereof.

10. **OTHER INSURANCE**

This insurance shall apply only as excess insurance over any other valid and collectible insurance which would apply in the absence of this policy, except insurance written specifically to cover as excess over the limits of liability applicable to Section II of this policy.

The insurance provided under Coverage E—Business Liability with respect to property in the care, custody or control of the **insured** shall also be excess over any valid and collectible property insurance (including any deductible portion thereof) available to the **insured** including but not limited to Fire and Extended Coverage, Builders' Risk Coverage or Installation Risk Coverage.

11. **INSURANCE UNDER MORE THAN ONE COVERAGE, PART OR ENDORSEMENT**

In the event that more than one coverage, part or endorsement of this policy insures the same loss, damage or claim, the Company shall not be liable for more than the actual loss, or damage sustained by the **insured.**

12. **REPLACEMENT OF FORMS AND ENDORSEMENTS**

If the policy period in the Declarations does not indicate a termination date, the policy being issued on a continuous basis, the Company may substitute or add forms and endorsements which are authorized for its use upon any anniversary date in accordance with rules of its manuals.

13. **WAIVER OR CHANGE OF PROVISIONS**

The terms of this insurance shall not be waived, changed or modified except by endorsement issued to form a part of this policy.

CONDITIONS APPLICABLE TO SECTION I

1. **REPLACEMENT COST**

   (a) With the exception of loss to Money and Securities, loss shall be adjusted on the basis of the replacement cost value of the property insured hereunder, but the limit of liability of the Company shall not exceed the least of:

      (1) the full cost of replacement of such property at the same site with new material of like kind and quality without deduction for depreciation; or

      (2) the cost of repairing the insured property within reasonable time; or

      (3) the limit of liability applicable to such property shown on the Declarations; or

      (4) the amount actually and necessarily expended in repairing or replacing said property or any part thereof.

   (b) The Company shall not be liable for payment of loss on a replacement cost basis unless and until actual repair or replacement is completed.

   The insured, however, may elect not to repair or replace, in which event loss settlement shall be made on an actual cash value basis rather than on a replacement cost basis. Should the insured elect this option, the insured's right to make further claim on a replacement cost basis shall not be prejudiced provided the Company is notified in writing within 180 days after loss of the insured's intent to make such further claim.

2. **DUTIES OF THE NAMED INSURED AFTER A LOSS**

   In case of loss, the named insured shall:

   (a) give immediate written notice of such loss to the Company;

   (b) protect the building and personal property from further damage, make reasonable temporary repairs required to protect the property, and keep an accurate record of repair expenditures;

   (c) prepare an inventory of damaged personal property showing in detail the quantity, description, replacement cost and amount of loss. Attach to the inventory all bills, receipts and related documents that substantiate the figures in the inventory;

   (d) exhibit the remains of the damaged property as often as may be reasonably required by the Company and submit to examination under oath;

   (e) submit to the Company within 60 days after requested a signed, sworn statement of loss which sets forth, to the best of the named insured's knowledge and belief:

      (1) the time and cause of loss;

      (2) interest of the insured and all others in the property involved and all encumbrances on the property;

      (3) other policies of insurance which may cover the loss;

      (4) changes in title or occupancy of the property during the term of the policy;

      (5) specifications of any damaged building and detailed estimates for repair of the damage;

      (6) an inventory of damaged personal property described in (c) above;

      (7) receipts for extra expenses incurred and records supporting the rental value.

3. **APPRAISAL**

   If the named insured and the Company fail to agree on the amount of the loss, either can demand that the amount of loss be set by appraisal. If either party makes a written demand for appraisal, each shall select a competent independent appraiser. Each shall notify the other of the selected appraiser's identity within twenty (20) days of receipt of the written demand.

The two appraisers shall select a competent, impartial umpire. If the appraisers are unable to agree upon an umpire within fifteen (15) days, the named insured or the Company may petition a judge of a Court of Record in the state where the insured premises is located to select an umpire.

The appraisers shall then set the amount of the loss. If the appraisers submit a written report of an agreement to the Company, the amount agreed upon shall be the amount of the loss. If the appraisers fail to agree within a reasonable time, they shall submit their differences to the umpire. Written agreement signed by any two of these three shall set the amount of loss.

Each appraiser shall be paid by the party selecting that appraiser. Other expenses of the appraisal and compensation of the umpire shall be paid equally by the named insured and the Company.

4. **COMPANY OPTIONS**

If the Company gives notice within thirty (30) days after it has received a signed, sworn statement of loss, it shall have the option to take all or any part of the property damaged at an agreed value, or to repair, rebuild or replace it with equivalent property.

5. **ABANDONMENT OF PROPERTY**

The Company need not accept any property abandoned by an insured.

6. **PAYMENT OF LOSS**

The Company will pay all adjusted claims within thirty (30) days after presentation and acceptance of the proof of loss.

7. **PRIVILEGE TO ADJUST WITH OWNER**

(a) Except as provided in (b) below, or unless another payee is specifically named in the policy, loss, if any, shall be adjusted with and payable to the named insured.

(b) In the event claim is made for damage to property of others held by the insured, the right to adjust such loss or damage with the owner or owners of the property is reserved to the Company and the receipt of payment by such owner or owners in satisfaction thereof shall be in full satisfaction of any claim of the insured for which such payment has been made.

If legal proceedings be taken to enforce a claim against the insured as respects any such loss or damage, the Company reserves the right at its option, without expense to the insured, to conduct and control the defense on behalf of and in the name of the insured. No action of the Company in such regard shall increase the liability of the Company under this policy, nor increase the limits of liability specified in the policy.

8. **SUIT**

No suit shall be brought on this policy unless the insured has complied with all the policy provisions and has commenced the suit within one year after the loss occurs.

9. **VACANCY OR UNOCCUPANCY**

(a) This Company shall not be liable for loss occurring while a described building, whether intended for occupancy by owner or tenant, is vacant beyond a period of sixty (60) consecutive days. "Vacant" or "Vacancy" means containing no contents pertaining to operations or activities customary to occupancy of the building, but a building in process of construction shall not be deemed vacant.

(b) Permission is granted for unoccupancy.

10. **MORTGAGE CLAUSE—APPLICABLE ONLY TO BUILDINGS**

This clause is effective if a mortgagee is named in the Declarations. The word "Mortgagee" includes "Trustee". Loss to buildings shall be payable to the named mortgagee, as interest may appear under all present or future mortgages on the buildings described in the Declarations in order of precedence of mortgages on them.

As it applies to the interest of any mortgagee designated in the Declarations, this insurance shall not be affected by any of the following:

(a) any act or neglect of the mortgagor or owner of the described buildings;

(b) any foreclosure or other proceedings or notice of sale relating to the property;

(c) any change in the title or ownership of the property;

(d) occupancy of the premises for purposes more hazardous than are permitted by this policy;

provided, that in case the mortgagor or owner shall neglect to pay any premium due under this policy, the mortgagee shall, on demand, pay the premium.

The mortgagee shall notify the Company of any change of ownership or occupancy or increase of hazard which shall come to the knowledge of the mortgagee. Unless permitted by this policy, such change of ownership or occupancy or increase of hazard shall be noted on the policy and the mortgagee shall on demand pay the premium for the increased hazard for the term it existed under this policy. If such premium is not paid, this policy shall be null and void.

The Company reserves the right to cancel this policy at any time as provided by its terms. If so cancelled, this policy shall continue in force for the benefit only of the mortgagee for ten days after notice to the mortgagee of such cancellation and shall then cease. The Company shall have the right to cancel this agreement on ten days notice to the mortgagee.

When the Company shall pay the mortgagee any sum for loss under this policy, and shall claim that, as to the mortgagor or owner, no liability therefor existed, the Company shall, to the extent of such payment, be thereupon legally subrogated to all the rights of the mortgagee to whom such payment shall have been made, under the mortgage debt. In lieu of taking such subrogation, the Company may, at its option, pay to the mortgagee the whole principal due or to grow due on the mortgage, with interest accrued and shall thereupon receive a full assignment and transfer of the mortgage and of all such other securities. However, no subrogation shall impair the right of the mortgagee to recover the full amount of said mortgagee's claim.

11. **RECOVERIES**

In the event the Company has made a payment for loss under the policy and a subsequent recovery is made of the lost or damaged property, the insured shall be entitled to all recoveries in excess of the amount paid by the Company, less only the actual cost of effecting such recoveries.

12. **LOSS CLAUSE**

Any loss hereunder shall not reduce the amount of this insurance.

13. **NO BENEFIT TO BAILEE**

This insurance shall not inure directly or indirectly to the benefit of any carrier or other bailee.

14. **NO CONTROL**

This insurance shall not be prejudiced:

(a) by any act or neglect of the owner of any building if the insured is not the owner thereof, or by any act or neglect of any occupant (other than the insured) of any building, when such act or neglect of the owner or occupant is not within the control of the insured; or

(b) by failure of the insured to comply with any warranty or condition contained in any endorsement attached to this policy with regard to any portion of the premises over which the insured has no control.

CONDITIONS APPLICABLE TO SECTION II

1. **ACTION AGAINST THE COMPANY**

   No action shall lie against the Company unless:

   (a) there shall have been full compliance with all of the terms of this policy; and

   (b) the amount of the **insured's** obligation to pay shall have been finally determined either by judgment against the **insured** after actual trial or by written agreement of the **insured,** the claimant and the Company.

   Any person or organization or the legal representative thereof who has secured such judgment or written agreement shall thereafter be entitled to recover under this policy to the extent of insurance afforded by this policy.

   No person or organization shall have any right under this policy to join the Company as a party to any action against the **insured** to determine the **insured's** liability nor shall the Company be impleaded by the **insured** or his legal representative.

   Bankruptcy or insolvency of the **insured** or of the **insured's** estate shall not relieve the Company of its obligations hereunder.

2. **FINANCIAL RESPONSIBILITY LAWS**

   This policy may not be certified as proof of financial responsibility under the provisions of any financial responsibility law.

3. **INSURED'S DUTIES IN THE EVENT OF OCCURRENCE, CLAIM OR SUIT**

   (a) In the event of an **occurrence,** the **insured** shall give to the Company or its authorized agents, as soon as practicable, written notice containing:

   (1) particulars sufficient to identify the **insured;**

   (2) reasonably obtainable information with respect to the time, place and circumstances; and

   (3) names and addresses of the injured and of available witnesses.

   (b) If claim is made or suit is brought against the **insured,** the **insured** shall immediately forward to the Company every demand, notice, summons or other process received by him or his representative.

   (c) The **insured** shall cooperate with the Company, and upon the Company's request, assist in the following:

   (1) making of settlements;

   (2) conducting suits;

   (3) enforcing any right of contribution or indemnity against any person or organization who may be liable to the **insured** because of injury or damage with respect to which insurance is afforded under this policy.

   (d) The **insured** shall attend hearings and trials and assist in securing and giving evidence and obtaining the attendance of witnesses.

   (e) The **insured** shall not, except at his own cost, voluntarily make any payment, assume any obligation or incur any expense other than for first aid to others at the time of accident.

SECTION II—DEFINITIONS

The Definition Section is an integral part of the policy and shall be applied as if the definitions appearing were included each time the words they define are used in the policy.

When used in the provisions applicable to Section II of this policy (including endorsements forming a part hereof):

automobile means a land motor vehicle, trailer or semi-trailer designed for travel on public roads (including any machinery or apparatus attached thereto);

bodily injury means bodily injury, sickness or disease sustained by any person which occurs during the policy period, including death at any time resulting therefrom;

completed operations hazard includes **bodily injury** and **property damage** arising out of operations or reliance upon a representation or warranty made at any time with respect thereto, but only if the **bodily injury** or **property damage** occurs after such operations have been completed or abandoned and occurs away from premises owned by or rented to the **named insured.** Operations include materials, parts or equipment furnished in connection therewith. Operations shall be deemed completed at the earliest of the following times:

(a) when all operations to be performed by or on behalf of the **named insured** under the **contract** have been completed;

(b) when all operations to be performed by or on behalf of the **named insured** at the site of the operations have been completed; or

(c) when the portion of the work out of which the injury or damage arises has been put to its intended use by any person or organization other than another contractor or subcontractor engaged in performing operations for a principal as a part of the same project.

Operations which may require further service or maintenance work, or correction, repair or replacement because of any defect or deficiency, but which are otherwise complete, shall be deemed completed.

The **completed operations hazard** does not include **bodily injury** or **property damage** arising out of (a) operations in connection with the transportation of property, unless the **bodily injury** or **property damage** arises out of a condition in or on a vehicle created by the loading or unloading thereof, or (b) the existence of tools, uninstalled equipment or abandoned or unused materials;

commercial automobile means an **automobile** of the truck type or other **automobile** designed for the transportation of material or merchandise over public roads;

contract means any written contract or agreement wherein the **named insured** has expressly assumed liability for damages to which this policy applies, provided, that such liability shall not be construed as including liability under a warranty of the fitness or quality of the **named insured's products** or a warranty that work performed by or on behalf of the **insured** will be done in a workmanlike manner;

insured means each of the following to the extent set forth below:

(a) if the **named insured** is designated in the Declarations as an individual, the person so designated but only with respect to the conduct of a business of which he is the sole proprietor, and the spouse of the **named insured** with respect to the conduct of such a business;

(b) if the **named insured** is designated in the Declarations as a partnership or joint venture, the partnership or joint venture so designated and any partner or member thereof but only with respect to his liability as such;

(c) if the **named insured** is designated in the Declarations as other than an individual, partnership or joint venture, the organization so designated and any executive officer, member of the board of trustees, directors or governors or stockholder thereof while acting within the scope of his duties as such;

Ed. 8-76

(d) any employee of the **named insured** while acting within the scope of his duties as such;

(e) any person or organization while acting as real estate manager for the **named insured.**

The insurance afforded applies separately to each **insured** against whom claim is made, or suit is brought, except with respect to the limit of the Company's liability.

This insurance does not apply to **bodily injury** or **property damage** or **personal injury** arising out of the conduct of any partnership or joint venture of which the **insured** is a partner or member and which is not designated in this policy as a **named insured;**

medical expenses means expenses for necessary medical, surgical, x-ray and dental services, including prosthetic devices and necessary ambulance, hospital, professional nursing and funeral services;

named insured means the person or organization named in Item 1 of the Declarations of this policy;

named insured's products means goods or products manufactured, sold, handled or distributed by the **named insured** or by others trading under his name, including any container thereof (other than a vehicle), but the **named insured's products** shall not include a vending machine or any property other than such container rented to or located for use of others but not sold;

non-owned automobile means an **automobile** not owned in whole or in part by, registered in the name of, hired by, leased by or loaned to the **named insured,** or if the **named insured** is a partnership, any partner therein;

occurrence means an accident, including continuous or repeated exposure to conditions, which results in **bodily injury** or **property damage** neither expected nor intended from the standpoint of the **insured** and with respect to **personal injury,** the commission of an offense, or a series of similar or related offenses;

personal injury means injury which arises out of one or more of the following offenses committed in the conduct of the **named insured's** business:

(a) false arrest, detention or imprisonment, or malicious prosecution;

(b) the publication or utterance of a libel or slander or of other defamatory or disparaging material, or a publication or utterance in violation of an individual's right of privacy; except publications or utterances in the course of or related to advertising, broadcasting or telecasting activities conducted by or on behalf of the **named insured;**

(c) wrongful entry or eviction, or other invasion of the right of private occupancy;

private passenger automobile means a four-wheel private passenger or station wagon type **automobile;**

products hazard includes **bodily injury** and **property damage** arising out of the **named insured's products** or reliance upon a representation or warranty made at any time with respect thereto, but only if the **bodily injury** or **property damage** occurs:

(a) after physical possession of such property has been relinquished to others; and

(b) away from premises owned by, or rented to the **named insured.**

However, if the business of the **named insured** includes the selling, handling or distribution of the **insured's product** for consumption on premises owned by or rented to the **named insured** part (b) above shall not apply.

property damage means (a) physical injury to or destruction of tangible property which occurs during the policy period, including the loss of use thereof at any time resulting therefrom, or (b) loss of use of tangible property which has not been physically injured or destroyed provided such loss of use is caused by an **occurrence** during the policy period.

Appendix E

AGE	LIVING AT BEGINNING OF YEAR	DYING DURING YEAR	DEATHS PER 1,000	AGE	LIVING AT BEGINNING OF YEAR	DYING DURING YEAR	DEATHS PER 1,000
0	10,000,000	70,800	7.08	50	8,762,306	72,902	8.32
1	9,929,200	17,475	1.76	51	8,689,404	79,160	9.11
2	9,911,725	15,066	1.52	52	8,610,244	85,758	9.96
3	9,896,659	14,449	1.46	53	8,524,486	92,832	10.89
4	9,882,210	13,835	1.40	54	8,431,654	100,337	11.90
5	9,868,375	13,322	1.35	55	8,331,317	108,307	13.00
6	9,855,053	12,812	1.30	56	8,223,010	116,849	14.21
7	9,842,241	12,401	1.26	57	8,106,161	125,970	15.54
8	9,829,840	12,091	1.23	58	7,980,191	135,663	17.00
9	9,817,749	11,879	1.21	59	7,844,528	145,830	18.59
10	9,805,870	11,865	1.21	60	7,698,698	156,592	20.34
11	9,794,005	12,047	1.23	61	7,542,106	167,736	22.24
12	9,781,958	12,325	1.26	62	7,374,370	179,271	24.31
13	9,769,633	12,896	1.32	63	7,195,099	191,174	26.57
14	9,756,737	13,562	1.39	64	7,003,925	203,394	29.04
15	9,743,175	14,225	1.46	65	6,800,531	215,917	31.75
16	9,728,950	14,983	1.54	66	6,584,614	228,749	34.74
17	9,713,967	15,737	1.62	67	6,355,865	241,777	38.04
18	9,698,230	16,390	1.69	68	6,114,088	254,835	41.68
19	9,681,840	16,846	1.74	69	5,859,253	267,241	45.61
20	9,664,994	17,300	1.79	70	5,592,012	278,426	49.79
21	9,647,694	17,655	1.83	71	5,313,586	287,731	54.15
22	9,630,039	17,912	1.86	72	5,025,855	294,766	58.65
23	9,612,127	18,167	1.89	73	4,731,089	299,289	63.26
24	9,593,960	18,324	1.91	74	4,431,800	301,894	68.12
25	9,575,636	18,481	1.93	75	4,129,906	303,011	73.37
26	9,557,155	18,732	1.96	76	3,826,895	303,014	79.18
27	9,538,423	18,981	1.99	77	3,523,881	301,997	85.70
28	9,519,422	19,324	2.03	78	3,221,884	299,829	93.06
29	9,500,118	19,760	2.08	79	2,922,055	295,683	101.19
30	9,480,358	20,193	2.13	80	2,626,372	288,848	109.98
31	9,460,165	20,718	2.19	81	2,337,524	278,983	119.35
32	9,439,447	21,239	2.25	82	2,058,541	265,902	129.17
33	9,418,208	21,850	2.32	83	1,792,639	249,858	139.38
34	9,396,358	22,551	2.40	84	1,542,781	231,433	150.01
35	9,373,807	23,528	2.51	85	1,311,348	211,311	161.14
36	9,350,279	24,685	2.64	86	1,100,037	190,108	172.82
37	9,325,594	26,112	2.80	87	909,929	168,455	185.13
38	9,299,482	27,991	3.01	88	741,474	146,997	198.25
39	9,271,491	30,132	3.25	89	594,477	126,303	212.46
40	9,241,359	32,622	3.53	90	468,174	106,809	228.14
41	9,208,737	35,362	3.84	91	361,365	88,813	245.77
42	9,173,375	38,253	4.17	92	272,552	72,480	265.93
43	9,135,122	41,382	4.53	93	200,072	57,881	289.30
44	9,093,740	44,741	4.92	94	142,191	45,026	316.66
45	9,048,999	48,412	5.35	95	97,165	34,128	351.24
46	9,000,587	52,473	5.83	96	63,037	25,250	400.56
47	8,948,114	56,910	6.36	97	37,787	18,456	488.42
48	8,891,204	61,794	6.95	98	19,331	12,916	668.15
49	8,829,410	67,104	7.60	99	6,415	6,415	1,000.00

Appendix F

Commissioner of Insurance
State of Alabama
Administrative Building
Montgomery, Alabama 36104
Tel. # (205) 832-6140

Director of Insurance
State of Alaska
Pouch "D"
Juneau, Alaska 99811
Tel. # (907) 465-2515

Insurance Commissioner
American Samoa
Office of the Governor
Pago Pago, American Samoa 96797

Director of Insurance
State of Arizona
1601 West Jefferson
Phoenix, Arizona 85007
Tel. # (602) 255-4862

Insurance Commissioner
State of Arkansas
400-18 University Tower Bldg.
Little Rock, Arkansas 72204
Tel. # (501) 371-1325

Insurance Commissioner
State of California
600 South Commonwealth
Los Angeles, California 90005
Tel. # (213) 736-2551

Commissioner of Insurance
State of Colorado
106 State Office Building
Denver, Colorado 80203
Tel. # (303) 839-3201

Insurance Commissioner
State of Connecticut
Room 425 State Office Building
Hartford, Connecticut 06115
Tel. # (203) 566-5275

Insurance Commissioner
State of Delaware
21 The Green
Dover, Delaware 19901
Tel. # (302) 678-4251

Superintendent of Insurance
District of Columbia
614 H Street, NW, Suite 512
Washington, D. C. 20001
Tel. # (202) 727-1273

Insurance Commissioner
State of Florida
State Capitol
Tallahassee, Florida 32304
Tel. # (904) 488-7056

Insurance Commissioner
State of Georgia
238 State Capitol
Atlanta, Georgia 30334
Tel. # (404) 656-2056

Insurance Commissioner
P. O. Box 2796
Agana, Guam 96910

Insurance Commissioner
State of Hawaii
P. O. Box 3614
Honolulu, Hawaii 96811
Tel. # (808) 548-7505

Director of Insurance
State of Idaho
700 West State Street
Boise, Idaho 83720
Tel. # (208) 384-2250

Director of Insurance
State of Illinois
320 West Washington
Springfield, Illinois 62767
Tel. # (312) 793-2420

473

Commissioner of Insurance
State of Indiana
509 State Office Building
Indianapolis, Indiana 46204
Tel. # (317) 232-2385

Commissioner of Insurance
State of Iowa
State Office Building
Des Moines, Iowa 50319
Tel. # (515) 281-5705

Commissioner of Insurance
State of Kansas
State Office Building
Topeka, Kansas 66612
Tel. # (913) 296-3071

Insurance Commissioner
State of Kentucky
151 Elkhorn Ct.
Frankfort, Kentucky 40601
Tel. # (502) 564-3630

Commissioner of Insurance
State of Louisiana
P. O. Box 44214
Baton Rouge, Louisiana 70804
Tel. # (504) 342-5328

Superintendent of Insurance
State of Maine
State Office Building
Augusta, Maine 04333
Tel. # (207) 289-3141

Insurance Commissioner
State of Maryland
One South Calvert Bldg.
Baltimore, Maryland 21202
Tel. # (301) 383-5690

Commissioner of Insurance
State of Massachusetts
100 Cambridge St.
Boston, Massachusetts 02202
Tel. # (617) 727-3333

Commissioner of Insurance
State of Michigan
P. O. Box 30220
Lansing, Michigan 18909
Tel. # (517) 374-9724

Commissioner of Insurance
State of Minnesota
500 Metro Square Building
St. Paul, Minnesota 55101
Tel. # (612) 296-6907

Commissioner of Insurance
State of Mississippi
P. O. Box 79
Jackson, Mississippi 39205
Tel. # (601) 354-7711

Director of Insurance
State of Missouri
P. O. Box 690
Jefferson City, Missouri 65101
Tel. # (314) 751-2451

Commissioner of Insurance
State of Montana
Mitchell Building
Helena, Montana 59601
Tel. # (406) 449-2040

Director of Insurance
State of Nebraska
301 Centennial Mall, South
Lincoln, Nebraska 68509
Tel. # (402) 471-2201, Ext. 238

Insurance Commissioner
State of Nevada
Nye Building
Carson City, Nevada 89710
Tel. # (702) 885-4270

Insurance Commissioner
State of New Hampshire
169 Manchester St.
Concord, New Hampshire 03301
Tel. # (603) 271-2261

Commissioner of Insurance
State of New Jersey
201 East State St.
Trenton, New Jersey 08625
Tel. # (609) 292-5363

Superintendent of Insurance
State of New Mexico
P. O. Drawer 1269
Santa Fe, New Mexico 87501
Tel. # (505) 827-2451

Superintendent of Insurance
State of New York
Two World Trade Center
New York, New York 10047
Tel. # (212) 488-4124

Commissioner of Insurance
State of North Carolina
P. O. Box 26387
Raleigh, North Carolina 27611
Tel. # (919) 733-7343

Commissioner of Insurance
State of North Dakota
Capitol Building, Fifth Floor
Bismarck, North Dakota 58505
Tel. # (701) 224-2444

Director of Insurance
State of Ohio
2100 Stella Court
Columbus, Ohio 43215
Tel. # (614) 466-3584

Insurance Commissioner
State of Oklahoma
408 Will Rogers Memorial Building
Oklahoma City, Oklahoma 73105
Tel. # (405) 521-2828

Insurance Commissioner
State of Oregon
158-12th Street, NE
Salem, Oregon 93710
Tel. # (503) 378-4271

Commissioner of Insurance
State of Pennsylvania
Strawberry Square, 13 & 14 Floor
Harrisburg, Pennsylvania 17120
Tel. # (717) 787-5173

Commissioner of Insurance
Puerto Rico
P. O. Box 3508
San Juan, Puerto Rico 00904
Tel. # (809) 724-6565

Insurance Commissioner
State of Rhode Island
100 North Main Street
Providence, Rhode Island 02903
Tel. # (401) 277-2223

Insurance Commissioner
State of South Carolina
2711 Middleburg Drive
Columbia, South Carolina 29204
Tel. # (803) 758-2185

Director of Insurance
State of South Dakota
Insurance Building
Pierre, South Dakota 57501
Tel. # (605) 773-3563

Commissioner of Insurance
State of Tennessee
114 State Office Building
Nashville, Tennessee 37219
Tel. # (615) 741-2241

Commissioner of Insurance
State of Texas
1110 San Jacinto Boulevard
Austin, Texas 78786
Tel. # (512) 475-2273

Commissioner of Insurance
State of Utah
326 South 5th East
Salt Lake City, Utah 84102
Tel. # (801) 533-5611

Commissioner of Insurance
State of Vermont
State Office Building
Montpelier, Vermont 05602
Tel. # (802) 828-3301

Commissioner of Insurance
State of Virginia
700 Blanton Building
Richmond, Virginia 23209
Tel. # (804) 786-3741

Commissioner of Insurance
Virgin Islands
P. O. Box 450, Charlotte Amalie
St. Thomas, Virgin Islands 08801
Tel. # (809) 774-2991

Insurance Commissioner
State of Washington
Insurance Building AQ 21
Olympia, Washington 98504
Tel. # (206) 753-7301

Addresses of
State Insurance
Commissioners

Insurance Commissioner
State of W. Virginia
1800 Washington Street, E.
Charleston, W. Virginia 25305
Tel. # (304) 348-3386

Commissioner of Insurance
State of Wisconsin
123 West Washington Avenue
Madison, Wisconsin 53702
Tel. # (608) 266-3585

Insurance Commissioner
State of Wyoming
2424 Pioneer
Cheyenne, Wyoming 82001
Tel. # (307) 777-7401

GLOSSARY

A

ACCIDENT: An event or occurrence which is unforeseen and unintended.

ACCIDENT AND HEALTH INSURANCE: Provides hospital, medical, surgical, and income benefits in the event of sickness, accidental injury, or accidental death.

ACCIDENTAL BODILY INJURY: Injury to the body of the insured as a result of an accident.

ACCIDENTAL DEATH BENEFIT: Provides additional benefit in case of death by accidental means.

ACCIDENTAL MEANS: The unexpected and unforeseen cause of an accident. The "means" which caused the mishap must be accidental in order to claim benefits under the policy.

ACQUISITION COST: The immediate cost of issuing a new policy, including cost of clerical work, agent's commission, and medical inspection fees.

ACTUAL CASH VALUE: The cost of repairing or replacing damaged property with other of like kind and quality in the same physical condition; commonly defined as replacement cost less depreciation.

ACTUAL DIVIDENDS: Policy dividends paid during a past period. See *Projected Dividends.*

ACTUARIAL COST METHODS: Systems for determining contributions to be made under a defined benefit retirement plan. In addition to forecasts of mortality, interest, and expenses, some methods involve estimates of future labor turnover, salary scales, and retirement rates.

ACTUARY: A person trained in the insurance field who determines premium rates, reserves, and dividends as well as conducts various other statistical studies.

ADJUSTABLE PREMIUM: A premium which an insurance company may modify under certain special conditions in accordance with a policy provision.

ADJUSTER: Person who settles insurance claims for property and liability insurance companies.

ADMITTED COMPANY: An insurance company licensed in your state.

ADVERSE SELECTION: The tendency of poorer risks or less desirable insureds to apply for or continue insurance to a greater extent than do the better risks.

AGE LIMITS: Stipulated minimum and maximum ages below and above which the company will not accept applications or may not renew policies.

AGENT: The *independent agent* is an independent businessman who represents two or more insurance companies under contract in a sales and service capacity and who is paid on a commission basis. The *exclusive agent* represents only one company, or a group of companies, usually on a commission basis. The *direct writer* is the salaried or commissioned employee of a single company or a group of companies.

AGGREGATE: The maximum dollar amount which may be collected for a single occurrence or during the policy period or during the insured's lifetime.

ALLIED LINES: A term for forms of insurance allied with property insurance, covering such perils as sprinkler leakage, water damage, and earthquake.

ALLOCATED BENEFITS: Benefits for which the maximum amount payable for specific services is itemized in the contract.

ANNUITY: A contract that provides an income for a specified period of time, such as a number of years or for life. The person receiving the payment is called an annuitant. Annuity payments are usually made monthly but can be quarterly, semi-annually, or annually.

APPLICATION: A signed statement of facts requested by the company on the basis of which the company decides whether or not to issue a policy.

ARSON: The willful and malicious burning of, or attempt to burn, any structure or other property, often with criminal or fraudulent intent.

ASSESSABLE: A policy which gives the insurer the right to require policyholders to pay additional premium.

ASSIGNMENT: Transfer of the ownership or benefits of a policy.

ATTORNEY-IN-FACT: One appointed to act for another; e.g., I give you power-of-attorney to sell my car and sign the required documents on my behalf.

AUTOMOBILE INSURANCE PLAN: A program under which automobile insurance is made available to persons who are unable to obtain such insurance in the voluntary market.

AUTOMOBILE LIABILITY INSURANCE: Protection for the insured against loss arising out of his or her legal liability when his or her car injures others or damages their property.

AUTOMOBILE PHYSICAL DAMAGE INSURANCE: Coverage for damages or loss to an automobile resulting from collision, fire, theft, and other perils.

AVERAGE CLAUSE: Requires the insured to buy insurance equal to a specified percentage of the value of the risk insured.

AVIATION TRIP INSURANCE: A policy protecting individuals as passengers of a scheduled aircraft. It is generally obtained at airports.

B

BENEFICIARY: A person or persons designated by the policyholder to receive a specified payment upon the policyholder's death.

BINDER: A temporary insurance contract made by an agent of the insurance company.

BINDING RECEIPT: A receipt given for a premium payment accompanying the application for insurance. This binds the company, if the policy is approved, to make the policy effective from the date of the receipt.

BLANKET CONTRACT: A contract of health insurance affording benefits, such as accidental death and dismemberment, for all of a class of persons not individually identified. It is used for such groups as athletic teams and campers, and includes travel policies for employees, etc.

BLANKET MEDICAL EXPENSE: A provision which entitles the insured person to collect up to a maximum established in the policy for all hospital and medical expenses incurred, without any limitations on individual types of medical expenses.

BLUE CROSS: An independent, nonprofit membership corporation providing protection against the costs of hospital care.

BLUE SHIELD: An independent, nonprofit membership corporation providing protection against the costs of surgery and other items of medical care.

BOILER AND MACHINERY INSURANCE: Coverage for loss arising out of the operation of pressure, mechanical, and electrical equipment. It may cover loss to the boiler and machinery itself, damage to other property, and business interruption losses.

BOND: Written contract in which one party (the surety) guarantees performance of an agreement between a second party (the principal) and a third party (the obligee). The surety makes the guarantee to the obligee on behalf of the principal.

BOTTOMRY: An agreement made in ancient Greece whereby a loan made on a ship was cancelled if the ship was lost. A similar agreement in which the cargo was collateral was called ''respondentia.'' Both these arrangements combined lending with insurance.

BROKER: Represents buyers of insurance. Deals with either agents or companies in arranging for insurance required by the customer.

BURGLARY, ROBBERY AND THEFT INSURANCE: Protection for loss of property due to burglary, robbery, or larceny.

BUSINESS INTERRUPTION INSURANCE: Coverage for loss of earnings in case the policyholder's business is shut down by fire, windstorm, explosion, or other insured peril.

C

CAPITAL SUM: The maximum amount payable in one sum in the event of accidental dismemberment. When a contract provides benefits for kinds of dismemberment, each benefit is an amount equal to, or a fraction of, the capital sum.

CAPTIVE AGENT: An uncomplimentary synonym for exclusive agent.

CATASTROPHE LOSS: A term applied to an incident or series of related incidents involving a loss of more than a million dollars.

CEDING COMPANY: An insurance company that shifts part or all of a risk it has assumed to another insurance company. The latter is the reinsurer.

CLAIM: A demand to the insurer by the insured person for the payment of benefits under a policy.

CLASS RATING: A system of premium rate determination in which all risks with similar characteristics are charged the same rate; e.g., all females the same age and in good health are charged the same rate per $1,000 of life insurance by a particular insurance company.

COINSURANCE: A policy provision which requires the insured to carry insurance equal to a certain specified percentage of the value of the property.

COMPREHENSIVE MEDICAL INSURANCE: Provides benefits of both a basic and a major medical health insurance policy. It is characterized by a low deductible amount, a participation clause, and high maximum benefits.

CONFINING SICKNESS: An illness which confines an insured person to his or her home or to a hospital.

CONSEQUENTIAL LOSS: Loss which results from a direct loss; e.g., a loss caused by fire causes loss of earnings while the damaged premises are being repaired.

CONSIDERATION: One of the elements of a binding contract. Consideration is what each party to a contract gives up to induce the other party to make the agreement.

CONSTRUCTIVE TOTAL LOSS: A partial loss so large that repairs would cost more than the insured property would be worth after being repaired. For example, it may cost more to repair an old car damaged by collision than to buy a replacement from a used car dealer.

CONVERSION PRIVILEGE: The right given to an insured person to change insurance without evidence of insurability.

COORDINATION OF BENEFITS (C.O.B.): A method of integrating benefits payable under more than one health insurance plan so that the insured's benefits from all sources do not exceed 100 percent of allowable medical expenses.

CREDIT INSURANCE: A guarantee to manufacturers, wholesalers, and service organizations that they will be paid for goods shipped or services rendered. It is a guarantee of that part of their working capital represented by accounts receivable.

CROP-HAIL INSURANCE: Protection against damage to growing crops as a result of hail or certain other named perils.

D

DEDUCTIBLE: A provision that requires the policyholder to contribute up to a specified sum per claim or per accident toward the total amount of the insured loss. Insurance is written on this basis at reduced rates.

DEFERRED ANNUITY: An annuity under which payment will begin at some definite future date, such as in a specified number of years or at a specified age.

DEFINED CONTRIBUTION PLAN: A pension plan which provides for an individual account for each participant and for benefits based solely on the amount contributed to the account—plus earnings and forfeitures and minus expenses. Also called a money purchase plan.

DISABILITY: Inability to perform one or more duties of one's occupation because of injury or illness.

DISABILITY INCOME INSURANCE: A form of health insurance that provides periodic payments to replace income when the insured is unable to work as a result of illness, injury, or disease.

DISMEMBERMENT: The loss of a limb or sight.

DIVIDEND: A policyholder's share in the insurer's divisible surplus funds apportioned for distribution, which may take the form of a refund of part of the premium on a participating policy.

DIVIDEND ADDITION: Paid-up life insurance purchased with a policy dividend and added to the face amount of the policy.

DOUBLE INDEMNITY: A life insurance policy provision which doubles the death benefit when death is caused by accident.

DREAD DISEASE INSURANCE: Insurance providing an unallocated benefit, subject to a maximum amount, for expenses incurred in connection with the treatment of specified diseases, such as cancer, poliomyelitis, encephalitis, and spinal meningitis.

E

EARLY RETIREMENT: A benefit which permits retirement of a participant prior to the normal retirement date, and usually with a reduced amount of annuity. Early retirement is generally allowed at any time during a period of 5 to 10 years preceding the normal retirement date.

EARNED PREMIUM: That portion of a policy's premium payment for which the protection of the policy has already been given. For example, an insurance company is considered to have earned 75% of an annual premium after a period of 9 months of an annual term has elapsed.

ELECTIVE BENEFIT: A benefit payable in lieu of another, e.g. a lump-sum benefit may be allowed for specified fractures or dislocations in lieu of weekly or monthly indemnity.

ELIGIBILITY REQUIREMENTS: This term refers to (1) conditions which an employee must satisfy to participate in a retirement plan, such as the completion of from 1 to 3 years of service with the employer, or (2) conditions which an employee must satisfy to obtain a retirement benefit, such as the completion of 15 years of service and the attainment of age 65.

ELIMINATION PERIOD: Number of days at the beginning of a period of disability for which no benefit is paid. Performs the same function as a deductible.

ENDORSEMENT: A document which modifies the protection of a policy, either expanding or decreasing its benefits, or adding or excluding certain conditions from the policy. Same as a rider.

EQUITIES: Investments in the form of ownership of property, usually common stocks, as distinguished from fixed income bearing securities, such as bonds or mortgages.

EQUIVALENT LEVEL ANNUAL DIVIDEND: The average of annual life insurance policy dividends paid (or projected) during a specified period, adjusted for interest at a specified rate.

EVIDENCE OF INSURABILITY: Any statement or proof of a person's physical condition and/or other factual information affecting his or her acceptance for insurance.

EXCLUSIONS: Specific perils or losses listed in the policy for which the policy will not provide benefit payments.

EXPENSE RATIO: Ratio of insurer expenses to premiums received.

EXPERIENCE RATING: Variation of the premium rate, computed on the basis of past losses and expenses incurred by the insurance company in the settlement of claims and other expenses involving a particular group of risks.

EXTENDED COVERAGE INSURANCE: Protection for the insured against loss or damage to his or her property caused by windstorm, hail, smoke, explosion, riot, riot attending a strike, civil commotion, vehicle, or aircraft. This is provided in conjunction with a fire insurance policy.

F

FACE AMOUNT: The amount stated in a life insurance policy to be paid upon death of the insured or the maturity date of an endowment policy.

FAIR PLAN: A facility, operating under a government-insurance industry cooperative program, to make property insurance available to those who cannot buy it through the regular market.

FAMILY POLICY: A policy which insures both the policyholder and his or her immediate dependents (usually spouse and children).

FEDERAL CRIME INSURANCE: Insurance against burglary, larceny, and robbery losses offered by the Federal Insurance Administration, an agency of the federal government.

FIDELITY BOND: A contract which indemnifies an employer for losses caused by dishonest or fraudulent acts of employees.

FIDUCIARY: One who exercises discretionary authority or control over management of a pension plan or disposition of its assets; renders investment advice for a fee with respect to moneys or property of a plan or has authority or responsibility to do so; or has discretionary authority or responsibility in the administration of a plan.

FINANCIAL RESPONSIBILITY LAW: A law under which a person involved in an automobile accident may be required to furnish evidence of financial responsibility, usually by auto liability insurance.

FIRE INSURANCE: Coverage for losses caused by fire and lightning, plus a variety of other perils, such as windstorm, hail, etc.

FIXED-DOLLAR ANNUITIES: An annuity under which the amount of each annuity payment is a fixed number of dollars.

FLEET: A group, as of automobiles. Or, a group of insurance companies operating under one management.

FLOATER POLICY: A property insurance policy in which the protection follows the property wherever it may be located.

FLOOD INSURANCE: Coverage against loss caused by the flood peril.

FRANCHISE INSURANCE: A form of insurance in which individual policies are issued to the employees of a common employer or the members of an association and the employer or association agrees to collect the premiums for the insurer.

FRATERNAL INSURANCE: A cooperative type of insurance provided by social organizations for their members.

FUTURE SERVICE BENEFITS: Benefits accruing for service after the effective date of coverage under a pension plan.

G

GENERAL AVERAGE: Maritime law that requires all parties to a voyage to bear their share of voluntary sacrifices made to save the ship and cargo in an emergency.

GRACE PERIOD: A period after a premium payment is due, in which the policyholder may make such payment, and during which the policy remains in force.

GROUP ANNUITY CONTRACT: A pension plan providing annuities at retirement to a group of persons covered by a single master contract, with individual certificates stating the coverage issued to members of the group.

GROUP INSURANCE: Any insurance plan under which a number of persons and their dependents are insured under a single policy, issued to their employer or to an association with which they are affiliated, with individual certificates given to each insured person.

GUARANTEED COST POLICY: A life insurance policy which does not pay dividends. Also called nonparticipating.

GUARANTEED RENEWABLE: A policy the insured has the right to continue in force by the timely payment of premiums to a specified age during which period the insurer has no right to make any change in any provision of the contract while it is in force, other than a change in the premium rate for classes of insureds. The term, "guaranteed continuable," is synonymous with the term "guaranteed renewable."

H

HAZARD: A condition that affects the probability of loss.

HEALTH INSURANCE: A generic term applying to all types of insurance indemnifying or reimbursing for costs of hospital and medical care or lost income arising from an illness or injury. Sometimes it is called Accident and Health Insurance, or Disability Insurance.

HEALTH MAINTENANCE ORGANIZATION (HMO): An organization that provides for a wide range of comprehensive health care services for a specified group at a fixed periodic payment. The HMO can be sponsored by the government, medical schools, hospitals, employers, labor unions, consumer groups, insurance companies, and hospital-medical plans.

HOSPITAL INDEMNITY: A form of health insurance which provides a stipulated daily, weekly, or monthly indemnity during hospital confinement. The indemnity is payable on an unallocated basis without regard to the actual expense of hospital confinement.

HOSPITAL-MEDICAL INSURANCE: Protection which provides benefits of any or all health care services.

I

INCONTESTABLE CLAUSE: A clause which provides that the insurer may not contest the validity of the contract after it has been in force for a specified period, such as two years.

INDEPENDENT ADJUSTER: A person who represents an insurer in settling loss claims but is not an employee of the insurer.

INDEPENDENT AGENT: An agent who sells insurance for several companies as an independent contractor rather than an employee.

INDIVIDUAL POLICY PENSION TRUST: A trust created to buy individual life insurance or annuity contracts to provide benefits under a pension plan.

INLAND MARINE INSURANCE: A broad type of insurance, generally covering articles that may be transported from one place to another as well as bridges, tunnels, and other instrumentalities of transportation. It includes in transit (generally excepting trans-ocean) as well as numerous "floater" policies such as personal effect, personal property, jewelry, furs, fine arts, and others.

INSURABLE INTEREST: If the occurrence of a loss, such as destruction of a house by fire, will affect you adversely, you have an insurable interest.

INSURED: In life insurance, the person on whose life a policy is issued; the subject of the insurance. In property and liability insurance, the person to whom, or on whose behalf, benefits are payable.

INSURING CLAUSE: The clause which sets forth the type of loss being covered by the policy and the parties to the insurance contract.

J

JOINT-AND-SURVIVOR ANNUITY: A contract that provides income periodically, payable during the longer lifetime of two persons. The amount payable may decrease at the death of one or the other or either person included in the contract.

K

KEY-MAN INSURANCE: Life or health insurance to protect the firm from loss caused by the death or disability of an employee who makes a significant contribution to the firm.

L

LAPSE: Termination of a policy caused by the policyholder's failure to pay the premium within the time required.

LEASEHOLD INTEREST: An interest that exists when a lease stipulates a rental that is greater or less than the prevailing market price for similar facilities.

LEVEL PREMIUM: A premium which remains unchanged throughout the life of a policy.

LIABILITY INSURANCE: Provides protection against loss arising out of legal liability resulting from injuries to other persons or damage to their property.

LIABILITY LIMITS: The stipulated sum or sums beyond which an insurance company is not liable to protect the insured.

LIFE ANNUITY: A series of payments that continue throughout the life of the annuitant but not beyond.

LIFE ANNUITY WITH 10 YEARS CERTAIN: An annuity which provides payments throughout the life of the annuitant, but not less than 10 years.

LIFE EXPECTANCY: The average number of years of life remaining for a group of persons of a given age according to a particular mortality table.

LIFE INSURANCE: Provides for payment of a specified amount at the insured's death, or at a specified date.

LIMITED POLICIES: Contracts which cover only certain specified diseases or accidents.

LIVERY: In automobile insurance, the carrying of passengers for hire.

LONG-TERM DISABILITY INCOME INSURANCE: Pays benefits to a disabled person for an extended period, to retirement age, or for life.

LOSS RATIO: Ratio of losses to earned premiums.

M

MAJOR MEDICAL EXPENSE INSURANCE: Pays for the expense of major illness and injuries. Provides large benefit maximums or no limit. The insurance—above a large deductible—pays the major part of all charges for hospital, doctor, private nurses, medical appliances, and prescribed out-of-hospital treatment, drugs, and medicines. The insured person pays the remainder.

MALPRACTICE INSURANCE: Liability insurance for professionals, such as physicians and surgeons, to protect them against the risk of claims for damages in connection with professional services.

MEDICAID: State programs of public assistance to persons regardless of age whose income and resources are insufficient to pay for health care.

MEDICAL PAYMENTS: A coverage included in some liability insurance policies, in which the insurer agrees to reimburse the insured and/or others, without regard for the insured's liability, for medical or funeral expenses incurred as the result of bodily injury or death by accident under the conditions specified in the policy.

MEDICARE: Hospital and medical insurance provided by Social Security.

MEDIGAP INSURANCE: Policies that pay for all, or part of, health care expense not covered by Medicare.

MORBIDITY TABLE: Shows the average number of illnesses or injuries befalling a large group of persons. It indicates the incidence of sickness and accident the way a mortality table shows the incidence of death.

MORTALITY TABLE: Shows the number of persons living, dying, and the death rate starting at a certain age, by year. It is used to calculate the probability of dying in, or surviving through, any period.

MULTIPLE PERIL INSURANCE: Policies that combine many perils previously covered by individual fire and liability policies.

N

NET PAYMENTS COST INDEX: A measure of the cost, including interest foregone, of a life insurance policy if you keep it in force until you die.

NO-FAULT AUTOMOBILE INSURANCE: A form of insurance by which a person's financial losses resulting from an automobile accident, such as medical and hospital expenses and loss of income, are paid by his or her own insurance company without concern for who was at fault.

NONADMITTED COMPANY: A company not licensed to write business in your state.

NONCANCELLABLE, OR NONCANCELLABLE AND GUARANTEED RENEWABLE, POLICY: A policy which the insured has the right to continue in force to a specified age, such as to age 65, by the timely payment of premiums. During the specified period the insurer has no right to unilaterally make any change in any provision of the policy while it is in force.

NONCONFINING SICKNESS: An illness which prevents the insured person from working but which does not confine him or her to a hospital or home.

NONDISABLING INJURY: One which may require medical care, but does not result in loss of working time or income.

NONOCCUPATIONAL POLICY: A contract which insures a person against off-the-job accident or sickness.

NONPARTICIPATING POLICY: A policy on which no dividends are paid to the policyholder. Sometimes called "guaranteed cost."

O

OCEAN MARINE INSURANCE: Coverage on all types of vessels, including liabilities connected with them, and on their cargoes.

OPTIONALLY RENEWABLE: A contract of health insurance in which the insurer reserves the right to terminate the coverage at any anniversary or, in some cases, at any premium-due date, but does not have the right to terminate coverage between such dates.

ORDINARY LIFE POLICY: Whole life insurance on which premiums are paid for life. Also called straight life.

OVER-INSURANCE: An amount of insurance larger than the loss that could befall the insured.

P

PACKAGE POLICY: A single insurance policy that includes several types of insurance, such as the Home-owners Policy.

PAID-UP POLICY: A policy that will remain in force without further premium payments.

PARTIAL DISABILITY: An illness or injury which prevents an insured person from performing one or more of the functions of his or her regular job.

PARTICIPATION CLAUSE: Requires the insured to pay for a specified percentage of the cost of health care services covered by a health insurance policy.

PARTICULAR AVERAGE: In maritime law, a partial loss that is borne by the person on whom it falls, rather than distributed among other interests in a voyage. See *General Average.*

PAST SERVICE BENEFITS: Benefits for service before the effective date of coverage under a pension plan, or prior to a date on which a plan is amended to improve benefits.

PERIL: The cause of loss, such as fire, flood, and theft.

PERMANENT LIFE INSURANCE: All forms of life insurance other than term. Actually a misnomer.

POLICYHOLDERS' SURPLUS: The net worth of an insurance company, adjusted for overstatement of liabilities.

POLICY LOAN: A loan made by the insurer to the owner of a life insurance policy, using its surrender value as collateral.

POLICY TERM: The period for which an insurance policy provides coverage.

PORTABILITY: The transfer of pension rights and credits when a worker changes jobs.

PRE-EXISTING CONDITION: A physical and/or mental condition of an insured person which existed prior to the issuance of his or her policy.

PREMIUM: The payment made for an insurance policy.

PREPAID GROUP PRACTICE PLAN: A plan under which specified health services are rendered by participating physicians to a group of persons, with fixed periodic payment in advance made by or on behalf of each person or family.

PRINCIPAL SUM: The amount payable in one sum in event of accidental death and, in some cases, accidental dismemberment.

PROBATIONARY PERIOD: A specified number of days after the date of the issuance of the policy during which there is no coverage for sickness. The purpose is to eliminate adverse selection.

PROJECTED DIVIDEND: A portrayal of future policy dividends based on current assumptions. Dividends cannot be guaranteed. See *Actual Dividends.*

PROXIMATE CAUSE: The cause actually responsible for the loss; the one that set in motion the events that led to a loss; e.g., a fire that led to water damage.

PUBLIC ADJUSTER: An adjuster who represents the insured in settling a claim for loss covered by an insurance policy.

PUNITIVE DAMAGES: Damages awarded separately and in addition to compensatory damages as punishment for the wrongdoer.

Q

QUALIFIED PLAN: An employee benefit plan which the Internal Revenue Service approves as meeting the requirements of ERISA and is entitled to certain tax advantages.

R

RECURRING CLAUSE: A provision in some health insurance policies which specifies a period of time during which the recurrence of a condition is considered a continuation of a prior period of disability or hospital confinement.

REGULAR MEDICAL EXPENSE INSURANCE: Coverage which provides benefits toward the cost of such services as doctor fees for nonsurgical care in the hospital, at home, or in a physician's office, and X-rays or laboratory tests performed outside of the hospital.

REINSTATEMENT: The resumption of coverage under a policy which has been lapsed.

REINSURANCE: Assumption by one insurance company of all or part of a risk undertaken by another insurance company.

RENEWAL: Continuation of coverage under a policy beyond its original term by the acceptance of a premium for a new policy term.

RESERVE: A liability entry on the balance sheet that recognizes a financial obligation.

RESPONDENTIA: An agreement made in ancient Greece whereby a loan made on cargo was cancelled if the ship was lost. This combined insurance with lending.

RIDER: A document which modifies the protection of a policy, either expanding or decreasing its benefits or adding or excluding certain conditions from the policy. Same as an endorsement.

RISK: Possibility of loss. Also used to refer to property insured; e.g., a building insured against loss is referred to as a risk.

RISK MANAGEMENT: An organized, formal approach to dealing with pure risks.

S

SELF-ADMINISTERED PLAN: A pension or profit-sharing plan funded through a fiduciary, generally a bank, but sometimes a group of individuals, which invests the fund accumulated instead of using the services of an insurance company.

SEPARATE ACCOUNT: A fund held by a life insurance company which is separate and apart from its general assets and is generally used for investment of pension assets.

SERVICE BENEFIT: An insurance benefit in the form of hospital or medical care services rather than money.

SHORT-TERM DISABILITY INCOME INSURANCE: A policy that pays benefits to a disabled person for a specified period not exceeding two years.

SOCIAL SECURITY OPTION: An option under which employees may elect higher annuity payments before a specified age (62 or 65) and lower payments thereafter to produce level annuity payments, including Social Security benefits when they start.

SPLIT FUNDING: An arrangement whereby a portion of the contributions to a pension plan are paid to a life insurance company and the remainder invested through a corporate trustee, primarily in equities.

STAFF ADJUSTER: An insurance company employee who settles claims for losses on its behalf.

STRAIGHT LIFE POLICY: Whole life insurance on which premiums are paid for life. Also called ordinary life.

SUBROGATION: Gives the insurer whatever right against third parties you may have as a result of the loss for which the insurer paid you.

SUBSTANDARD RISK: A risk with higher than average probability of loss, such as a person with a physical impairment who applies for health insurance or a person with a bad driving record who applies for auto insurance.

SURETY BOND: An agreement providing for monetary compensation should there be a failure to perform specified acts within a stated period. The surety company, for example, becomes responsible for fulfillment of a contract if the contractor defaults.

SURGICAL EXPENSE INSURANCE: Health insurance policies which provide benefits toward the doctor's operating fees. Benefits usually consist of scheduled amounts for each surgical procedure.

SURGICAL SCHEDULE: A list of cash allowances which are payable for various types of surgery with the maximum amounts based upon the severity of the operations.

SURPLUS LINE: Insurance not available in the regular market from admitted companies. May be placed in the surplus lines market with a non-admitted company under special provisions of state law.

SURRENDER COST INDEX: A measure of the cost, including interest foregone, of a life insurance policy if you keep it in force for a specified period and then surrender it for the cash surrender value.

T

TEMPORARY LIFE ANNUITY: An annuity payable while the annuitant lives but not beyond a specified period, such as five years.

TOTAL DISABILITY: A disability which prevents a person from continuously performing every duty pertaining to his or her occupation or from engaging in any other type of work for remuneration. (This wording varies among insurance companies.)

TRADITIONAL NET COST: A measure of the surrender cost of a life insurance policy which ignores the cost of interest foregone.

TRAVEL ACCIDENT POLICY: A contract that covers loss caused by an accident that occurs while an insured person is traveling.

U

UMBRELLA LIABILITY POLICY: A form of insurance protection against losses in excess of amounts covered by other liability insurance policies; also protects the insured in many situations not covered by the usual liability policies.

UNALLOCATED BENEFIT: A policy provision providing reimbursement up to a maximum amount for the costs of all extra miscellaneous hospital services, but which does not specify how much will be paid for each type of service.

UNDERWRITING: The process by which the insurer decides whether or not and on what basis it will issue a policy.

UNINSURED MOTORIST PROTECTION: Indemnifies an insured who is injured by a hit-and-run motorist or a driver who is at fault but has no liability insurance.

V

VALUED POLICY: One in which the value of the property insured is agreed upon and specified in the policy.

VALUED POLICY LAW: Statute that requires payment of the face amount of the policy in the event of a total loss, regardless of the actual value of the property.

VARIABLE ANNUITY: An annuity under which the amount of each periodic payment varies according to the investment experience of the insurer.

VESTING: A provision concerning the right of pension and profit-sharing plan participants to contributions made by the employer.

W

WAITING PERIOD: Time between the beginning of an insured's disability and the beginning of benefit payments.

WAIVER: An agreement attached to a policy which excludes from coverage certain disabilities or injuries which are normally covered by the policy.

WAIVER OF PREMIUM: A provision which exempts the policyholder from paying premiums while totally disabled.

WARRANTY: A statement made by the applicant for insurance which, if false, provides the basis for voidance of the policy.

WHOLE LIFE POLICY: A life insurance policy which remains in force throughout the life of the insured.

WRITTEN PREMIUMS: Premiums on policies issued during a specified period, as opposed to earned premiums.

Index